Photo Greg Cornell

Keith Morton is an outdoor enthusiast, instructor and writer. During 45 years of recreating he has travelled to every part of North America, from Nova Scotia to Alaska, from Southern Ontario to the High Arctic, as well as to many other parts of the world. He guides canoe trips, ski tours and arctic raft trips and instructs a wide range of outdoor topics including group trip organization, emergency situation management, canoeing, backpacking, skiing, outdoor cookery, map and compass, and avalanche safety. He is currently the New Products and Equipment Editor for *Explore* magazine. Morton lives with his librarian wife Mary Enright in Calgary, Alberta.

Rocky
Mountain Books

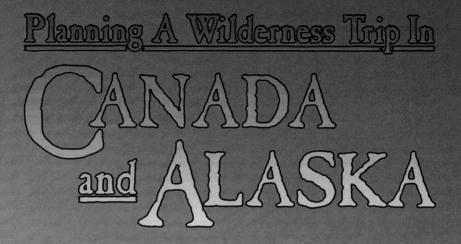

Planning A Wilderness Trip In
CANADA and ALASKA

Keith Morton

Cover: Shore ice on a fjord in Ellesmere Island, photo John Dunn.

Front inserts—clockwise from top left: Caribou, photo Ken Ellison; Backpacking in the Canadian Rockies—Burstall Pass, photo Gillean Daffern; Ice climbing in southern Alberta, photo Eric Hoogstraten; Canoe tripping on the Castle River, photo Mary Enright.

Back inserts—clockwise from top right: Ski mountaineering on the Wapta Icefields—Canadian Rockies, photo Alan Kane; Sled hauling on Arctic sea ice—Ellesmere Island, photo John Dunn; Horse packing in the northern Canadian Rockies, photo Gillean Daffern; The summit of Sir Sandford—Columbia Mountains, photo Tony Daffern.

Title page: Sled hauling on Arctic sea ice—Ellesmere Island, photo John Dunn.

Cover by Zac Bolan

The publisher gratefully acknowledges the assistance provided by the Alberta Foundation for the Arts and by the federal Department of Canadian Heritage

The Alberta Foundation for the Arts   **Alberta** COMMUNITY DEVELOPMENT

COMMITTED TO THE DEVELOPMENT OF CULTURE AND THE ARTS

**Published by
Rocky Mountain Books
#4 Spruce Centre SW**
RMB **Calgary, AB T3C 3B3**

Canadian Cataloguing in Publication Data

Morton, Keith.
  Planning a wilderness trip in Canada and Alaska

  Includes index.
  ISBN 0-921102-30-5

  1. Wilderness survival--Canada, Northern. 2. Wilderness survival--Alaska. 3. Outdoor life--Canada, Northern. 4. Outdoor life--Alaska. I. Title
GV191.46.N7M67   1977   796.5'09719   C96-910821-4

Contents

Acknowledgments

My early interest in the outdoors was fostered by the Scout movement in the UK, and thanks go to Jean Street, Barbara Loten, Ian MacBean, Ken Owen, Ben Clark, Doug Beresford, David Armstrong and Jack King who put the "out" in ScOUTing around Alderley Edge in Cheshire; A.D. Siddall, my far-sighted phys.ed. teacher in Macclesfield who saw beyond conventional team sports. He didn't write off the asthmatic uncoordinated kid, and encouraged me into outdoor pursuits, helping me develop confidence and a lasting love of the outdoors. Thanks also to Don Robinson at Leeds University whose foreign expeditions and Outdoor Education class for trainee teachers opened new horizons; Harold Wilson's government for keeping UK teachers in such penury that I fled to a teaching job in Canada and began to experience the real wilderness; Mike Exall at Seneca College for guidance and some great opportunities to develop outdoor, instructing and guiding skills; John Rudolph, a classroom teaching and outdoor education partner in Hamilton with whom I shared some of my most rewarding outdoor tripping teaching experiences; John Aikman and John Heaslip for some great academic outdoor education experiences; Klaus Streckmann who inspired me to visit the Nahanni in 1973 for my first taste of real Wilderness; Ron Riffel and Derrick Wright in Calgary who gave me the scope to develop skills in adult outdoor teaching and course development; numerous friends, students and clients who shared happily (and sometimes justifiably unhappily) in countless trips; my mum who encouraged every outdoor endeavour and somehow managed to look cheerful as her only son took off on a decrepit motorbike to go rock-climbing; and last but not least, my wife Mary Enright who for 22 years has been sharing trips with me to all corners of the earth and encouraged me during the writing of this book.

Introduction

Canada and Alaska are among the best places on earth for outdoor recreation, and this book aims to help you enjoy the opportunities they offer. There are still vast areas of relatively unpeopled and unspoiled wilderness country to visit; a wide range of activities can be enjoyed year round because of the variety of seasons, climates and terrain; and security and logistics are relatively minor concerns in these stable first world countries. Although the wildness of these lands is a major attraction, it does mean that once you set off into the backcountry you are on your own. There will be scant opportunities for resupply, retreat, or for obtaining rescue or medical assistance. You therefore need to be skilled, organized, well equipped and self reliant. This book leads you chapter by chapter through the steps in planning and executing a trip in remote wilderness country. It tells you what you must know to have a comfortable, enjoyable, safe and low impact stay in the magnificent but unforgiving Canadian and Alaskan wilderness. If you make mistakes and experience a wilderness emergency, the guidelines in the book will help you to resolve the situation effectively.

The ideas presented here are from a lifetime of personal outdoor experience, formal learning and discovery. Everyone, from beginners to seasoned wilderness travellers will find useful ideas, techniques and new perspectives to help them have a successful trip.

Some recreationists would prefer that people did not write "how to" books and guide books that encourage more people to visit these often fragile wilderness lands. It is a dilemma, but the numbers of people heading into the backcountry will increase regardless. That sounds like a cop-out, but another aspect of the dilemma is this: The wilderness will survive longer if more people have learned from books such as this that you really can "tread lightly" and enjoy wild country very comfortably without resorting to motors and high-impact facilities. Although people always have some impact, the wilderness may be saved from a far more destructive industrial impact if it acquires a constituency and local value as a sustainable low impact tourism generator. Information in this book will help you to organize your own trip or choose a suitable outfitter and live comfortably and safely in the outdoors with minimum impact. That way the priceless legacy of Canadian and Alaskan wilderness might survive for a few more generations.

Happy travels in the greatest outdoor playground on earth!

Spring ski touring in the Icefield Ranges, west Yukon.

Chapter 1

Recreational Opportunities

Self-propelled backcountry recreation in Canada and Alaska is a big topic because Canada and Alaska are big countries. Alaska is five times larger than the British Isles or Germany, and Canada is six times larger than Alaska. The area extends from the latitude of Rome to within 800 kilometres of the North Pole, and covers nearly one third of the earth's circumference. You can encounter anything from cold desert to temperate rainforest; from low-lying plains to soaring 6000 metre ice-clad peaks. The variety of outdoor recreation opportunities is endless.

Chapter One is an overview of some of the regions in this vast area and the recreational opportunities they provide. Subsequent chapters will help you plan and carry out a memorable trip in the Canadian or Alaskan backcountry with minimal environmental impact.

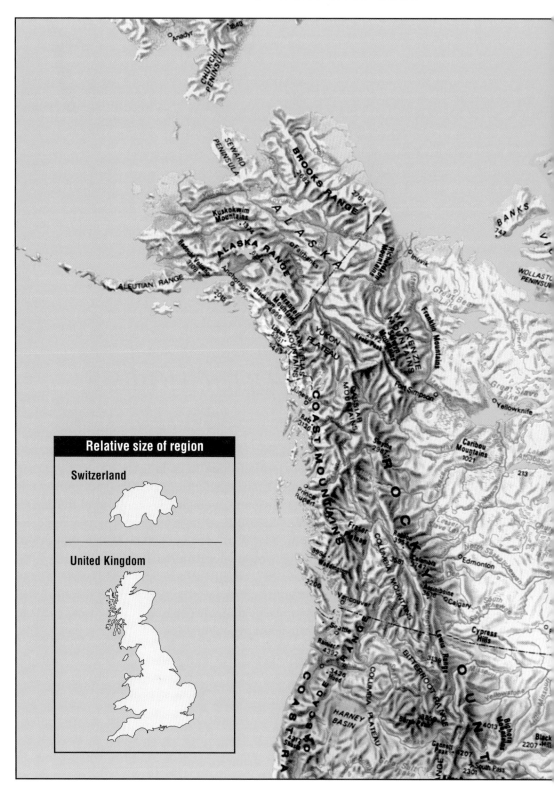

Relative size of region

Switzerland

United Kingdom

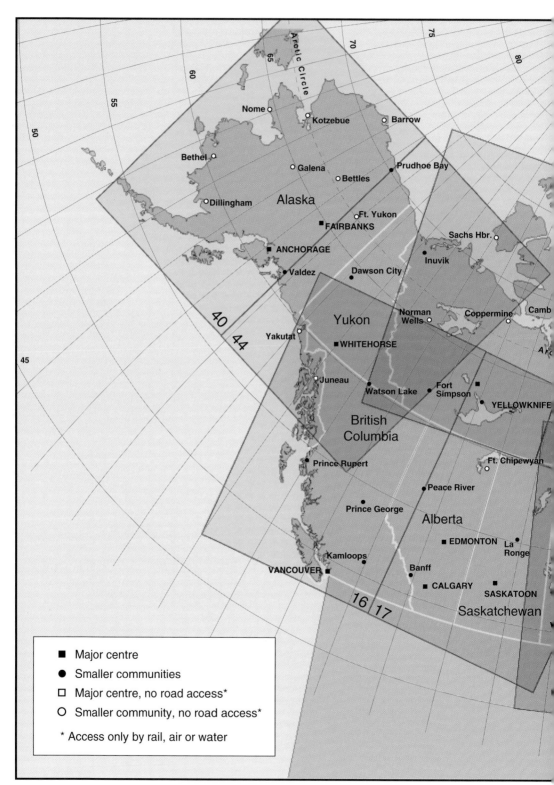

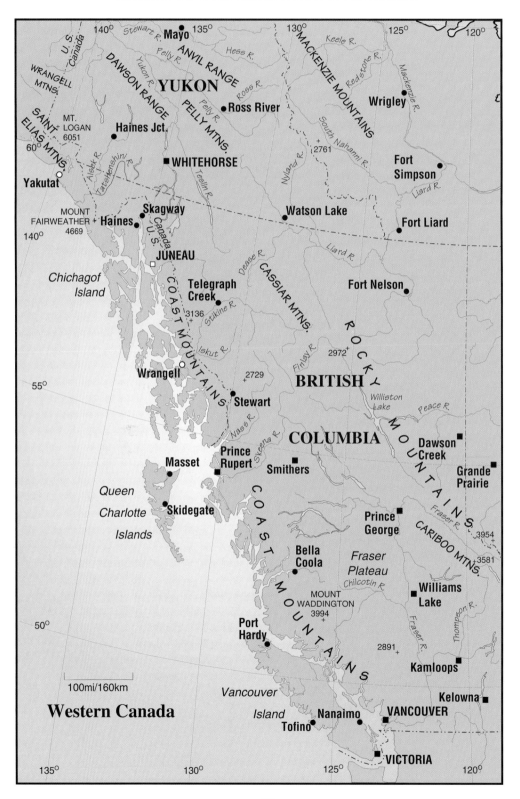

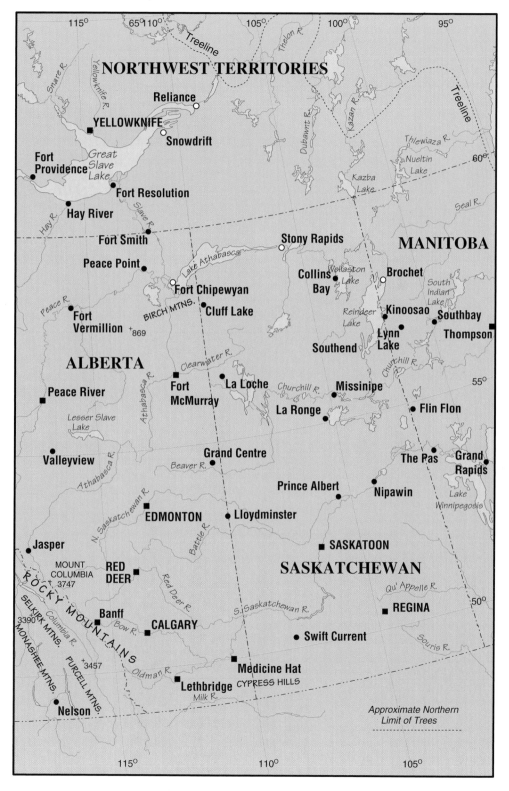

Alsek River, Alaska Panhandle.

The Regions

Canada and Alaska can be divided up into a number of regions on the basis of physical geography, climate and vegetation. These factors greatly influence the type of recreational activity to which they are suited.

The West Coast of Canada and the Alaska Panhandle

The West Coast of Canada is flanked by mountains reaching as high as 4000 metres. At the north end of the panhandle Mt. Fairweather rises nearly 5000 metres and is only 20 kilometres from tidewater. Everywhere long spectacular fjord-like waterways lead back into the mountainous interior. Pushing through to the coast are major rivers like the Tatshenshini/Alsek, Stikine and Skeena. Many offshore islands, some quite mountainous with steep shorelines and few beaches, form sheltered archipelagoes, but there are also sections of very exposed coastline with no shelter of any kind.

The climate is notoriously wet with lots of dull weather and a relatively small seasonal temperature variation. However, because it is a mountainous area, rain shadow effects are common. For example, Juneau airport has little more than half the rainfall of the town 13 kilometres away. Sunnier and drier areas include the southern part of Vancouver Island and the Sunshine Coast north of Howe Sound. Weather conditions get harsher farther north on the Pacific side of Vancouver Island and particularly north of Vancouver Island around the Queen Charlotte Islands. Over most of the area, February to June is the driest time, after which the rainfall steadily increases.

Generally the warm, wet, dull winters are not attractive, but keen, well-equipped people do sail, kayak and ski. Although the maritime influence generally prevails, a period of northerly winter winds can bring very cold interior air over the icefields and down the passes to the coast. This is especially the case in the northernmost parts of this region.

Even in summer the fjords are swept by cold katabatic winds (called takus in some areas) that funnel down from the high snowfields with considerable force. Because of this cold air drainage, temperatures at valley bottom can be much colder than at places a few hundred metres up the valley sides. The water is very cold except in Desolation Sound, and tends to generate summer fog.

While I have experienced days of torrential rain on Vancouver Island, I have also had several early September holidays where we have fried day after day in tropic-like sunshine in the same area. A sea kayaking guide we met on one of those roasting trips recounted how two weeks earlier she had spent five days pinned down with her clients by a summer storm that had the power of a winter storm. Be prepared for anything and everything in the way of weather!

Thick temperate rainforest covers most of the west coast shoreline in B.C. and the Alaska Panhandle. Exposed coastal islets generally have dense, almost impenetrable scrub that hinders progress inland from the beach. In less exposed areas, giant cedars, Douglas fir and spruce can still be found, although much of the coast has been logged. Vast areas of old growth forest have been laid waste, and in many places erosion is making regrowth impossible. Where regrowth is occurring it is often a completely unnatural monoculture. The moderate climate means that treeline is high with treeline brush rather than the open meadows of drier areas.

The area provides splendid opportunities for kayakers and sailors, and even for canoeists with seaworthy fast craft equipped with full spray covers. The fjord coastline is spectacular, though the steep sides and deep water mean there are relatively few landing beaches and anchorages. Strong winds along the channels and fjords, fog and some very powerful tidal currents in some areas demand skill and caution. Glacier Bay is accessible from Gustavus by charter boat and tour boat. It is popular with large cruise ships as well as with smaller sightseeing motor boats, and finding a solitary wilderness experience takes some effort. Good anchorages in the southern part of Vancouver Island tend to be crowded in the high season of July-August. They are also frequented by vast motor cruisers, some of which arrive complete with noisy, smelly generators, megawatt stereos and a cargo of annoying toys such as jet-skis and waterski boats.

Lower-lying and more exposed outer coasts and islands that tend to have more beaches can be utilized by kayaks and small boats, trailered or carried by ferry or float plane to the area. Larger craft would have to brave long, open coastal passages to reach these areas and would not have the option of going ashore in bad weather.

The most popular backpacking route, the West Coast Trail on Vancouver Island, has a user quota system. Because of the wet climate and rough terrain, this trip demands a high level of skill. Like so many high-profile trips, it tends to attract people who do not have the necessary skills, and without skills it's difficult to have a particularly rewarding time.

Generally, though, wilderness walking and backpacking are not high profile activities on the coast. The combination of rugged terrain, dense forest and dense undergrowth including devil's club means that unless there is a trail, making headway is impractical. It's often difficult and time consuming to climb into open terrain with views. Logged areas are, of course, more open, and provide views if you can handle the close-up view of the devastation.

Active and disused logging camps are found along the coast, especially where there is a natural harbour for shipping logs. From these camps a network of logging roads, which may or may not connect with a public road system, provide foot access to the interior. Logging camps may be served by air or ferry service so, along with the roads, can be useful to backcountry travellers.

There can be tension between user-groups in these forests, however. Skiers who emerged from a spring icefield tour at one of these camps were asked very pointedly if they were environmentalists before they were accorded any civility or assistance. Also, remember that you could be looked on as a person who will see and report illegal logging activities. New laws in B.C. provide for more significant penalties for illegal logging practices like logging to the edge of salmon streams, logging of identified and agreed-on biodiversity protection areas and scenic buffers, and logging of erodible areas. The key will be enforcement of the new laws.

The Coast Ranges of British Columbia

The Coast Ranges of B.C., rising to 4000 metres, are bordered by the Pacific Ocean on the west and the Interior Plateau, Fraser Plateau and Fraser River on the east. Because of enormous snowfalls, large icefields and glaciers are present despite a moderately warm climate. Valleys are steep-sided and glaciated and long fjords penetrate the range from the ocean. The Fraser, Skeena and Stikine are major rivers piercing the ranges as they flow to the coast from the interior.

The warm maritime climate produces enormous precipitation, as snow in winter and rain in summer. May is one of the drier months out of 12 very wet ones.

Consequently the vegetation on the west slopes is a thick, temperate coastal rainforest of cedar, Douglas fir and spruce characterized in many places by an almost impenetrable shrub undergrowth including devil's club. Drier forest is found in the rain shadow over to the east. Treeline is high and the trees often fade out into scrub rather than meadow. Vast areas have been logged.

The thick growth makes off-trail hiking below treeline tedious or impossible, so you must seek out trails. Woodland trails provide little in the way of wide vistas, but if you can get above treeline or to a viewpoint the terrain is spectacular—that is if you are lucky with the weather and can see anything through the rain and cloud. North of Whistler, access is difficult because there is no road up most of the coast side of the range. Access is by ferry to villages or logging camps. Logging roads give access from the east.

Plenty of crag and alpine rock climbing is available as are mixed rock and ice routes. Steep glacier-scoured valley walls form popular crags such as at Squamish, but there are plenty of others, some only accessible by boat. The rock is igneous and superior to that in the Rockies—when it is dry and not covered in lichens, that is. Reaching the alpine is the main problem for mountaineers and access by air often makes sense. Helicopters and fixed wing ski-wheel aircraft are used in winter, and float planes in summer. Many of the major peaks such as Waddington remained unclimbed for so long because of the difficulty in reaching them without aircraft.

Snowfalls are heavy and frequent in winter, the snow tending to be wet and heavy. Ski touring is possible, but trailbreaking is hard work and reaching the treeline is not easy. In spring, the weather improves and the snow consolidates. Classic high-level tours such as the Spearhead traverse above Whistler can be done in April and May in spring snow conditions. The huge icefields north toward Mt. Waddington are worthy objectives for fly-in spring touring. More accessible areas such as the Pemberton Icecap are accessible to snowmobiles, so you may not have a pleasant mountain experience in this area. You may have to endure periods of rain and wet snow that makes camping above treeline a chore even for the well-equipped expert. In the more northern regions, accessible glaciers such as the Juneau Icecap and Stikine Icefield provide expeditionary-style spring ski touring and rugged summer hiking and mountaineering.

The heavy precipitation in the Coast Ranges ensures there is lots of water for the whitewater paddler on rivers draining both sides of the range. Paddlers even go out in winter in the coastal areas. The Grand Canyon of the Stikine where it punches through the range is generally regarded as being unrunnable.

Opposite
Top: View from Mt. Argowitz into Radient Basin, Coast Ranges. Chic Scott photo.
Bottom: Toquart Bay, Broken Islands.

Ascending Canoe Glacier, Cariboo Mountains. Alf Skrastins photo.

The Central Ranges of British Columbia

The south Central Ranges, rising to 3500 metres, include the Selkirks, Monashees, Cariboos and Purcells, which are separated from the Rockies by the Rocky Mountain Trench and from the Coast Ranges by the south-flowing reach of the Fraser River and the Fraser Plateau. In northern British Columbia the Central Ranges are represented by the Skeena and Cassiar mountains. Volcanic cone mountains are also found in the north near Dease Lake. Large glaciers and icefields are a characteristic of the Central Ranges.

Because these ranges are farther from the coast, the climate is drier and colder than in the Coast Ranges. There are more clear days, and the snowfall is less. The trend continues as you head east to the Rockies—compare 1000-2000 centimetres (yes, centimetres!) annual snowfall in Rogers Pass at 1300 metres in the Selkirks to 400 centimetres at Lake Louise in the Rockies. Winter weather rarely gets as cold as in the Rockies (-23°C at Rogers Pass caused considerable surprise during Christmas '93). Dampness and cloudiness keep summer temperatures moderate. The driest month in Revelstoke is May with 56.5 millimetres of precipitation; the rainiest month is June at 73 millimetres. July, August and September are in the 60-65 millimetres range.

The warmer, wetter climate results in a higher treeline and denser growth of bigger trees than in the Rockies, but lower and less dense than in the Coast Ranges. Cedars and Douglas fir are the dominant species with dense undergrowth containing the thorny devil's club. Treeline can be scattered trees and meadow or can incorporate nasty scrub thickets.

Little of the interior ranges is protected by readily accessible major parks so it is generally a multi-use area allowing logging, hunting and motorized recreation. Summer hiking is popular, but because of the heavy snow accumulations there can be deep winter snow still lying at quite low elevations into July. Snowfalls can render the mountain trails temporarily treacherous at any time in the summer season.

For climbers, the rock in these ranges is mostly igneous and metamorphic, which provides excellent summer mountaineering. The granite spires of the Bugaboos in the Purcells are a legendary rock-climbing mecca. Good mixed-route mountaineering is available in areas where glaciers are present.

In the south, there are many whitewater rivers descending from the mountains to the big rivers of the intermontane valleys. Most of these side valleys have roads or logging roads that provide access. In the north, major rivers such as the Stikine provide scope for long wilderness trips.

The warmer winters and the heavier snowfall produce a snowpack more suited to powder skiing than that in the Rockies, and with better weather than the Coast Ranges. There are a large number of remote huts and lodges, usually accessed by helicopter, which are popular locations for week-long, powder-skiing trips.

Unfortunately the big-money heli-skiing outfits have been allowed to lease virtually all the good ski terrain in the B.C. interior ranges in the southern half of the province. This was intended to prevent competition between them for territory, but the result has been that opportunities for self-propelled powder skiers have been curtailed. Unpleasant confrontations have occurred when helicopter groups have chosen to ski over terrain that touring parties have worked hard to reach. On the brighter side, there have been notable examples of cooperation where tourers have helped rescue heli-skiers and vice-versa.

Later in the season in March/April the heli-skiers depart, the weather stabilizes and the snow consolidates enough for easier long-distance touring on classic routes such as the Bugaboos to the Rogers Pass traverse or the Cariboo traverse. The high level parts of the Grand Traverses are viable into late May. However, without helicopter or ski plane access you can be faced with horrendous low-level approach and egress conditions in a rotted snowpack.

Lack of proper regulation and increasing machine power means that snowmobiles are able to penetrate high into the mountains up resource access roads. Their presence above the treeline in the alpine meadows, coupled with inconsiderate use by some riders is having an adverse effect on the ski touring experience in some areas.

The Canadian Rockies

The Canadian Rockies proper are the eastern-most range lying between the prairies and the Rocky Mountain Trench (a rift valley occupied by the north-flowing leg of the Columbia River and continuing northwest with the north-flowing arm of the Fraser, Parsnip and Finlay rivers). The highest peaks are almost 4000 metres, with many around 3000 metres. Extensive glaciers and icefields are found in the higher areas of the Rockies along the Continental Divide, which is also the British Columbia–Alberta boundary.

Because they lie in the rain shadow of the Central Ranges, the climate of the Rockies is drier than that of the ranges farther west. Lake Louise at 1500 metres near the Great Divide has an annual precipitation of 68 centimetres and around 400 centimetres of snow, which is much less than that of the western ranges. The Rockies' own rain shadow effect ensures that the east side of the range is even drier, especially in winter. Banff, 50 kilometres farther east of Lake Louise, has only about 47 centimetres of precipitation and only 250 centimetres of snow. In winter the Rockies are protected from warm, wet ocean winds by the ranges to the west, but are subject to the influence of cold, dry prairie air, which is particularly strong on the east side. However, warm, dry chinook winds play havoc with the snow on the east side of the Rockies. The extensive glaciers are a result of a combination of low temperature and moderate snowfall.

In summer, weather will not always be better farther east. "Upslope" conditions can exist in which moist air from the east dumps precipitation on the east side. This usually occurs in late spring. Heading west is then a good option if you have a choice. July tends to be drier with temperatures reaching the high 20s Celsius and August to be less stable, but in the mountains you can never be sure what you'll get. By September the nights are cool or frosty but you can still have warm, sunny days into October. On the other hand, you can have snow in any month, too.

The Rockies are well forested on lower slopes, especially on the wetter side where there is also a dense understorey similar to that found in the Central Ranges. Lodgepole pine is common, along with Engelmann spruce and Douglas fir. At treeline the trees thin out to islands of trees in meadows.

Much of the Canadian Rockies is protected by the national parks of Waterton, Kootenay, Banff, Yoho and Jasper and by provincial parks and wilderness areas such as Elk Lakes, Assiniboine and Mt. Robson parks in B.C., Peter Lougheed Provincial Park, the White Goat Wilderness and the Ghost River Wilderness area in Alberta. These are large areas for backcountry recreation without heli-skiers, hunters or ATV drivers and snowmobilers. On the other hand, Kananaskis Country is a wildland recreation area with separate zones for non-motorized and motorized recreation.

Summer hiking and backpacking are popular, especially in the parks where there are many hiking trails. High-altitude trails near the Great Divide are wet and fragile, even snow covered, well into July. The farther east you go toward the prairies, the drier the overall climate, with hiking good from May onwards.

Rock is sedimentary or metamorphic and of variable quality for rock climbing. There is sound quartzite, good limestone and vertical scree. Use a guidebook! Sport climbing is becoming increasingly popular in the southern half of the region. Excellent mixed alpine mountaineering opportunities exist on the icefields and on glacier-clad peaks. Accessibility is quite good from the Icefields Parkway.

Whitewater opportunities abound, though most of the rivers are short and more suited to car-supported day trips than multi-day trips, particularly because roads parallel the rivers in most valleys. In the southern third of Alberta alone, there are a dozen or so easily accessible rivers flowing out of the mountains onto the prairies, providing up to three-day whitewater paddling weekends on Class 2, 3 and 4 water.

Compared to the ranges to the west, winter weather is more often clear and the snow lighter and fluffier, which makes for good ski touring. Unfortunately, high winds are common in the longer periods between snowfalls, and these soon hammer much of the powder into breakable crust or boilerplate. In addition, low winter temperatures and shallow snowpack cause the formation of depth hoar and deep snow instabilities. Consequently, avalanche danger makes skiing hazardous to those unfamiliar with the conditions. More stable snow and more settled weather make March/April the prime season for ski touring and ski mountaineering up on the glaciers or in the Alpine.

The Canadian Rockies. The flower gardens of Rockwall Pass looking toward Tumbling Pass and Tumbling Glacier. Gillean Daffern photo.

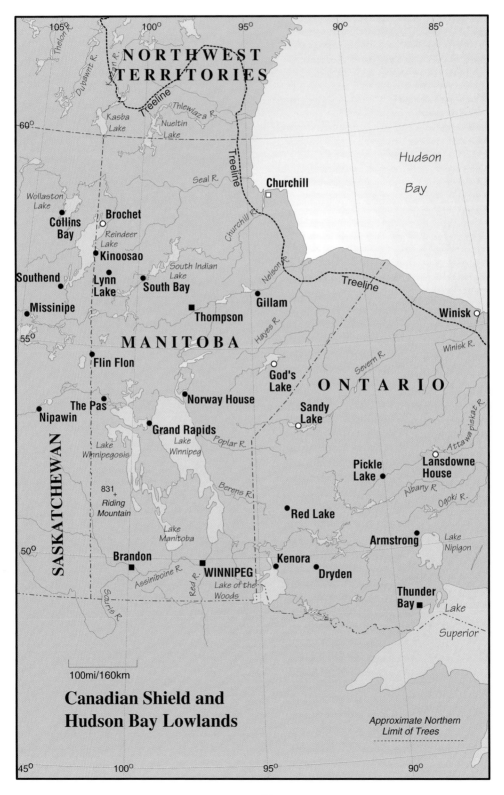

**Canadian Shield and
Hudson Bay Lowlands**

100mi/160km

Approximate Northern
Limit of Trees

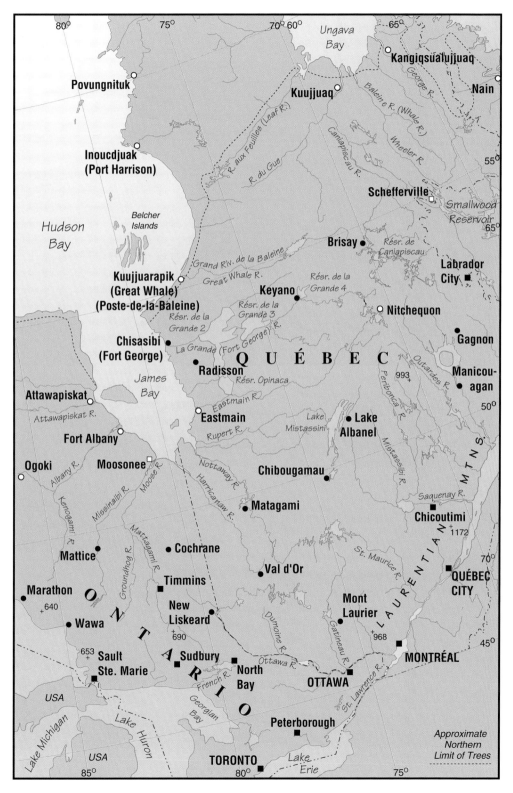

Eskers provide raised campsites in low-lying northern Manitoba

Liard River, approaching the Mackenzie River.

The Prairies and Mackenzie Lowlands

The Prairies are generally regarded as being the flat and rolling treeless plains of Alberta east of the Rockies, southern Saskatchewan and southern Manitoba. However, technically the area also includes the forested lands of northern Alberta and the Mackenzie Valley. Some uplands exist, such as Riding Mountain and Duck Mountain in Manitoba, the Cypress Hills in southeastern Alberta and the Swan Hills in northern Alberta.

The climate is continental with extremes of temperatures ranging from -40°C in winter to +40°C in summer in southern regions. Northern regions can still experience +30°C summer temperatures, but cold, sleet and rain are equally possible. Rainfall is low in the south, often falling during thunderstorms that are associated with high winds, hail and even tornadoes. Similarly winter snowfall is light in the south but heavier farther north and west.

Vegetation varies from arid grasslands through scattered clumps of cottonwoods on river banks and in sheltered areas to aspen forest and black spruce/muskeg terrain farther north and west. Upland areas such as Riding Mountain are generally forested.

While the unforested parts of the Prairies are largely private farmland or public land leased to ranchers for grazing, there are areas important for recreation. The eroded coulees and spectacular badlands of southeastern Alberta and western Saskatchewan can be visited on foot or by canoe and raft from the rivers that flow through them. The rivers are generally silty flatwater, though some have a good current. There are historic, prehistoric and palaeontology sites of interest along many of these rivers like the Milk or the Red Deer. Lakes are often shallow and swampy and busy with motor boat traffic, so lake canoeing is not a prime option. Large lakes are also subject to high winds, which, coupled with the shallow water, soon whip up dangerous waves. Uplands such as Riding Mountain and the Cypress Hills provide hiking opportunities. An area of natural rolling grasslands is preserved in Grasslands National Park in southern Saskatchewan. The forested northwestern region is not a recreation mecca because of generally flat terrain, forest, muskeg and bugs.

Rivers such as the Mackenzie and its tributaries that traverse the area are used by canoeists, but day after day of bugs, often poor camping, muddy banks and not much scenic variety is not my idea of a good way to spend holiday time. However, people do find the native culture along these rivers interesting. The larger rivers are wide enough to present major wind problems, either headwinds or large waves whipped by the wind blowing against the current.

Snow accumulations are light in the treeless south, the small amount of snow generally windblasted and unappealing to skiers. Winter recreation opportunities such as cross-country skiing and snowshoeing are better farther north in the forested regions where the climate is wetter. Little of the region is protected by park regulations so snowmobiles will be encountered.

The Hudson Bay Lowlands

The Hudson Bay Lowlands surround Hudson and James bays in a crescent. The country is generally flat, liberally dotted with swamps and bogs and, for many people, monotonous. The coastline is also mostly low-lying with vast mud flats at low tide. Because the area is subject to isostatic rebound after melting of the ice-sheets, there are many raised beaches along the shoreline.

The inland part of the lowlands is subject to both hot interior continental summer weather and to cool, damp weather from the north. Coastal areas are apt to be cool and foggy, the bay moderating summer temperatures until ice forms on the ocean. Winter conditions are extremely cold because of Arctic and continental influences.

South of the treeline there is mile after mile of muskeg and black spruce forest, with little change or variety. In summer this is serious bug country. The Hudson Bay Lowlands are not most people's choice as a recreation destination. However, some major classic canoe routes pass through the region en route to the coast from the more interesting Shield country.

Be aware that the Churchill and Nelson rivers have been seriously disrupted by hydroelectric stations, as have many of the rivers on the Quebec side in the notorious James Bay project.

Some parties try to navigate the Hudson Bay coast from the mouth of rivers such as the Seal to the town of Churchill for exit by rail to the south. Because much of the exposed coast is low-lying and featureless, navigation is difficult. Problems are compounded by shallow choppy water, fog and vast areas exposed at low tide. Attempting the route has resulted in deaths, so an air or boat charter is advisable.

The forest generally extends right to the river banks. Low river levels later in the season may provide more open, windy and less buggy sand bar or gravel bar camp sites. Eskers, which may be marked on topographic maps, tend to form sandy beaches and raised camp sites with views.

The terrain is generally unappealing to walkers because of poor drainage, bugs and large numbers of polar bears that move ashore once the ice melts. However, a walking route has been planned along the James Bay coast from Moosonee to Cape Henrietta Maria. The route is along raised beach ridges that provide good walking and birdwatching opportunities. It is only usable in May and June before the polar bears come ashore.

Winter expeditions have been made along the coast and also inland, on snowshoes pulling traditional toboggans or using dog teams.

Low tide on the low-lying coast of Hudson Bay at the mouth of the Seal River.

Shield country—rock outcrops, lakes and mixed forest.

The Canadian Shield

The Canadian Shield is characterized by vast numbers of lakes of all sizes, connected by streams and rivers that may or may not be navigable. Between the lakes are swamps and uplands, often with exposed outcroppings of Precambrian granite or ancient quartzite. In most regions the Shield is a rugged undulating plain or plateau with little overall relief. The few hilly locations include the Thunder Bay area, the La Cloche Range north of Lake Huron, the 1200 metre-high Laurentian Mountains north of Montreal and the 1200 metre-high Monts Groulx north of Baie Comeau. Major rivers traversing the Shield flow into James Bay, Hudson Bay, the Arctic Ocean, Labrador Sea and the Gulf of St. Lawrence. In some areas such as the uplands of Quebec, the rivers run in deep, narrow gorges.

Weather conditions and the timing of the seasons vary considerably because the Shield extends in a wide swath across Canada. In the southern regions of the lower Great Lakes and the St. Lawrence Valley, the ice is gone from the lakes in April, and hardy types may be swimming in June. Hot, steamy 30°C weather seeping up from the U.S. is quite common during July and August. Although the weather can be pleasant well into October, be prepared for anything from snow to 20°C weather in fall.

Farther north the summer season is progressively shorter, with ice remaining on the lakes until June or even later. Mid-summer temperatures can still reach the high 20°C range, usually without the nasty humidity of the south. However, temperatures in the teens are more common. In the far northwestern areas of the Shield north of Great Slave Lake, I have experienced everything from snow to 25°C weather in July. Rainfall varies across the region, but it is certainly high on the Shield of Labrador and eastern Quebec.

Winter temperatures are variable but are more consistently cold and dry farther north and west. Areas adjacent to the southern Great Lakes and St. Lawrence Valley are subject to periodic winter thaws caused by warm, damp weather spreading north from the U.S. These thaws are unpleasant but do have the advantage of settling the snowpack to improve travel conditions. Snowfalls are heavier and wetter farther east. Large bodies of water such as the Great

Lakes not only exert a local temperature-moderating influence, but also generate locally heavy snowfalls in the early part of the winter before they freeze over.

Most of the Shield is forested with scattered pockets of agriculture and occasional larger pockets such as the "Clay Belt" in the Timiskaming region of Ontario/Quebec. Forests are a mixture of hardwoods (maple, oak, birch, poplar) and softwoods of spruce and pine in the south, giving way to boreal forest of spruce, birch and poplar in more northerly regions. Ice-scoured ridges of bare rock and exposed esker tops have sparse vegetation, thus allowing views and easier travel. Although the Shield extends beyond the latitude treeline, higher elevations are generally below treeline. Even at high points like Mt. Tremblant at 1200 metres there are trees on the ridge tops. Farther north, such as on the plateaux of the Monts Groulx, there is both tundra and alpine forest.

Poor drainage on the Canadian Shield provides excellent breeding conditions for mosquitoes and blackflies. It's not easy to find open, bug-free gravel bar camping along the waterways.

Much of the summer recreation in the Shield country is water-based. Many of the lakes are connected by old, established portage trails, making long journeys by canoe possible. Light canoes and equipment are required to make portaging ("the noble torture") less of a chore and to allow single carries of a week's worth of gear.

Because there is so much exposed bedrock, the rivers are usually the "pool and drop" type. Consequently, there aren't many of the long, uninterrupted stretches of rapidless water that appeal to motorized river travellers. Navigation generally requires whitewater expertise or strenuous portaging. The better rivers within 300 kilometres or so of cities are very popular and crowded, especially on long weekends. However, "crowded" is a relative term and you rarely encounter the mob scenes characteristic of some U.S. rivers. Rafting is also popular and can sometimes create an unpleasant atmosphere. Good camping spots are few and therefore heavily used, but small parties with small, free-standing tents, good sleeping pads, a water carrier and stoves, have a better selection of sites and can also easily move up and away from the water.

Many of the Shield rivers have been devastated by hydroelectric developments. The most notorious of these lie on the Quebec side of Hudson Bay where whole landscapes have been changed and drainage patterns entirely altered. In Manitoba, the Churchill River system has had major diversions and now flows into the Nelson. Some rivers draining south into the St. Lawrence have also been altered. The Shield is extensively logged for lumber and pulp and paper manufacturing. Some rivers are protected by unlogged scenic corridors. Many rivers downstream from pulp mills are noticeably polluted and eating the fish is not recommended.

Touring in sea kayaks, canoes with spray covers and sailboats is possible where the Shield abuts large lakes such as Huron, Superior and Great Slave. This is especially the case where the coasts are sheltered by islands. Unfortunately, the same places are also attractive to motor boaters. The best boating is generally away from the main channels and in shallow, rocky areas where motor boats are less likely to go.

Summer travel on foot is less appealing than travel by canoe because of rugged terrain, bugs and the fact that in many areas you cannot walk far without encountering a watery obstacle. Old logging roads provide some hiking routes, but are usually at low elevations without views and are also used for motorized recreation. Long-distance hiking is best on walking trails such as the Rideau Trail in eastern Ontario and the Voyageur Trail around the upper Great Lakes. In drier and hillier areas there is more scope for impromptu routes.

The Shield country offers tremendous opportunities for winter recreation because the frozen lakes and the portages between them provide a network of through routes. Old logging roads also permit easy travel, and in some areas the forest is open enough to allow easy progress. Travel on skis and snowshoes or by dogsled can be very rewarding. Note that except in parks, this same terrain is also heavily used by snowmobilers, often creating unpleasant conditions for skiers and snowshoers. Networks of groomed and trackset cross-country ski trails exist in southern Ontario and Quebec and around some northern communities. Some trails are linked hotel to hotel.

Kayak touring on the northeast coast of Lake Huron.

Granite outcroppings provide good opportunities for rock climbing. In certain areas, especially within reach of urban centres, the cliffs are becoming popular and crowded, but there are still plenty more to be explored in remoter places. Blackflies and mosquitoes can make climbing miserable—on a hard move a blackfly in your ear can be hell! Early spring and late summer are more pleasant when fewer bugs are around. Likewise, waterfall ice climbing is increasing in popularity. New climbs are being sniffed out all over the accessible areas of the Shield, particularly around Thunder Bay. Crags on private land pose access problems. This is partly because rock climbing and ice climbing are relatively new activities and there is no "mountain tradition." They are looked on as fringe activities and many landowners are concerned about their exposure to liability lawsuits if people are injured on their land.

There are a number of large and famous parks in the Shield region, such as Algonquin, Quetico, La Verendrye and Prince Albert. Some are not pristine wilderness areas and allow industrial and motorized activity. Algonquin is a prime example of a renowned park that people expect to be a protected area. In fact, much of it is being or has been logged, and half is open to aboriginal hunting. One section is even open to hunting by private hunting clubs. Check the status of parks before you go.

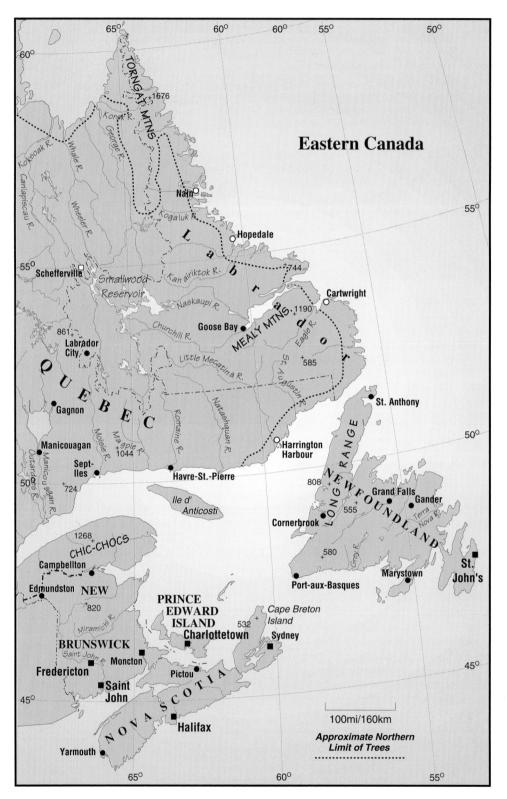

Eastern Canada

100mi/160km

Approximate Northern
Limit of Trees

Eastern Canada

The east coast has a wide variety of landscapes. In southern Nova Scotia the coastline is generally indented and low-lying. Inland the relief is also low with many small rivers, lakes and swamps. Farther north the Cape Breton Highlands, a plateau dissected by deep valleys, rise 500 metres from the ocean. Similarly the rolling country of New Brunswick rises to around 850 metres in the north of the province. The coast of the Bay of Fundy is a mix of cliffs and tidal flats, backed by hills and rolling country. The St. Lawrence estuary shoreline is generally not indented except in the areas of the Mingan Archipelago and the Saguenay estuary, which are of interest to recreationists. On the Gaspe peninsula, the Chic-Chocs are an extensive region of uplands rising to 1300 metres.

The agricultural Prince Edward Island is quite developed and mainly of interest to tourists attracted to sandy beaches and relatively warm ocean waters. The north shore has extensive sandspits with protected lagoons behind them.

Newfoundland is known as "The Rock" with good reason—the coastline is rocky with many coves, fjords and bays. The west coast is backed by the 600 metre-high hills of the Long Range, which drop precipitously from the plateau to spectacular fjords in the Gros Morne National Park region. The interior is varied with open uplands and lowland forests and swamps. Labrador has a similar shoreline. In the northern part the rugged Torngat Mountains rise to 1600 metres behind a coast characterized by deep fjords and islands.

The area's climate is generally classified as cool maritime, becoming cooler as you head north. In coastal areas the climate is influenced by the warm Gulf Stream and the cold southerly-flowing Labrador current that brings cold Arctic water and icebergs from the Davis Strait. Summer fogs are a common occurrence, and a day that is warm and sunny at the head of a bay or a few miles inland can be decidedly cool and dank out on the coast. Inland, with less of a moderating influence from the ocean, continental influences are stronger, so winter temperatures are colder and summer temperatures warmer.

The valley of the Kogaluk River cuts into the Labrador Plateau. Ken Ellison photo.

Cape Chignecto, Bay of Fundy. Photo courtesy of Scott Cunningham—Coastal Adventures, Tangiers, Nova Scotia.

While the Atlantic coastline of Nova Scotia and Newfoundland experience considerable precipitation—about 100 centimetres annually, the western side of Newfoundland has barely two-thirds as much, and northern Labrador less than half that amount. The coastal summers can be very wet and grey, especially on Newfoundland's east side. Throughout the area, even relatively low hills create relief precipitation effects in all seasons because of proximity to the ocean.

Winter conditions vary depending on whether the dominant influence at the time happens to be cold dry continental, warm damp maritime or cold wet northern. There are snowbelts where winds off the ocean combine with land relief to cause localized heavy snowfalls. Particularly heavy snowfall areas include southern Labrador, the highlands of northern New Brunswick and the western uplands of Newfoundland. On the open uplands such as the Chic-Chocs and Gros Morne, arctic blizzard-like conditions can occur, made more unpleasant by dampness due to the proximity of the ocean. Drifted snow stays on these uplands well into April and even later.

In the more sheltered areas deciduous and coniferous forests flourish to the shoreline, but are not as thick and lush as the dense rainforest of the Pacific coast. Coastal vegetation thins out farther north, and much of the Labrador coast is devoid of trees. The treeline is quite low over much of the area, and at even 600 metres in Gros Morne, the vegetation has an arctic-alpine quality. As treeline is approached, and in exposed coasts and uplands, harsh growing conditions result in dense, stunted growth of spruce and fir that is impenetrable. This is known in Newfoundland as tuckamore. The mainland interior is likewise densely forested with a mixture of deciduous and coniferous trees, the actual density depending on local climate and soil. Most of the area has been heavily logged. Poor drainage and generally wet summers mean that most of the region is prime habitat for mosquitoes and blackflies.

Sea kayakers have a wide variety of opportunities. On the populated coasts of Nova Scotia, Quebec, New Brunswick, Prince Edward Island and some parts of Newfoundland, road access is available to many launching places. The remoter areas with their small, isolated fishing communities are served only by ferries or air. Since 1949 centralization of settlements and services has meant that many of these communities have been abandoned, especially in Newfoundland and Labrador. In the fjord coastline of northern Labrador, very remote, expeditionary sea kayaking opportunities exist. Access is by ferry, charter boat or aircraft, so it takes time and/or money to get there. The Voisey's Bay region near Nain is now the hub of a major mining and prospecting boom. In the Bay of Fundy, the extremely large tidal range is a factor to be reckoned with.

Expeditionary hiking and mountaineering is possible in the Torngat Mountains of northern Labrador, where open terrain makes for easier travel. The sea cliffs of west Newfoundland are largely unexplored as a rock climbing venue. Other, more accessible uplands such as the Chic-Chocs and the Cape Breton Highlands provide good backpacking opportunities. In the gentler terrain in other parts of the region most of the hiking is below treeline on trails and old logging roads you will often have to share with ATVs and 4x4s. In Newfoundland, Gros Morne and the ridges of higher ground above interior boggy plateaus offer good walking, especially where not covered in tuckamore. However, intervening swamps and tangled spruce forest can make foot travel unpleasant, especially in a wet year. Getting to the good walking may be a challenge, and as elsewhere, if there is a trail it will likely be open to motorized travellers. While fall is a good time for hiking in most areas (no bugs), there are hazards associated with being in the woods at the same time as hunters.

Canoeing is rewarding in many parts of the region, with opportunities for lake canoeing, lake-and-portage canoe trips and river trips. Some of these trips take you through private land, which can create camping problems. Labrador, especially, has many opportunities for serious, long-distance river wilderness canoe tripping. In remote areas access and egress is often difficult, expensive and time consuming unless you have folding craft that are easier to transport by air. Some people have found it worthwhile to group together and buy canoes to leave in Labrador. Over a number of years and trips, the initial transport expense becomes insignificant. As elsewhere in Canada, hydroelectric projects have affected vast areas

Palmer River valley, Torngat Mountains. Ken Ellison photo.

and have diverted whole watersheds. Check carefully before you pick a river. Churchill Falls in Labrador and the Bay d'Espoir project of southwest Newfoundland are major developments to be aware of.

Good cross-country skiing and snow-shoeing can be enjoyed all over the region. I still fondly remember my first forays on cross-country skis in the uplands around Wentworth Valley in Nova Scotia. Unfortunately, as in so many regions, conditions that are good for cross-country skiing and snowshoeing are also good for snowmobiling. Some of the parks even allow snowmobiling, so check before you go! More adventurous, mountain-style ski touring can be found in the highlands such as the Chic-Chocs of the Gaspe, and the Long Range and Gros Morne in Newfoundland. Hut to hut skiing is available in the Chic-Chocs and in some lowland parks such as Kejimkujik in Nova Scotia.

The Alaska Interior

The Central Interior straddles the Arctic Circle between the Alaska Range and the Brooks Range. It includes the basins of major rivers such as the Kuskokwim, Yukon and Koyukuk. Parts of these basins are very wide low-lying marshy plains, such as the Yukon Flats. In other areas low wooded hills are interspersed with wetlands. There are ranges of higher hills such as the Kuskokwim Mountains, the Kokrines Hills and the uplands east of Fairbanks toward the Yukon border. The west coast of this region extends from the Alaska Peninsula to the Arctic Circle and is generally low-lying, very different from the coasts farther east and south. The vast deltas of several big rivers are major features.

The area has a semi-arid continental climate with extremes ranging from -50°C to +30°C. In Fairbanks, for example, temperatures in summer range from 2°C to 30°C. In winter temperatures can fluctuate even more, from -50°C when a cold Arctic air mass is stationary over the area to +7°C, when warm southerly winds occasionally come over the Alaska Range to produce a warm, dry, chinook effect. Spring is generally the driest time, with the most rain falling in thunderstorms in July and August. That's less than five centimetres for the month. Farther west in the region and nearer the coast, temperatures are moderated by the ocean.

Treeline approximates the Arctic Circle and then dips south approximately paralleling the coast to the Alaska Peninsula. Farther south, vegetation is only present up to 800 metres, and ranges from scattered deciduous and coniferous forest in favoured locations through alder and willow thickets to tundra. Bugs are fierce in this region during summer months. The first frost can arrive in August and then most of these pests are eliminated.

The numerous rivers are the highways of the region, used in summer by boat and in winter by snowmobiles and dogsled. Long-distance water travel along these rivers by canoe and raft is popular. Although the generally lower-lying terrain means that many of these rivers do not have the spectacular grandeur of mountain rivers, they do traverse some wild and beautiful country. Some areas, such as the Yukon Flats downstream of Circle, are very flat and marshy. Other areas,

like the Yukon-Charley Reserve, have more interesting relief along the riversides. In this region of few roads, access by air is often necessary. Rafts and other inflatables are cheaper and easier to transport this way than canoes.

The larger rivers such as the Yukon are very wide in their lower regions—several kilometres in some cases. This, coupled with flat open country means they are very subject to the effects of high winds. A friend reported two metre-high waves kicked up into a dangerous short chop by the wind against the current of the lower Yukon. In summer, the banks are often low-lying and muddy, making camping difficult.

Hiking and long-distance backpacking is possible, especially above treeline or using old gold mining exploration roads. In the western coastal regions of low-lying rolling tundra the main attractions are the wildlife and the archaeological interest associated with the Bering Land Bridge.

Winter recreation is popular within the limitations of short winter days (five hours in mid-January at Fairbanks), and low temperatures. In some areas shallow snowpacks coupled with low temperature can result in recrystallization rather than consolidation of the snow making off-trail travel poor. However, opportunities still abound for cross-country skiing, snowshoeing and the great Alaskan tradition, dogsledding.

Raft on Kendik River. Photo Peter Fitzmaurice.

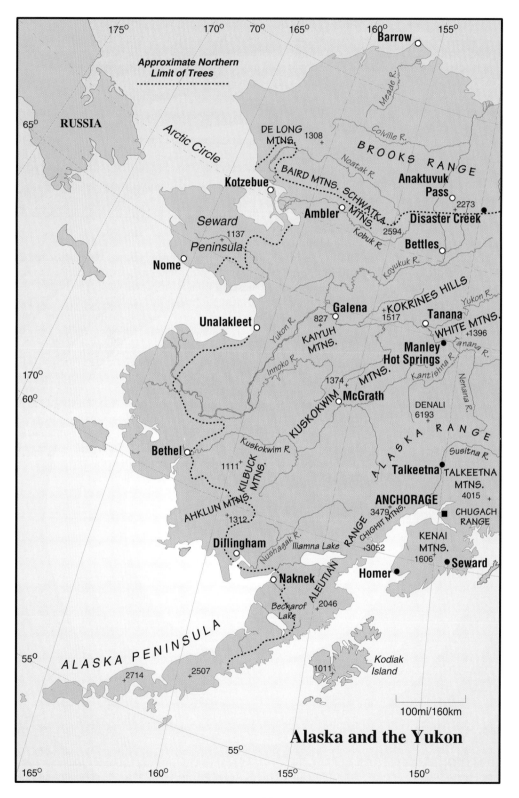

Alaska and the Yukon

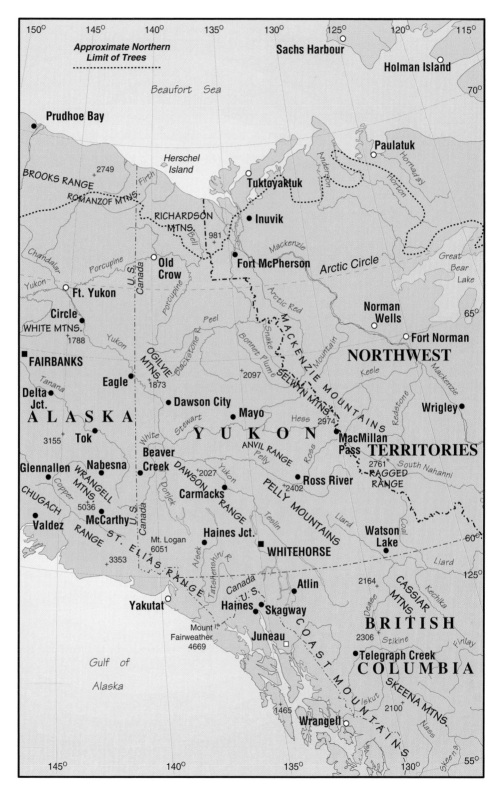

150° 145° 140° 135° 130° 125° 120° 115°

Approximate Northern Limit of Trees

Sachs Harbour

Holman Island

70°

Beaufort Sea

Prudhoe Bay

Paulatuk

BROOKS RANGE

+2749

ROMANZOF MTNS.

Firth

Herschel Island

Tuktoyaktuk

Anderson

Hornaday

Horton

RICHARDSON MTNS.

Inuvik

981 +

Mackenzie

Chandalar

Porcupine

U.S.
Canada

Bell

Old Crow

Fort McPherson

Arctic Circle

Great Bear Lake

Yukon

Ft. Yukon

Porcupine

Arctic Red

Norman Wells

65°

Circle

WHITE MTNS.

+1788

Peel

Bonnet Plume

Shake

Mountain

Fort Norman

Yukon

OGILVIE MTNS.

Blackstone R.

+2097

MACKENZIE MOUNTAINS

Keele

NORTHWEST

Redstone

Mackenzie

■ **FAIRBANKS**

Tanana

Eagle

+1873

SELWIN MTNS.

Delta Jct.

Dawson City

Mayo

Stewart

Hess

2974 +

Wrigley

A L A S K A

3155 +

Tok

White

Y U K O N

ANVIL RANGE

MacMillan Pass

2761 +

South Nahanni

TERRITORIES

Glennallen

Nabesna

WRANGELL MTNS.

Beaver Creek

DAWSON RANGE

+2027

Yukon

Pelly

Ross River

+2402

Ross

RAGGED RANGE

Copper

CHUGACH

5036 +

McCarthy

Donjek

Carmacks

PELLY MOUNTAINS

Liard

Watson Lake

Coal

60°

Valdez

RANGE

ST. ELIAS RANGE

Mt. Logan 6051

Haines Jct.

Teslin

■ **WHITEHORSE**

Liard

+3353

Alsek

Tatshenshini R.

Canada
U.S.

Atlin

2164 +

CASSIAR MTNS

Kechika

125°

Yakutat

Haines

Skagway

Dease

Stikine

Finlay

Mount Fairweather 4669

Juneau

2306 +

C O A S T   M O U N T A I N S

BRITISH

Gulf of Alaska

Telegraph Creek

COLUMBIA

SKEENA MTNS.

Iskut

2100 +

Nass

+1465

Wrangell

Skeena

55°

145° 140° 135° 130°

Katmai National Park. Valley of the 10,000 Smokes area. Jill Fredston photo.

Yukon River, Five Finger Rapids. Paul Bezooyen photo.

The Alaska Peninsula and the Aleutians

The Alaska Peninsula and the Aleutian chain extend like a narrow finger far out into the north Pacific. Much of the terrain is very rugged with volcanic mountains showing signs of recent volcanic activity reaching nearly 3000 metres. Other landscapes include tundra-covered hills and plains, lakes and wetlands, short wild rivers and ocean cliffs.

The Alaska Peninsula and particularly the Aleutian chain are renowned for miserable weather with high winds, grey skies, fog and rain the norm. However, what you actually experience depends on whether you are there when Pacific weather is moving north or when Bering Sea weather is moving south, and whether you are on the Bering or Pacific side. Temperatures are moderated by the ocean.

The exposed climate means the Aleutians and southern peninsula are treeless, except for small trees and scrub in a few favoured locations.

For backpackers, the harsh climate and remoteness makes the area very demanding. The volcanic mountain areas are of interest to a small number of highly skilled, experienced and self-sufficient backpackers. The Chigmit Mountains across Cook Inlet from Anchorage provide climbing opportunities, but must be accessed by air. Becharof National Wildlife Refuge and the adjacent Katmai National Park are renowned for dense grizzly bear populations. The rivers are short and fished heavily by grizzly and fishermen seeking salmon. Be aware that although much of the area is a Maritime wildlife refuge or wildlife refuge, this does not mean that hunting is necessarily prohibited.

Southern Central Alaska

The Kenai, Robinson and Chugach mountains separate the Southern Central Alaska interior lowlands from the coast. These ranges are generally around 1500 metres, but with peaks reaching 3000 metres, and extensively glaciated. Separating the Chugach and Robinson ranges is the vast Copper River, which punches through to the coast from its lowland basin north of the mountains.

The inland side of the mountains is drier and sunnier than the coast side because of the rain shadow effect. The difference is dramatic, with a tenfold increase in rainfall between the two areas. In winter the interior is colder because of a somewhat more continental climatic influence. However, the Alaska Range to the north helps keep out the really cold winter air from the Arctic. This is particularly the case on the higher ground between the Copper River basin and the Susitna basin to the west. Early summer is driest, with rainfall increasing after mid-June. By July and August, in Anchorage for example, there is a 60 per cent chance a day will be cloudy and a 30 per cent chance it will rain. September is the wettest month. The fall season is brief, extending from mid-September to mid-October, depending on altitude and local influences. Snow becomes more frequent in October, and even a 500-metre elevation change increases the snowfall considerably and extends the snow season.

In wetter areas with a coastal influence there is spruce and hemlock rain forest giving way to spruce and hardwood forest in the drier areas.

Mountain weather anywhere is unpredictable, but it is even more so in this area. It is close to the stormy Gulf of Alaska and far enough north to experience severe weather at any time.

Many of the rivers provide excellent canoeing, kayaking and rafting opportunities. Although summer can offer shorts and T-shirt weather, hypothermia is a possibility even on a fine day because Alaska river water is extremely cold. In the event of a capsize, a wet suit or dry suit will reduce the chance of hypothermia.

Access to mountains farther east for climbing and other recreation is possible by road from the Glenn, Richardson and Edgerton highways. The Wrangell-St. Elias Park area is relatively accessible but so far little developed, thus providing opportunities for expeditionary mountaineering, canoeing and kayaking, and rugged backpacking. Travel by air taxi to the numerous gravel airstrips is a common means of access.

Brooks Range. Jill Fredston photo.

Brooks Range. Jill Fredston photo.

Brooks Range and Arctic Plains

The Brooks Range, rising to 2800 metres, separates the Interior from the Arctic Plains that extend to the Arctic Ocean. Except for the granite spires of the Arrigetch Peaks, the limestone mountains are more rounded than the mountains farther south, with fewer glaciers reflecting a drier climate. The Romanzoff Mountains at the east end of the range are the highest and most glaciated. Major rivers on the south side of the range include the Kobuk and tributaries of the Koyukuk and Chandalar. The Noatak flows west between the two arms of the Brooks Range. The north side is drained by the Colville and its tributaries, flowing to the Beaufort Sea across the plains, a vast area of often poorly drained windswept tundra.

The oceans produce some moderating effects in summer after the ice melts. Summer may not start until July, and even then, conditions are cool and often wet and windy. There is a marked increase in precipitation in the mountains compared to Bettles just to the south, which has only 37 centimetres annual rainfall. By mid-August, temperatures well below freezing are likely. Winter temperatures are so extremely cold, in the -50°C range, that some areas are uninhabited.

Anomalies in the permafrost allow the growth of isolated patches of spruce trees well beyond the normal treeline. There is limited taiga vegetation at lower elevations and in sheltered locations and river valleys on the southern side of the range. The northern side is much colder and is virtually treeless. As with most northern regions the bugs can be bad in summer.

Backpacking is generally expeditionary type because access is usually by air and only longer trips justify the travel costs. The mountain terrain is open, permitting easier travel than in forested areas. However, walking through scrub in valley bottoms can be very difficult. Tundra terrain that looks innocent from a distance can be horrendous to walk over if it is tussocky—you are either on the unstable tops of the tussocks or in the bog between them. Impromptu trails from foot traffic have developed on some of the more popular routes. You should consider the ethics of contributing to the erosion problem by using these trails or of even going into some of these areas at all. Special care is needed in this fragile environment to practise minimum-impact travel and camping. The terrain and the lack of sheltering vegetation means travellers must be equipped and skilled enough to cope with strong, cold winds and rain without shelter or fires. The Arrigetch Peaks and Romanzoff Mountains are the areas of most interest to mountaineers.

Rivers are a popular way to see the area. Boaters can carry more gear, food and creature comforts than can backpackers. This makes it easier to deal with the harsh climate, especially if you get a period of bad weather, and you can still go on hiking or backpacking forays away from the river. Air charter outfitters in communities such as Bettles and Ambler can provide items such as canoes and rafts, which is a great help when staging points are only accessible by air or winter road. Be aware that Alaska has more private aircraft per capita than any other state, and boaters will encounter fly-in fishermen and weekenders.

There are plenty of whitewater rivers and rivers whose attraction lies more in their remoteness and unspoiled landscapes than in their adrenalin-high-inducing properties. Some, such as the Kobuk, have scattered settlements and homesteads.

Mount Fairweather from Alsek Lake.

The Alaska Coast

The Alaska coast from the Alaska Peninsula to the north end of the Alaska Panhandle is largely a region of mountainous islands and spectacular deep fjords flanked by glacier-studded mountains. The glaciers descend close to sea level in some areas such as Glacier Bay, Yakutat Bay, Icy Bay and Prince William Sound. Low-lying coastal plains are only of significant size between Cross Sound and Cordova. The Copper River with its vast delta enters the coast east of Cordova.

The Alaska coast is warmer than one would expect for the latitude because of the warming effect of ocean currents. The coastal winters are, in fact, quite mild. Glaciers are more the result of enormous snow accumulations in the mountains that rise behind the storm-lashed coasts than of low temperatures. Annual precipitation ranges from 200 to 500 centimetres, with snowfalls in the nearby mountains of 1000 centimetres and more. Even though June and early July is the driest time, the summer season is still best described as warm, cloudy and wet. A pilot with whom I flew out of Dry Bay, near Yakutat, told me that my flight was only the third of about 300 he had flown when there was not a low overcast sky. Parties have spent weeks in the area and never seen the mountain backdrop. As with any large expanses of inland icefields, cold air drainage off the ice is common, and fog can be expected quite often. The morning of our spectacular clear flight out of Dry Bay we had canoed in thick fog through a glacial lake full of icebergs before the fog burned off.

The vegetation is coastal wet forest, as dense as one would expect in a warm (considering the latitude), wet climate. The terrain is open where glaciers have retreated and the ice-scoured land not yet vegetated.

The coastal region is a mecca for sea kayakers, excepting the more open low-lying coast between Cross Sound and Cordova. Marine parks, national parks and wildlife refuges protect some of the area. Kayakers must be skilled and well equipped to deal with Gulf of Alaska weather and water conditions, including fog and tidal bores. They must always be prepared to wait out a period of bad weather. Prince William Sound and the Kenai Fjords are very popular because of easy road access from the Anchorage area. Kayak rentals are available and there are plenty of air and boat charters to get you to your starting point. The Sound is, of course, well known as the site of the infamous Exxon Valdez oil spill, but is recovering.

Because of lush coastal vegetation, walkers generally need trails. These are few and far between except near main centres and in some parks, but where trails exist, walking can provide spectacular ocean views if you are lucky with the weather. Careful scouting from the water can reveal worthwhile scrambles where the vegetation is thinner over more exposed terrain. From what I have seen of glaciers in the Glacier Bay region, their broken nature makes them unappealing as routes to the mountains.

Blackstone Bay, Prince William Sound.
Jill Fredston photo.

Mount Hunter from southeast fork of Kahiltna Glacier. Dave Clay photo.

The Alaska Range and Interior Mountains

A rugged range of high mountains arcs across south-central Alaska. They start from the west side of Cook Inlet and extend north and eastward through the Denali region where peaks reach up to 6190 metres. Farther east the Mentasta and Nutzotin ranges are considerably lower. The Wrangell Mountains, separated from the coastal Chugach Mountains by the Chitina River, contains America's largest concentration of high peaks in the 5000 metre range. Unlike the coastal mountains, where extremely heavy snowfall is the main factor, the area's many glaciers are the result of both heavy snowfall and low temperatures.

The Alaska Range forms the boundary between the arctic/continental climate to the north and the more maritime influences of the coast to the south. While the coastal mountains reduce the coastal influence they are not sufficient to stop storms tracking in off the Gulf of Alaska. On the high peaks, arctic conditions generally prevail. Spells of -40°C temperatures with high winds are not uncommon in the spring and summer climbing seasons. However, warmer spells can occur, especially in the spring period of fine weather.

Lower elevations are forested with treeline much lower than in the coastal mountains, making the alpine relatively accessible. Willow and alder brush as well as boggy and tussocky tundra can be as big a hindrance as dense forest, so routes and terrain must be carefully selected.

The Alaska Range contains Mts. Denali (McKinley), Foraker, Huntingdon and numerous equally worthwhile and challenging but less crowded peaks. The prime climbing season for major peaks is May to early July. Weather becomes more unsettled through July and August, leading to heavy snow high up and rain and melting snow bridges lower down. Access by foot to the major peaks from the Glenn, Richardson and Denali highways is possible for the purists, the masochists or the broke. However, charter flying makes more sense because arduous approach on foot is more likely to wear people out than prepare them physically for the climb. I'm glad I turned down an invitation to participate in an ascent of Denali on foot from the road. It was 23 years ago, but if I remember rightly, the party took 36 days of relaying horrendous loads to reach the summit. Meanwhile, I was spending my precious holiday time having a much more pleasant five weeks on the South Nahanni River!

Denali Park and preserve publishes excellent information for climbers. There are regulations to be complied with in advance, and restrictions on aircraft landing and air drops in the park. See page 124, Regulations.

East of the Denali region, the mountains are not as high but offer excellent opportunities for mountaineers. The lower elevations and proximity to highways make access easier but conditions shouldn't be underestimated. The region is, after all, close to the Arctic Circle and to the notoriously storm-lashed Gulf of Alaska, so extremely severe conditions can occur at any time.

Be aware that mountaineers are more affected by altitude in these northern latitudes than they would be at a similar altitude nearer the equator in the Himalayas or South America.

There are also plenty of opportunities for serious backpacking adventures beyond treeline in national and state parks. Even in Denali, much of the hiking is trail-less, "general route only," to preserve the permafrost. More self-sufficiency and navigation skill is required than on the signposted trails in southern national parks! There are many opportunities for hiking and backpacking outside the parks as well. However, be aware that Alaskan hiking *routes* can be very different from hiking *trails*, especially trails in the more heavily used southern states backcountry. River crossings can be a challenge because bridges are rarely provided in remote, little-used areas.

Canoeing, kayaking and rafting opportunities abound on the rivers draining north and south of the range. Some of these rivers are very challenging, others are much easier. Some have road access, others are fly-in. Generally the weather is more appealing for summer boating on the drier north side of the range.

With the northern latitude producing short winter days (five hours in January) and low winter temperatures, the later part of the season (March-April-May) is the best time for ski touring, snowshoeing and expeditionary ski touring and mountaineering using fly-in access.

East ridge of Mount Steele, Icefield Ranges. Summit is at top left. Tony Daffern photo.

Dall sheep near Kluane Lake, western interior ranges. Gillean Daffern photo.

The Icefield Ranges

The Icefield Ranges in the western Yukon and at the north end of the Alaska Panhandle include the largest nonpolar icefields in the world, with a vast array of peaks including Mt. Logan (5960 metres), Canada's highest peak, Mt. St. Elias, Mt. Vancouver, Mt. Lucania and Mt. Fairweather. Inland of the high ranges is an extensive area of lower, more rounded mountains and uplands extending east to the Yukon Valley.

Because they are so close to the coast, the Icefield Ranges have unpredictable weather. Extreme storms can occur at any time. The best months to visit are May and June when there is a reasonable balance between liveable temperatures, clear weather and firm enough snow for travelling. The lower mountains and uplands to the east lie in the rain shadow of the high peaks and have a drier, more continental type climate. This climatic transition between the Icefield Ranges and the interior is dramatic. Within a few days of returning from a three-week Icefield sled-hauling ski trip at the end of May, we were canoeing whitewater in shorts near Haines Junction. Admittedly that was a warm spring, and it could have snowed on us.

Moist forests of coniferous and deciduous trees as well as copious alder scrub cloak the western reaches of some of the major valleys such as the Tatshenshini and Alsek. They are pathways along which coastal moisture creeps inland through the Coast and Icefield ranges. Farther inland there is drier forest of lodgepole pine and spruce with less scrub at treeline. Extensive areas are above treeline, which is at about 1000 metres, and covered mostly in tundra-type vegetation or ice.

The Icefield Ranges are a magnificent area for serious expeditionary mountaineering, ski touring and ski mountaineering by strong, skilled and self-sufficient parties. Access is usually by ski-equipped fixed wing aircraft or helicopter from Kluane Lake or Whitehorse. Occasionally parties access the ranges on foot from the Alaska Highway. Much of the region is protected in the largest continuous international protected zone in the world. Various jurisdictions are involved—the Wrangell-St. Elias National Park and preserve (U.S.), Kluane National Park, Canada, Kluane Game Sanctuary, the newly protected Tatshenshini Provincial Park (B.C.) and the Glacier Bay National Park and preserve (U.S.). It is essential to contact the parks well in advance to find out about regulations and advance booking requirements. You should also make use of the wealth of information they can provide.

Western Yukon Interior Ranges

The Interior Ranges or "front" ranges east of the Icefield Ranges contain many lakes and rivers that provide opportunities for canoeing, kayaking and rafting. A number of very large mountain lakes and connecting lake systems also provide access by water to hiking areas. These big lakes are subject to unpredictable winds and must be navigated with more care than comparable sized lakes in less mountainous areas, especially as they are so cold. The spectacular and very demanding Tatshenshini-Alsek rivers rise in the front ranges, piercing the Icefield Ranges barrier to reach the Pacific.

Ski touring is not as good as one might expect because shallow snow and low temperatures contribute to a rotten snowpack with widespread depth hoar. The spring period of freeze-thaw consolidated snow is short. Some of the better touring is in road-accessible areas in the transition zone between coastal and interior snowpacks.

Excellent above-treeline hiking exists in the front ranges, some of it in Kluane National Park. However, there are few roads into the area and four-wheel drive vehicles or fly-ins to lakes are sometimes necessary. The historic Gold Rush Chilkoot Trail over the mountains is a popular backpacking route.

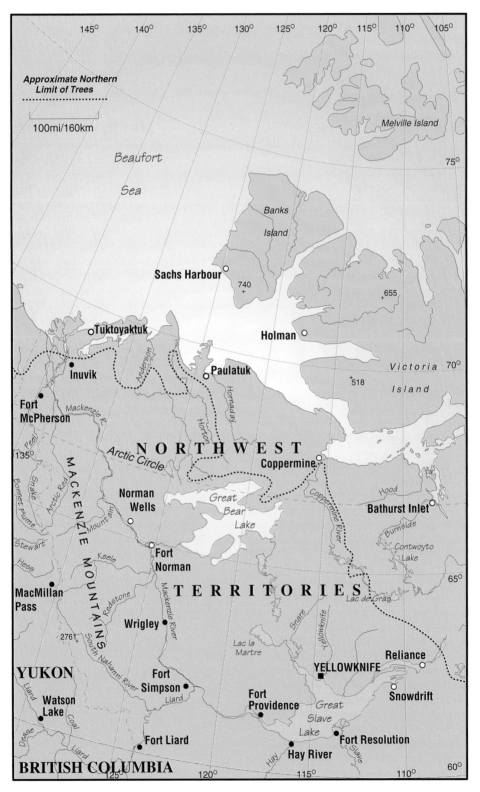

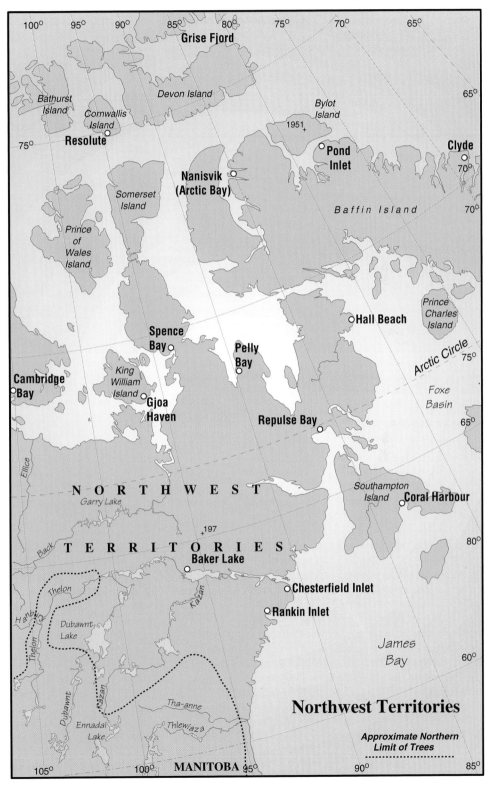

100°   95°   90°   85°   80°   75°   70°   65°

Grise Fjord

65°

Bathurst Island

Devon Island

Cornwallis Island

Bylot Island

1951 +

75°

Resolute

Clyde

70°

Nanisvik (Arctic Bay)

Pond Inlet

Somerset Island

Baffin Island

70°

Prince of Wales Island

Prince Charles Island

Hall Beach

Arctic Circle

75°

Spence Bay

Pelly Bay

Foxe Basin

Cambridge Bay

King William Island

65°

Gjoa Haven

Repulse Bay

65°

Ellice

N O R T H W E S T

Southampton Island

Coral Harbour

Garry Lake

Back

+ 197

T E R R I T O R I E S

80°

Baker Lake

Chesterfield Inlet

Thelon

Kazan

Rankin Inlet

Hanbu...

Dubawnt Lake

James Bay

Thelon

60°

Dubawnt

Kazan

Tha-anne

Ennadai Lake

Thlewiaza

Northwest Territories

Approximate Northern Limit of Trees

105°   100°   **MANITOBA** 95°   90°   85°

Upland lake, west central Yukon. Photo courtesy Primrose Wilderness Encounters, Whitehorse.

Central Yukon/Western Northwest Territories

The central Yukon is an area of upland to 2000 metres containing the Dawson Range, Pelly Mountains, and farther north, the Ogilvie Mountains. It is dissected by the north and west flowing tributaries of the Yukon River such as the Teslin, Big Salmon, Pelly and Stewart. Farther east, the Mackenzie Mountains, rising to almost 3000 metres, represent the continuation of the Rockies and form the border with the NWT. They eventually drop down to the interior plains of the Mackenzie Lowlands. The Mackenzie Mountains are predominantly sedimentary and there is a large area of karst country north of the lower reaches of the South Nahanni River. However, the spectacular Ragged Range or Logan Mountains (not to be confused with Mount Logan in the Icefield Ranges near the coast) have 3000 metre peaks with 1000 metre granite walls. The Tombstone Mountains farther north are yet another dramatic igneous intrusion. The Mackenzie Mountains drain east into the Mackenzie via major rivers such as the South Nahanni and Mountain. To the west, they drain into the Yukon via the South Macmillan and Hess and to the north via the Bonnet Plume and Snake.

This a fairly dry region because of its location to the east of high coastal mountains. The interior of the Yukon around Whitehorse is considered semi-arid. The mountains in the eastern parts of the region, like most mountain ranges, create their own weather. This is especially true in summer, when afternoon convective rain and thunderstorms are common. Partly for this reason, July and August are in fact the wettest months, with 90 and 60 millimetres respectively in the Mackenzie Mountains at Tungsten. Abrupt weather swings are possible. On one Nahanni trip I experienced day after day of wearing almost nothing in hot sunshine, but then a day later I was wearing everything I owned in sleet and snow. I recently read an account of a summer "canoe trip from hell" on the Natla River during which the party endured five days of snow. Average July/August temperatures at Tungsten are around 10°C, but about 15°C at the lower altitudes on the plains to the east.

Winter temperatures are of course very low because of the northern latitude and continental influences. However, occasional chinooks moderate the temperatures in western areas.

Virginia Falls, Nahanni River. Peter Jowett photo.

Because of the northern latitude, the treeline is low. There can be nasty alder and willow scrub at treeline in many wetter places and in valleys, making access to the alpine unpleasant. Spruce forests with occasional clumps of aspen are found in lowland areas, with the surrounding hills rising above treeline.

Good hiking is possible from the roads in the eastern part of the Yukon, especially once you are above treeline. In some areas the willow or alder scrub can make access to the treeline slow and tedious. Innocent-looking flat areas can be very unpleasant to hike if they are in fact spongy, wet tundra. Canoes allow access to high-quality hiking that is not road-accessible. The above-treeline hiking from some of the rivers in the eastern mountains is especially good. Walking the 350-kilometre Canol Heritage Trail is a very serious undertaking because of its remoteness and the difficult river crossings. Many parties have had serious difficulties on this route.

For canoeists, interior rivers such as the Yukon, Pelly, Big Salmon and Stewart provide long-distance wilderness trips that do not require such high-level paddling skills as some of the rivers in the more mountainous areas to the east. Road access is possible. The steeper tributaries running westward from the mountains into the Yukon basin are more challenging, and some require air access. In the Dawson area many of the tributary streams have been disturbed by placer mining and resulting siltation.

Rivers flowing eastward into the Mackenzie basin such as the South Nahanni, Bonnet Plume, Mountain and Ogilvie-Peel are more remote and demanding, and many require access and egress by air or chartered motor boat. North beyond the treeline in Northern Yukon (Ivvavik) National Park there are some very demanding rivers in very remote areas.

The granite walls of the Ragged Range have been a climbing mecca for many years, with climbers generally using air access. Some parties have walked in from the South Nahanni, and some have walked out to the road at Tungsten.

Winter travel is difficult unless there is a packed trail, because low temperatures and relatively low snowfall promote the formation of an unconsolidated recrystallized snowpack. Friends who did a circle trip around the Ragged Range one March reported horrendous trailbreaking conditions in bottomless snow.

Ogilvie Mountains, Yukon. S. Fleck photo.

Trees in a sheltered Barrens valley.

The Barren Grounds

The "barren grounds" is a region of generally open country on the Shield, beyond the treeline. Some areas of hillier terrain, such as the Coppermine Mountains, rise a few hundred metres above the surrounding terrain, but generally the area is low relief, scattered with lakes of all sizes and traversed by major rivers draining into the Arctic Ocean and Hudson Bay.

The area is sparsely populated with no road access. Motor boats, snowmobiles and all-terrain vehicles are used by native people for hunting and trapping. Access is by chartered float plane or ski plane or by scheduled aircraft to native communities. There are isolated mines and exploration camps, but overall there is very little industrial activity so water quality is generally good. Recently there has been a flurry of diamond exploration activity in the Lac de Gras region north of Yellowknife and there is some concern about its implications for the Coppermine basin.

The time between the ice leaving the lakes and the onset of wintry (by southern standards) weather is a short period between early July and late August. During this short six weeks or so of summer, temperatures can reach the high 20s, or it can snow. Strong winds are common. The winter is characterized by very low temperatures (down to -40°C), high windchills, low snowfall, relatively shallow snowpack and wind-whipped ground blizzards.

The region is not entirely devoid of trees, there being occasional isolated groves such as the famous Warden's Grove on the Thelon. Patches of trees found in sheltered locations such as river valleys may consist of willow scrub, poplar and spruce. Poor drainage, made worse by permafrost, provides ideal breeding conditions for insects. These pests and the cost of access protect the area from heavy summer use. The subspecies in these northern regions are active at much lower temperatures than insects farther south.

The region is famous for long (three to six weeks) canoe routes. Periods of strong winds across the open terrain can be a boon if you want relief from the insects, but can pin canoeists to shore for days, especially on big lakes. You need good tents to withstand these winds. The near-absence of trees means that firewood is very scarce so your equipment must be good enough to make drying or warming fires unnecessary even in poor weather.

Long-distance foot travel is impractical in many parts because of numerous ponds, lakes, creeks and swamps. The tussocky terrain also makes walking arduous, though one party completed a 100-day walk from Yellowknife to Coppermine between April and July in the mid-1980s. However, short hikes during canoe trips can be very rewarding if you choose your route and terrain carefully. Eskers, for example, provide wonderful walking with fewer bugs. High regions such as the Coppermine Mountains provide interesting tundra hiking with views.

The open windswept terrain of the barrens is not very appealing for winter recreation because of high windchills and low temperatures.

The Arctic Islands

The islands of the eastern Arctic—Baffin, Bylot, Devon, Ellesmere and Axel Heiberg—are a vast wilderness of mostly mountains and glaciers. The coastlines are rugged and the surrounding ocean frozen for much of the year. The western Arctic islands are generally lower and flatter without glaciers.

A few scattered settlements are generally served by scheduled air services, which may or may not be able to bring large amounts of your excess baggage on the same flight with you. Transportation is a major cost in this area as you will likely have to charter aircraft or possibly boats. In these remote and unforgiving surroundings with difficult communications you must have the skills and equipment to be self-supporting for long periods. Accommodation and food are very costly, if available at all.

Summer is a short one- to two-month period around July. You could experience clear, sunny weather or cold, grey or wet weather, depending on your luck. As a friend once said about a summer trip to Axel Heiberg Island, "We had a miserable winter up there that summer!" Mid-winter conditions are extreme with very low temperatures around -30°C to -40°C, short days if any daylight at all, high windchills and ground blizzards. The area is a cold desert with less than 15 centimetres of rainfall, and snowfalls ranging from 200 centimetres in mountainous parts of Baffin Island to as little as 50 centimetres in northern Ellesmere Island. In spring (April-May-June), the days are warmer and longer (16 hours in mid-April in northern Baffin). The snow is also warmer and

Shore ice on a fjord in Ellesmere Island. John Dunn photo.

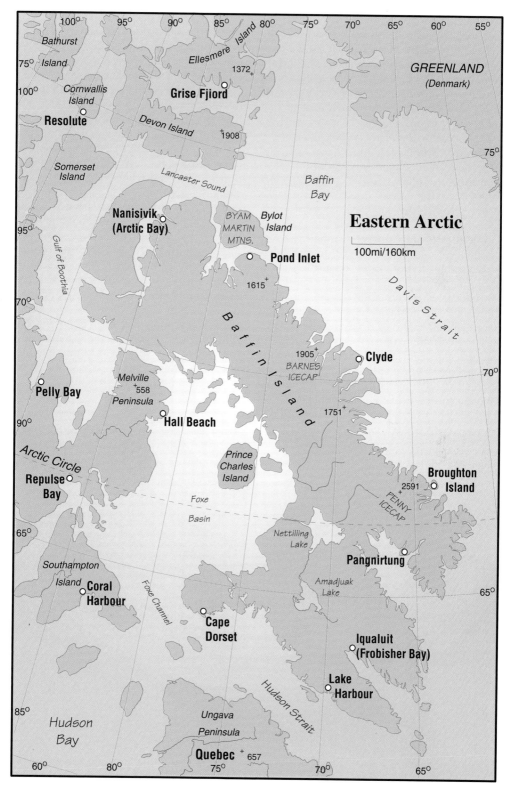

THE ARCTIC ISLANDS

Bathurst
Island
75°
100°

Cornwallis
Island
Resolute

100°

Ellesmere Island
80°
1372

Grise Fjord

Devon Island
1908

75°

GREENLAND
(Denmark)

75°

Somerset
Island

Lancaster Sound

Baffin
Bay

95°

Gulf of Boothia

Nanisivik
(Arctic Bay)

BYAM
MARTIN
MTNS.

Bylot
Island

Pond Inlet

1615

Eastern Arctic

100mi/160km

Davis Strait

70°

B a f f i n   I s l a n d

1905
BARNES
ICECAP

Clyde

70°

Pelly Bay

Melville
558
Peninsula

Hall Beach

1751

90°

Arctic Circle

Repulse
Bay

Prince
Charles
Island

Foxe

Basin

Broughton
Island

2591
PENNY
ICECAP

65°

Nettilling
Lake

Pangnirtung

65°

Southampton
Island Coral
Harbour

Foxe Channel

Cape
Dorset

Amadjuak
Lake

Iqualuit
(Frobisher Bay)

Lake
Harbour

85°

Hudson
Bay

Ungava
Peninsula

Hudson Strait

Quebec 657

60°

80°

75°

70°

65°

less "sandy," providing easier travel by ski. As summer progresses the thin snowpack rapidly rots and disappears in many areas, so the transition time between good travel and not enough snow can be short. You could be caught with insufficient snow and have to backpack gear and sled. Spring travel has the advantage that bad weather is still likely to be snow, which is easier to cope with than cold rain.

Vegetation is sparse on the Arctic islands, and what there is consists mainly of tundra. However, there are a few areas such as the Soper Valley on Baffin Island where willows reach several metres in height.

In the eastern Arctic there are tremendous possibilities for expeditionary trips involving mountaineering, ski touring or extended backpacking. Some river canoeing opportunities exist, but the cost of canoe transportation means that travel by raft or folding kayak is more affordable. Ocean travel in sea kayaks, small motorized inflatables or rigid craft depends on sea ice conditions at the particular location *and* the particular year. Check the sea ice maps in the *National Atlas of Canada.* By the time the ice has melted—if it melts that year—it could be mid August. We visited an area with sleds, skis and hiking equipment in June and were able to

travel on sea ice, glaciers and dry land. Friends were in the same area in August and were unable to use their inflatable boats and had shorter days and worse weather. Days are getting shorter, nights colder and weather can be quite wintry. Because of the northern climate and fogs along the coasts, you need first-rate equipment and a high level of skill at living and travelling under difficult conditions. There is little shelter and no firewood for warming up or drying out. Polar bears are a significant concern, especially in coastal areas and when travelling the ice-foot along the coast.

The lower-lying western islands are not as popular. However, the wide-open spaces certainly have an appeal of their own, and there is lots of wildlife to see. Hiking in the open terrain is generally good though some people might describe it as monotonous. In spite of the region being technically a desert it can be cold, rainy, windy and snowy, so good gear is a necessity. Some canoe trips have been done, but the period between breakup and low water and then freezeup is very short. The region has little to offer in the way of winter recreation because of extreme conditions and short days.

Climbing above a fjord on Ellesmere Island. John Dunn photo.

Chapter 2

Choosing Your Companions

"As an outdoorsman, you frequently run the risk of finding yourself locked into a week-long stay at a remote camp with a person you barely know. By the end of the week you know the person very well indeed, and may wish fervently that you didn't." P. McManus, *The Grasshopper Trap*, published by Henry Holt.

If a wilderness trip is to be a good experience, participants must be compatible. They are most likely to be compatible if you assemble the group yourself. However, this requires care and much effort. There must be good communication of personal aims, objectives and expectations, and an understanding of potential sources of friction. This is a lot of work and it is much easier to go with a wilderness outfitter on a fully packaged trip. The disadvantage of going with a commercially organized group is that you lose control over who your companions are. You also still need to research the organization carefully about their overall philosophy, the competence of their guides, their requirements of participants in terms of fitness and ability, and the maximum group size.

Assembling a Compatible Group

The history of wilderness expeditions is peppered with stories of major dissent and confrontations. C. F. Hall was poisoned with arsenic by his expedition physician in 1871. A food-stealer was shot during the Greeley expedition. In more recent times an international Himalayan expedition that assembled some of the world's best mountaineering talents was wracked by infighting and dissent. During a tough stage of his 30,000-kilometre canoe odyssey, Verlen Kruger highlighted the problem when he said, "The mistake most people make is that they fight themselves and each other. If we fight anything it's got to be the circumstances. We're in the business of staying alive."

The problems of interpersonal relations are not limited to major expeditions. The success of any trip of any length and group size can be drastically influenced by the interactions between the participants. Internal strife can mean that the best-planned and best-equipped event fails to meet its objectives and is not an enjoyable experience. Worse still, strife can lead to poor decision making, resulting in accidents. Choose your companions carefully!

In Canada and Alaska, because distances are large and wilderness areas are real wilderness, you cannot risk splitting your incompatible party into subgroups that are too small for safety. Not only might they be too small, but also they may lack expertise in such subjects as rescue, first aid, etc. It may be difficult to split first aid or rescue gear for the two groups. There may be no safe alternative other than to continue the trip together. The situation is very different from that in the more populated outdoor recreation regions of the world where it would be relatively safe to split an incompatible party or for some of the party to return to civilization.

In the unpeopled and remote wilderness, it's hazardous to sidestep the companion selection problem by travelling alone.

You must take the time and trouble before a trip to assemble your group carefully. This is particularly important for long trips and expeditions where you could be with people for days or weeks. In their *Mountaineering Handbook for Denali*, the U.S. parks' service points out that having personnel who work well together as a group is as important as having people with individual technical skill.

Four main factors should be considered when selecting participants:

- their awareness and acceptance of the style and objectives of the trip.

- their technical skill and fitness relative to the technical and physical demands of the trip.

- their personal style, motivation and objectives, and how they fit in with the other participants.

- leadership hierarchy, if any, and the leader's style, motivation and objectives.

One of the most important steps in assembling a compatible party is to discuss clearly, frankly and thoroughly all aspects of the trip. If people really understand and agree on what they are letting themselves in for, you stand a better chance of assembling a compatible group. You must be clear and forthright in your discussions because people can become so obsessed with the idea of doing a particular trip that they see only the appeal and lose sight of what it really entails.

In another of McManus' humorous books he writes, "...Outdoorsmen, and outdoorswomen for that matter, are the best of bad company. They have these wild and terrible enthusiasms that inevitably lead to catastrophe. I don't much care for catastrophe, but getting there can be a lot of fun.... What usually happens is that the person of sensibilities becomes caught up in a wave of enthusiasm generated by bad company and gets swept along toward a catastrophe he doesn't expect and isn't mentally or emotionally prepared for. Some people just don't have the nerves or stomach for catastrophe."

Trip Style and Objectives

Interpersonal problems on trips often result because the trip style and objectives were never properly established and clarified with all the members before the trip. Different people often read totally different meanings into the same general trip title or description. They are left to make assumptions if the objectives and methods of a trip are not clearly conveyed. The resulting conflicting aims and expectations leads to strife and dissatisfaction during the trip.

I remember the planning meeting of one five-week canoe trip where we seemed to agree we would do some hiking into the mountains. Unfortunately, my understanding of the term "hiking" included a four-day bushwhacking backpack into some spectacular country, but others interpreted "hiking" in a totally different way. This led to dissension on the trip. More recently, a telemark ski week at a remote cabin was a fabulous week for those of us who understood correctly that it was to be a steep-and-deep, powder yo-yo skiing week, not a touring week. One individual who assumed otherwise and expected to go touring in gentler terrain did not have such a good time.

You should, therefore, talk through and clarify the trip purposes and objectives carefully and in detail before the trip. Reach agreement or compromises at this stage. Some participants may decide the trip is not for them, and may leave and join a different trip, but that's fine if it means they'll have more fun. Then you have to trust that the agreements and compromises you made will be adhered to during the trip!

Clarifying the trip objectives is important for every type of excursion, whether it is a few hours' walk with friends, a club trip or a major expedition. My wife has learned the hard way to question me carefully if I am suggesting a walk. How long is the walk, is it for exercise or for conversation or for photography or for wildlife viewing? Is it a trail walk, a bushwhack, a scree scramble or a tundra trot, and what is the likelihood of it escalating into a major epic? I've not been allowed to forget a certain "afternoon walk" 15 years ago on the flats of Prairie Creek on the Nahanni, which escalated into an eight-hour foray into the mountains and canyons beyond!

The leader or trip instigator must form a clear idea in their own mind as to what the trip will

Just saying you are going on a "canoe trip" means different things to different people.

entail. Only then can they convey the information effectively to others in trip planning meetings. It is particularly important for organizations such as clubs to require participants to contact the trip coordinator ahead of time and not just communicate for the first time at the trailhead. Problems are more likely to occur on club trips because people do not know each other well (if at all) and will inherently have a variety of aims, objectives and styles. If a trip does not unfold as expected, participants soon get grumpy and snarly and start focusing on all the other little negatives. The atmosphere becomes tense and nasty, the group splits up and the classic club trip coordinator nightmare ensues, with subgroups scattered all over the backcountry.

I remember one club trip where the leader's stated purpose was to snow camp in a spectacular area, ski some great powder and maybe bag a certain peak if the conditions were good. Most of the participants seemed to understand and accept this, but a few others focused on climbing the peak as a prime objective. Camping and powder skiing were not objectives, but chores in the way of their goal, which was bagging the peak. A beautiful weekend was marred with tension and acrimony.

Examples of Trip Styles

The following are some examples of trip styles that will help you to identify and clarify in your own mind the types of trips you like to participate in.

Instructional Trips

Some organized trips are actually described as courses, which implies that people should attend with the express purpose of learning something. However, sometimes they arrive with a very casual attitude that is confusing and disconcerting for the instructor. I remember one individual complaining to the supervisor of a college where I taught a ski touring course that she objected to being expected to learn things. Apparently she just wanted to go on a cheap guided ski tour!

Holiday or Get-There-or-Bust?

Two trips to the same location can be entirely different in spite of having the same general title. My wife and I recently returned from a fabulous sea kayak holiday on the west coast of Vancouver Island. When asked before the trip where we were going, our general reply was "Clayoquot Sound and Hotsprings Cove." Our discussed and agreed intention was to have a holiday and enjoy the scenery, lay back, and get away from the pressures of everyday life. If we reached the hotsprings, that would be a bonus, but not an objective for which it was worth putting in slog days in poor weather. Another group did a similarly described trip, but the leader was focused on reaching the hotsprings. He was a "cap feather collector" who liked to boost his ego by reaching objectives that he felt had brag value. The party endured slogs against weather and tides, along with discomfort and acrimony. Their trip was salvaged only when the group split up to meet different people's needs.

Exploratory

Another important characteristic to discuss is whether the trip will be exploratory or will have a well-researched itinerary. Some people enjoy exploratory trips where there is uncertainty and they continually have to adapt to whatever the environment throws their way. They thrive on the uncertainty and the mental and physical challenge. They may like to provide input and be part of ad hoc decision-making rather than following a preordained route.

Others prefer trips that have been researched and organized right down to the last detail and where there are no surprises. Personally I like to strike a middle ground—it's nice to know whether there are any nasty surprises such as unrunnable river ledges or cliff bands that block a ski route and do not show on the map. However, I don't want to ski or hike a route with all the decisions made for me in advance by a guidebook. For me, part of the pleasure comes from the mental exercise of assessing a situation, forming a plan of action and executing it. (And quickly obtaining incontrovertible feedback about whether my assessments and actions were correct!)

People may just want their cross-country skis to be a means to get to somewhere nice to relax in the sun and admire the view, or (photo p. 66) they may see them as a source of exercise and competition.

Expeditions

Sometimes a trip is described as "an expedition," and this can have all sorts of connotations. The famous explorer H. W. Tilman, who preferred small, light, fast and tightly knit teams, said, "When a trip becomes an expedition there are too many people." To others, expedition may mean a very high level of organization with a rigid hierarchy. It could mean a Scott of the Antarctic-style trek, complete with heroic but futile gestures and sacrifices. Sometimes a person calling the trip an expedition is simply unskilled, so that a routine trip takes on a high level of seriousness for that person. I was intrigued to read in the foreign press of an "expedition" down a stretch of a Canadian river on which my wife and I had experienced a very pleasant "holiday." The group in the article had made the trip unnecessarily difficult by bringing unsuitable canoes, tents without mosquito nets and low skill levels. The dynamics of this type of trip may or may not be your scene, so inquire carefully why it's termed "an expedition"!

Epics

Some people seem to deliberately set out to have survival epics in the backcountry. Maybe it's because by contrast it's so nice when they get back home to the rat race. Maybe it's for brag value in the bar or lecture hall surrounded by similarly macho types or those who don't know that there is a better way. The audience may not know that the epic hardships were the result of incompetence or poor planning. Epic tales seem to be more common on well-known routes such as the Nahanni River or the West Coast Trail. Perhaps because these routes are so well known they catch the imagination of the unskilled and uninformed. Perhaps, too, they have an inherent brag value for those who want it. Another reason for perpetrating survival-type trips is a team-building or character-building agenda—to "prove oneself." Or perhaps these epic adventures are simply a result of ignorance about how to organize and live and travel comfortably and safely, or an unwillingness to make the effort to train, prepare and organize properly for the realities of wilderness travel.

Epic adventures are fine as long as everyone in the party wants that type of trip and the group doesn't become a burden on the rescue authorities or other groups. They should also make sure they don't leave a mess behind them. I know of one group of incompetent yahoos out for a "Deliverance" adventure on a northern river who left a trail of burnt forest, cut trees, abandoned equipment and inconvenienced authorities.

Strenuous or Relaxing

The strenuousness of a trip should be considered and discussed. Strenuousness must be carefully matched to the capabilities and objectives of the participants. An easy trip for some is a marathon for others. Remember that it is possible for trips to become more strenuous than expected as a result of headwinds, heavy trailbreaking or unexpected detours. Some people want to go back to work after a trip pleasantly exercised and not exhausted!

Bash-on-Regardless

A friend recently recounted how on a guided mountaineering trip one of the participants wanted to bail out when the going got a bit uncomfortable in poor weather. The guide laid down the law quite bluntly and told the client something along the lines of "you knew that mountain weather could be uncomfortable when you signed up for the trip so get a grip and come on." Perhaps what the client was not used to was the idea of going on in bad conditions when they were not having fun. Some people know from past experience that they can tough it out if they have to, but would rather not bother proving themselves again. They figure they'd be better off going home and painting the kitchen or tidying the basement instead.

It can be enormously frustrating for members of a party to find that other members want to abort the trip. This usually occurs when the going gets rough, maybe bad weather or bad bugs. Whatever the reason, departure of some of the group can make life difficult for the rest of the party if there are insufficient numbers remaining to continue safely. As I write this section, my wife and I are debating whether to join a group for a long-weekend hike. We are realizing that if the weather is poor we would rather do chores around the house than have a rough trip. To retain the flexibility to chicken out at the last minute we are considering a trip for just the two of us, so we will not adversely affect others if we drop out.

High and Low Risk

There will be stress and tension unless there is some discussion and consensus beforehand about the levels of risk (real and perceived) the group will face. This consensus may result in formulation of a policy to, say, always ski roped on a glacier, or to scout every rapid, or to never leave camp alone or always wear a helmet. This consensus is important because participants must realize that their own risk-taking affects the rest of the group. The attitude that "it's my neck and if I die it's my problem" just won't do in a group. Someone getting hurt or dying on a trip can spoil people's appetite for their sport for a long time.

If you engage in risk-taking beyond the agreed levels for the trip, you adversely affect the party even if your activity does not result in an accident. The rest of the group can end up worrying all day rather than enjoying themselves. I recall a memorable ascent of a high, glaciated, but relatively low-risk peak in the Rockies. After the ascent, part of the group stopped to sunbathe at a high pass while others took the easy route up an adjacent peak. Unfortunately, one individual decided to solo climb a steep, exposed ice slope in full view of the sunbathers. The skill level of the soloist and the steepness and quality of the ice were hard to assess, making it difficult to determine the level of real risk. The sunbathers **perceived** a high level of risk and had a tense time watching the climber, and eyeing the bergshrund into which he could fall. This was not what they had bargained for on this low-risk peak, and they would rather have relaxed to enjoy the Indian

summer weather and some pleasant conversation. Undoubtedly the perceived risk was much greater than the **actual** risk, but the point was that the day was spoiled for some of the group.

Commitment and Electronics Communications

Trips with an extremely committing style can lose some of their atmosphere of seriousness and commitment if modern aids such as radios and satellite location systems are carried. Some people feel very strongly that the mere presence of a two-way radio or an emergency beacon spoils the atmosphere of the trip. This should be discussed by the group. However, I suggest it would be stupid to have someone die or suffer pain and perhaps permanent damage for want of a modern communication system.

Participant Skill and Fitness

The skill and fitness level of participants can have a large impact on the success of your trip. The progress of the trip can be put in jeopardy if just one member of the party has inadequate skills and fitness to meet the technical demands of the trip. You should take the time to assess all prospective members' capabilities carefully. Some suggested methods and criteria follow.

Experience as a Skill Indicator

Remember that evidence of experience is not necessarily a reliable indication of skill. People can be very experienced at doing things incorrectly and be experienced at simply being very lucky year after year. I once went on a trip with people whom I had been assured were "experienced." They were experienced in procedures contrary to what they would have been taught by a reputable training organization. It was, to say the least, an unnerving trip. Skill comes from a suitable mixture of both training and experience.

The term experience is used rather loosely, too. A recent report about backcountry avalanche fatalities referred to a high proportion of victims as "experienced" skiers. This as-

sumption was made because they were skiing steep slopes. In fact, the only reliable prediction to be made about these people was that they were probably technically skilled at pointing skis down a hill. The skill did not necessarily come from experience, and certainly not necessarily from relevant mountain backcountry experience. Unless they were just unlucky, they were unskilled and inexperienced in what mattered—snow stability evaluation and routefinding.

This is not to say that experience is always an inadequate teacher. Some people learn much of value from their experiences, while others learn little. I always remember a famous Himalayan climber talking about his climbing life and recounting tales of the desperate epics and major horror shows of his early career. What came through loud and clear, time and again, was the phrase "but we learned…from that experience." For him the epics were not just things to brag about in the bar, but experiences to think about and to learn from, and from which to formulate improved procedures.

Certification as a Skill Indicator

If you are using someone's certification as a skill indicator, make sure that the certification really relates to the needs of the trip in question. If all you want to know is how well they ski or paddle, fair enough, but on a wilderness trip you will need to know how skilled they are at the daily activities associated with conducting themselves safely and comfortably in the backcountry. I have encountered qualified cross-country ski instructors who rarely leave the controlled environment of groomed trails and ski hills. Their certification therefore gives little indication of their competence on a serious backcountry trip.

The same problem applies to people who are uncertified but whom you know to be highly skilled. They may be skilled only in a narrow field—the 5.12 cragrat who only climbs near the road and has no alpine experience, the Class V expert paddler who only paddles an empty boat on competitive courses, the hot dog skier who only skis resorts. These people can be dangerously lacking in wilderness skills.

As well as physical strength, some trips require psychological strength just to keep going for hour after hour when you don't have landmarks to gauge your progress. John Dunn/Arctic Light.

Psychological Suitability

Some people with excellent technical skills honed on roadside crags and rivers are psychologically affected by the remote environment of Canada's and Alaska's wilderness, and as a result do not function well. The feeling is summed up well by Maurice Herzog in his book *Annapurna*, about the first successful ascent of that mountain in 1950. "Everything was so new, so utterly unprecedented, it was not in the least like anything I had known in the Alps where one feels buoyed up by the presence of others—by people of whom one is vaguely aware, or even by the dwellings one can see in the far distance."

I remember conversing by radio with a party who were climbing nearby on Mt. Logan in the St. Elias Range. We were in high spirits, but we could sense their low morale and the fact that they were overwhelmed by the scale and remoteness. Although probably technically capable of making the climb, their psychological state brought them to a standstill.

If the effect of remoteness is simply to make people more cautious and keep a wider safety margin, that's good because of the desperate seriousness of a mishap in remote places. However, if it actually adversely affects performance, safety margins diminish and you have a recipe for disaster. This is another reason to check that people have had successful experiences of the type they will encounter in Canada or Alaska.

Questioning Prospective Participants

Quizzing people is not easy and some people will definitely take exception to queries about their skills and experience. Those people are often the ones to be most wary of. If they do not want to give information or don't see why you need it, you should see "red flags": the person has something to hide, or a nasty ego problem or a poor understanding of safety in the outdoors, or a combination.

- Ask where people have been before, with whom, under what snow/water/bugs/ weather conditions, what role they took, how long the trip took and of course the time of year. The same trip under different conditions can make entirely different demands on people's skill levels.

- Questions about how someone handled a route or trip you're familiar with can provide revealing answers.
- Try to corroborate the information so you won't be misled by a fabricated resume.
- In preparation for longer trips, nothing beats a preliminary shakedown trip to find out how competent people are and whether the group will be compatible and work well together. If this is not possible, checking references and using the outdoor network to find out more about prospective participants is time well spent. Make sure you have a very clear idea about your needs and preferences so that you ask useful questions.
- If weeding out becomes necessary, a positive approach to the process such as "I don't think you'll have much fun on this trip" rather than a judgmental "You are too slow/can't paddle/can't ski well enough" one, is easier on both weeder and weedee. Even though what you really mean might be "**We'll** have more fun if you don't come," the result is the same but with less argument and acrimony. Often the individual is already having second thoughts and can back out without losing face. Leave doors open with suggestions for more appropriate activities or future trips.

People may be very interested in the flowers or birds and may want to spend time getting to know them.

Participant Style and Objectives

As well as finding out about a person's fitness and technical ability, you must find out other key information that will affect the group as a whole.

Participant's Motivation

When Valerie Fons was asked why she was embarking on a canoe circumnavigation of Baja California, someone spoke up from the audience and said, "If you know the reason why you are doing something, it may not be worth doing. Let the adventure happen to you." There was a spontaneous burst of applause. I think, however, you really must sit down and get to the bottom of people's reasons for wanting to go on a trip. One of the best trips I have ever been on was originally conceived as a guided ski circuit of Mt. Logan. However, because we all did some serious talking before the trip it became clear that in fact we were not particularly motivated to go and "ski around Mt. Logan" as an objective. It became apparent that we were not really keen to travel every day no matter what the weather and to suffer a grunt trip just to be able to "cut brag notches in our ski poles" and say that we had skied around Mt. Logan. We were actually more interested in three weeks of good ski touring in the spectacular area near the mountain, travelling when the travelling was good, powder skiing if it was good and sleeping and drinking tea if the weather was bad. That is exactly what we did and we had the trip of a lifetime.

For many people, the motivation is the opportunity to be in the wilderness environment, something that provides them with considerable satisfaction and enjoyment. Whether or not they reach a summit or other objective is of minor importance to them and they get satisfaction from learning how to anticipate and accommodate all that nature throws at them.

For others, wilderness on the way to a goal is not a special pleasure, and they get most of their enjoyment if and when they reach that goal, beating nature into submission along the way. The backcountry becomes an outdoor gymnasium where they show off or test their physical prowess. They are often very fit and technically excellent as climbers, paddlers, cavers and skiers but are not really what I call "wilderness people." Wilderness is an inconvenience on the way to their goal or testing ground. They do not tune in to the architecture and decor, and the wilderness surroundings are just the unnoticed foyer and hallways on the way to the gym and maybe the winner's podium. A great part of their enjoyment may in fact come later, recounting their exploits to a dazzled audience.

Discussing this difference in motivation brings to mind the case of a high-profile international adventurer who was having an epic expedition "beating the wild Canadian wilderness into submission" on a "desperate" northern river, and filming it too. Apparently he was quite miffed to find a youth group having a marvellous holiday, canoeing the same river. Because of their approach, training, skill and preparation the youths' trip was not taking on the characteristics of a newsworthy epic. Just calling a trip an "expedition" rather than a "holiday" or a "trip" has a certain connotation that may attract people for more ego-centred reasons.

Some people are even "testosterone-poisoned" or "adrenalin junkies," motivated by being on the edge and pushing the limits. Others are show-offs. I've been on intermediate whitewater trips where ego-tripping individuals have paddled falls everyone else portaged. They had an audience to perform for, but their activities caused considerable anxiety among the portagers and spoiled the trip for many of them. Find out what categories your group members belong to! Some don't mix very well!

Safety and Risk-Taking

People who are casual about their own safety neglect to consider the risk to which they put others who may have to rescue them. They also overlook the general unpleasantness created for everyone when an unnecessary mishap occurs. An acquaintance recounted trying to dissuade a person with a serious heart condition from coming on a strenuous trip. Their comment, "If I die, I die," completely overlooked the unpleasantness, inconvenience and possibly even liability implications for the rest of the group.

Ask what equipment people take with them, when they last did an avalanche transceiver exercise, or took a first aid course or practised crevasse or river rescue. Beware of those who say "We don't take much" or "We've never had any trouble." These "It'll never happen to me" comments indicate a lack of awareness of the potentially serious consequences of backcountry mishaps. Such people likely will be no use in an emergency, so question whether to include them unless they have a lot to offer in another aspect of the trip. Because a team approach is critical, be aware that anyone who says things like, "I'm not bringing my avalanche shovel—there are enough in the group already" is really saying, "I'm all right if I'm buried, and to heck with you guys if you get buried."

A friend described a similar mind-set on a river canoeing trip. He was the only person with a rescue rope throw bag, an item that responsible river canoeists regard as a crucial piece of rescue equipment for every canoe. He handed the throw bag to the occupants of the other canoe, who asked, "What will you use if we are the ones who capsize?" His reply was, "I don't know, you're the ones who screwed up and didn't bring a throw bag!"

Another way to find out about people's safety attitudes and awareness is to ask about their experience on a trip you are both familiar with. Their answers may indicate their ability to recognize hazards and clarify their attitude toward those hazards. If they ran a certain rapid successfully they were either skilled or lucky, and you are not much the wiser. However, if they portaged instead, asking why they did so could actually reveal far more useful information. If the answer is something like, "The group was tired and we realized that the risk of a capsize was not worth the consequences of possibly destroying the boat and having a nasty swim through that monster hole," you know you are talking with someone who has the ability to recognize the overall level of hazards. Not only that, but they will take appropriate action to avoid dangers. If they say, "We just didn't think we could make it without capsizing," you know you are talking with someone who knows their own limitations but who perhaps didn't tune in to there being more of a risk than just getting wet in a capsize. Someone who failed to reach a summit because they had the guts to turn back in the face of dangerous conditions may be a better candidate than someone who summited, but only because they were lucky.

Leader Style, Motivation and Objectives

Once the leader and the group have agreed on the trip style and objectives, leadership style should be decided on. Incompatible or unsuitable leadership styles can be a source of major dissension. Participants should be wary of a prospective leaders' hidden agenda!

Leader, Organizer or Both?

A trip may be instigated and organized by one person who also expects to be in charge of the trip in the field. As a prospective participant, you should examine that person's objectives and their personal style before committing yourself. Remember that a good trip instigator or organizer may not be the best person to run the actual outing. If they are not on an ego trip they will hopefully relinquish their position in the field if there is a better qualified person. The Footsteps of Scott Expedition to the South Pole is a good example. The leader during the organization phase knew enough to relinquish his position on the actual trip in favour of more qualified field people.

Leader's Safety Attitudes

A particularly important factor to consider is a prospective leader's attitude toward safety. If participants feel insecure and unhappy about how safely the trip is led, they will not have a good time. Similarly, people will be unhappy if they feel the leader is overzealous and safety precautions hinder their enjoyment of the trip. Be very wary of leaders who say things like, "I've never had any problems so I don't take rescue gear," or "Usually everyone has a repair kit" or "I keep my lifejacket in the boat just to satisfy regulations."

A good leader will lay down safety rules he feels comfortable with before the trip; for example, helmets and lifejackets to be worn at all times on the river, or an avalanche transceiver check to be done every morning or the party to be roped at all times on the glacier. If people don't want to go along with the restrictions, they have the option of not going on the trip. Remember that a good leader feels some responsibility for the party. The leader should also be aware that he or she has more legal responsibility and exposure to liability than do the group members. The leader may therefore want to lean well on the safe side of safety concerns, and participants should understand the reasons for this.

Other Attitudes and Values

The leader represents other values besides safety that must be clearly communicated and agreed on. If the values in an organization or group are not compatible, chaos ensues. I once worked as an outdoor professional in an organization that was an offshoot of two others, one with bureaucratic roots and the other with professional roots. The values in the organization were confused. The manager intended the organization to have the values of an entrepreneurial, initiative-oriented, competitive operation with the bottom line being to support professionals in their efforts to deliver the best possible services to the community. A lower-level supervisor came from a bureaucratic background. The bureaucratic, egocentric, control-and-dominance oriented style of management was at odds with the manager and was unsuitable for managing professionals who had to deliver front-line professional excellence and service to customers. The effect was many confused, dissatisfied and unhappy professionals.

Leader's Motivation

Although most trip organizers are motivated simply by a desire to share a fun trip idea with other people, there can be other reasons why they organize a trip. An organizer with an ego problem looks at the trip as an opportunity to boss people rather than lead them. Others want an opportunity to show off their skill, so they plan a trip with less able individuals who make them look good by comparison. There are still others who simply like to organize and look upon the trip as an organizational challenge and exercise. They may organize the fun and spontaneity out of the trip.

Still others are motivated to lead trips within organizations because they can't get people to go with them any other way, the reasons for which sometimes become painfully obvious! Then there is the mercenary approach of those who want a free trip, their share paid for by clients.

On the positive side, there are people who organize and lead trips to "put something back in" to an organization or run trips simply because they want to share a wilderness experience with people and are willing to do the considerable work required. They may also be glad to provide instructional assistance if the participants wish and are receptive.

Leadership Styles

Regardless of the motivation for leading, leaders can do the job in a variety of styles. Leadership styles range all the way from autocratic (authoritarian, dictatorial) through varying levels of democracy to a nonleadership, laissez-faire (let things drift along) style. Bullying, power tripping, stroke-my-ego-or-else leadership/management styles are not acceptable to most people and are counterproductive in the outdoors. At the other end of the spectrum is the trip that has no real leader at all. Everything may work out fine, but if an emergency arises the lack of leadership will probably be manifested in chaos.

One leadership style is not necessarily "better" than another style. Circumstances affect how participants will respond to and accept various leadership styles.

An **authoritarian, dictatorial style** is generally more effective under the following circumstances:

- In emergencies
- When the skill level of participants is marginal for the conditions
- For short-term tasks
- For simple tasks
- When actually completing the task, getting the job done is crucial
- When people are fatigued, cold or otherwise performing below par
- When people are stressed
- If the group is large and democracy is too unwieldy or time consuming
- If participants want a guided or instructed rather than participatory trip
- If motivation is low.

A **democratic style** or absence of a leader is generally more effective or acceptable when:

- Participants are expecting a participatory, shared adventure trip
- The skill level of the group is ample for the conditions
- Tasks are longer-term
- Tasks are complex but well understood
- Completing a task is less important than the process by which it is completed
- Everything is going fine and there is plenty of time
- Groups are small so democracy is not too slow and unwieldy
- The objective is a growth/learning/challenge experience
- Group members are well motivated.

Changing Leadership Style to Suit the Circumstances

What type of leadership will work, therefore, depends on the circumstances. Some of these are known in advance, some arise during the trip as it evolves. A good leader can and must change their style to suit the circumstances. A leader who is unable to adapt in this way will lose their leadership to someone who emerges from the group with a leadership style appropriate for the circumstances.

Effective leadership of a trip requires leaders to continually evaluate the situation and to switch their style dramatically if necessary. If there is no designated leader in an emergency, someone must quickly take charge with an authoritarian style to get things done fast enough. In an avalanche accident, the laid-back leader must snap to attention and bark orders to stimulate the group into coordinated rapid action. If he does not he will either be usurped by someone with an appropriate style or will find himself presiding over a disaster.

Insecurity and lack of confidence can result in either bullying authoritarian leadership or in the opposite, shy withdrawal. Leaders should minimize their insecurity by leading trips that are familiar or well within their capability. This will reduce their stress level and allow them to operate in a wider variety of leadership styles.

Being a Good Leader

Regardless of leadership style, there are some fundamental aspects of leading. Successful leaders believe that, as St. Luke said, "A leader is one who serves." Good leaders believe that "Leadership is for the benefit of the people being led, not for the aggrandisement of the leader" (David Townshend, *Up the Organization*). A good leader regards their job as "liberating people to do what is required of them in the most effective and humane way possible" (Max De Pree in *Leadership is an Art*).

The signs of good leadership appear primarily among the followers. Are they reaching their full potential? Are they having fun? Are they learning? Are they achieving personal goals? Newcomers to the outdoors who lack the skill to discern, or who lack the network to be forewarned, may end up under the influence of questionable leaders.

On one of our first trips with an outdoor club the large group was divided up under a number of leaders. We were aware of some jockeying for position, but being new to the organization and knowing no one we found ourselves in the clutches of an individual who was, to be charitable, authoritarian, abrasive and egotistical, and not very skilled, either. Luckily we knew enough to realize that this wouldn't be a typical style in a club like this, otherwise we would have left the club immediately. Less knowledgeable newcomers, however, could easily have been very discouraged.

Paul Brickhill, writing about Squadron Leader Leonard Cheshire, in his book *The Dam Busters*, sums up leadership very well: "The ground crews were liable to frustrations which could only be soothed if they could be assured of their value, and Cheshire delicately gave them those assurances. When he landed in the early morning after a raid, his driver usually found him under the wing sharing a cocoa and sandwiches with his ground crew. As anxiously as they asked him how he had got on, he would ask in return if they had managed to get any sleep while he was away, or thank them for the performance of the aircraft, all with a friendly touch and a few jokes thrown in. With flying crew or ground crew, he was a leader and never a driver, never bullying, overdriving or petty, though his tongue could be quietly dev-astating if you merited it. His air crews almost worshipped him, and the ground crew's feelings were probably deeper because he treated them with warm consideration, and they were not used to it." Imagine what our institutions could achieve with more leaders like that.

So, if you go on a trip with a designated leader, make sure you really figure out what the leader's objectives, motivations, style and expectations are before the trip. Make sure that the person plans to fulfil the role you expect of them in an acceptable manner. If things don't fit, choose a different trip and group.

Sources of Friction

Now that you have selected a basically compatible group, you need to pay attention to the small details that affect how the members will interact. Small sources of friction have a habit of escalating or joining together to cause major dissension. However, an awareness of what some of these minor aggravations can be will help you avoid them or bring them into the open for discussion. Here are some potential sources of friction.

Personal Space

Many trips in Canada and Alaska are long ones. Trips that force everyone into close proximity for extended periods with no opportunity for escape are likely to allow minor differences to fester and coalesce, resulting in major acrimony in the group. Minimize, whenever possible, the extent to which people are forced to be together. Allowing for smaller tenting/eating groups, providing scope for people to go away from the main group to do their own thing on a rest day, and generally giving people a chance to be alone occasionally are good strategies. Then when conditions do force everyone together there will be some reserve of patience and tolerance.

General Behaviour Norms

Norms of behaviour vary considerably with the type of trip. I remember on one nature-oriented, two-week trip I guided, there were two individuals who were expecting it to be an all-male, macho, boozing, bragging and bullshitting event. They were most chagrined to find that there were women on the trip, especially women 20 years their senior who were fitter, more able and more competent in the unforgiving environment of an extended northern camping trip. Even before we left the float plane dock at the start of the trip the macho misfits were pouring themselves tumblersfull of liquor to build up some courage.

Joining us on another similar nature-oriented trip were a few rah-rah-rah yahoo yellers, much in the style of some whitewater rafting outfits, but totally not the style of the organization running the trip or the rest of the group, who wanted to see wildlife and enjoy peace and quiet. To make matters worse, the yellers were encouraged by one of the guides, who was more interested in currying favour with individual clients from whom tips might be forthcoming than in upholding the advertised norms and image of the organization.

Photography

Photography can cause friction in a group. Participants don't appreciate being asked to pose or wait unless pictures are needed for expedition fundraising, obligations to sponsors or similar group-centred purposes. If you take personal photographs don't be intrusive and don't make too many demands. A competent photographer with adequate equipment can usually obtain good shots without intruding significantly.

TRY AND MAKE IT LOOK DIFFICULT

Posing for the camera can be tiresome and photographers need to be considerate. Jim Watson, *On Foot and Finger*, Cicerone Press, U.K.

Some people simply do not want their picture taken, especially if they are recognizable or scantily clad, and it is polite to ask people at the start of the trip how they feel about their photograph being taken. Written permission is usually required for publishing photographs in which individuals are recognizable.

On a lengthy round-the-world trip we took pictures of everyone and everything, and had been surprised about occasional hostile reactions. Shortly after our return from that trip I looked out my window and saw the incredible sight of a rather strange neighbour in even stranger garb herding three geese down the middle of the road. I grabbed my camera and headed for the door. I was almost onto the porch when I stopped and thought, "Some nerve to stand there and take a picture." Then I realized that's exactly what I'd been doing for the last six months in all those other countries. I slunk thoughtfully back indoors and put the camera away.

Sharing the Load

People get very grumpy if they think the weight of the group gear (as opposed to personal gear) is unfairly distributed. I remember being furious on one remote glacier ski trip where I was carrying the additional weight of a comprehensive first aid and repair kit, as well as a rope. I was left behind by people travelling lighter without any contingency gear. The problem arose partly because there had been no prior discussion and agreement on what level of preparedness the group would have, and what gear would be taken and designated as group gear (some people even thought a rope was unnecessary).

This type of problem is solved in two stages. The first is to decide what group gear is to be taken, and what, if any, other gear is to be designated as "group" (for example, the official trip photographer might expect the team to designate some of his additional photography gear as "group" and to take on some of his additional load). The second stage is to pool the group gear and divide it up, possibly even using a small pocket spring balance to ensure the division is fair. If there are couples, you might want to divide the gear equally among the couples and let them split the weight as they like within each couple.

Group Benefit Tasks

There are other types of work to be done on a trip besides carrying gear. At the risk of overorganizing for a holiday trip, identify the group benefit tasks and maybe even write up an organized roster to keep things fair. A trip with two couples works really well if each is responsible for their own breakfasts and lunches but produces dinner for four on alternate nights. Make sure both couples agree on the menu and that one pair doesn't produce gourmet four-course dinners and the other produce freeze-dried one-pot glop! Some cooks create vast amounts of dirty cook pots so you may want to make the cooks responsible for cleaning dishes, too. On the other hand you may wish to subdivide the workload and have the others wash.

Tidying People's Gear

One person's "organization" is another person's pigpen. It should be understood that nobody touches or moves another person's gear unless there is a hazard, and then must inform the person that it was moved. Moving people's gear can create real problems, as well as wasted time when people can't find things. If people have identical equipment items, mark them clearly. We have a large number of sea kayak dry bags, many of the same make and colour. I distinguish mine from my wife's simply with a piece of flagging tape tied to the fastener. A magic marker works well for some items.

Alcohol

Some people drink for taste, others for "effect." Some people are very uneasy about alcohol consumption on trips, perhaps because of the penchant in North America to equate drinking with an intention to become significantly impaired. Sharing with my wife a bottle of good beer to complement our ham and cheese at lunch time was viewed askance by some members of a group we recreate with. Right or wrong, it was against their "norms," and you have to establish, communicate and pay attention to group norms. Some friends were alarmed that my wife and I would take four litres of white wine (the equivalent of a good glass a day each) to drink with our fresh caught fish on a 10-day sea kayak trip.

Caffeine

Make sure that you accommodate some individuals' need for a caffeine fix; withdrawal symptoms can be very unpleasant for caffeine addicts. Some people are bothered by the diuretic and other effects of caffeine drinks and wish to avoid caffeine, so provide a variety of drinks to satisfy everyone's needs and tastes.

Smoking

I find even the slightest smell of cigarette smoke on the wilderness wind to be most unpleasant, and I certainly won't tolerate it in my tent. I feel particularly uneasy around smokers who throw butts on the ground instead of in the fire or into a tin box in their pocket. Apart from the fire hazard, it's littering. I feel uncomfortable when people disobey the cardinal rule of outdoor smoking, which is to sit down in one place when smoking to control where any glowing embers go.

Affection

Conspicuous displays of affection can really aggravate others in the group who are without their partners and are still three weeks from home!

Travelling Pace

Incompatible travelling pace is a great source of frustration in a group. Rates of progress can be evened out if faster individuals take time to fish, take photographs, take side trips to secondary peaks, yo-yo ski or play with empty boats in rapids. I used to accommodate different speeds on a backpacking course by stopping at the top of a pass where the gung-ho types could do a side trip to a peak and those who were already tired could sit and rest while admiring a great view. If some people are fit and fast and capable, but want to spend time taking pictures or on other pursuits, it may be reasonable to let them stop for their activity while the rest of the party continues, and then let them catch up. You don't want to risk them taking a wrong turn, though, so wait at junctions. When the overall trip style and objectives are discussed the group should decide if it will be a fast-moving trip or a more leisurely paced one.

Delaying the Party

When someone delays the group unnecessarily, considerable friction can result. Slower travellers can, however, take steps to avoid delaying a group. Some elderly people with whom we have skied do not delay the party appreciably. Though they move relatively slowly, they are highly organized—boots and gaiters on, skins are already on the skis, packs ready—so when they arrive at the trailhead they head off up the trail immediately. They've had a substantial head start by the time the rest of the group get going, and it takes a long time to catch up to them. Also, they don't stop and fiddle around on the trail much. In a recent incident, an individual who moved slowly incensed the rest of the group, who had been waiting two hours for him to catch up, by proceeding to fiddle around for 3/4 hour in the hut at lunch time. An apology and eating quickly might have been more appropriate.

Keeping people waiting beyond an agreed departure time is an annoying habit of some people. It is simply bad manners, especially when other people may have made personal sacrifices to be on time. I hate waiting beyond departure time while someone brushes their teeth or heads off to the woods for a protracted bathroom event when with that extra time, I could have had an extra cup of tea, stayed in bed longer, waxed my skis better, fixed some gear or even brushed my teeth, too. Organize yourself to always be on time.

If you handle incompatible pace by splitting the group, make sure that you can easily meet up again, and that both groups are adequately equipped with first aid, repair, food, cooking and camping gear. If slow individuals are slow because they are ill or exhausted, or because they keep falling when skiing or capsizing when canoeing, do not split the party.

Daily Schedules

Some people like to get up and on their way early in the morning with minimal time spent cooking breakfast, and with no time to dry the dew off their tents. They like to be finished travelling by early afternoon so they can sit around and relax and dry their gear. In the early days before good drybags were available it made sense to finish summer canoe days with lots of time to dry out gear before bedtime.

Other people prefer a relaxed morning with a good breakfast and a leisurely second cup of coffee, and don't mind travelling until late afternoon. An alternative is to make a fairly early start but have a number of stops during the day to fish, swim, do side trips and still finish in late afternoon. An early start is essential on short winter days, when travelling into the darkness at the end of the day reduces your safety margin.

In far northern areas in summer with 24-hour daylight, it is easy to allow the day's schedule to get out of step with your biological clock. People overtax themselves and become irritable because they are active for too many hours. A conscious effort is required to keep to an approximate time schedule and to eat and sleep regularly.

Environmental Ethics

Divergent environmental ethics can be a source of aggravation. I remember going on a long trip with two people we did not know well but who were recommended by an environmentally sensitive acquaintance. We assumed (!) they would be sensitive, too. Their propensity for lighting fires at every opportunity, and even two fires (one for cooking, one for drying socks) was a continual source of aggravation. This was especially tiresome because we were cooking entirely with a stove in this sensitive area and were trying to be meticulous about no-trace camping.

Insensitive practices include cutting green wood, cutting standing dead trees (habitat for birds), dragging canoes over rocks and leaving coloured marks, burning plastic garbage and careless disposal of organic garbage such as food scraps.

On one glacier tour I was reprimanded for not burning my toilet paper. I was puzzled—charred materials last forever, as any archaeologist will tell you. There have been incidents where people burning toilet paper in the woods has caused forest fires. Talk these and other pet peeves over, and come to a reasonable consensus, bearing in mind fire hazard, dryness/coldness and other factors affecting decomposition rates, esthetics, intensity of use of the area, insects and hygiene.

Nudity

Some people don't care, others are quite uncomfortable. Use discretion.

Fires

Some people are compulsive fire-fiddlers—just when the fire is burning clear and smokeless they poke it and start the smoke billowing all over everyone again! Others are pyromaniacs with a propensity for building bonfires that serve no useful purpose, burn up the limited wood supply and leave a big scar or a pile of unburned charcoal that persists for years. Worse still, they burn up the cook's supply of firewood. Others treat the limited fuel supply with respect and use small efficient fires, burning only when needed. Still others prefer to use stoves exclusively.

Sharing Utensils

Sharing cups, plates and cutlery bothers some people more than others and is unwise anyway. Play it safe by using marked personal items (magic marker or tape) to minimize spreading germs. Mixing unfamiliar personal flora can lead to intestinal unhappiness and is an unnecessary risk.

Snorers

Sleep disturbance caused by snorers can lead to fatigue and accidents. Some people jokingly advocate taking earplugs and a bag—you put the earplugs in your ears and the bag on the snorer's head! Of course you would not use the bag, but earplugs are a big help. Try to locate all the snorers away from the rest of the group.

Horseplay

Horseplay can relieve tension or boredom that can arise if you are camp-bound in poor weather. However, I personally feel uneasy around horseplay. Although the benefits can be considerable, if something goes wrong you may have a serious problem on your hands as well as feeling or looking very stupid. One hilarious tent-bound horseplay session during a three-day storm resulted in someone's glacier goggles being broken. A football match in a remote area left one member with a severely sprained ankle, luckily at the end of the trip while waiting to fly out. A wild, high-speed sail along a remote glacier, pulled on skis by a billowing tent fly, was hilarious and a memorable event, but could have resulted in injury or in someone skiing over the fly and cutting it.

Ribaldry and Teasing

This may be OK in small doses, depending on the group, but take care not to offend or go too far. One group of guys I encountered was sufficiently familiar with each other that they knew of one member's perennial bush constipation problem and ran a pool on the date and time he would obtain relief! On another occasion I was bathing with reasonable decorum when a rather attractive young lady in the party yelled across the gravel bar "Get 'em off, Morton!" This sort of thing might offend some people, though our group, including my wife, took it in good humour.

Scary Stories

Be careful with wolf stories, bear stories and generally scary talk. You really need to know the people in your group well before getting into these topics. Some people will pretend amusement while in fact they are quite disturbed by the stories. They may end up uneasy and not have any fun. Sleepless nights lead to chronic tiredness and people becoming accident-prone. Remember that what to you is obviously a tall tale to be taken with a grain of salt, might not necessarily be perceived the same way by people with less experience or knowledge. Also, people have associated fears you couldn't even imagine. For example, I remember one individual whose fear of bears was made much greater because he could not face the idea that something (other than worms) might actually eat him after death!

Language and Standards

Some people let their language deteriorate and their standards drop while on a bush trip, and the trend can spread among the group in ways and to extents that they might individually regret.

You won't always be doing your trips with the same old familiar gang (it gets dull after a while anyway!). It's nice to recreate with new people now and then even though some may regard newcomers as potential liabilities. No trip is perfect, but hopefully this chapter will have increased your awareness of human and group dynamics factors so you will more easily organize happy and successful trips.

Joining Commercial Trips

There is a wide range of commercial trips available, and by simply paying a fee you have a ready-made organizer, leader and group of companions. However, organized trips have numerous advantages and disadvantages that you should consider carefully.

Advantages

There are many good reasons for joining an organized trip. You may not have the time to organize the trip properly yourself, or the logistics of transporting gear, canoes and kayaks especially, may be too complex, too time consuming or uneconomical. It therefore makes sense to use the outfitter's gear and let them worry about getting it to and from the start and finish of the trip.

A common problem that is easily circumvented by joining an outfitted trip is the difficulty of assembling a big enough group of people who want to do the same trip at the same time.

Some outfitters have lodges, huts or cabins in prime areas, and it makes sense to buy in to their package if you want to use those areas. This is particularly the case with ski-touring and mountaineering outfitters in the western mountains.

If you have limited holiday time at your disposal, you want to ensure that no time is wasted at each end of the trip. A well-organized outfitter will be slick with the logistics so you won't waste time getting into the backcountry. The second time I went to the Nahanni I had the time to do the work an outfitter would do myself. The result was that my wife, who did not have as much holiday time, could fly out from Toronto in the morning and be on the river the same evening.

The outfitter's guides will know the area well so that you get straight to the best powder snow, the best viewpoints, the best fishing, the best side-hikes and the best camping. You won't waste time on cruddy snow and horrid bushwhacks, or find yourself camping in a marginal site when there is a superb one half a

The outfitter has done all the preparation work involved in getting the group and the gear to the start of the trip.

kilometre farther on. They should also know the hazards of the area so you will be safer than if you were on your own.

Certainly a feeling of confidence and security is a major reason for going on a guided trip. It's also occasionally nice to have someone else there who will do the thinking about avalanche hazard, routefinding or what to have for dinner, so you can just relax. However, you should never drop your guard completely—stay alert and keep thinking in case the guide has a lapse. Hopefully, the guide is more skilled than you are, but that is not necessarily always the case, and everyone can make mistakes.

Disadvantages

Expense is a disadvantage of an outfitted trip, but the savings by doing it yourself may be less than you think, especially when you factor in your time saved. An outfitted trip can look like a good deal when you add in all the additional expenses you might incur alone, and particularly if you include a price for blood pressure and worry.

You have no knowledge of or control over the skill levels and compatibility of the rest of the party when you sign up for the trip. You can end up being part of a mobile horror show, as it is difficult for outfitters to preassess the skills of their clients. They may not even bother inquiring carefully about prospective clients' skills, because economic necessity may dictate that they take anyone who can pay the fee.

Occasionally the skilled clients end up spending their holiday helping to nurse along someone who shouldn't really be on the trip in the first place. Sometimes a skilled pair of tandem canoeists will end up being split up so they can each take care of the members of a pair whose skills are inadequate. While the competent pair would be entitled to refuse to split, particularly if they had indicated a desire to paddle together at time of booking, splitting might be the only practical action to enable the trip to proceed safely. Similar problems can occur on backpacking, skiing or climbing trips. Someone's poor skiing skills may mean that you don't get to ski the steep-and-deep you would otherwise enjoy.

Remember that one reason people join organized trips is that they do not, for one reason

or another, have partners for trips of their own. The reasons may be quite innocuous, but could on the other hand merit investigation! Occasionally you end up with people on the trip who just catalyze strife and dissension and set people on edge. In a club situation or with commercial operations it is difficult to keep control over who is coming on the trip.

I remember lines from a song from the fifties called "Don't Bring Lulu":

She's the kind of smarty / who breaks up every party / hullabaloo—loo, don't bring Lulu / she'll come by herself!

Some people just cannot help stirring up trouble, but others take a perverse delight in deliberately creating problems. A solution that works well is for party members to take turns with the troublemaker, tactfully keeping him occupied away from the group. That way only one of the party is driven crazy at a time and the others can meanwhile get some peace.

Another disadvantage is that you may find yourself hampered by being part of a group with overall low outdoor living competence. A guide commented to me recently that many of her sea kayaking clients were not only lacking in basic small boat skills and water sense, but also lacked basic camping skills and the ability

A remote fly-in lodge in the Yukon. Primrose Wilderness Encounters, Whitehorse.

to stay dry and comfortable on land. These types of problems can mean that the scope of the trip must be curtailed, to the frustration of those who have taken the time and trouble to prepare, train and equip themselves for the trip. The frustration is likely to be experienced at both ends of the skill level spectrum. The person who is out of their depth will also not be happy. They may feel continually stressed, out of their "comfort zone" and possibly embarrassed at being "a burden."

I would feel far more comfortable signing up for an outfitted trip if the outfitter asked me some searching questions about my skill levels. I would feel there was less chance of me getting in over my head or of there being a lame duck on the trip who would spoil it for everyone. However, this doesn't always work. I remember a guide describing how a client had totally fabricated the resume that got him onto a polar expedition. He also described how another had listed a number of trips he had been on, but it turned out that these were as a total "passenger" on guided trips.

Outfitted groups tend to be larger than private groups, and large groups can diminish the "wilderness feeling." However, a large group increases your chances of finding a kindred spirit if that is important to you. Always ask how many people will be on the trip, and also ask how many guides will be along. This is because more than one guide enables the group to engage in different activities simultaneously. For example, you can split into a fast group and a slow group or a fishing group and a hiking group if there are two guides.

Another factor to consider is whether you really want all the services in the "outfitting package." Often guiding comes as part of a package, along with logistics handling, food organization and preparation, equipment, and perhaps the use of a lodge or other facility. Some people want the services, but would rather do without the actual guiding. They really want to "do their own thing" on the trip. They want to ski off by themselves, choose their own route through the rapids or walk their own path, rather than be "guided" and told where to go.

For a variety of reasons including safety and liability, this independence is often not permitted on guided trips, so it can be a source of friction and dissatisfaction. Usually this dissatisfaction is misplaced, because the guide probably knows something the client doesn't—the location of the best ski run, or the most scenic path. The really good guide may try to assess the capability of the group so that an appropriate balance of challenge, autonomy and risk (real or perhaps just perceived) is reached to keep everyone satisfied.

A friend recently returned from a ski lodge whose resident guide is felt by some to be rather restrictive. My friend commented that he perceived that if the guide felt he could trust the group to do exactly as he said and they would ski under his control, then he would take them to better skiing on more challenging but riskier terrain. As a result of perceiving an unwillingness of the clients to do what they were told, he was only prepared to take them where the consequences of them disobeying were not so serious.

The Role of Participants

As a client on a commercial trip you are not entitled to significantly alter the operation of the organization. You are even less entitled to do so if there are other clients who are not part of your group. My wife and I have experienced some great ski holidays with a guide who runs a remote ski chalet and guiding operation in the western mountains. We are aware of the "norms" of such guided operations and are quite comfortable with them. We don't fret about what, to some people, are regimented trail procedures. We go with the express purpose of paying someone else to make all the decisions for a change. Other people, unaware of the norms, are irked by the restrictions. They perhaps think of the chalet simply as a hotel operation rather than as a complete package with guiding.

Chapter 3

Planning Your Trip

You can plan your trip to be entirely self-sufficient and independent of assistance from other people or organizations. On the other hand, using the many different services available to recreational travellers may save you a great deal of time and money during both the planning and the execution of your trip. If you choose the types and levels of service carefully you will be able to meet your own personal need for autonomy and independence. It may be as minimal as acquiring up-to-date information crucial to the success of your trip. The planning stage also includes procurement and careful examination of appropriate maps, air photos and charts. An awareness of problems related to compass use in the north and of the potential applications of GPS devices for navigation is also important.

Services for Recreational Travellers

A wide range of services is available to assist recreational travellers. Even the most independent and self-sufficient recreationists will often find that these services can save time and allow the trip to run much more smoothly. This section provides information about the types of services available.

Services in Small Communities

Foreign visitors especially must be aware of how small some isolated communities are, and how limited the services and facilities may be. Some small scale maps and atlases can be very misleading in that they may mark a tiny village in the far north with the same size lettering as a fair sized town in the south. Remote settlements are likely to have very limited foodstuffs available and will usually not have banks or money-changing facilities. Cash will be required and credit cards are not likely to be accepted except possibly by air

charter companies. For example, in the whole of the Canadian eastern Arctic, the only banking facilities are at Iqaluit (formerly Frobisher Bay). Medical facilities will be very limited, possibly only a nursing station. There may or may not be a public phone. Accommodation will be nonexistent or limited, and certainly extremely costly. Sometimes accommodation can be arranged through Inuit Co-ops in the far north. Some small villages have a recognized camping site with limited facilities. These sites may not be satisfactory if they are frequented by large numbers of local children or semiwild dogs, as well as by local "partiers." There may be guiding and outfitting operations based in the communities, but they tend to be more often of the hunting-fishing variety. Major trip outfitting organizations are usually based in larger centres. See Choosing Outfitters and Guides, page 86.

A native community in northern Manitoba.

Outfitters

A wide range of "outfitting" services are available. Some outfitting organizations just rent equipment, others provide fixed-site food, accommodation, equipment and guiding. Still others provide complete tripping equipment/food/route plan/transport packages and maybe guiding as well. It is a good idea to make very sure you understand exactly what service the organization you are dealing with will actually provide for your money. Many outfitting services advertise in outdoor magazines and can be found through tourism listings.

Guides

This term is applied rather loosely in North America and does not necessarily imply a high level of training. It is applied to a range of individuals, from someone who just has some knowledge of the area all the way to highly trained alpine guides. It is often taken to mean a hunting or fishing guide, whereas in Europe it generally means a qualified mountain guide. See Choosing Outfitters and Guides, page 86.

Wilderness Schools

Wilderness "schools" and other training organizations have an education mandate and generally provide a more learning-oriented experience than do guides or outfitters. Their courses may involve a period of training leading up to a final trip, maybe learn-as-you-go trips, or maybe simply courses of instruction. One advantage of these organizations is that if someone's skills are not good enough for a trip, the staff know how to remedy the situation. Guides, on the other hand, are not necessarily good instructors because instructing is not their primary function. These organizations advertise in outdoor magazines and can also be found through tourism listings.

Clubs

Outdoor clubs run a large number of trips in both their local areas and farther afield. My local canoe club runs about 100 canoe trips each summer and about 50 winter ski trips. The service the clubs provide is usually a designated "trip coordinator" who organizes the logistics of the trip and keeps track of participants. Usually the coordinator has done the trip and is familiar with the route, so the trip logistics run smoothly. They are not expected to take on the responsibilities of a guide but may, however, act in some capacity as a guide or mentor. Some clubs such as the Alpine Club of Canada organize longer trips or "camps" with a more formal leadership structure, sometimes with professional guides. Many clubs also organize skills instruction sessions. You can contact clubs through state, provincial and municipal recreational umbrella organizations, and many are listed in large city Yellow Pages.

Expediters

These organizations are found in the "gateway" communities that are jumping-off points and transportation hubs for remote hinterlands. Their exact functions and modes of operation vary somewhat but basically they act as agents in town for people in the bush, arranging procurement and delivery of items ordered by people in the bush. They can arrange anything from bush orders of groceries to delivery of equipment and machinery parts needed by miners and prospectors. They have a good knowledge of where to get what and how to get it to remote places and can usually be found in the Yellow Pages. Although the tourism industry is not a large part of their clientele, they may be able to provide a vital link in your trip logistics and planning.

Lodges, Camps, Campsites, Chalets, Cabins and Huts

There are many different outdoor recreation facilities. While the divisions are not cut-and-dried, lodges tend to be the more luxurious, full-service facilities, sometimes with a single large building or else with a main base building and a number of separate high-grade cottage-style sleeping units. Camps are much the same but generally more rustic. However, whereas the term "lodge" is applied equally to huntin'-fishin' places and to skiing or wildlife viewing facilities, the term "camp" when applied to facilities tends to refer to either huntin'-fishin' places or to children's outdoor recreation institutions.

The term "camp" does not necessarily imply tented facilities, and can involve the whole range of structures from tents, through wood floor/canvas roof combinations, all the way to permanent buildings.

A camp*site* or camp*ground* is distinct from a camp and is a place to which you bring a tent, trailer or recreation vehicle. Many of them do not regard people with tents as a major part of their clientele, and I recently even saw a sign saying "no tents please" outside a campsite! Campsites tend to be more spacious than those in many other countries. Tent sites are often nonexistent or else are gravel pads that require a good sleeping pad and nails for tent pegs. Take a plastic tarp to put under your tent because people with RVs often let grey water (and worse) run onto the ground. You may find yourself paying a hefty camping fee because the site provides all sorts of frills like showers, flush toilets and free firewood. Paying this high fee can be aggravating for people who are on a budget and who only need a pit toilet, a tap to fill a washbasin and a legal place to pitch a tent. One advantage of private campgrounds is that they tend to be better supervised. The cheaper, more rustic, but usually unsupervised park or forest service campsites may be more pleasant locations.

Chalets, cabins and huts are more like the European mountain huts. Chalets are generally more luxurious than huts, though the term may be used simply because of the mountain location. European visitors in particular should be aware that Alaskan and Canadian huts are generally more primitive than European alpine huts and don't usually have a custodian, food, cooked meals or bedding available to casual arrivals.

Because services range all the way from "bring your own food and bedding and be self-catering and self-guiding," all the way to "full service," it is essential to find out what your prospective facility will actually provide. Advance booking is required for virtually all these backcountry facilities in Canada and Alaska. Some are so popular that you can only obtain bookings if you are successful in a booking lottery.

A traditional mountain hut in the Canadian Rockies.

A privately operated backcountry chalet in the Selkirk Mountains offering complete transport, catering and guiding packages. Ruedi Beglinger/Selkirk Mountain Experience, Revelstoke.

Huts operated by the Alpine Club of Canada may or may not have a custodian, may be locked and only provide foam sleeping mats, limited pots and cutlery, and cooking stoves without fuel (naphtha). Heating, if present at all, is usually with wood stoves. Bookings must be made to obtain a key, so at least one person in the party must be an ACC member. There are a small number of huts still operated by the national parks in western Canada. These require overnight use permits from the park offices.

Quebec has a number of small (4-10 people) huts in remote areas for skiers and wilderness travellers. A chain of huts in the Charlevoix region is operated by the Quebec Mountain Federation. Vehicle shuttles and food transport can be arranged. There are also huts in the Chic-Chocs region of the Gaspe Peninsula.

Hostelling International Canada (formerly the International Youth Hostel Association) has numerous hostels in Canada. However, unlike Europe, they are not all within walking or cycling distance of each other, because of the size of the country. They tend to be clustered in specific areas of interest such as the mountains of Alberta. The association runs a shuttle bus that can carry bikes from Calgary to the mountain hostels.

Hostelling International U.S.A. (American YHA) also operates hostels in Alaska. There are also about 200 cabins available for public use in Alaska, operated by various agencies.

Some lodges and air charter companies operate "outpost camps"—remote cabins, usually on lakes. They are often provided with a boat of some kind since they are intended primarily for fishermen and hunters. You don't, of course, have to hunt or fish to use these facilities.

A popular modern hut on the Wapta Icefield, operated by the Alpine Club of Canada.

Choosing Outfitters and Guides

If you decide to go with an outfitter or guide, you should research them carefully. A large proportion of them cater primarily to trophy-hunting and fishing clientele. You need to have a clear picture of exactly what they will provide and obtain some feeling for such factors as their competence and environmental sensitivity.

Levels of Service and Luxury

When choosing an outfitter you must consider how much service and luxury you want, and how much you are prepared to pay for. More important still is to consider whether the impact on the wilderness values of the area through providing that luxury is acceptable. Generally, the more comfort and services, the higher the impact.

However, there are lodges run by people whose hearts are in the outdoors as much as in business, and who provide quite comfortable facilities with much reduced environmental impact.

We occasionally use an unobtrusive 7- by 12-metre two-storey backcountry lodge catering to 18 guests. My conscience is relatively comfortable with the small basic rooms, an outside toilet system, sauna rather than showers and no running water. Maybe I would like some other luxuries, but I know I don't *need* them, and I certainly can't justify their impact on sensitive areas.

Tents and sleeping bags provided by outfitters for their clients vary considerably in quality. I'm used to the comfort of a top-quality sleeping bag and a reliable, easy-pitching tent, so I prefer to take my own gear. If you want to take your own, a prudent outfitter will ask you the make and model to make sure that it is suitable.

Besides comfort, the other value-added service is the interpretive information a guide can provide, which enables the clients to better tune into and use the area's true values. It is worth paying for a guide who knows the history, geography, geology and biology of an area, so that you obtain more value from your trip. Sadly, many people go to special or sensitive areas understanding little of what they see and obtaining little value from their passage. It's rather like occupying a space in a crowded, high-quality restaurant and only eating a roll and butter.

More and more outfitters are providing educational components to their trips, and special interest groups such as the World Wildlife Fund sponsor and organize trips with a particular flavour. An outfitter who supplies a bibliography and a list of other trip references to clients is probably one with a more cerebral attitude to the wilderness experience. He wants his clients to derive the most benefit from the experience.

Operating Styles

The operating styles of outfitters are many and varied, even though they provide basically the same services. It therefore pays to do some careful research to ensure you choose an organization whose ethics and style are acceptable.

The lack of environmental sensitivity of a licensed local fishing and hunting guide on a guided canoe party of which I was a member made some participants unhappy. He cut green wood for camp structures and built big redundant fires in an area of limited wood supply and slow regeneration.

On the other hand, some organizations have no-trace ethics and practices that are superior to those of most backcountry travellers. They have a vested interest in preservation of wilderness in the area where they make a living. Friends who recently canoed the Grand Canyon reported on the impeccable standards of their own outfitter and of the one who used each campsite immediately before them. There was not a scrap of litter or wood ash or toilet paper, and even the footprints in the sand were raked over. Those standards need to apply everywhere.

Ask your prospective outfitter the sort of searching questions that will really indicate how environmentally friendly his operation is. If they just say, "we are environmentally friendly," ask for specifics about their environmental friendliness. Ask about their procedures for human waste disposal. Ask whether they use fires, and if so what they do to minimize their impact (fire boxes, small fires or driftwood only). Ask what they do to avoid disturbing the flora and fauna and their habitat. Ask about their maximum group size. Twenty people in a group is hardly what you call environmentally friendly.

It may also be useful to find out more about the guide's other duties with the organization or their off-season activities and interests. A guide who is an environmental biology student or ski touring guide in the off season may cater better to your

A cozy mountain hut with basic facilities allowing enjoyment of the mountains with minimal impact.

needs and be more to your liking than one who is a hunting guide or logger. An organization that hires guides and staff locally and is part of the local economy immediately has some environmental friendliness because it is providing employment in a sustainable and nonconsumptive sector of the economy.

However, just because the guide or operator is a resident of a place that is your idea of heaven, don't assume they view and treat it the same way you do. The no-trace or at least minimum trace school of camping seems, paradoxically, to be an idea often espoused more by urban people than by many rural residents.

There are still organizations catering to both snowmobilers and skiers. Skiers should inquire carefully before booking. A group of us recently used a motel advertising "ski tourers welcome," but they were also catering to snowmobilers so our stay was not pleasant.

In British Columbia much of the best mountain terrain is allocated to Heli-ski operators. Friends recently went telemark skiing from a lodge renowned for its superb terrain, but the guide refused to take them to the best runs because they were "reserved for heli-skiers"! Heli-skiing is a pervasive intrusion in much of the ski-touring terrain in British Columbia, so inquire. My experience has been that heli-ski operators show little courtesy toward people who have laboriously broken trail into an area.

Outfitter Competence

As well as having ethics and attitudes acceptable to you, the outfitter you choose must be competent enough to look after you and provide the services to maintain your safety.

Regulation of guiding and outfitting organizations and the level of training required before being allowed to guide in the outdoors varies across the country. Organizations listed in state and provincial government publications usually meet certain basic requirements, but these can be minimal, and are geared more to health and safety of facilities than to field competence. National and provincial parks have more stringent regulations governing guides and outfitters operating within their boundaries. In British Columbia, the rafting industry is stringently regulated, requiring operators to be highly trained, certified, licensed and insured. Mountain guides belonging to the International Association of Mountain Guides (UIAMG) are trained to the highest standards.

You therefore need to ask about the training and skill levels of the guides. However, no matter how good the training, remember that even within the confines of the same outfitter's organization, individual characteristics of different guides can create widely differing atmospheres on a trip. Add the dynamics of a randomly assembled group of clients, and regardless of the guide's skill, your enjoyment of the trip can definitely involve a component of luck.

An inquiry to one provincial government official indicated there was nothing to worry about because the outfitters listed in their brochure were "experienced" and had been in business for extended periods. Unfortunately, experience isn't always a measure of competence.

The statement "Competence only comes with training, practice, experience and the development of judgement" succinctly sums up the situation. The problem is that people can be very experienced at doing things in a manner contrary to what they would have been taught through a reputable training organization. They can also become very experienced at being very lucky. Sooner or later the luck runs

Your guide needs to be able to do many things, including preparing good food in an appetizing and hygienic manner.

out. Consequently, if you ask an outfitter about the guide's competence or read in the brochure that the guides are "experienced" rather than trained or qualified, be wary.

You must ask your prospective outfitter some searching questions about their guides' training and experience. If you get a response like, "Oh we don't worry much about first aid—we've never had any problems," beware. It indicates a lack of responsibility for the clients. Though they are perhaps unlikely to become injured, they would probably be in an environment where the consequences of an inadequately treated injury would be serious. Guides should have a wilderness first aid qualification that trains them for the difficult outdoor first aid situation and for the long period before help arrives.

Ask about safety precautions and procedures. Beware if the organization equates *first aid* with *safety* and says, "We have a big first aid kit and well-trained first-aiders." A first aid kit is not a safety precaution—it's what you use when safety precautions and practices to prevent injury have been inadequately followed! If they say, "Don't worry—we're insured," then beware! You'd rather be safe than hurt and making insurance claims, though knowing there is insurance (which there may not be) can be some consolation.

If, on the other hand, they say things like, "We use saws instead of axes" or "No one leaves camp alone or without saying where they are going" or "The guides go to annual updating courses in snow stability evaluation" or "We

Hopefully your outfitter's guides will have gone through comprehensive training and practice in carrying out rescues.

spend the entire first day doing canoe instruction and self-rescue drills," then they are displaying a better attitude. Better still is if they say that all the guides are qualified in the various disciplines by organizations you can recognize. You would like to hear that they do a group training and practice session at the start of each season and carry out surprise emergency procedure drills at intervals through the season.

Be aware that a guide must be a master of many trades, not just the physical skills of getting up the rock face or skiing down the hill or paddling through the rapids. That famous climber, skier, paddler or adventurer may not be a good guide. According to Don Vockeroth, a UIAGM guide, "A guide must be a teacher, demonstrator, advisor, good at the technical aspects of the activity, navigator, outdoors enthusiast, diplomat, weather expert, repairman, doctor, comforter, tower of strength and shining example."

As previously mentioned, two guides allows for splitting into fast and slow groups or less ambitious and more ambitious groups. There is also a better safety margin with two guides because an emergency may be too much for one guide to handle or it might be the guide who is injured. Statistics show that a surprisingly high proportion of accidents happen to trip leaders.

No matter how good the guides, the organization must provide them with good equipment and organizational support so they can concentrate on the true professional's prime duty of looking after the needs of their clients. Unfortunately, these aspects of an operation are hard to judge until you arrive for the trip.

The food prepackaging and organization by a rafting outfitter I guided for was superb, and I never had to waste time worrying about quantities or whether everything was there. I could be absolutely certain that the "Day One" package really did have everything in it for 10 people for Day One. That removed one of the many headaches inherent in guiding, enabling me to spend more time with the clients.

Although most outfitting organizations are run by professionals, the pressures of economics and business can result in cost cutting, which puts more pressure on the guides. There are lots of ways to cut costs that can result in guides being overworked and unable to give the necessary attention to their clients. The same rafting company I worked for provided their guides with excellent quality, easy cleaning cookware, including good nonstick fry pans—an extra cost item but one that made the guides' task easier and gave them a few minutes more time for the clients.

Certifying or Regulating Bodies

- Trade Association of Sea Kayaking—has guidelines for safety.
- ACMG—Association of Canadian Mountain Guides
- UIAGM—International Association of Mountain Guides
- Canadian Association of Nordic Ski Guides
- Canadian Recreation Canoeing Association
- CRCA or Provincial Affiliates—leader and instructor training and qualifications
- Rescue 3 Swiftwater Rescue
- Red Cross Wilderness First Aid
- B.C. Professional Rafting Association
- CISSR Canadian Institute of Safety, Search and Rescue
- Ski Patrol/Nordic Ski Patrol
- Red Cross Wilderness First Aid
- B.C. Industrial First Aid
- Ontario Rock Climbing Association
- National Parks—rules vary, but generally guiding activities are closely controlled by licensing, quotas, the requirement of insurance, and variable testing or monitoring of competence.
- Provincial and State Parks—rules vary. Some are very loose, others require licensing, testing or monitoring of competence, and require insurance, impose quotas, etc.
- Alpine Club of Canada. Courses in mountaineering skills.
- Canadian Avalanche Association Avalanche Training
- Alaska Wilderness Recreation and Tourism Association, Juneau. Trade association with directory of members with good credentials who follow association's ecotourism guidelines.
- American Mountain Guides Association
- American Canoe Association.
- Universities in Canada and Alaska offer outdoor and guiding programs.

Sources of Information

Up-to-date local information can be crucial to the success of your trip; things change much more quickly in Canada and Alaska than in older, more established countries. An access road may have ceased to exist, be gated or subject to seasonal closures. A new road, cutline or trail may save you miles of bushwhacking. A bridge may have been washed out, an area may have been devastated by recent logging, or a river drained by a hydroelectric project. An area that looks appealing on the map may in fact be a multi-use area shared with snowmobilers, heli-hikers, four-wheel drivers, heli-skiers or jet boaters. There may be restrictions on random camping or on access at certain times of year to protect wildlife from poachers and other disturbances. Permission will be required to travel through private land, Indian Reserves and other special jurisdictions.

You also need to know about the weather conditions to expect in your destination. There can be local weather effects such as chinook winds, williwaws, fogs and treacherous combinations of winds and tides. Different areas have vastly different snowpack structures and attendant avalanche hazards. An unusual preceding season may make your trip difficult. For example, a heavy winter snowpack may delay the opening of hiking trails or may make rivers dangerously high. An unusually dry season may mean there is a high forest fire hazard and that areas are closed to travel. So, don't be afraid to ask people! A particularly tragic disaster happened to a school party canoeing a lake that local people could have told them was subject to sudden violent squalls, if only they had been asked.

A few phone calls can quickly yield valuable information. Although phoning long distance from overseas is more costly than writing letters, it offers the advantage of an immediate reply; you may not get replies to your letters from some individuals and organizations. While they may see no benefit to spending a half hour on a written reply, they may be willing to talk for five minutes on the phone. Visitors from abroad should realize that the telephone is used much more widely in North America than in most other countries.

The following are useful sources of information. You won't necessarily need to use all of them

for any given location, but hopefully they will enable you to obtain the information you need.

Park wardens, rangers and information officers. When approached in the right way, these people can provide very useful information. However, remember that they know nothing about your expertise or your intentions, and consequently may be cautious or even discouraging about a trip if they are unsure of your expertise. All sorts of people ask them for information and then get themselves into trouble. Giving a fair indication of your skill level without bragging helps them provide relevant information. Valuable information that park officials can usually provide is whether there is a large group already using an area, and also about trail closures.

Many rangers and wardens spend time in the backcountry, and some are likely to be practitioners of backcountry activities and will be glad to provide valuable information. A group of wardens met with leaders of our local outdoor community and made it clear that they do not want to be seen as "representatives of officialdom and bureaucracy" or as "cops of the backcountry," but rather as sources of information and assistance to help people have quality outdoor experiences.

On one occasion, I wanted specific information about avalanche conditions on a particular section of a route. A quick phone call put me in touch with a ranger who had been there recently and who could tell me that all the threatening slopes had already slid. After the trip the ranger who "de-registered" us inquired specifically about conditions we found, to add to his knowledge for future reference.

It is advisable to first obtain basic information from information officers who can answer such questions as group size limits, closed areas, can and bottle bans, special fishing regulations and camping restrictions. Only then should you approach wardens with specific detailed technical questions.

Information officers in my experience vary greatly in their ability to help the serious backcountry user because they deal with the whole gamut of park visitors, most of whom don't venture more than 100 metres from the road.

They generally don't have detailed firsthand information for the backcountry user, but you may just strike lucky and be served by someone who is a practitioner of your activity and who has the information you need.

When writing to parks for information and for brochures you will not always be sent all that is available or all that you need at the first approach. There are sometimes excellent documents that are in short supply and not distributed unless officials are reasonably sure they will be used. Study the first mailing to narrow down your needs, then ask for more specific items. Preferably obtain a list of available documents. Make sure you start your inquiries long enough ahead of the trip to allow time for several mailings.

Tourist information bureaus may not be good sources for specific backcountry information, but they can often provide good general information and leads to other sources of information. They may have guidebooks or lists of guidebooks, tourism and recreation maps, and certainly brochures for guiding, outfitting and equipment rental organizations. Also air and boat charter operators who might be able to assist with transport. Brochures can give you good ideas on areas to visit, or avoid as some of them

CAUTION
Bear in area.
Travel with caution

Wardens and rangers will be able to forewarn you about conditions before you get to the trailhead.

may promote outdoor activities you find unpleasant. State and provincial tourism bureaus are a good starting point. However, bureaus are also often organized on a local regional basis by tourism associations. They can have names that can make them hard to track down, for example, Mystery Country in northern Manitoba or Rainbow Country around Manitoulin Island. Ask the state or province to put you in touch with these organizations, too. Allow plenty of time. It could be weeks before you receive an initial mailing of basic materials and even more time for followups once you send off additional specific requests. A document list is one of the most useful things to request in your first mailing.

Libraries. Your own library should have catalogues of books in print for the U.S. and Canada to help track down guidebooks, etc. However, some good guidebooks seem to be conspicuously absent, perhaps because they are small, locally published items. General background books are easy to track down this way. The catalogues of books in print are expensive and may not be purchased every year by smaller libraries so they may not be up to date. Many libraries now have online search capabilities that you can use to browse the collection of the library and possibly of associated libraries. In libraries near to the region of interest you may find historic and other books pertaining specifically to that region. For example, I was able to read a reference copy of an old publication of explorer Samuel Hearne's diary in the Yellowknife library before a trip. You may find a university library with a good reference collection of topographic and other maps and maybe even air photos.

Clubs and associations can be extremely useful sources of local information. If you are a new resident in the area, join the local clubs. If you are a visitor and approach a club for information, you may find that some individuals are rather protective and secretive about their local area. They may be reluctant to share information with unknown outsiders, so be prepared to talk at some length while they sound you out a little. Most people are quite open and realize that sharing information works both ways, and that sooner or later they may themselves want information on your home area.

The club may invite you to participate in its trips and activities if they feel comfortable with your skill level and feel you won't be a liability. Clubs to which I belong have welcomed occasional trip participants visiting from other areas. A friend who occasionally has to visit another part of the country on business skis and paddles with their local groups.

Track down local clubs through retailers, municipal government recreation departments, even directly through the Yellow Pages. You can also track them down through national, state or provincial sporting organizations such as Cross Country Canada, The Canadian Recreational Canoeing Association, The American Canoe Association or the Federation of Mountain Clubs of B.C.

Local enthusiasts can be very helpful sources of information, but can unintentionally be misleading by failing to give crucial information. Having canoed extensively in eastern Canada before moving west, I have a good perspective on the differences between eastern and western conditions. I therefore have a better insight into what to tell a visiting eastern paddler than does someone who has only a western perspective. For example, a western mountain whitewater paddler may be so used to paddling in a wet suit that he wouldn't think to tell an easterner to bring one. Only a westerner with prior eastern experience would be aware that wet suits and dry suits are not automatically part of eastern summer paddling. Similarly, to someone from blackfly and mosquito country, summer outdoors means bugs, and they may forget to tell visitors from bug-free areas to come prepared with head nets and impregnated bug shirts. By all means, use local people as a source, but make sure you ask enough questions.

Be careful when asking local hunters and fishermen for information. They may well regard your presence on "their" turf as competition they would rather not have, even out of season. Others may regarded you as an "environmentalist" who is against the consumptive industry from which they make a living, so any information provided may not be very useful. Whoever you talk to, remember that the information will be from a perspective influenced by their level of skill or fitness, which may be very different from yours.

Local retailers. Retailers can be a mine of information on local outdoor recreation opportunities, but please remember that their business is to sell equipment, not to chat, so make sure you do the decent thing and buy something after you have picked their brains! To find likely retailers, look in the Yellow Pages in your library, or check magazines that cater to your activity for a list of retailers that sell the magazine. That way you can zero-in on stores that concentrate on your outdoor activity. Remember that "sporting goods" stores may be catering primarily to people whose outdoor recreation involves fishing, motorized activities or hunting, and not low-impact recreation. It can be useful to find out from these sources where **not** to go!

A phone call to the specialty equipment retailer in that area can quickly and cheaply provide much vital information. They likely stock local guidebooks, some of which may be small local productions, not widely distributed, and generally unobtainable outside the immediate area. If you can find a specialty store, it might be staffed by people involved in the local recreation scene who can provide a multitude of tips. They will also usually be able to put you in touch with local clubs and outfitters, and generally advise and give you more "leads" to pursue. When my wife and I were ski-touring in British Columbia, a visit to a skiing/backpacking/canoeing store quickly informed us that the area we had in mind for touring was not appropriate for us because it was popular with snowmobilers. We were told that many of the local skiers had to resort to using snowmobiles themselves to gain access to remote steep terrain not used by snowmobilers.

Local hotel and motel owners can be a very useful source of information. Make sure you phone at a time when the owner is likely to be there. People in the hospitality business usually know lots of people in the community even if they themselves cannot help you directly. In more remote areas they may also cater to other needs of travellers such as transportation and supplies, often through subcontractors. You may pay more than you would had you engaged the subcontractor yourself. However, a subcontractor has more incentive to do a good job for a local business than he does for a one-time-only client whom he will never see again.

Local Chamber of Commerce offices. You can pick up leads here but they are not generally the best sources of specific outdoor information.

Local industries. Liaison with these organizations and especially with some of the larger forest companies can be surprisingly helpful. Providing recreation information is good public relations for them, and is a way of mollifying an increasingly aware and concerned public. They can tell you where logging roads provide access, and may provide you with maps. They know where active logging is and locations of recently logged areas you may wish to avoid. Active logging operations should be avoided—driving on a logging road in company with logging trucks is apt to be unpleasant and unhealthy, and the companies prefer that the public stay away from these areas.

The local tourism information office, chamber of commerce or provincial forestry department will be able to tell you what companies are active in which areas so you can contact them in advance.

Forest services. Forest services are not necessarily only concerned with supporting the logging industry. They are often involved in outdoor recreation and can provide information, maps and local industry contacts. British Columbia Forest District Recreation maps, for example, are very useful because logging roads open to the public are marked, as are trails, campsites, gates and impassable areas. In Alaska, the forest service has a large amount of recreation information and manages backcountry cabins for public use.

Guidebooks. Guidebooks are a tremendous help to outdoor enthusiasts, but they must be used with caution. A well-written guidebook will have key information on trailhead locations, access practicality and legality, trip difficulty, time required, camping spots, hazards, points of interest, sources of water or supplies, best time of year and up-to-date information on new roads, trails or bridges, and changes in features marked on older maps.

A good guidebook includes information specifically geared to the mode of travel for which the guidebook is intended: "Ski down through the trees rather than trying to stay on the summer

trail" or "The land on the narrow isthmus is now private so you cannot use the ancient traditional portage and must paddle around the exposed point." Marked topo maps and especially the marked photographs in a guidebook can be a tremendous help for finding routes, especially in bad weather. A photograph of the terrain provides far more information than does a map, and the oblique photos in such publications as *Ski Touring the Wapta Icefield* and *Ski Trails in the Canadian Rockies* or Bill Wolferston's *Cruising Guide to British Columbia* are a tremendous help, especially in poor visibility.

That said, we must remember the potential drawbacks of guidebooks. First of all, bear in mind that one person's mosey is another person's marathon, and that one person's rapid is another person's waterfall. In other words, the perspective of the writer may be very different from yours. They may have a different skill and fitness level, have used vastly different equipment or experienced very different conditions. Consequently, estimates of time required and difficulty should be viewed with caution.

A group of very fit and strong ski friends on a trip the guidebook indicated should take four to eight hours, recently spent an extra night in the woods because of horrendous trailbreaking conditions. However, at least that particular guidebook did give time ranges varying by a factor of two to accommodate different conditions and skill levels. Any guidebook should probably give a time spread of that order if it is realistic about variability of skill levels and conditions.

Compounding the subjectivity of the guidebook writer's assessments is the fact that the author may not be writing on the strength of their own firsthand information. Also, guidebooks are rarely absolutely error free, as either the writer makes an error or something changes after the book goes to press.

Finally, there is the risk of becoming over-reliant on the guidebook, so that you do not tune in adequately to the actual information your eyes and ears are giving you about the route as you proceed along it. If you let this happen, you can be in serious trouble, especially if there is a guidebook error or a change in the terrain, or, as surprisingly often happens, you misread the guide. Without the guidebook you would be more cautious and would be reading the terrain, so would probably detect warning signs and take steps to avoid trouble. For example, the guidebook warns of big rapids, but your erroneous interpretation of the guide leads you to believe it is still a kilometre ahead. Relying on your guidebook, you ignore the loud roaring sound from just round the next corner and end up swimming as a result of your mistake.

I have no qualms about annotating my guidebooks. I have also converted some to a loose-leaf format with a sharp knife. That way I can take just the pages I need, tucked in my map case. Have the book punched by your local friendly printer, or clamp it tightly between two pieces of scrap wood in a vise and drill holes through the wood and the book. Then use long twist ties or loose rings to hold the loose pages in the book between trips.

Maps and air photos. Air photos provide a lot more information than maps, and photos are often more up-to-date, so new features such as logging roads, burned areas, cutlines, beaver flooding, bridges, etc. are visible. Forest type is recognizable, open areas in forest show up, as do crevassed areas, trails, even rapids on rivers. The disadvantage of air photos is that a stereoscope is required to see topographic detail. I discuss using a stereoscope later in this chapter.

Canada and Alaska are well mapped with topographic maps, special purpose maps and marine charts for both maritime areas and major inland bodies of water. The chief limitation is the ability of the user to interpret them to their best advantage and obtain information from them. Always keep in mind the date of the map when considering man-made features. See the discussion of map reading later in the chapter.

Phone books and yellow pages. Major libraries will have the Yellow Pages and telephone books for most of the country. White pages should be consulted for services in small communities. A sample test of this on a small northern community yielded a lodge, a general store, local community college, local air and coastal ferry services, and the local radio communication society. Two construction companies listed could also be useful as owners of transport vehicles and barges. A few minutes on the phone can open up a lot of possibilities.

Journals. The *Canadian Alpine Journal* (CAJ) and the *American Alpine Journal* (AAJ) are annual Alpine Club publications that chronicle in detail explorations of mountainous areas. CAJ photographs are high-quality and with captions provide a wealth of information for mountain travellers. A subject index is available. Other club newsletters can be a source of trip descriptions or can help you track down people who have been to a particular area.

Books. Books about an area can provide useful information even if not intended as guidebooks. I just finished reading *Arctic Passages* by John Bockstoce, Hearst Marine Books. It gave tremendous insight into the problems of navigating the Arctic coastline of Canada, weather and ice conditions, bugs, fogs, feasible travel seasons, history, etc. However, be wary of information from books that are not intended as a guide and critical information source. Also be aware of the influence of people's skill level, toughness, equipment and motivation on their portrayal of a trip.

Another potential source of information is coffee-table books and other picture books. They may have very useful photographs showing crucial parts of a route.

Magazine articles. Magazine articles can provide information about trips or ideas for trips and new areas to go to. However, as with books, be aware that the article is not intended as a guide and critical information source. Some of these, such as the Canadian magazines *Explore* and *Canadian Geographic*, and the American magazines *Canoe* and *National Geographic,* have a cumulative index available so you can find articles about specific areas easily. *Explore*'s index is arranged by subject and by issue.

Internet. Recent development on the Information Highway have tremendous potential for those seeking information. World Wide Web sites catering to your type of recreation can easily be found using one of the many search engines available. You can also put out feelers for information through suitable news groups. Once you have made contact with a source of information you can communicate at virtually no cost through e-mail.

Maps, Charts and Air Photos

Maps, charts and air photos are easy to obtain and can provide you with a wealth of crucial information to help you plan and carry out a successful trip.

Maps and Map Reading Skills

The amount of information you get from maps depends on your map reading skills. A map "speaks" to a skilled reader, just as a book speaks to someone who can read text. The skilled map reader interprets the symbols and squiggles and builds a mental picture of the area and what it will be like to travel through.

Acquiring map reading skills requires some effort—reading books or taking courses, and above all, practising with your map and compass in the outdoors.

A worthwhile exercise is to orient the map to the ground using a compass and then correlate visible ground features with what's on the map. That way you develop your skills of building a mental picture of the landscape from the map.

You should practise compass techniques for following compass bearings in times of bad visibility. Map and compass exercises should be done often enough so you can carry out the techniques when you really have to, without error and without thinking.

You must also be thoroughly familiar with compass declination, the difference between true north and magnetic north. Although in some parts of Canada declination is negligible, in other regions it can be 40 degrees or more. Also, declination is easterly in some areas and westerly in others, so you must also know when to add or subtract.

I remember one client on a northern river trip commenting that we had been going northwest for several days and asking when we would turn north toward the ocean. I was puzzled, since we were on one of the most north-oriented sections of river. Questioning him further, I discovered he was oblivious to the concept of declination, and certainly to the possibility of the 42 degrees easterly declination, which made him think we were going northwest! See page 108.

Take a map and compass course or go out and practise by yourself until you are proficient.

There are a number of excellent map reading books available (see list), and canoeists should read *Maps and Wilderness Canoeing* from Canada Surveys and Mapping Branch. Marine charts contain crucial safety information, and marine travellers should take a coastal navigation course or read some books and learn to interpret charts and tide tables.

Map Accuracy

Always check the date of a map, which is usually in the bottom margin just left of centre or at the bottom left corner of Canadian maps, bottom right of U.S. maps. You will see a copyright date and a publishing date. What matters, though, is the date of the information from which the map was made, not the copyright or publishing date. For example, the map in front of me was published in 1985, which sounds quite recent. However, it is an update of an earlier map using air photos taken in 1977 and 1979, eight years before publishing. A culture check—a check of man-made features—was done in 1981.

In Canada, an authorized dealer will have the latest edition of government maps because unsold old editions are removed from store shelves. Unauthorized retailers, however, such as small sports stores or lodges, may still be selling old editions.

Canadian maps are surprisingly detailed and accurate considering the vast, uninhabited areas they cover. However, over the years I have found a few inaccuracies in representation of natural features. One of the more memorable of these was on a hike that abruptly ended in a raging glacial meltwater creek. However, to be fair, areas near the toes of glaciers are subject to quite rapid change, and the drainage pattern could have changed since the making of the map. Glacial recession or advance can also be quite rapid, particularly in coastal Alaska. Other features that change are river channels, which can alter drastically with floods. The marking of rapids on rivers is improving somewhat and some older Canadian maps have been overprinted with rapids and portages in purple. However, a canoeist should never assume that all rapids are marked and should keep their eyes and ears open. They certainly should not make any assumptions about the difficulty of particular rapids, although a succession of rapids symbols is likely to indicate a staircase of more continuous rapids.

The names of features are occasionally changed. Creeks have been renamed on some Yukon 1:250 000 series. The changes are made in a rather faint grey on Yukon Land Resource inventory maps, though changes are usually in purple on topographic maps. Some glaciers in the St. Elias Range were incorrectly named on old 1:250 000 series maps, and directions of flow were not correct in some cases. This led to confusion about dropoff and pickup locations by air charter operators. Recent 1:50 000 maps of the area have correct names. Beware when comparing old trip accounts with new maps in that area. Peaks are occasionally incorrectly named, for example, Mt. Barbette at the north end of the Wapta Icefield in Banff National Park is named on the wrong peak on the map and Mt. St. Nicholas in the same area was also wrongly marked, but has been crossed out in purple.

To avoid similar problems you need to be very careful when describing locations to support people—use grid references or latitude and longitude as well as names. Also be aware of local names that are not "map" names, especially as you will meet local people who know the land very well but who do not use a map. Major confusion can arise when talking with such people as they sound very familiar with the area, but their firsthand familiarity might be difficult to translate to features on your map.

Man-made or cultural features change considerably between map updates, and this is where information from more recent guidebooks, air photographs and local people can be very useful. A trail no longer in existence, a road no longer maintained or a trail that exists but is not shown can make a huge difference to your trip. In areas where there is tourism development, logging, mineral exploration, or oil and gas exploration, there are likely to be many trails and roads not shown.

Remember that maps do not usually show road closures or resource roads that have been reclaimed. Travelling in the mountains of British Columbia, I have used air photos to pencil in logging roads and cleared areas on my map. Even old air photos show many features that don't appear on the maps that were drawn from them since there is a limit to the detail that can be incorporated in a map.

The depiction of a road or trail crossing a creek does not necessarily mean there is a bridge. It may be long gone if there ever was one. It's not like in Europe where some bridges have been in place for centuries. Creeks that were easily forded by vehicles during the winter logging or drilling season may be dangerous or impassable on foot in the high water of spring and summer. Many backcountry roads were designed for use in winter when the ground and waterways are frozen solid. In western Canada especially, remember that the traditional mode of transport was the horse, so there will not necessarily be a bridge where a trail crosses a creek.

Bridges also wash out, so check locally whether a crucial bridge is still there. A bridge providing road access to one side of a large park was washed out recently, eliminating access to an excellent section of intermediate whitewater. The side benefit of the washout is that it prevents vehicular access by hunters and poachers to the terrain adjacent to the park, and it seems unlikely it will be replaced.

Choosing Appropriate Maps

A variety of map types is available for planning and carrying out your trip. You may require more than one type to obtain all the information you need. For example, a B.C. Forest District information map will give you information on the passable logging roads and location of campsites, but you need a topographic map once you get in there and want to hike or paddle. If you are kayaking on the coast you must have a marine chart, but if you want to go ashore and hike or explore you will want a topographic map. Do not try to navigate on the ocean with a topographic map! It's not like lake navigation because there are tidal currents and bottom features exerting a big influence on ocean travellers. Kayakers have died using topos when charts would have warned of the dangers.

If the map shows a trail crossing a river, it does not necessarily mean there is or ever was a bridge.

Canadian Maps

The main types of maps are described below, but you should obtain both provincial and federal map and publication catalogues from the addresses listed on page 371, as well as catalogues from the provincial government departments responsible for tourism, mining and forestry. Some of the more obscure maps listed may provide crucial information. Provincial catalogues vary from a few typed pages to the 52-page book put out by Maps Alberta.

Topographic maps 1:50 000 are the most useful maps for recreation, and almost the entire country is mapped at this scale, which translates into 2 cm to 1 km or approximately 1-1/4 inches per mile. Sheets cover an area about 35 kilometres wide by 27 kilometres high (30 minutes of longitude by 15 minutes latitude). Contour intervals vary between 25 feet and 100 feet and on metric maps between 20 metres and 40 metres.

Warning! Some maps have two different contour intervals on the same sheet! The interval on a number of maps around Jasper National Park is 20 metres on land below 2000 metres and 40 metres on land above 2000 metres! This makes it almost impossible to recognize a peak or landmark from its profile and gives the impression that all the mountains have gently sloping summits.

The UTM grid appears on the 1:50 000 maps at one kilometre intervals so positions can be described using UTM grid references, easily estimated to within 100 metres. See page 109. The grid is also useful for estimating distances. There are no latitude and longitude lines across the maps, but the margins are marked at one-minute (of angle) intervals.

These maps show treed areas shaded in green, but the boundaries can be a little vague near treeline because a decision as to what constitutes forest is somewhat subjective. What the maps definitely do not tell you is the type of trees and what the travelling through the bush will be like.

Local knowledge, air photos and even forest inventory maps can help you find out whether that four-kilometre stretch of trail-less bush is a pleasant hour's walk through mature forest or a horrendous four-hour grunt through young lodgepole pine and deadfall in an area recently burned.

The relatively close contour interval paints a reasonable picture of the topography, but still

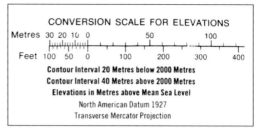

CONVERSION SCALE FOR ELEVATIONS

Metres 30 20 10 0 · · · 50 · · · 100

Feet 100 50 0 · · 100 · · 200 · 300 · 400

Contour Interval 20 Metres below 2000 Metres
Contour Interval 40 Metres above 2000 Metres
Elevations in Metres above Mean Sea Level
North American Datum 1927
Transverse Mercator Projection

Beware of maps with two different contour intervals. It is extremely difficult to recognize mountains by their profile from these maps.

has its limitations in that the land or river can have gradual slopes between contour lines or alternatively can be stepped, with a series of waterfalls or headwalls that make progress difficult. With 50-foot contour intervals a 49-foot cliff does not necessarily show on the map! Creeks and small streams as well as rivers are shown, and it is usually possible to distinguish braided streams (easier to cross but questionable boating) from single channels. Intermittent streams are distinguished from year-round streams, though in some areas a year-round stream can vary enormously in its flow rate and navigability or crossability. In the dry interior of northern Canada the spring runoff can be very short-lived and in a dry year, streams can become prohibitively low for navigation. One foreign canoe party in the Barrens simply ran out of water and had to be flown out.

Marshes, lakes and intermittent lakes are distinguished on the maps, and conditions will vary with the time of year and the wetness of the particular season. These areas can also

The map shows both forests the same way, yet one would provide easy travelling, the other a bushwhacking nightmare.

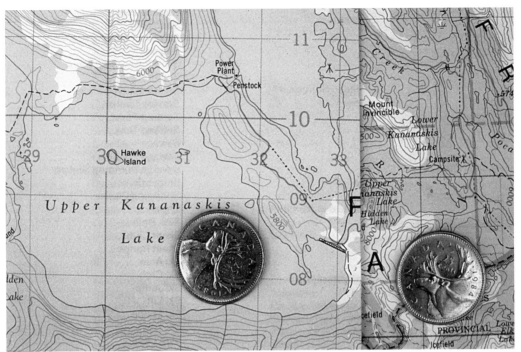

The same location is shown at 1:50 000 scale on the left and 1:250 000 on the right — notice the big differences in detail.

be subject to tremendous changes caused by beaver activity in the area. High water levels behind beaver dams can make navigating through a chain of ponds an easy prospect, but if the water level drops you can have a nightmare of mud and debris to contend with. Air photos and local knowledge help here.

Topographic maps 1:250 000 scale are useful for overall planning, and are also nice to have when you are up on a peak on a clear day and you want to identify really distant landmarks. They cover an area about 150 kilometres wide east to west (at the latitude of Calgary) and 110 kilometres north to south. (They are actually two degrees of longitude wide and one degree of latitude high.) The maps are progressively lower value for your money when you go north, as two degrees wide is only 80 kilometres at the Arctic coast! In the far north the maps expand to four degrees wide.

The 1:250 000 scale translates into four miles per inch or 1 centimetre to 2.5 kilometres. While it is a good scale for overall planning, it is not a large enough scale to provide sufficient detail for convenient foot travel, skiing and most canoeing. However, it will suffice for long canoe trips on big rivers such as the Nahanni or Coppermine where carrying larger scale maps would be a burden because of the sheer numbers required. The contour interval is correspondingly large, so topographic detail is limited. The UTM grid is at 10 kilometre intervals. Positions can be described as UTM grid references, but the mm scale on the edge of your compass is needed to do this accurately. There are no latitude and longitude lines across the maps, but the margins are marked at five minute intervals. There are also + marks on the body of the map at 15 minute intervals. Latitude and longitude lines can be drawn in using these marks, and positions can then be determined with a roamer.

One very useful way to use a 1:250 000 scale map is as an emergency backup. If you used a 1:250 000 map for planning but use 1:50 000 maps on your trip, give the 1:250 000 map to someone else in the group. If the 1:50 000 map is blown away or lost in a canoe wipeout or avalanche, you still have a map of sorts, which is much better than nothing.

Orthophoto maps are air photos with contour lines superimposed on them, greatly facilitating their use in the field. They are not readily available but it is worth inquiring, and even a chance to look at one can provide an enormous amount of information you can transfer to your topo. Sometimes these are available more readily through municipalities rather than through provincial or federal offices.

County and municipal district maps indicate public land, Indian Reserves, public land leaseholders' and landowners' names for titled lands.

Recreation maps. An excellent example is the British Columbia Forest Recreation map series. Maps are produced for each forest district showing logging roads, trails, campsites, points of interest, etc. The entire back of the sheet has text and information such as canoeing access, etiquette and regulations. There is no topographic information. The Invermere Forest District map at a scale of 1:250 000 covers a region about 225 kilometres by 150 kilometres. They can be obtained free from the B.C. Ministry of Forests or through district forest offices. Another useful series is produced for various districts in the Rockies by Map Town Ltd. in Calgary. There are topographic maps with hiking trails, etc., marked. Chrismar Mapping in Uxbridge, Ontario makes similar products for eastern Canada.

Yukon land resource inventory 1:250 000 maps. These topographic maps are overprinted with a variety of information. Each sheet has only one or two types of information, so for a given area there can be numerous sheets. One map shows mineral claims, including placer mining. The silting and disruption of placer mined areas may well be something to avoid, but on the other hand there could be a road or trail providing access to an interesting area. Oil and gas wells are shown on another sheet, and unlicensed airstrips are shown that might be usable for a fly-in to a hiking, paddling or climbing area. They might also be useful for rescue, so find out from local aviators or aviation officials about the usability of the strip. Also investigate the reason for the strip's existence—you may find yourself in the midst of a mining exploration operation during your wilderness holiday!

The Historic Travel Routes and Historic Sites category of Yukon Land Resource Inventory maps may be of particular interest to those looking for themes and background for their trips. For example, the Tatonduk and Porcupine River Route is marked on the Ogilvie River map sheet. Beside each feature marked on the sheet there is a number that can be cross-referenced with the Yukon Land Resource Inventory Bibliographic Index. This route has the number 15-0122 beside it. When you look this up in the Bibliographic Index you're referred to the book, *The Klondike Gold Rush Through Edmonton.*

Forest inventory maps. These are usually blueline (Diazo) maps on a large scale that give details about the type of forest cover that could provide crucial information about the feasibility of a section of a particular route. Alberta maps, as an example, are on a scale of 1:15 000 and indicate species, height, crown density, burned areas, deadfall areas, etc. and are available from provincial forestry offices.

Resource extraction maps. These show locations of logging roads, oil and gas well sites, pipelines, etc. They can be very helpful for access to or egress from areas. For example, a canoe trip we did was only feasible in the time available because we used a gas well road to obtain access to the riverbank. These are provincial maps so contact provincial government branches.

Provincial access maps. The Alberta series shows roads and trails but on a scale of 1:250 000 and with no topographic detail, so it is difficult to extract useful information.

Park maps. Some parks produce excellent large-scale maps, such as the canoeing maps of some of the Ontario parks. However, some do not have grids, making it difficult to use a compass. The 1:200 000 scale maps of some of the national parks (e.g., the Banff Kootenay Yoho sheet) are useful for an overview and planning and can in a pinch be used on the ground if you stay on trails and annotate the maps with campsite information from brochures. Expect to pay for the larger and more useful maps. They are not randomly distributed with your initial inquiry, so be sure to ask for one if required. The quality of paper is often poor compared to topographic maps, so you may wish to laminate them. Also ask for and look carefully at the list of publications from the park.

Northern land use information series. These maps are part of a major systematic environmental-social research and information program for the Canadian north. The wildlife maps outline critical and important areas, migration routes, nesting and calving areas, seasonal ranges, etc. This information enables you to plan your trip so you won't adversely infringe on wildlife at critical times. Other topics include Native Land Use, Ecological Land Classification and Forestry including recent burns. Socioeconomic information and cultural data include such topics as community information, breakup and freezeup dates, archaeological sites, mining and mineral resources, and existing and proposed development areas. These maps are now available only in libraries.

Atlases and books can be very good value for money and provide excellent planning information. A *Map of the Province of Nova Scotia* from Lands and Forests Government Services covers the entire province at 1:250 000 scale with 46 topographic maps for only $10. It also includes an index of geographical names. *The Atlas of Alberta* provides a wide variety of information. The Locations of Pulp Mills and Sawmills page is useful to canoeists who wish to avoid polluted rivers. The Forts of Alberta page showing fur trade forts could be useful to plan a trip with an historic theme. Climate pages are less useful in that precipitation is given as mean annual rather than monthly. Mean annual snowfall is useful for winter recreation, though in Alberta the warm chinook winds can prevent significant accumulation. Other pages show gas fields and agricultural activities.

National Atlas Of Canada. *The National Atlas of Canada* covers a myriad of topics including vegetation patterns, precipitation, runoff, physiographic regions, temperatures, snow cover and day length. The transportation section includes some "frontier roads with public access or limited public access." The air transportation network information dated 1984 has a number of inaccuracies I know of from firsthand experience, but it does show the locations of air charter services. Another section shows the location of pulp and paper mills for canoeists wishing to avoid the polluted waters downstream of these industries. Be aware that the map showing generating stations only shows those of 400 MW and greater and so does not show the smaller ones that nevertheless devastate some rivers. Coastal classification maps describe the shoreline and the land immediately behind it. Maps are available individually.

Orienteering maps. These large-scale maps cover only small areas that have been specially mapped for orienteering competition. They are on a very large scale and very detailed. They do not look like topographic maps and do not require declination adjustments. People who have learned their skills on this type of map will have to adjust to using topographic maps.

Hydrographic maps are available for lakes and are useful for canoeists who may need to be wary of choppy conditions over shallows. All Alberta lakes are covered and contour lines rather than specific soundings are used. Marine charts are available for all coastal areas of Canada and the larger inland lakes.

Obtaining Canadian Maps

Three National Topographic Series Index Sheets cover the entire country. These are small-scale maps of the country with the boundaries and dates of various topographic maps superimposed on them and numbered. They are updated approximately every 18 months. Unfortunately, the index map for the 1:50 000 sheets is small scale and the only reference points are rivers and major towns. Each 1:50 000 sheet is shown at about half the size of a postage stamp so it is difficult to decide exactly which maps cover your area of interest. If time allows it may be worthwhile ordering the 1:250 000 map of an area and using it to decide exactly which 1:50 000 maps you need. Each 1:250 000 map area comprises 16 1:50 000 maps, which are arranged and numbered as shown in the following example:

Example: 1:250 000 sheet 82 J

82 J/13	82 J/14	82 J/15	82 J/16
82 J/12	82 J/11	82 J/10	82 J/9
82 J/5	82 J/6	82 J/7	82 J/8
82 J/4	82 J/3	82 J/2	82 J/1

By folding or ruling the map into 16 squares you can determine which sheet covers the area you are interested in. When ordering 1:250 000 scale maps, do not be confused by the name of the sheet, which may be some obscure place distant from your area of interest.

Nova Scotia produces a 1:000 000 index map with detail that makes it much easier to choose the right sheet.

These index sheets also list the other available maps from Ottawa, including *National Atlas of Canada* loose map titles, and national park special maps. Map order information is available on page 371-372.

Alaskan Maps

The most useful maps are produced by the U.S. Geological Survey (USGS), who produce a wide variety of maps. Other specialty maps are produced by various organizations, as discussed below. See page 372 for addresses.

Alaska topographic maps are standard topographic maps except that they do not have either UTM grid lines or latitude/longitude lines superimposed on them. This comes as a nasty surprise to people from countries who are used to having these crucial lines shown on topo maps. Without the lines it is difficult to use UTM grid references or latitude/longitude for accurately describing locations or to use the maps in conjunction with compasses and GPS devices. However, on many maps a square one-mile grid is present, which can be used to estimate distances and as a true north reference using a compass. The one-mile squares are numbered so a location can be defined as being within a one-square mile area, but not as accurately as with UTM or latitude and longitude squares. You may encounter older maps that lack even these lines.

If you want to rule in UTM or latitude/longitude lines, UTM grid ticks and latitude/longitude reference ticks are present along the edges of the map. Take time and care and use a good

metal straightedge on a flat, smooth surface. If you have access to a drafting table, use it. Ruling lines on your map will be difficult to do if you buy your map on the way into the backcountry, so buy ahead of time! Fine point micro-ball pens give a nice fine line but with no chance to correct a slip. The more waterproof the ink the better, so test the pen on scrap paper and find a good one. Do the line marking before you laminate or waterproof the map. Make sure your waterproofing liquid does not smudge your lines.

If you end up with earlier maps with no lines on them, you could rule in a few magnetic north reference lines similar to those on orienteering maps. Then you do not have to make adjustments when changing map (grid) bearings to ground (magnetic) bearings.

The disadvantage of drawing in magnetic north reference lines is that declination changes over time as the position of the earth's magnetic field changes. In practice, however, the changes are small relative to the accuracy with which most people can use a map and compass. Unlike Canadian maps, Alaska topographic maps do not indicate the annual rate of change of the declination. Consequently, you cannot calculate the current declination for a map on which declination was specified at time of printing, which may be many years ago.

Some topographic maps have extra contour lines drawn as dotted lines where the relief is low. For example, the map may be drawn with 100-foot contours over most of its area but in the flatter, often low-lying areas, 50-foot contours may be dotted in. This seems to be a better way of solving the cartographer's problems than the diabolical Canadian method of using two different contour intervals on the same map, but using the same style of line.

Alaska topographic maps 1:250 000 (1 cm to 2.5 km or approximately 4 miles to 1 inch). All of Alaska is available at a scale of 1:250 000. A map of Denali Park is produced on this scale.

Alaska topographic maps 1:63 360. Alaska topographic maps are also available at a scale of 1:63 360 (one inch to one mile). These maps are known as "15 minute" maps because they cover 15 minutes of latitude. This is an unusual scale and people used to the more common internationally used scale of 1:50 000 will have to make some mental adjustment. Some Alaska maps have a one-mile (1.6 kilometre) grid superimposed on them, which helps keep track of distances, but you still really have to concentrate and remember these are 1.6 kilometre squares and not the more familiar one kilometre squares. A small number of maps are metric. Some are still only rated as Provisional maps. A noticeable difference on these maps is that the glaciers are not distinguished by blue contours or blue shading. Some of the Alaska 1:63 360 maps are very old, dating back to the 1950s.

Alaska topographic maps 1:24 000. More populated areas are also covered at a scale of 1:24 000. These maps are known as 7.5 minute maps because they cover 7.5 minutes of latitude. The scale is close enough to the standard 1:25 000 to avoid too much confusion.

Orthophotoquads are black and white photo images compiled from air photos. They have been rectified to eliminate image displacement from terrain relief. They are prepared in 7.5 minute (1:24 000 see above) format and have a reference grid and some names for orientation. They are very useful in conjunction with topo maps and are available for about half of the Alaska 1:63 360 maps.

Land use and land cover maps. Only seven of these 1:250 000 maps are listed in the USGS Alaska catalogue.

Alaska boundary series maps. This series includes maps of national monuments, national parks and national preserves. Scales are 1:4 000 000 or 1:250 000.

Native lands and private lands. A small-scale map that shows approximate locations of native lands is available. More detailed information is available from Status Plats, which are large-scale maps available at the same address, or from the Bureau of Land Management. Also make local inquiries.

Trails Illustrated Recreation Maps are specially customized copies of USGS topographic maps. They are updated before each annual or biennial printing, and have text useful to map users. They are printed on durable, waterproof, paper-like plastic.

Current Alaska issues include Denali Park at 1:133 000 and Kenai Fjords at 1:105 600. Prince William Sound and Kenai National Wildlife Refuge will soon be available. Be very careful when using these obscure scales that you do not lose sight of the overall size of the terrain.

Alaska Atlas and Gazetteer. One hundred and forty pages of full colour topographic maps at about 1:300 000 scale. Western coast, Brooks Range and N. Slope are at about 1 inch to 22 miles. Includes information on trails, campgrounds, parks, wildlife refuges, etc.

From Wild Rose Guidebooks:
Map of Kenai Fjords National Park and surrounding area including Chugach National Forest approximately 1:100 000. Waterproof, with additional information.

Denali National Park and Preserve Map one inch to five miles overall plus details of permit areas at one inch to three miles.

Map of Mt. McKinley. Reprint of Bradford Washburne's classic map. 1:50 000, 100-foot contours.

Map of Kachemak Bay (Kenai Peninsula) 1991 1:62 500.

Kenai River—Skilak Lake to Cook Inlet 1988 1:25 000. Mostly fishing information.

Kenai Lake and vicinity including part Kenai River 1987 1:62 500.

Kenai Peninsula NW portion 1980 1:62 500.

Recreation Map and Guide—Anchorage and Eagle River 1993.

Alaska road and recreation maps. Parks Highway 1/6 inch to 1 mile, Kenai River at 2.5 inch to 1 mile, Kenai Peninsula one inch to one mile, Kenai Lake one inch to one mile, Kachemak Bay one inch to one mile, Big Lake and Pt. MacKenzie one inch to one mile and Matanuska Valley one inch to one mile are available.

Forest service maps. Tongass and Chugach Forest Visitor Map, Road Guide Maps for Prince of Wales, Mitkof Island, Wrangell Island and Hoonah area, Canoe/Kayak Route Maps for Cross Admiralty, Kuiu Island and Stikine River, and Wilderness/Monument Maps for Misty Fjords and Admiralty are available.

National park maps. Request a special index for U.S. park map coverage. The 1991 Alaska map catalogue shows only Denali at 1:250 000.

Small-scale topographic maps. These are available at a scale of 1:1 000 000.

Satellite image maps. These are available at a scale of 1:250 000 for about 30 areas in Alaska.

Major ecosystems of Alaska map. Published by the Joint Federal and State Land Use Planning Commission for Alaska, 1973, this map shows the locations of different ecosystems such as moist tundra, wet tundra, alpine tundra, high brush, coastal hemlock or spruce forest.

Obtaining Alaska Maps

Obtain the booklet, *Alaska Index to Topographic and Other Map Coverage* and the *Alaska Catalogue of Topographic and Other Published Maps,* with order forms. The 1:2 500 000 *Alaska 1:63 360 Quadrangle Names'* sheet indicates 1:250 000 map names and boundaries.

The *Alaska Catalogue of Topographic and Other Published Maps* lists 40 Alaska map dealers scattered over the state. Prices may vary from USGS (1993 prices) of $2.50 for 1:63 360 and $4 for 1:250 000.

The *Alaska Index to Topographic and Other Map Coverage* booklet makes it reasonably easy to choose the correct 1:250 000 or 1:63 360 scale map for the area in which you are interested. Each page has an index map at a scale of about 1:1 250 000, or about 20 miles per inch. This means that the land covered by a 1:250 000 sheet is shown at about 12 centimetres wide by 9 centimetres high. Reference details such as major peaks, rivers or settlements help you determine which is the correct 1:250 000 sheet, and reference squares and numbers make it easy to select which 1:63 360 sheets you need.

The *Alaska 1:63 360 Quadrangle Names'* sheet lists the 1:63 360 sheets to order, but does not have enough background detail for you to be sure of ordering the correct sheet. You could use it to order the appropriate 1:250 000 sheet first as it does indicate 1:250 000 map names and boundaries. Allow lots of time if you are mail ordering. Be careful to note that the number of 1:63 360 sheets across the longitude of a 1:250 000 sheet could be five, six or eight depending on which 1:250 000 sheet you are looking at, so check the *Names'* sheet and divide it up appropriately.

USGS publishes an annual list of the year's publications. It is not cumulative so the publication you want may be in a previous year's catalogue. There are 15 volumes of these Yearly Publications' catalogues available.

Map depository libraries in Alaska:

Anchorage-Municipal Library, the University of Alaska, Alaska Resources Library USDI

Fairbanks-University, Rasmusan Library

Juneau-Alaska State Library, University of Alaska Library

Ketchikan-Community College Library, Public Library, Palmer Community College

Marine Charts

Marine charts are essential for all marine recreation including kayaking. Tidal currents and shallows where breakers can form in otherwise fairly calm areas are among the many types of vital information provided. A tide table is also essential. Land information on charts is limited to basic topographic data, which is enough to recognize landforms from the water but not enough for land use. They are updated periodically, sometimes with stuck-on overlays, sometimes with overprinting, sometimes just through "Notices to Mariners." Some popular recreation areas are charted on very large scales; for example, Barkley Sound in Pacific Rim National Park is available at 1:20 000.

Costs are considerably more than for topographic maps so it is well worth laminating charts or waterproofing them with Map Seal, Nikwax Map Proof or Canadian Tire Vinyl-Silicone tent waterproofing liquid or even Thompson's Water Seal. Use a chart case, too. The Ortlieb models are flexible in cold weather and the Velcroed roll-top closure is convenient and reliable.

The longitude lines you need for true north reference are quite widely spaced. This presents no difficulties if you are in a big boat with a chart table and a course arm protractor and other instruments to work with. However, it is inconvenient if you are in a kayak or small boat working with one hand on a folded chart with a small Silva-type baseplate compass. It is therefore worth ruling in some additional lines of longitude on the chart at home before your trip.

Obtaining Canadian marine charts. There are four catalogue sheets. See page 372 for address.

- Atlantic Coast to Cape Chidley (northern tip of Labrador)
- Pacific Coast
- Great Lakes (including southern half of Manitoba and southeast Saskatchewan)
- Arctic

Charts and tide tables can be obtained from local map and chart dealers or by mail order.

Obtaining Alaska marine charts. Local sporting goods and marine suppliers usually stock the charts. However, in popular areas and at busy times of the year they may be out of stock, so get them ahead of time by mail order. Ask for Index #3 for Alaska, see page 373 for address. Note the different address for foreign mail orders.

Air Photographs

Air photographs are available to the public and can be a useful supplement to maps.

Advantages and disadvantages of air photos. When maps are made from air photographs, information has to be omitted to avoid cluttering the map. The original air photographs will therefore often provide information useful to you that is not on the map. Another advantage of air photos is that they may be more recent than maps because some areas are photographed more often than they are mapped, usually for forestry, agricultural or land use purposes. New features such as logging or mining roads, burned areas, cutlines, beaver flooding, bridges, airstrips, glacial advance or retreat and logged areas may show up on photos. Other useful features you can see include glades and openings in the forest, rock outcroppings, the type of vegetation and forest, crevassed areas on glaciers, rapids, eskers, beaches and trails. Air photos are particularly useful for places like the Hudson Bay Lowlands, which have vast areas of relatively featureless landscape and for which little relief detail shows on conventional maps. On one occasion I checked air photos and found

a logging road that made a crucial difference to a ski-out from a glacier at the end of a spring ski tour. Without that logging road we would have spent another night in the bush. Another photo revealed that a river we wanted to canoe dropped into a deep, narrow canyon and that there was a clearcut we could portage through. Neither were shown on the map.

Air photos do have some disadvantages. They are difficult to interpret because no labels and symbols are used, and topography such as valleys and mountains is difficult to see without a stereoscope. You need to determine the north-south direction and mark it on them. You cannot easily detect gates or vehicle traps on roads that are closed, and buildings may be obscured in forest.

Air photo types and scales. Air photos are available in black and white, colour for some areas and "false colour" (infrared). Infrared is used mainly to assess crop and forest health.

Scales are from 1:10 000 to 1:60 000. Photos can be ordered enlarged up to about 10x without being grainy because the standard size prints at 10 inches square are contact prints, not enlargements of narrow film.

Scale is not usually marked on air photos but you can calculate it. Measure the distance between two well-spaced features on the photo with a ruler and compare it to the distance between the same features on a map. Use the following formula:

Scale of Photo =
$$1 : \frac{(\text{Map scale large number x map distance})}{\text{Photo distance}}$$
$$\text{e.g. } 1 : \frac{(50000 \times 2.0)}{4.0} = 1:25\ 000$$

Stereo interpretation of air photographs. Topographic detail shows up on air photos when a stereoscope is used, but the vertical scale is exaggerated so it is difficult to gauge actual steepness. Pocket stereoscopes can usually be obtained from drafting, surveying or mapmaking equipment suppliers for around $25-50. Air photo libraries will usually have large mirror-type stereoscopes available.

To use a stereoscope, you need two overlapping photographs of the same point on the ground. It takes some practice to position them correctly and to use the instrument. With a

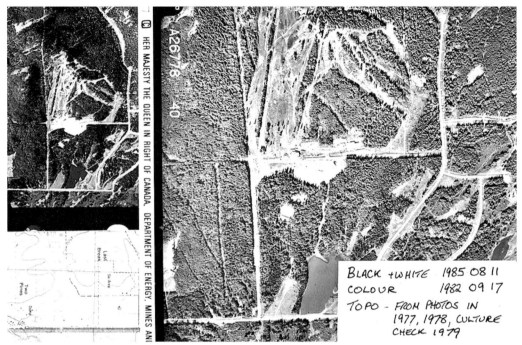

The same location shown on a 1:50 000 topo map, a small scale colour air photo and a larger scale black and white air photo.

pocket stereoscope you need to position the two images so that each one is under a lens. Because they overlap, it can help to fold up the edge of one photo. Mirror stereoscopes are easier to use because the photos do not have to be overlapped or folded.

You will see the stereo image more easily if you illuminate the photos from the same direction as the sun when they were taken. You can deduce this from looking at the shadows on the photo. Stereo is also easier to see if the shadows fall toward you. Make sure the photos are in line and not twisted relative to each other or to the line joining the centre of the stereoscope lenses. If you accidentally reverse the left and right photos, the stereo image will be reversed so valleys appear as ridges.

Some air photo interpretation tips.

- Smoother surfaces appear lighter in colour—even black asphalt.
- The shape of tree shadows helps distinguish conifers from deciduous trees.
- Shadows of buildings, hydro or radio towers, etc. may show up better than the objects themselves.

- Man-made features tend to be regular in shape with smooth curves and distinct sharp borders. Natural features tend to be the opposite.
- If shadows obscure the details you need, a photo taken at a different time of day may provide the necessary information.

Obtaining air photographs. You may be lucky and have a library nearby with a collection of air photos accessible to the public for viewing. I have used photos in my local university reference library quite extensively, and the library has high-quality stereoscopes available for use on site. You may also be able to view photographs in forestry and other government offices.

Air photos can be mail ordered, or bought over-the-counter from the appropriate government department, usually in provincial or state capitals. Air photos may be produced by different levels of government. For example, in Canada they are produced by both provincial and federal governments. Instant prints from over-the-counter sales may be lower quality than true contact prints, which take more time to produce.

If ordering in person you may be given access to actual prints or to a microfilm reader that you can use to preview and select the frame number you want.

If you are mail ordering without reference to a previewed photo, you should send a marked topographic map. Put your name on the map and they'll return it. A photocopy of a topographic map will do as long as it shows the map number and the margins for grid referencing or latitude/longitude referencing. The UTM grid references of the corners of the area also helps. Indicating what you want to see or the type of information you need will help the person filling the order choose appropriate photos if several series of photos exist. Photos taken at different seasons or with different sun angles show different details. If you send for an index map, it will have the aircraft flight lines marked on it and the serial numbers of the photos at each point along the flight line will be superimposed. Don't forget to indicate whether you need stereophoto pairs or whether single photos will do.

U.S. air photos can be selected by ordering the USGS Index to National Aerial Photography Program (NAPP) from USGS. There is also an index to National High Altitude Photography (NHAP I) and another to National High Altitude Photography (NHAP II). Leaf-on photos are available from USGS. See page 373 for address.

Aerial obliques of northern Canada were taken before 1950 and are filed in the National Air Photo Library, Ottawa. Unlike conventional vertical photos, they are more of a "pilot's-eye view." Prints are available, and provide useful information for recreationists.

Aerial obliques of the Alaska Range. Most modern aerial photography is done vertically, but high-quality oblique air photos of peaks and routes in the St. Elias and Alaska Range are available. This classic set is of enormous value to climbers. See page 373 for addresses.

A full set (over 150) is available for viewing at Talkeetna Ranger Station and at Denali Park headquarters.

Protecting Maps

Maps are costly and soon deteriorate under the rigours of outdoor use so it is worth protecting them. Ortlieb's map case is the best I have used; it is soft and supple but strong and has a reliable roll/Velcro waterproof closure. You can also laminate your maps with products such as transparent Colorsplash from the kitchenwares aisle of your supermarket. Laminating adds weight and stiffness. Map Proof liquid by Nikwax works well, as does Map Seal by Aquaseal. Both are aqueous so there is no nasty smell and no organic solvents polluting the atmosphere while they dry.

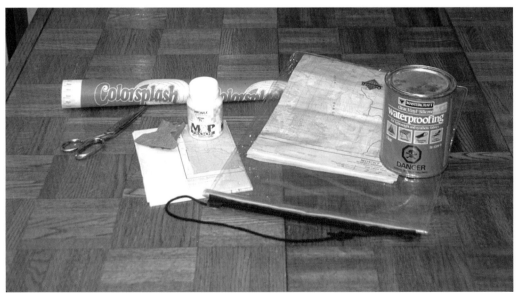

Protect your maps and charts with a good case or by laminating or coating with waterproofing liquids.

Magnetic Declination and Its Effect on Compass Use In the North

In most parts of Canada and all of Alaska there is a considerable difference between the direction to which a compass needle points (magnetic north) and the direction of north on a map (true north or grid north, depending on the map). This is because the Magnetic North Pole is nowhere near the true or geographic North Pole. The magnetic pole is in the region of Ellef Ringnes Island in the Canadian Arctic at a latitude of only about 77 degrees north and about 1500 kilometres from the North Pole. Actually, the compass needle does not point directly toward the magnetic north pole; the magnetic lines of force with which it actually aligns itself curve toward the magnetic pole.

The difference between grid and magnetic north is referred to as magnetic declination and can be as much as 45 degrees, which could really get you lost if you are not aware of it! Each degree of error will put you off course by 17 metres for every one kilometre travelled. Neglecting even a 10 degree declination can put you a long way off course.

Ellef Ringnes Island and the magnetic pole is at longitude 100 W, which is the longitude of Thunder Bay on Lake Superior. In the Thunder Bay area there is consequently very little declination because the same straight line north from Thunder Bay goes through both the magnetic and geographic poles. Locations to the *west* of Thunder Bay therefore have *easterly* declination, i.e. magnetic north is off to the *east*. If you travel east of Thunder Bay, declination is westerly, i.e. magnetic north is off to the west of true north. When converting between magnetic (ground) bearings and map (grid or true) bearings you must remember whether to add or subtract the declination.

Remember that:

Declination EAST makes magnetic LEAST

Declination WEST makes magnetic BEST

Then add or subtract declination to conform to the rule.

As declination varies from place to place and with time, you must check your map for the current amount of declination. With Silva Ranger and similar compasses you can dial-in an adjustment that corrects for declination. Remember to reset the adjustment when away from your home area.

On Canadian topographic maps a declination diagram and information for calculating the current declination is found on the upper end of the right margin. On U.S. maps it is on the lower margin. Be aware that the declination diagrams are not drawn as an accurate visual representation of the angle. On some U.S. maps

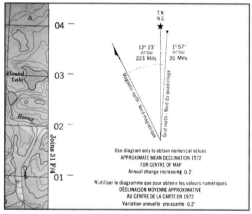

Declination diagrams on Canadian maps.

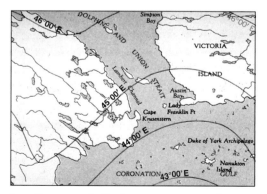

In northern areas, declination can vary enormously even on a single map sheet. There may be a small inset mini-map like this in the margin to show how declination varies across the sheet.

there is no diagrammatic representation of declination at all, but the declination appears in writing in the lower left of the sheet. If you trim your maps before laminating them, make sure you transfer this vital information to an appropriate part of the sheet before trimming!

Declination near the North Magnetic Pole

The nearer you get to the North Magnetic Pole, the greater the declination is and the more variable it becomes, to the point where a magnetic compass can have marginal value. Instead of having a declination diagram, northern maps may have a mini-map that indicates the declination in various parts of the main map.

In these areas of uncertain declination, you must check the declination frequently for accurate navigation and position-fixing with a compass. Do this by comparing the map bearing between two visible identifiable landmarks and the observed compass bearing between them. If you are travelling in the far north you should be prepared to use a variety of navigation methods making use of the compass, sun, map features and now Global Positioning Systems (GPS). See page 110 on GPS.

The "north" end of the compass needle is pulled downward toward the earth's surface as well as in the general direction of magnetic north. The needles are counterbalanced to overcome this effect so that they do not jam. Compasses built for the southern hemisphere are counterbalanced differently to allow for a stronger pull at the "south" end of the needle "down under." These compasses may tend to jam in the northern hemisphere. New "Turbo 20" models from Recta have a special system to eliminate the need for counterbalancing, but most manufacturers counterbalance for up to five different "zones" across the globe, and compasses do not work so well outside their intended zones, and especially near the magnetic poles.

Compasses calibrated in mils are perfectly usable on regular maps, though it can be difficult to cross reference with other people's compasses and their bearings. There are 18 mils in a degree.

The UTM Grid

Many topographic maps have a square grid of blue lines superimposed on them called the Universal Transverse Mercator grid. It is made up of one-kilometre squares on 1:50 000 scale maps and 10-kilometre squares on 1:250 000 maps. The squares are exactly square, so the orientation of their sides cannot be quite parallel with the longitude lines that form the boundaries of the map sheets. The lines are therefore oriented to an artificial "Grid North."

The grid is extremely useful in several ways. First, the grids provide you with a direct representation of distances all over your map. The one-kilometre squares are printed everywhere, and you can easily estimate distances against them by eyeballing. This is particularly easy if the distance you are measuring is parallel with the sides of the squares. The distance diagonally from corner to corner is 1.4 kilometres on 1:50 000 or 14 kilometres on the 1:250 000 scale.

Another use for the UTM grid is as a basis for accurate position descriptions called grid references. Using a six-digit number you can specify a position to within 100 metres or less on 1:50 000 scale maps and about 500 metres on 1:250 000 maps.

In an emergency you can use a grid reference to pinpoint exactly where the injured party is. Many guidebooks use grid references to indicate exactly where a hut or a peak or other feature is on a map. If you are talking with someone over the phone you can describe positions in terms of grid references. When using a GPS device you can key in the grid reference of the location you wish to visit and the device will tell you range and bearing to the point and help you stay on course. There is a diagram on the right margin of Canadian topographic maps that explains how to work out a grid reference.

If you have U.S. maps without the grid squares you are denied all these conveniences. However, you can rule-in grid lines using "ticks" along the edge of the map that indicate UTM positions. Use a fine, waterproof pen and check that it will not smudge with your map waterproofing compound.

Global Positioning Systems

Imagine yourself in a sudden whiteout in the middle of an icefield. You're completely disoriented and you have only a vague idea of the way back to camp. The temperature is plunging, it's starting to snow and the light is failing. This sounds like the opening lines for one of those epic horror shows; three days wandering in the murk, thousand dollar tents lost to the snows and a heroic struggle to survive. However, you pull out your small, handheld Global Positioning System (GPS) receiver, about the size of a telephone handset, and press a few buttons. Within seconds it tells you your position to within 30 metres. You press another button and the range and direction to your camp appear on the screen. Then, as you proceed toward camp, the device indicates if you are straying off course. Half an hour later you are drinking tea in the tent! This technology is available for outdoor recreation at ever decreasing prices—now as low as $300.

The GPS navigation system is available worldwide, 24 hours a day. It determines your position using signals from three or more of 24 satellites orbiting about 20,000 kilometres above the earth. The receiver measures range by determining the time taken for signals to travel between satellites and your receiver. Fixes may be three-dimensional, including your current altitude as well as your surface location, but sometimes the position of satellites is such that only a two-dimensional fix can be obtained.

GPS technology was originally intended for military use, and played a key role in the Gulf War. In that conflict it was essential for soldiers to know their position accurately in featureless desert. While the special military signals are more accurate, the signals to which the public has access will give you accuracy of between 15 and 100 metres. I found that all the units I tried read to within 30 metres of a survey marker of known position.

Latitude/longitude positions from the GPS are fine for aviators and mariners because they use charts marked latitude and longitude. Land users will find UTM grid references to be much more usable. Do not buy a GPS receiver for land-based use that does not support UTM grids.

Cold weather storage and operation capabilities vary but are a significant consideration. You may have to keep the unit warm under your clothing at all times in winter conditions. Carry a spare set of batteries, because battery power consumption is high in some use

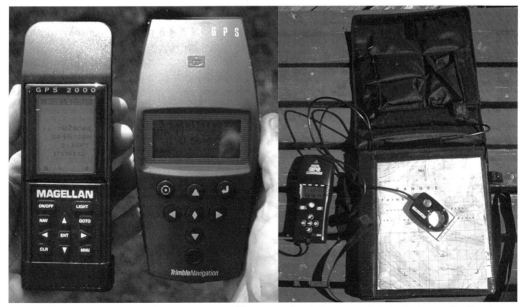

GPS receivers. Left to right: Magellan GPS 2000, Trimble Scout, Silva GPS compass. Missing is the popular Garmin 38.

modes. On U.S. topographic maps that have no grid lines, position fixing is much more difficult. You can rule in lat/long lines or you can use Trimble's "over and up" method with their Scout model. First of all you key-in the latitude/longitude of the bottom right corner of the map or of a map point nearer to where you are on the map. This is your reference point. You also key in the scale of the map and whether you will use inches or centimetres. Locations on the map are then expressed as distances measured from the reference point "over" (across the map) and then up the map.

The new Silva GPS system incorporates a special map case connected to the GPS. A transparent mouse-type device with crosshairs is moved over the surface of this special case to send map position information to and from the GPS. This is great for U.S. maps with no UTM grid or latitude/longitude grid.

As well as simply determining position, GPS units have numerous more complex navigational capabilities. For example, if you are at a position to which you wish to return later, you can press a button to name and store that position as a waypoint in the device's memory. When it's time to return, you call up the appropriate function, and key in the name you gave the way point. The device will then give you information on the bearing to follow, and the range (distance) back to the way point. That waypoint could be your camp, a hut, your cache, an injured person, a hot fishing spot, a good river crossing or your car on that backcountry road.

Then, as you travel, a "CrossTrack Error" indicator tells you whether you are left or right of the straight line back to the stored waypoint. This function is useful on land where it is nice to follow paths of least resistance such as animal trails that are going in the correct general direction. Sooner or later you need to know whether you have strayed left or right of your route. However, the indicator is not sensitive enough for travellers on foot to use effectively by itself. You will follow a very energy-consuming zig-zag if you try! Use your compass to indicate general direction and the GPS periodically to indicate your drift.

When boating, your travel on a bearing is subject to wind and tidal currents, and the "CrossTrack Error" indicator will help you stay on course. Some indicators respond to a few metres of straying, others to a few hundred metres. In the far north where compass declination is large and variable, and compasses are unreliable, this feature is particularly useful. However, satellite coverage is not as good in the far north as it is over the more populated areas.

You can store a series of waypoints as a route in the receiver's memory. Each change of direction is stored as a separate named waypoint. You can follow a route from waypoint to waypoint in poor visibility or reverse a route to return to your starting point.

You should not become overconfident in GPS receivers to the extent that you risk travel in conditions that are unsafe for reasons besides the tricky routefinding. Boating in fog exposes you to risks of being run down by other traffic or of the party becoming separated. Travelling on snow in whiteouts may cause you to stray into dangerous crevassed or avalanche-prone areas—ones you would studiously avoid if you could see what you were getting into. The weather may be such that staying holed-up until visibility improved would expose the party to less risk of hypothermia, frostbite or injury.

GPS receivers greatly enhance your ability to navigate a route. However, when my map reading class suggested GPS would soon put me out of business, I pointed out that you still need to be able to read a map. It's the map that tells the trained reader what's there on the ground. You need that knowledge so that you can determine **where** you should go and **what** will be an appropriate **route** to follow with your GPS.

Used properly, GPS will help you navigate better, though it won't make you a better navigator, just as better skis let you ski better but don't make you a better skier. Don't neglect the fundamental principles of using map and compass—after all, map and compass are reliable technology with no batteries to run down!

In order to learn how to use handheld GPS receivers in outdoor recreation you should read *GPS Made Easy* by Lawrence Letham. It contains some excellent examples of how to use receivers in different outdoor situations. You should read this book if you have not already purchased a receiver for its advice on necessary features for recreational use.

Chapter 4

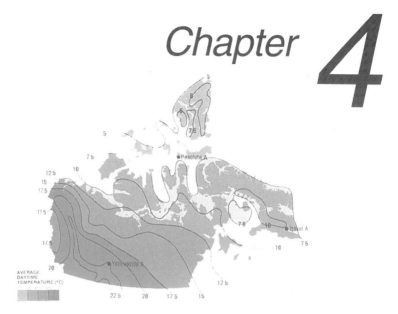

Things to Think About Before You Go

In many respects the Canadian and Alaskan backcountry is still very wild. There usually isn't any shelter nearby to retreat to when the weather turns bad, so you should plan to handle whatever nature throws at you. You should be aware of the extreme conditions you could encounter and how to cope with them. You need to know how to obtain weather forecasts and how to interpret them.

On the other hand, the backcountry is not so wild that you can just head off into the wide blue yonder and do as you please. There are often regulations that affect your activity, and you must find out about them. It's not necessarily an advantage to seek unregulated areas, because the regulations are rarely a significant imposition, and they often have the advantage of prohibiting activities by other people that could make your stay unpleasant.

The wilds have not kept the spectres of litigation and liability at bay. Although the backcountry was traditionally where people were expected to be responsible for themselves, you must now be aware of personal liability implications. You also need to think a little about crime, personal security and the security of your gear. In the event of an accident or injury you need to be sure your insurance will cover ambulance evacuation in remote areas and the medical fees.

Canadian and Alaskan Weather

Weather has a big effect on most outdoor trips, but more so in Canada and Alaska than in the more populated areas of the world. There is often no easy escape from a spell of bad weather because of the vastness of the backcountry, which is unpeopled and undeveloped. It is not like Europe where the mountains are scattered with huts and hotels with well-trodden trails leading to them, and probably a ski lift back down to the populated valley. Weather is a force to be carefully reckoned with when planning and equipping your trips—it can transform a pleasant jaunt into a survival epic.

Choosing the Best Season

For all trips, especially major ones, it is advisable to find out what time of year will usually provide the best conditions. Use local contacts, rangers, wardens, guidebooks and tourism and weather publications as information sources. Unfortunately, the same month one year can be very different the next year, so while it is useful to do your research and travel at what is statistically the best time, nothing is guaranteed. A ski trip in the St. Elias Range of the western Yukon was planned for May, as the weather and snowpack are usually best at that time. The unusually warm, clear weather was even better than expected, and we had a fantastic trip. The good weather continued too long, however, and resulted in horrendous conditions for a group who went into the range shortly after our return, in what would normally have still been prime season. Rotten snow bogged their aircraft, and snow bridges collapsed into water-filled crevasses.

On another occasion I travelled the Nahanni in day after day of hot weather; a few years later at the same time of year it rained every day of the trip. Last year on the west coast, there were weeks of poor weather and a full-scale winter-style storm in mid-summer. This was just before a week of tropical weather in September. On the Tatshenshini River in the southwest Yukon/Glacier Bay area we went expecting and equipped for 11 days of rain, but instead we had one short shower and many days of hot sun. I could have used more than the one cotton T-shirt I packed among all the gear for the cold and wet.

Be prepared for any weather—a ski party sweating it out near Mount Logan.

Local Knowledge

Local knowledge is very important and can provide crucial information you might otherwise have overlooked, so ask! A group planned a late-season canoe trip in the N.W.T., ending on the Arctic coast. They wanted to go late in the season to avoid the bugs. However, it was only when they searched out local knowledge that they discovered there would be more fogs on the coast at that time of year, making their prearranged float plane pickup unreliable.

Many northern canoe trips must be planned for the short period between ice thaw on the northern lakes and the time when winter weather starts to make travel difficult. Check with knowledgeable local people such as air charter operators who will know when areas are usually clear of ice. With the narrow window of opportunity for some northern trips, there will be years when your planned itinerary may not be possible, so it is advisable to have an alternative plan ready.

A few years ago a group ran into major low-water problems on a canoe trip in the N.W.T. It was a trip on which they would have had marginal water levels at best. It was a drier year than normal, but they set off anyway. There simply was not enough water and they had to abort the trip and be flown out.

Local people will also know of dangerous local weather effects such as the line squalls and white squalls of the Great Lakes, the Squamish winds of the west coast, fogs, rivers prone to flash flooding, etc. Some years ago a fatal canoeing accident occurred at a place the locals know is notorious for squally winds. A recent mountaineering accident may have occurred because the victims did not know that the valley was a notorious cold trap, and while the temperature low down was a safe -8°C, it would in fact be warmer higher up. The snow on a snowfield in the warm air above weakened and eventually avalanched on them.

Don't be afraid to ask direct, specific questions of coast guards, rangers and other sources as to whether there are specific local weather hazards. If you are using a guidebook, don't neglect to read the "General Information" or "Introduction" sections—too often people skip this vital part of the book and go straight to the route descriptions. Consult publications like *Marine Weather Hazards along the British Columbia Coast*.

Misleading Photographs

A trap to be wary of is the impression of weather in an area you get from sunny photos in books or in people's slide shows. These photos can paint an unusually rosy picture that is misleading—most of the pictures may have been taken on one or two days of their trip! I've recently been drooling over my photographs of the Fairweather Range in southeast Alaska and dreaming of skiing and climbing escapades. I have to come back to earth and remember a pilot's comment that in about 300 flights in the area he remembered only three occasions when it was as clear as we saw it.

Weather Extremes

Having chosen a time when weather and conditions should statistically be best, it is still essential to find out what weather conditions you may have to cope with if you encounter a period of extremes. You can then plan your route, level of commitment, itinerary and equipment accordingly.

Route planning and Weather

Route planning must be done with some thought as to how the weather will affect the route's safety and feasibility. You should consider such factors as wind, poor visibility, heavy precipitation, unusual temperatures and changing conditions during the trip. Consider the effect of changing weather on snow stability or on water levels in rivers. If possible, you should make alternative plans for inclement conditions.

A year ago, friends planned a fly-in/ski-out holiday to one of the remote icefields in the Canadian Rockies. Their only possible return route was a three-day ski back to the road, no matter what the conditions. The weather could and eventually did have an enormous influence on the feasibility of this exit. After four days in a tent on the icefield in a raging wet blizzard, they had no alternative but to set off and persevere with their only route out. A horrendous three-day journey to the road ensued. Unusually warm weather and rain at the lower levels had rotted the snowpack, and

Wind and drifting snow can make a glacier tour a very different proposition to the trip shown on page 114.

rain-swollen creeks necessitated frequent detours and hazardous fording. Every aspect of their considerable skill and fitness was taxed to the utmost to reach the road.

There are ways to plan your routes to allow for bad weather. With due consideration for the potential impact of weather, a three-week ski tour in the Yukon's St. Elias Range was planned so that it would not depend on totally clear flying weather to either fly in or fly out. We were not committed to fly in over high ground, and there was a low-level flying route to our intended dropoff. Had the weather been bad on the way in, we could have landed lower on the glacier and travelled farther on foot. At the end of the trip, a couple of extra days' travel would have brought us farther down the glacier to a point that was accessible even in quite poor flying weather, or in a pinch we could even have reached the road. We had also allowed time in case poor weather forced us to sit in the tent and drink tea and read for a few days. As it happened we had marvellous weather for most of the trip, but at least we were prepared.

Wind

Wind can change the character of a trip tremendously. Some canoe routes north of the treeline are directed much more into the prevailing winds than others and need more careful time allowances for windbound days. Even if the wind is not against you, it can raise waves that make progress dangerous on inland lakes as well as on the ocean. A northern lake that is basically clear of ice can present big problems if the wind happens to push all the remaining ice to the side you wish to paddle! On one raft trip I guided in the Arctic, there was a strong headwind blowing on the very first day. Fortunately, we had planned our itinerary with enough time flexibility to stay put, rather than having to spend an exhausting and frustrating day fighting our way down the river. We didn't waste our day worrying or chafing at the weather either, but instead enjoyed bracing, bug-free hikes across the windswept tundra. Ocean kayakers need to be particularly aware of how wind can affect a crossing, and must also take into account the compounding effects of wind, tides and shallow water on wave size.

Hiking or skiing into the wind or with the wind can be vastly different, especially if the wind is driving rain or snow before it. As I write this I am contemplating a ski tour for the weekend that will entail a section through a long windswept pass. The return journey will be with the prevailing winds, so I am less concerned about the likelihood of becoming trapped on the wrong side of the pass by icy headwinds. I have to also consider how the wind will influence the avalanche hazard along our route.

Wind can produce cooling effects out of all proportion to the actual temperatures. Consequently, when planning clothing for your trip you should not just go by the temperature statistics. This is particularly important if the trip will entail travel above or beyond the treeline or in other exposed areas. Wind slows you down or can be bad enough to make travel without face masks and goggles almost impossible, so always keep them somewhere in your pack.

Remember also that you may want to camp in windy places to escape the bugs, but the wind can make it miserably cold. Summer mountaineering at high altitudes in arctic regions such as on Mt. Logan or McKinley exposes you to astronomical winds and very low temperatures, much like Himalayan winter conditions. If you will be camping in exposed places, make sure your tent will withstand high winds—you cannot afford to have a tent destroyed on a wilderness trip!

Visibility

Visibility, and as a result, routefinding, is also affected by weather. Threading your way through a crevasse field might be easy if you can see, but exasperating and time consuming, as well as dangerous, in a whiteout. I remember seeing the tracks of a ski party in the St. Elias Range who had obviously been moving through a crevassed area in poor visibility. We could see how at almost every crevasse they had turned the wrong way and wasted a lot of energy on unnecessarily long detours.

It's tempting to stay out and enjoy spring sunshine, but the avalanche hazard rises enormously in late afternoon on these sorts of days.

Poor visibility affects canoeists, skiers and hikers and in fact anyone who must navigate accurately. Paddling into the delta of an Alaskan river in a fog, we were at risk of missing the channel that would take us to the airstrip. Luckily, our Garmin GPS satellite navigation system confirmed our estimated position and we found the right channel. The intricate navigation required in avalanche terrain is particularly difficult in poor visibility. Alternate routes that can be easily and safely followed in poor visibility should be planned, or you should have enough food, time and equipment to wait until the weather clears.

Avalanches and Weather

Snow stability is particularly influenced by changes in the weather. I remember one trip where we were close to the cabin that was our destination, but could not reach it because the weather had created a high avalanche hazard over the final kilometre. The wind had risen gradually during the afternoon and created a large area of wind slab overlying powder snow, a very unstable condition. Because we had started early in the day, we still had time to retreat and make a long detour to reach the cabin by a different but safer route. On another ski trip we knew we had to pass close below a steep south-facing slope that would undoubtedly warm up if the spring sunshine continued, and start to avalanche by early afternoon. We were glad of our early start, because sure enough, less than two hours after we passed below the suspect slope, the first slides reached our tracks.

Precipitation

Prolonged periods of precipitation can make life tedious and adversely affect morale. Keeping enough equipment and clothing dry can tax the skills and equipment of the best prepared and equipped party if precipitation continues for several days without respite. Hence the popularity of the 200 or so public cabins in Alaska. Compared to much of the world, there are relatively few convenient riverside inns or public mountain huts into which you can retreat to dry out! Precipitation can also slow a group considerably, by making trails slippery, navigation on swollen rivers nerve-wracking

and stream crossings difficult, unpleasant or hazardous. On one autumn backpack we had trouble finding and staying on the trail because it was obliterated by early snowfall.

Weather Changes

Often it's not so much the weather itself that creates safety hazards and crisis situations, but rather the **changes** in the weather. Usually if the weather is poor from the outset, people modify their route or are well equipped for the conditions, or do not set off at all. However, if the weather is good at the start but later deteriorates, people are more likely to be caught out on a route they cannot complete or reverse, or without sufficient equipment to deal with the deteriorated conditions.

A classic weather-change scenario that involved a sudden drastic drop in temperature almost caused a disaster a few years ago in the mountains of Alberta. A group of school children had been ski-touring, based at a remote cabin for several days in relatively mild weather. On the morning of their 23-kilometre ski-out back to civilization, a ferocious arctic front moved in, causing temperatures to drop sharply. The wind rose and visibility deteriorated. They set off anyway, but luckily were persuaded by a mountain guide in the area to return to the safety of the cabin. The temperature soon plummeted into the -30°C range, and the group would likely have suffered serious frostbite injuries and worse had they continued in the storm. They were eventually evacuated by helicopter.

You need to be particularly careful to allow for the impact that changed weather conditions can have on the return leg of a trip. This means allowing plenty of time and devising alternate routes. Fog can move in very quickly on both the Atlantic and the Pacific coasts, as well as certain parts of the Great Lakes. Fog not only causes the temperature to drop considerably, but creates major navigational problems for all watercraft. That pleasant morning paddle away from your base camp in, say, the Broken Islands on Vancouver Island's west coast, can quickly change into a navigational nightmare as you grope through the fog trying to find your way back to your campsite. I've heard sobering stories of lost paddlers searching for hours for their camp, and of people in

Weather signs and portents such as these lenticular clouds will give some information about what to expect, but you should obtain information from forecasters whenever possible.

dinghies frantically looking for the sailboat they left anchored an hour or two earlier to go gunkholing. A friend met some people in the cloud on the Columbia Icefields who had been wandering about for 1-1/2 days looking for their camp. They had left it in clear weather to make a quick ascent of a peak, and the weather had closed in while they were away.

A worthwhile precaution is to take enough gear to bivouac in case conditions change enough to prevent a return to camp. That way there is less incentive to push your luck against dangerous conditions to get back to camp. On day sea kayak trips away from base camp I have a good reserve of food, clothing, water, a pot, the stove and a tarp. On one occasion the winds rose in the afternoon and caught us away from camp on the wrong side of a wide wave-torn channel. Because we had dinner with us there was no rush and it was no hardship at all to wait into the evening. When the wind dropped and the tide changed, we had a safe paddle back to camp just before dark. People often ignore weather conditions that tell them to "stay put and wait," and instead leave a safe place and push on at great risk to reach some haven, and end up in big trouble as a result.

For skiers, weather changes such as rain over deep, cold snow can create a waxing nightmare and progress becomes slow and frustrating.

Similarly, a ski descent will only be quicker than the ascent if the snow conditions remain manageable. Return travel becomes hard work after a heavy snowfall obliterates your nicely broken ski trail, and routefinding can become quite tricky. Remember that in the real wilderness of Canada and Alaska, there is not likely to be another group ahead of you breaking trail. Also, heavy snowfall may make the route unsafe because of avalanche hazard, and poor visibility makes the intricate routefinding needed for safe travel in avalanche terrain more difficult.

Weather Differences En Route

Unfortunately, access to much of the high country requires substantial travel at low levels along valley floors before you gain altitude. This is a particular problem in winter when logging roads usable in summer are often impassable in cars. Unlike California and Colorado and the European Alps, there are few high altitude roads. Warm spring days render the valley bottom access routes unpleasant or impassable on skis long before the skiing deteriorates high up. A route out of the Premier Range of B.C.'s Cariboo Mountains after a spring glacier tour turned into a horrific slog—rain and deep, rotten snow on the valley floor after enjoying powder higher up.

Obtaining Weather Information

Weather reports provide vital information for trip planning. As I write this section, it is a beautiful autumn Monday morning, but I can already see the forecasted major snowstorm approaching on the horizon. Friday's forecasts indicated that yesterday would not have been a day to push your luck and "go out on a limb," because getting out of trouble today or carrying out a rescue will soon be a nightmare. Today would certainly not be a day to set out on a trip. Three days later I read in the paper that two people were trapped in the backcountry by the storm, which deposited 60 centimetres of snow on their trail and cut off their retreat. It was lucky they had no other problems apart from being stranded, because even so they barely survived.

Long-Range Weather Forecasts

If you are planning a short trip of up to five days, check the long-range weather forecast. If the forecast was for deteriorating weather, you would want to take that into account when planning your turnaround point. You'd want to allow more time for the return leg in worse conditions so you'd turn round before the halfway point. If on the other hand, the weather is foul at your starting time, but is destined to improve, you could consider setting off anyway. However, long-range forecasts should not be relied on to the point of neglecting normal prudent safety precautions and procedures—they have been known to be wrong! Also, don't neglect to consider the detrimental effects "improving" weather may have, such as streams becoming swollen with meltwater and difficult to ford.

Media Forecasts

Newspaper, radio and TV weather forecasts vary in completeness and usefulness because of time and space constraints. Large city forecasts tend to be very local, and this is frustrating for recreation planning. In Calgary, for example, forecasts are for Calgary and Banff townsite. Anywhere farther west or at higher altitude is ignored, in spite of the fact that many Calgarians travel over the Rockies into southeastern B.C. for their recreation.

Weather Office Reports

Recorded general forecasts for different areas are available free by phone. A phone call to your local weather office using a 1-900 number —for which you will be charged—will produce more precise information. Better still, phone the weather office in the area you plan to visit. Your local office will provide phone numbers. I tell them exactly where I am going, when I am going and what I will be doing there, to help them decide what information is appropriate. Better still, if you know a little meteorology and can convey that to them by asking a few good questions, you may get even more detailed and practical information.

For example, if I tell them I am planning to be at 3000 metres on the Columbia Icefields, they will tell me the expected cloud base, and the temperature and wind direction to expect at that altitude. The conditions in Banff townsite or at home in Calgary can be totally different to those on the Icefields; a relatively thin, cold air mass over the prairies can produce -25°C temperatures in Calgary, but the mountain peaks can be above the cold air in a surprisingly warm air mass. When I lived in southern Ontario and taught courses farther north, I would tell the weather office I would be, for example, "winter camping with a group of teenagers north of Parry Sound near the lake" or "canoeing and hiking with an adult education class in Killarney Park." This information helped them provide me with an appropriate forecast.

Continuous Weather Forecasts

Continuous weather forecasts are broadcast from weather offices in many parts of North America. Weatheradio Canada and the U.S. National Weather Service transmissions are on special VHF frequencies of 162.4, 162.475 or 162.550 MHz. They can be received on some portable VHF transceivers and on some cable TV channels. The frequencies are not available on most domestic FM radio receivers, but small specially designed Weatheradio receivers are widely available.

Special low-cost VHF receivers available from radio stores enable you to receive continuous forecasts from Weatheradio Canada, the coastguard and the U.S. National Weather Service.

Most of these low-cost receivers are designed to be installed in a residence or large boat, but I have used mine for sea kayaking, protected in a plastic bag and dry bag. A marine VHF transceiver can receive weatheradio signals.

Generally the transmission range is only around 50-60 kilometres, and provides line-of-sight reception only. However, over water I have received transmissions from stations much farther away, when nearer stations were masked by high ground. Numerous repeater stations increase the coverage. My radio comes with a 60-centimetre telescopic antenna and a socket for a wire antenna that improves reception of weak signals. When experiencing weak coastal reception I find orientation of the antenna to be quite critical—it is worth experimenting. It also seemed to be influenced by proximity to the ground, the tent and people, with no apparent reason or pattern.

The Weatheradio Canada forecasts and U.S. National Weather Service transmissions are quite detailed, and usually include an explanation of what is actually going on in the weather systems. If you have any meteorological background it's good to have this information. The broadcasts may include recreation information like ski reports and boating conditions. Weather warnings are also transmitted, and some of the receivers can be set to emit a warning sound or to flash a warning light that tells the operator to turn it fully on and listen for a weather warning.

Coastguard Forecasts

In coastal areas, the Canadian Coastguard transmits weather forecasts on Channel 21B 161.65 MHz and Channel 83B 161.775 MHz, with some local variations. In Alaska, the coastal forecasts are announced on VHF Channel 16 (the emergency channel that everyone monitors) and broadcast on Channel 22. Check with the local coastguard in the area in which you will be operating before you leave. Marine VHF transceivers will receive these broadcasts, and there are plenty of small, light handheld units available that can be used by recreationists. However, since these units operate on VHF frequencies, they are still line-of-sight devices and you can easily enter areas of poor or nonexistent reception in high-relief coastal terrain. A licence is required if you use a transceiver. It makes sense to obtain this licence so you can transmit emergency calls on the international emergency frequency 156.800 MHz, Channel 16.

Other Radio Weather Transmissions in Alaska

The U.S. National Oceanic and Atmospheric Administration produces the handy *Marine Weather Services Chart MSC-15*, which lists weather broadcast stations and their transmitting details. These include the NOAA Weatheradio stations, commercial AM and FM stations, HF broadcasts and Upper Sideband 4125 kHz broadcasts. Weather office telephone numbers and operating hours are also listed. It also includes a sketchmap showing sea ice positions at various times of the year. See page 373 for address.

Weather Forecast Terminology

Terms such as "Blizzard" and "Heavy" rain mean different things to different people. They are among a number of terms used by forecasters that actually have quite specific meanings. You should know what the various terms mean, and particularly what they might mean for you out in the wilderness!

Weather Advisory

An **advisory** is issued when actual or expected conditions may cause general inconvenience or concern, but do not yet pose a big enough threat to warrant issuing a weather **warning**. Advisories may be used when conditions are showing signs of developing into the "severe" category, but the situation is unclear or too far in the future to justify giving a weather warning.

For example, a Cold Wave Advisory indicates that the temperature will drop 20 C degrees or more within 18 hours.

Weather Watches

Watches are to advise that conditions are favourable for the formation of severe weather. For example, a severe thunderstorm watch or a tornado watch.

Weather Warnings

Warnings advise that severe weather is occurring or that hazardous weather is highly probable. Examples of weather warnings are:

Severe thunderstorm warning. A severe thunderstorm has developed with one or more of: heavy rain, damaging winds, large hail >20 millimetres or intense lightning. People outdoors should be aware of the potential for flash floods, washed out backroads, footbridges washed away, unfordable streams, roads blocked by fallen trees, trees falling on tents, tents blowing away or being damaged, injuries from hail and the possibility of lightning strike injuries, especially in the mountains or in wide open plains. Foreign visitors should be aware that thunderstorms in Canada and Alaska can be very violent events.

Tornado warning. One or more tornadoes are occurring in the area specified and you should be on the alert for the development of additional ones or the development of severe thunderstorms. The expected speed and direction of existing tornadoes may be given. Tornadoes are a most frightening weather phenomenon, but a person in open country may actually be safer than a person in a building that could collapse and certainly safer than a person in a vehicle that can be thrown around.

Blizzard warning. Snow and/or blowing snow with strong winds, visibility less than one kilometre, windchill of >1600 W/sq m, (Canada) and expected to last for more than four hours. With a windchill of >1600 W/sq m, frostbite can occur with prolonged exposure and good winter outer clothing is essential. Blizzards can easily result in people becoming lost or stranded and unable to travel to shelter, resulting in exhaustion, frostbite, hypothermia and even death. Even if vehicles can be reached, driving conditions may be impossible, especially on backroads used for recreation access. Foreign visitors not used to Canadian and Alaskan winter driving need to be wary of these conditions. See Chapter Eight, Using Vehicles. See also Heavy Snowfall Warning below.

Freezing rain warning. Freezing rain covers everything with ice, knocking trees and power lines down and making driving, walking, skiing, snowshoeing, riding and cycling dangerous. Horrid conditions to be caught out in— the backroad used for access may become glazed and impassable for a long time unless you have tire chains. The snowpack may become glazed and provide the ultimate slippery, breakable crust.

Heavy rain warning. Heavy rain is likely to cause local or widespread flooding. A warning is issued if the expected amount is 50 millimetres in 12 hours or less or 80 millimetres in 24 hours or less. Beware of flooding, road and bridge washouts, impassable roads and trails, rivers becoming dangerously high for navigation, creeks and streams unfordable.

Heavy snowfall warning. Accumulation of 10 centimetres or more (15 centimetres in Ontario) in 12 hours or less. Heavy snowfall causes poor driving conditions that can maroon travellers in late fall on remote backcountry roads that will not be plowed, and on any road in winter. Visibility is usually poor, making off-trail navigation difficult. Trailbreaking often becomes difficult. Avalanche hazard may skyrocket. But, the skiing may be fabulous in a few days when stability returns! Heavy snow accumulations on lakes may push the ice down, so water comes up through cracks, leading to overflow and icing problems for travellers on skis or snowshoes. If the temperatures are warm, travellers will be soaked by the falling snow.

Wind warning. Wind warnings are issued when winds will blow steadily at >60 km/h or when winds will gust to >90 km/h, for more than one hour. Just as the threshold for windchill warnings is higher in northern areas, so the wind warning threshold is higher in windy Alberta where gusts to 100 km/h are required and even windier southern Alberta where winds must be 70 km/h with 120 km/h gusts. High winds can make travel on foot and by boat difficult or dangerous, and can produce a significant windchill factor. Shoreline campsites can become unusable because of waves and spray. Water levels will rise considerably at the downwind ends of long lakes. Falling trees are a hazard to consider.

Winter storm warning. Issued in Ontario when two or more winter conditions reach warning levels.

Windchill warnings. Windchill warnings take into account the way wind produces a greater rate of cooling of the body than one might expect for the actual temperature. The actual temperature may be -20°C but because of the wind, there is a cooling effect equivalent to being at -40°C in still air.

In Canada the windchill is measured in watts/sq metre, while in the U.S. it is given as a Fahrenheit temperature equivalent.

1800 to 2000 W/sq m is equivalent to approximately -30°C or -22°F in still air. Frostbite of exposed areas can occur in a few minutes, so layers of good winter clothing are essential for protection.

2000+ W/sq m is equivalent to approximately -40°C or -40°F in still air. Unprotected skin can freeze in one minute, face masks or hoods with good face protection are needed. Outdoor recreational activities are not advisable.

2200+ W/sq m Face protection mandatory. Outdoor activity is hazardous.

2300+ W/sq m is equivalent to approximately -50°C (-58°F) in still air. Outdoor conditions become dangerous. Buddy system required for safety.

When the warning is issued, conditions are deemed hazardous to human activity. The threshold values at which warnings are issued vary with the part of the country, for example, 1800 W/sq m in southern Ontario up to 2500 W/sq m in the N.W.T., Yukon and northern Quebec.

In those northern areas the people are more likely to be equipped with the clothing and have the skills required to deal with the conditions. Lower levels of windchill are so common that frequent warnings at the lower level would lose their effectiveness. High windchills generally make life in the outdoors much less pleasant and all tasks more difficult. You must be more conservative about risk-taking because handling an emergency becomes much more difficult. Preventing an injured person from becoming frostbitten or hypothermic is often a bigger problem than dealing with the original injury. Your fitness, acclimatization, competence and particularly the quality and design of your clothing will influence your ability to cope with such conditions.

Regulations

The wilderness areas of Canada and Alaska are certainly wild, but not so wild that they are devoid of regulations. You should find out about specific local regulations, because many of them exist to protect the wilderness, and because penalties for infractions can be heavy.

Permits

Many parks require that overnight users, and even winter day users, obtain permits for which there may be a charge. Vehicle entry permits are also required for any vehicle stopping in the Canadian mountain national parks. While this seems bureaucratic, it serves a number of useful functions that should counteract any feelings of loss of freedom. Getting a permit brings you in contact with wardens or rangers who can provide you with useful local information. They will know about such problems as bridges that are washed out, avalanche hazards, grizzly activity, large groups in the area and other parties on the same climbing route.

Permits may or may not be associated with mandatory "registration," whereby your route and expected return time are recorded and a search initiated if you do not return. This is obviously to your advantage, but make sure you de-register on your return. There will be a heavy penalty for not doing so.

Regulations vary widely from place to place. For example, Denali climbers are required to register and pay a $150 fee. On the other hand, backpackers on the north side of the Alaska Range are required to have permits to limit the numbers of parties and their impact on the tundra. Many parks limit group size (minimums for bear safety, maximums for impact and esthetics). Permit and quota systems are increasingly common on popular routes, including the South Nahanni River, West Coast Trail and the Tatshenshini River.

A permit for some areas may require detailed documentation of your group's equipment, and members' names and skills. You may also need to acquire your permit a long time in advance—three months for climbs in the Icefield Ranges of Kluane Park in the Yukon. You may be required to alter some aspects of your plan to obtain a permit.

Rights-of-way and Private Land

Waterways are usually rights-of-way, and the land up to the high water line (vegetation line) is public. The exception is some Indian land where the water is not public. Check Canadian topographic maps and marine charts that show reserve boundaries, and inquire about navigation status. In Alaska, the boundaries of native corporation lands are not yet on many topographic maps, so you should obtain maps and information from the Public Information Centre of the Department of Natural Resources (see page 372 under Native Lands and Private Lands for address).

The Alaska Land Status Map shows the entire state at a scale of 1:2 500 000 (1 inch to 40 miles) and indicates the status of land at the Township level.

Private land above high water line may effectively exclude access to or egress from the water. Ancient portage rights are sometimes interrupted by private lands. Old rights-of-way are not as jealously guarded and maintained by

Ancient rights-of-way are not as well protected in North America as they are in Europe. La Vase Portages—Canada's history for sale. Courtesy Paul Chivers, Restore the Link, North Bay, Ont.

the public and by statutes as they are in, for example, the U.K. In one case a canoeist who was denied permission to carry his canoe over a portage trail died while running the rapid he wanted to portage.

Fencing and/or signage is the usual indication that land is privately owned. However, some public land leased at low cost for grazing is fenced even though it is not owned, and the right to exclude the public from that land is a contentious issue. Many landowners are quite amenable to public use of their land if they are first approached in a civil manner.

Land claims' settlements in the N.W.T. have limited non-native access to some areas of land. In the Nunavut territory of the N.W.T. (roughly east of longitude 110°W) the boundaries of these areas are shown at 1:3 000 000 scale on a map available with booklet R32-134/ 1993E ISBN 0-662-20725-4 from the Department of Indian Affairs and Northern Development. A shorter summary pamphlet is also available. Topographic maps are also being overprinted with the boundaries of the affected land parcels. The Nunavut boundaries come into effect on 1999 April 1.

Full details and maps of the 35,000 square miles of Western Arctic Claim affected area may be found in the Department of Indian Affairs and Northern Development (DIAND) publication QS-5201-001-EE-A2, "The Western Arctic Claim."

As more land claims are settled, recreationists should remember to check their right-of-access, although so far there has been little difficulty.

Camping and Fires

There may be time limits on the number of consecutive nights you can camp in one place—it can be as low as four nights in some Alaska state parks.

There are often regulations prohibiting leaving a camp unoccupied for more than a certain number of days. Such a law is not usually enforced in a remote area if mountaineers establish a basecamp and are away on a route for four or five days. Random camping is not permitted in the wilderness area of some parks and in some areas fires can be lit only in official firepits. Leaving a fire unattended is certainly wrong and is usually an offence. Some parks

A fire should never be built or left like this, and in many parks it is illegal to light a fire anywhere other than the firepits provided. High forest fire hazard conditions may result in the imposition of a total camp fire ban.

require campers to carry bearproof food containers and some parks ban canned or bottled food and drink in the backcountry.

Restrictions may apply on the numbers of people who can camp in one place. There may be minimum sizes to reduce the likelihood of bear problems or, more likely, maximum sizes to reduce impact.

It is undesirable to camp on or close to trails because of the risk of an animal encounter. There may be rules enforcing a minimum distance from a trail—in one area it is 500 metres to keep people away from other people on the through route.

Firearms

Handguns are prohibited in Canada and cannot be transported through the country to Alaska by U.S. citizens. Strict rules apply to transporting firearms through Canadian national parks. Firearms must be sealed or dismantled and ammunition stored separately.

Firearms for protection from animals are subject to regulation. See page 296.

Hunting

There are definite hunting seasons and licence requirements. Some species such as rabbits, which are vermin in other countries, have game status and regulated hunting seasons in North America. Killing animals for survival is illegal if the situation results from poor planning or incompetence. It is illegal for non-natives to live off the land.

Roadkill is the property of the government—and usually they're welcome to it!

Wildlife

Feeding, approaching or harassing wildlife is certainly wrong and dangerous, and in many places it is an offence. The days of an evening's entertainment feeding the bears are long gone. Collecting discarded animal parts such as antlers is frowned on everywhere and is illegal in many parks (antlers are an important source of minerals for small rodents). Possession of migratory bird feathers could get you into trouble because you couldn't prove they were simply lying on the ground. You could come under suspicion of obtaining the item by means detrimental to the

Certain areas and trails can be closed completely or to certain activities. Check before you go because the closures are not necessarily indicated at the trailhead.

You should not collect even discarded horns and antlers, because their minerals are important to rodents. It is illegal to collect them in many parks.

bird or illegal because the bird is out of season. Bird egg possession is highly illegal.

Closed Areas and Trails

Areas of parks and public land can be closed by authorities for various reasons. These include: public safety for protection from bears, avalanches, etc., avalanche control with blind-firing artillery, forest fire prevention, protection of wildlife, preservation of sensitive areas, strict entry regulations to caves and military test areas. Certain trails may be closed to activities such as equestrian or mountain biking. Check before you go.

Fishing

Fishing licences are required even in the ocean. Some types of bait, hooks or lures are prohibited in certain waters or at certain times of the year and there is often a limit to the number of hooks or lines a person can have in use. Unattended lines may be illegal. It is illegal to place fish guts back in the water in some areas, but this practice is recommended in other areas. Catch and release rules may apply, and possession limits and catch limits often exist. Size limit restrictions may apply. Some areas may be closed to fishing for health reasons or to protect breeding stocks.

Limits exist and licences may be needed for crustaceans (crabs and lobsters) and molluscs (such as clams), which are loosely grouped under the term "Shellfish."

Useful leaflets can often be obtained from provincial or state authorities. For example, the *B.C. Tidal Waters Sport Fishing Guide*, produced by Canada Fisheries and Oceans, is free from fishing licence vendors and includes illustrations of different species, fishing methods and details of regulations. Ocean kayakers and sailors should read this carefully as there are a surprising number of restrictions on catching ocean fish and shellfish. Freshwater fishing guides are also available from the relevant authorities.

Boating

Some areas still require that approved personal flotation devices only be "present" in the vessel. However, most intelligent paddlers wear theirs all the time. They realize that when you are thrashing around in cold northern water, finding your PFD and putting it on is not a practical option.

Many good PFDs are not "approved," that is to say they do not have U.S. Coastguard Approval or Canadian Department of Transport approval. An excellent item may not be approved simply because the manufacturer did not want to pay for the approval process. However, some are not approved because they are not a high-visibility colour. Also, the large pockets for survival equipment on some raises concerns about people possibly overloading or unbalancing the garment. These last two features are recognizable from a distance and you could be ticketed. You'd deserve the ticket if you were using a low-visibility fashion colour PFD. However, survival gear pockets are so useful, I would take my chances with officialdom. I like my flares, radio and survival kit on my person, not buried in the boat I could be washed away from.

Some sea kayaks are long enough to fall into a category that technically requires them to carry certain signalling and rescue devices such as life rings. These rules have so far not been applied to kayaks, though sensible boaters carry warning devices such as whistles and signalling devices such as flares.

Alcohol

Visitors, particularly from Europe, should be aware of very different attitudes and laws concerning alcohol. Consumption of alcohol in public in Canada is an offence. This means anywhere other than licensed premises, a home, motorhome or your campsite. However, I have never encountered law enforcement officers looking for illegal drinking unless people draw attention to themselves with drunken behaviour. A discreet sip of wine or beer with lunch is not likely to attract attention.

Consumption of alcohol by passengers in a vehicle, even if the driver is sober, is an offence in most Canadian provinces. An open case of beer or an open alcohol container inside a vehicle is also illegal. If you are stopped for some other reason you should not be surprised if the officer looks inside the vehicle. Keep empties and full containers in the trunk, or well back in the rear of a van or sports-utility vehicle where it is not readily visible or available to driver or passengers.

A permit is required to bring more than a small amount of wine, spirits or beer into the N.W.T. In addition many northern and remote communities have strict regulations relating to alcohol. Some are Prohibition Communities in which no alcohol is allowed within 20 kilometres. Controlled Communities regulate the use of alcohol and you are required to obtain permission from the community Alcohol Education Committee to bring alcohol in. Other communities are open and subject to normal liquor laws. Do **not** give alcohol as gifts.

You must be aware of liquor prohibitions around some northern communities.

Pets

Pets, particularly dogs, are banned from the backcountry in some areas. The prohibition varies from park to park and may vary with the season to allow dogsledding.

Collecting

It is an offence to remove any items whatsoever from national parks and most provincial and state parks. That includes picking flowers, collecting rocks and fossils, and certainly collecting or disturbing historical artifacts and wildlife parts such as discarded antlers. Removing items of interest from an area impoverishes the area for others who come after you, and in the case of wildflowers and hunting trophies, actually depletes the gene pool of those species.

Geological Specimens

Alaska law prohibits the removal or disturbance of fossils without a permit. Similar laws also exist in Canada and are especially strict about mining or removing fossils from their original location. Removing anything from a national park is illegal.

Gold Panning

Panning for gold is part of the northern mystique for many people. It is permitted on most public lands but not on other people's claims. Usually the claims are clearly marked, but check their locations at the mining recorder's office. Some streams in Alaska are closed to panning because of the disturbance of critical salmon spawning beds. Check with fish and game departments. Even if areas are not closed, you should be aware that panning is environmentally very unfriendly. Never dig into stream banks or areas where the gravel bars have been stabilized by vegetation. Never let the silt from washing go directly into the stream where it settles on spawning beds.

It's nice to have your special canine friends along on some trips, but check park regulations first.

Historic Artifacts and Sites

Disturbing historic sites and artifacts is a serious offence both morally and legally. Visitors should realize that non-native history is quite short in Canada and Alaska and that recent ruins, even if they look like abandoned property and junk, are of considerable historical importance. Cold temperatures and a dry atmosphere can also mean that artifacts weather quite slowly and are in fact older than they look. "Abandoned" cabins can also be seasonally used trapping cabins. People who use these cabins rely on them and their contents.

Alaska has state and federal laws prohibiting the removal of any historic, prehistoric or cultural materials without a permit. Similar laws exist in most parts of Canada. In Alaska the law extends to cover tidal areas, so beachcombers beware. Native historic sites and prehistoric sites are commonly found by tourists, especially in the Barren Grounds of the N.W.T. These sites are protected, and disturbance of them or possession of stolen artifacts, including stone arrowheads, is an offence. Report the exact location of your find to the state, provincial or territorial museum who will investigate and document it if it is a new find.

In most places it is illegal to disturb or remove historic artifacts, and they should be left for others to see and enjoy. Top: Inuit stone circle. Middle: One of the infamous lead-soldered food cans from the Franklin Expedition era. Bottom: Arrowhead.

Importing Equipment and Food

Visitors bringing recreational equipment into Canada may be required to pay a deposit at the border equivalent to the taxes and duties due on that equipment, even though the item is for personal use and is to be re-exported. A smaller deposit may be accepted, but either way, it could be a substantial amount on, say, a $5000 folding kayak or even a $2000 canoe.

Normally payments are required in cash or certified cheque, but major credit cards are also accepted. Either way, it could be a nasty unexpected addition to your holiday expenses. If the item is later stolen or wrecked, make sure you make a full report to the police and in the case of a wreck, obtain photographic proof if possible. An American friend who wrecked a canoe on a remote Ontario river and was thankful to get out alive, had his financial loss compounded when customs would not believe his story and tried to retain the duty and taxes.

As of January 1994, there is no customs restriction on bringing noncommercial quantities of food into Canada from other countries, so you should have little problem with the prepackaged rations for your expedition. However, it would be a good idea to package food unsuspiciously in clear plastic and not to seal daybags or other packages until after customs inspection. Bring your tape and ties with you. It's easier to seal stuff for the first time than to reseal items broken open for customs inspection! Transport of foods into the U.S. is similarly straightforward as long as you are bringing noncommercial quantities.

However, there are agriculture restrictions on importation of meats, vegetables, plants, etc. These restrictions are taken seriously in order to prevent the introduction of foreign pests and diseases. Items that are of greatest concern are those that are fresh and perishable and therefore could contain live disease organisms or pests. Meats and dairy products are a particular hazard if they have not been preserved by canning where the processing has killed everything. Do not try to cross borders with such items as sausage, salami or cheese, even if vacuum packed. Vacuum packing does not sterilize food products and there can be live organisms within a vacuum package. Fresh fruits and vegetables have strict restrictions.

Radio Use and Licences

Licences are required for operators of marine VHF two-way radios and the set itself must also be licensed.

Visitors bringing their own devices should be aware that licensing of the set requires an approval number. Gaining approval for your own device may be quite time consuming.

Operators of HF single sideband radios do not need a licence, but the set itself must be licensed. (See the section on radio communications.)

Unauthorized use of frequencies is an offence except in a genuine emergency. Ordering more beer over a parks' frequency would be definitely frowned on, but calling for help in a wilderness emergency would be viewed more favourably.

UHF walkie-talkies are supposed to be licensed by the purchaser by filling in a form. Operators of these radios do not require a licence.

CB radios are widely used and widely available, but their short range limits their usefulness.

Make sure you have appropriate station and operator licences for your radio communications.

Legal Liability in the Outdoors

You go into the outdoors to enjoy yourself and to get away from all the trappings of daily life. However, even in the backcountry you cannot escape from your responsibilities and liabilities. Recreation pursuits seem to be increasingly placing people in positions where someone could sue them as a result of their acts or omissions. The North American propensity for suing people at the drop of a hat has reached ludicrous proportions and some people (not just lawyers) see a lawsuit as a quick route to a fortune. The concept that when something happens to us "it can't possibly be our fault and someone else must be held accountable and made to pay" is pervasive in North American society.

General Considerations

Following are some sobering points to consider.

Someone you regard as a "friend" on a joint adventure trip could decide to sue you if they thought they were injured or suffered loss as a result of your actions. It's amazing what "friends" will do, particularly if they think they can get a whole lot of money out of an insurance company and maybe even out of your pocket!

When a liability suit is filed, it will name everyone who is even remotely connected with the incident. For example, as a club official or director you can be named in a suit for something that happened on a club trip even if you were not there.

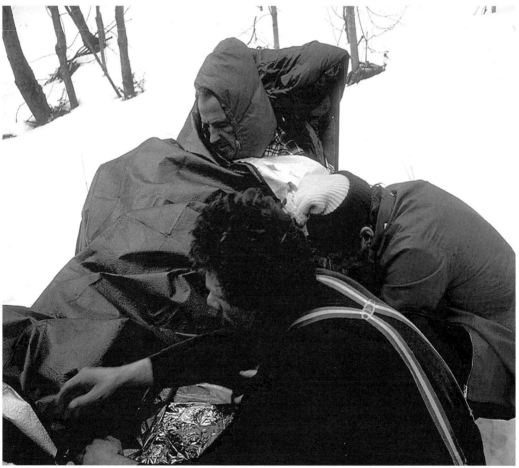

A wilderness accident can have serious liability implications besides being serious in itself.

As a volunteer leader or instructor you can be sued. As a paid instructor you can certainly be sued and your homeowner's policy may not protect you because you are paid.

The more formally trained and skilled you are, the higher the performance expectations the courts will have for you. The more trained you are, the easier it is for expert witnesses to show that you made a mistake and are liable.

You are not obliged to help at the scene of an accident involving someone with whom you are not connected (for example, another party you encounter on the trail). However, once you start helping you take on some liabilities and responsibilities, the main one being that you cannot then abandon the situation unless you are in danger yourself. As long as you do your best **within your skill and training level**, you are unlikely to get into liability problems. The Good Samaritan approach to the law (in Canada, at least) is reasonable protection.

In Canada, a well-written waiver **is** worth the paper it is written on. You **can** protect yourself against being sued with a good waiver. Conversely, if you are a client on a guided trip you will probably have to sign a waiver removing **your** right to sue as a condition of joining the trip. Many provincial governments in Canada require the clients of outfitters on public land to sign a waiver that expressly protects the province as landowner. A waiver, if it is well worded and correctly administered, will prevent the signer from having any recourse even in the case of negligence. (See Delaney vs. Cascade River Holidays, B.C. 1983.) Even the printed waiver on the back of a ski lift ticket is being upheld by Canadian courts, despite the fact that you do not have to sign it.

Where children are involved you have to be extremely careful. This is because lower expectations are placed on their level of responsibility and correspondingly higher expectations are placed on the supervisor's level of responsibility. Juries tend to be more sympathetic to children and to assess financial settlements in their favour.

See page 375 for a sample waiver form of the type used by some Western Canadian guiding organizations.

Protecting Yourself Against Liability Claims

Think along the lines of "how would this look when portrayed to a jury by a smart-ass lawyer whose questionable morality is further distorted by being on a contingency fee and having $ signs in his eyes" and conduct your operations accordingly. Take the trouble to learn and follow proper safe practices so that the likelihood of you causing anything to go wrong is minimized. Ensure that you have the appropriate safety equipment for the activity and the conditions.

Do not portray yourself as an expert in something in which you are not. Not only is the delusion likely to lead to a mishap, but people are also entitled to have higher expectations of you—ones that you cannot live up to. Do not attempt to take on responsibilities beyond your training and skill level.

If you are in any type of leadership role, do not mislead the people for whose safety you are liable and responsible about the risks they face. In fact, as part of the waiver and/or trip briefing, you should leave participants in no doubt as to what they are getting into, and give them a chance to back out gracefully.

Learn to handle mishaps properly to minimize their consequences. You thereby reduce the likelihood that someone will suffer significant injuries that would justify a claim against you.

Never admit you were at fault if an accident occurs.

Check with your Homeowner's Insurance to see if you are covered for the types of liabilities to which you expose yourself, and get a ruling in writing. They may even cover you if you are occasionally paid by a club to instruct.

If an incident occurs, take photographs and document the incident in writing as soon as possible after it occurs. Your written and photographic record will carry more weight later in court than someone else's vague, undocumented recollections. Remember, it can take a long time before a case gets to court and memories dull or distort over time. If you can get signed statements from witnesses to back you up, do so; for example, witnesses to attest that you had specifically and clearly told the victim not to do what caused the accident.

Guided groups may have to be quite regimented for safety and liability reasons.

Reduce your risk of a liability claim by learning to handle accidents well so you can minimize their consequences. These club trip leaders on a training exercise have splinted a "broken" leg, protected the victim from frostbite and hypothermia, dispatched a well-briefed message party for help and are all safe and warm with the victim in a snowshelter at +7°C.

Encourage members of your group (especially clubs) to purchase Personal Accident Insurance. Investigate the costs of a group plan. It's much easier and quicker for a victim to claim against their own accident insurance than it is to sue someone else and prove their liability in court. What the victim needs is swift compensation for their injury, and it should not matter to them where it comes from unless they are vindictive.

Clubs can save themselves a lot of grief by purchasing liability insurance to protect club assets and officials personally against the consequences of liability suits.

Waivers

Good waivers that will stand up in court have the following characteristics:

- A good waiver will make it very clear that by signing it you give up the right to sue anyone who might, by even the most tenuous of connections, be liable. This may even extend to the governments on whose lands activities are carried out. It also makes it clear that the signer's relatives have no recourse either.
- The waiver will clarify to the signer the nature of some of the risks to which they will be exposed. This helps the signer better recognize trouble and stay out of it, but the list on the waiver will probably refer to "risks including but not limited to" because not all the conceivable risks can be listed.

  Remember that newcomers to the outdoors can be very naive about risks that trained and experienced people recognize as a matter of course and carefully avoid. A visitor from the southern U.S. sued a glacier bus tour operator because they did not tell him that ice was slippery. After he fell and was injured, he successfully contended that it was not reasonable to expect him to know that ice was slippery because it never snowed where he came from. The list of risks and hazards also makes it more difficult for a plaintiff to say things like, "I didn't know bears were dangerous and not cuddly." It also puts some onus on them to ask for more detail about the hazards.

- A good waiver will require that you initial it in several places to acknowledge that you have read and understood each paragraph.
- The waiver must be signed and the signature witnessed.
- People should know well in advance that they have to sign a waiver before they are allowed to go on the trip. If they are already committed and are just setting off and are then unexpectedly presented with a waiver, they can be deemed to be signing under duress, and this makes the waiver less valid. Waiver forms are becoming a common part of outfitters' brochures.
- It is better if the actual signing of waivers is done by all members of the party, together and under the same circumstances after the same briefing.
- Club "short waiver" forms signed by the participants on each trip are not as effective as a full waiver form. Full waiver forms should be signed each year as part of membership renewal. However, short forms should be kept on file. If a club can produce a collection of forms with a person's signature acknowledging their acceptance of risk, that person would have difficulty in front of a jury saying they didn't really know about the risks. They'd acknowledged their existence on numerous occasions but not done anything to find out more about them.
- There may be occasions when the injured plaintiff has a legitimate complaint, perhaps of gross negligence, and they deserve compensation. A waiver could prevent a claim and may therefore prevent the injured party from getting something to which they actually have some entitlement. This makes it all the more important that people carry personal accident insurance that pays up quickly regardless of fault.

For more information on this topic, see *Outdoor Pursuits Programming: Legal Liability and Risk Management,* Glenda Hanna, University of Alberta Press. See page 375 of this book for an example of a waiver form.

Security

After more than 20 years of backcountry pursuits in North America, I'm pleased to say I have had very few "negative people experiences" or confrontations. Incidents do occur, however, and precautions must be taken, because confrontations with other people can be very upsetting. Vandalism or theft of equipment can also have a very serious impact on your holiday or wilderness trip.

Personal Security

If you are sure you will be alone in the backcountry, you are unlikely to have people encounters of the wrong kind. Generally speaking, the farther you are from motorized access, and the more difficult or obscure the travel, the less likely you are to encounter people at all, and even less likely to encounter the type of people who will cause problems. Criminal types generally don't go in for significant physical exertion, so you don't often encounter them in the backcountry if there is no motorized access.

There are a few cases where "strange" individuals or people with dubious, if not outright criminal, pasts are living rough in remote areas. Some have a reputation for being unpleasant toward people invading "their" territory. Locals will probably warn you about such individuals so you know whether to approach or avoid a person, cabin or area. Be aware that substance abuse is rife in many remote areas and people may be acting strangely or with unexpected violence as a result. The "idyllic" northern surroundings can hide some disturbing realities.

On the subject of substance abuse, if you happen to stumble into a marijuana patch hidden in the bush, leave the area immediately in case its owner shows up. Keep your eyes open for booby traps.

Hunting season is a time to be particularly wary. Most hunters are law-abiding citizens, although you may disagree with their choice of outdoor activity. However, the season attracts some individuals who will try to discourage people from recreating in what they perceive as "their" area. It is an offence to interfere with legal hunting.

Poaching for illegal trophies and animal parts such as bear paws and gall bladders for oriental traditional medicine trade is big business. Meat poaching is often on an organized scale for trafficking rather than the occasional person putting a deer in the freezer for the family. The perpetrators are often habitual criminals, many with a history of violence. With increased penalties for poaching in force, they are playing a higher stakes game, so I would certainly not risk my life by confronting an armed poacher in a remote area. I would avoid letting the person know I had seen anything. If contact with the person is unavoidable, show disinterest or lack of awareness that an offence has occurred. If you can leave the area without them being aware of your presence or of your suspicions, do so and alert the authorities as soon as possible.

I've only had two experiences where my personal safety was threatened, both at trailheads on country roads. On one occasion I was asleep in my vehicle at the road-end and a gang of drunken four-wheel drive types arrived in the middle of the night and made it unpleasantly clear they wanted me to leave. The other occasion was also an encounter with an impaired individual who felt we were trespassing on reserve land when we were not even in the reserve. In such cases, it's best to avoid any physical confrontation and to acquiesce and retreat.

Landowners can have a disconcertingly belligerent initial approach, but bear in mind that, innocuous as your particular trespass may be, they may be fed up with abusive hunters and partiers and be classifying you in the same genre.

If you are actually attacked, your capsicum bear spray may be a tempting weapon, but remember that like mace, or any other weapon for that matter, it could be turned and used against you. When used against people, capsicum bear spray is a prohibited weapon in Canada.

Avoid these situations at all costs—courts have not always been particularly sympathetic to the innocent person who has fought back. If you are uneasy, obey your instincts and just leave—there's plenty of room in the backcountry.

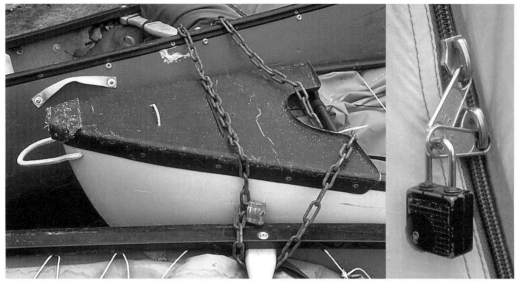

Locking several canoes into an unwieldy bundle with a cable or chain is a handy way to discourage theft. Locking your tent zipper may discourage casual theft.

Equipment Security

With increased motorized activity in the backcountry, your vehicle parked at the road-end is more at risk than it used to be when fewer people were making backcountry forays. Your 4x4 or sport truck is a particularly appealing target for joyriders, thieves or people looking for parts such as custom wheels with good tires. It's debatable whether it's better to hide the vehicle completely or to park it in a very open, conspicuous place where it is visible to many other people. Vehicle antitheft alarms will likely discourage thieves since they probably don't know how far away you are.

A locking hood on the vehicle is essential to prevent battery theft, and external spare tires should be locked onto their carriers. Small readily saleable items such as cameras and binoculars must be kept out of sight, preferably in a hidden compartment. If you are in the habit of leaving your vehicle, and particularly for paddlers or others who may wish to leave wallets behind, it's a good idea to set up a hiding place for valuables. Explore your vehicle carefully for suitable hidden or awkward places. A small nylon pouch can be attached to all sorts of obscure places with some Velcro. Glue the Velcro in place or glue it to a piece of wood that can be screwed in place. A pouch attached to a crocodile clip (electrical supplies

store) could also be used. Do not leave your ownership and insurance in an obvious place—keep them hidden but make sure authorized drivers know their location.

Items that particularly appeal to thieves, such as radar detectors and fancy stereos, should be hidden as much as possible. High quality, high-tech recreation equipment is now also a target, and I know of incidents where canoes, kayaks and of course backcountry skis have been stolen. Skis can simply be locked inside the vehicle or out of sight in a ski box. Canoes can be locked to roof racks by a piece of chain around the seat or thwart and the rack. Locking devices to fit into the cockpit of closed canoes and kayaks are now available if there is nothing to thread a chain or cable through. A padlock and a length of chain or steel cable with an eye spliced in each end is a useful item for canoeists to carry, especially if they will have to leave boats unattended during a car shuttle. A suitable cable is easy to make using galvanized or stainless steel cable from a hardware store, perhaps threaded through clear plastic piping to protect your gear. Have the eyes swaged by your local wire rope supplier, or use the swaging ferrules from a hardware store and a hammer. You can even use screw-type wire rope clamps and then hammer the threads after tightening, to prevent them being undone. If the roof rack is too easily removed to be worth locking to, pass a long cable through slightly opened windows and lock the ends together inside the vehicle. Several canoes or kayaks can be locked together in an unwieldy bundle or locked to a tree. Paddles should be inaccessible to discourage casual joy-riding. It's best to take them with you, but they can be locked to the boat with a short piece of chain and a padlock, as can packs using the pack grab handles. Paddles can also be hidden well back in the bush, preferably hoisted off the ground because porcupines will gnaw them if they are left for long.

I know that a quick search around the wheels and inside the bumpers of vehicles at a trailhead would almost certainly produce a set of keys. It amazes me to see people, particularly canoeists, still using places like this to leave their keys. Never do it with vehicles that might appeal to joy-riders. Take your keys with you, on a lanyard around your neck but under clothing so it can't snag and strangle you. Or pin them securely inside a pocket with a safety pin. Some packs and garments have a ring or clip inside pockets for keeping keys. Keep a spare door key for the vehicle taped as inconspicuously as possible on the outside of the vehicle. Duct tape is less conspicuous than a magnetic key box, and can be attached to a wider variety of surfaces. It becomes more easily camouflaged by mud, too. Add to your security by keeping the ignition and gas tank keys hidden separately inside the vehicle. Give your trip partners your spare keys so they can get into the vehicle without you if necessary, or tell them where the emergency key is hidden.

If you have to leave a vehicle in or near a community, check with local police to locate a safe place. They will usually be able to advise you, though it may mean paying a fee for parking in a secure area.

Thefts around campsites do occur. Sometimes the culprits are people who have deliberately set out to steal something, and sometimes they are people who succumbed to the irresistible temptation of an "easy mark." You can't do much to protect against the former except by leaving nothing to steal, but you can make it more difficult for them. You can protect yourself against spontaneous casual thieves by keeping temptations out of view,

and even a token lock provides some protection. Breaking into something or cutting something open requires more serious intent than does casual theft or "just picking it up"—it's a bigger psychological step for the perpetrator. Also, by at least making an attempt to lock items, you put yourself in a better position when dealing with your insurance company. A small lock on the tent zipper weighs only a few grams, and its presence would force a thief to cut their way into the tent—serious intent. However, Canadian police tell me the charge if caught would still only be theft rather than break and enter. The lock should be inconspicuous so that it doesn't catch someone's eye and make them wonder what's inside to require the lock! The risk is, if they are only after money, which isn't in the tent anyway, you could end up with a damaged tent and possibly having to abort your trip.

Outdoor clothing and gear is costly—packs are around $300, and good tents and sleeping bags easily cost $500 apiece—so you can be leaving several thousand dollars worth of gear in your campsite. A group of canoeists recently had $15,000 worth of camping gear stolen from a campsite off a dirt road in the backcountry. It's easy to indelibly "customize" your tent with a magic marker to make it recognizable and therefore less attractive to thieves. The same can be done to a sleeping bag or pack. Most household insurance can be

Take your valuables with you when boating. Use a waterproof fanny pack such as the Seal Pak by Cascade Designs, the MiniSafe or SeaSafe by Basic Designs, or the SurfSafe. (Clockwise left to right—SeaSafe, MiniSafe, SurfSafe [middle], Seal Pak [bottom right].)

endorsed to cover Off Premises Theft. Check the limits, though—your $1,600 canoe may need to be itemized on the policy, and there may be a limit to the total value on one claim. You might be surprised at the actual replacement cost of all your gear.

There are generally fewer "undesirables" in the backcountry. However, trailheads and viewpoints are often deliberate targets of criminal activity. For this reason, theft warning signs are often posted in these locations. Even technical equipment like climbing ropes and hardware is stolen from vehicles, and people's vehicles have been completely emptied. Generally, the farther off the beaten track you are the better.

It's wise to be very careful about your gear, money and valuables in huts and hostels, too. Use a money belt or small fanny pack that goes everywhere you do. A waterproof fanny pack (Cascade Designs), waterproof money belt (Ortlieb) or fanny box (Basic Designs) even allows you to take your valuables into the shower, pool, lake or ocean, so someone doesn't have to stand on guard.

In hostels, keep your gear together, and in your pack or a plastic bag. Don't leave gear in a communal drying area longer than you need. Distinctive markings on look-alike items like ski skins can avoid bleary-eyed morning confusion in a poorly lit hut. Keep your food bag tightly closed and put away. Even be careful with your fuel—there was an incident where someone's carefully calculated fuel supply for their trip was raided to run the hut lantern for a late-night card game and they consequently had to abort their trip.

Medical Insurance

An injury in a remote area can prove very expensive unless you have appropriate medical insurance. Check whether costs of evacuation from medical emergencies are covered by your medical insurance plan. Ambulance services are sometimes not included or have limits. If you are going outside your home province there may or may not be a reciprocal ambulance cost coverage. If you buy travel insurance, check the small print on ambulance services carefully. Insurance usually includes "local" ambulance service, which to most people

in most travel situations just means a conventional ground ambulance. However, in remote roadless areas it often means an aircraft. Check with your insurer that this will be covered. Try to make them understand the difference between this type of "air ambulance" for primary evacuation in a remote area and what they are more used to dealing with as an "air ambulance." They are more familiar with a specially equipped aircraft used to transport a person from a medical facility back to their home country or home medical facility. They generally insist that this be preauthorized after consultation between an attending doctor and the insurance company. Obviously if you are out in the wilderness needing primary evacuation, you are not likely to be able to enter into discussions with doctors and insurance companies! Document everything and use common sense and usually things can be sorted out satisfactorily if the case is legitimate. In the meantime you might run up a big credit card bill. Make sure you have plenty of credit available before you set off on your trip, just in case.

Check carefully that the activities you will be engaging in are covered. You may have to pay additional fees or have difficulty obtaining coverage for activities such as mountaineering, hang gliding, etc. Also check what they really mean by "mountaineering," "canoeing," "skiing," etc. For example, a British travel insurance plan for one of my visitors excluded "canoeing." I realized that in Britain, "canoeing" really means kayaking, so I wrote to the company. In fact they did include what we in North America call "canoeing." See also Paying for Rescues, page 358.

The contents of this chapter perhaps strike a sombre note. However, regulations are rarely burdensome to those who are treating the wilderness and other people with respect. Liability claims are not common (at least in Canada), and like personal or equipment security problems, you can prevent most of them with a little forethought and care. Take precautions, stay wary and keep your eyes open. Then you've done all you can, there is no point in worrying about it, so get on with enjoying yourself.

Chapter 5

Clothing and Equipment

Modern clothing and equipment has made it possible for many more people to enjoy the outdoors than in the past. Because of the availability of lightweight, high performance, reliable and comfortable gear, the outdoors is no longer the preserve of the very fit, the very strong or the masochistic. However, with outdoor recreation becoming more popular there is more equipment available to choose from and quality and design are not always good. Because of the remoteness of the backcountry in Alaska and Canada, and the difficulty of escape or resupply, the gear you choose must have *maximum effectiveness and maximum reliability*. You certainly cannot afford to have equipment fail in the middle of a trip. Because you are likely to be out for a long time and have to allow for a variety of weather, the equipment must also have *maximum versatility* and *minimum weight*. You should therefore spend the time and money to outfit yourself well.

Clothing

In Canada and Alaska "abnormal" extremes of weather are normal! You may be stripped down to shorts and singlet under a blazing sun. A short time later you may be wearing jackets and overpants to cope with cold, wind and rain. In bug country, special clothing may be needed to fend off swarms of blackflies or mosquitos. Versatility is essential to cope with weather changes, especially when you have to keep weight down. On serious trips you simply cannot afford the weight of inefficient clothing such as cotton jeans or thick cotton shirts and sweaters. Not only is cotton a poor insulator for its weight, it is useless in wet weather. In spite of what the marketers of a lot of cotton "outdoor" clothing would have the uninformed public believe, knowledgable outdoorspeople in Canada and Alaska have little use for heavy cotton garments, unless they have a lodge to retreat to. The best way to ensure comfort and keep weight down is to buy high quality clothing and to use a system of layering made of modern, functional, technical fabrics.

Underwear

A young lady once accosted me on a ski trail and announced, "That underwear you told me about changed my life!" This of course aroused considerable interest from my wife, until it became apparent that the lady was an alumnus of one of my ski courses! Modern synthetic moisture-transporting "technical" underwear fabrics have revolutionized outdoor comfort, eliminating chilling after you build up a sweat. The polyesters seem to be the best, and of these, I have had most success with Patagonia Capilene, Nike ACG and particularly the new Polartec 100 series BiPolar next to skin fabrics. There are numerous other fabrics in various weights for various activity levels and with varying prices and washabilities. These include Blue Johns and other chlorofibres, Lifa and other polypropylenes, Thermax, Thermastat and Duofold. Cotton underwear is useless except in hot weather when you want to stay cool. It has been appropriately dubbed "killer cotton" at inquests into hypothermia deaths. It absorbs sweat or rain water into its fibres, destroying their insulation properties. Moisture is held against the skin where it causes large amounts of cooling through evaporative heat loss and usually at times when you don't want it.

Insulation Clothing

Synthetic piles and fleeces (usually polyester) outperform wool in terms of their insulation for a given weight. They also absorb very little water and dry quickly. Even when wet they continue to insulate. Several thin layers are better than one thick because they dry faster and you also have more versatility in terms of choosing the desired amount of insulation for the conditions and exertion level. Fashion garments tend to be too short in the body and too baggy in the sleeves for optimum performance in the backcountry.

Thick, quilted down and synthetic jackets are useful for around camp and possibly for travel in extreme conditions. Remember that down loses much of its insulation if damp with condensed sweat or exterior moisture. One thick jacket does not provide the versatility and quick drying of several thin ones, and goes against the principles of layering. In cold conditions it is essential to avoid a buildup of frozen body moisture in the insulation, by avoiding sweating. It happens to some extent anyway, but by layering, condensation can be confined to a single outer garment that can be dried independently of the others.

Shells

A reliable waterproof shell jacket and pants are essential in spring, summer and fall, because if you get wet you can quickly become hypothermic in a rainstorm. Waterproof-breathable materials are versatile because one garment serves as both crucial, lifesaving raingear and also as windgear. My experience, and that of everyone I talk to who does not have an axe to grind, indicates that GoreTex still has the best ratio of waterproofness to breathability for active recreational travellers in most climates. If you choose one of the cheaper waterproof-breathable fabrics, remember that the fabric must be waterproof and all the seams must be tape-sealed. **Except** in winter, you are safer with something that is waterproof and has poor breathability than you are with something not waterproof with good breathability.

In winter, breathability takes precedence over waterproofness except in warm, wet, coastal climates. For windproofness and breathability while retaining adequate water repellency, modern, tightly woven microfibres

Cotton absorbs and holds sweat against the skin, causing a chilling effect when you stop, so it is of little use except in hot weather.

A well-designed hood with enough fullness to protect the side of the face and to cover a hat without the whole jacket hanging off the top of your head.

such as Super Microft and Hydrenaline are very effective even as a light fabric. They are not quite as windproof as GoreTex or Gore Activent, but I have had great success with a one-piece Super Microft shell suit for ski touring in all but the worst weather.

You must decide whether you need a lot of durability for your particular activity. Some heavy-duty shell clothing is heavy and if the durability is not needed, you can save a kilogram of weight with lighter garments. Shells do not have to be thick and heavy anymore to provide needed protection. The effective part of Gore Activent and GoreTex is a very light membrane, and the fabric to which it is applied can be very light without compromising effectiveness. Patagonia's Gridstop, a fabric reinforced with aramid (Kevlar is an aramid), is very light and extremely durable and has a Gore membrane applied to it.

Look for adequate length in the body and sleeves for freedom of movement without riding up. Really long sleeves that will cover your hands when hiking in the rain are useful. Also look for hoods big enough to protect the side of the face and to do up properly over a hat without the jacket hanging off the top of your head. Look for a bend built in to the pant knees and bum, and into sleeve elbows to provide freedom of movement. Also look for full-length separating zippers on pant legs to make them easy to get on and off over muddy boots.

Sun Protection Clothing

Wide-brimmed hats such as Tilley Hats and cowboy hats work well. Baseball-style caps, like so many fashion items, are of little use. All they do is keep the sun out of your eyes, and there are numerous cases of skin cancers around the ears to prove it. If you really must wear this style of cap, use a bandanna, French Legionnaire style. Many light fabrics are surprisingly transparent to UV, especially when wet or worn skin tight. See page 275 in Health section.

Good rainwear will usually allow you to enjoy yourself no matter what the weather.

Boots

In response to a surge in demand for "outdoor look" products, the range of boots available has expanded enormously. Unfortunately, everything that looks like a hiking boot is not actually a hiking boot and buyers must beware. While there are some excellent products available, there are some similar-looking products that do not work well for serious hiking, especially in the backcountry.

Boots must provide adequate grip for safety and must protect your feet from bruising through the soles and sides on rough ground. You should test to get some indication of the sole's resistance to distortion and of the ease with which rocks will be felt through it. Test for this by pressing with your thumbs to see if you can push the middle of the sole upward. Also flex the sole and look for a steady bend all along the sole rather than a sudden "hinge-like" flex under the ball of the foot where the stiff shank ends.

It is important to have support to keep the ankle from rolling and to keep the foot from distorting, particularly when carrying a load. Many people push their luck by using boots that provide inadequate support for backpack-ing. The extra load in your pack increases the likelihood of injury, and you need support to prevent this. By definition, a backpacker will be farther from help when injury occurs. Check for a good, stiff heel cup or "counter" by squeezing the heel and ankle area of the boot. Try twisting the boot along a lengthwise axis, too.

Fabric-leather composite boots are popular, but have limitations in weatherproofness. They do not usually keep the wet out because of their multitude of seams, although GoreTex linings can help. The stretch GoreTex oversocks by Rocky are a handy item to use in wet weather. Fabric-leather boots do not necessarily breathe all that well either, depending on the type of fabric.

Leather technology is changing all the time with new proprietary treatments improving waterproofness and breathability of leather boots. Good quality leather keeps its shape well, is durable, highly water repellent and breathable, and absorbs less moisture, but cheap leather performs poorly in these respects.

You can buy both fabric and leather boots with absorbent synthetic linings. The linings do absorb sweat well, but they also draw leakage in from outside if the boot leaks at all. I'd

Insulated booties are great in your tent or sleeping bag. Knee-high cover (right) enables you to step outside.

Waterproof-breathable oversocks make your light hiking boots much more versatile for a variety of conditions. Left, GoreTex socks by Rocky and SealSkinz by DuPont.

Bama Sokkettes will keep your socks dry in rubber boots, and mesh insoles will keep your feet drier by keeping your liners out of the frost or condensation layer.

rather have the option of a less absorbent lining and removing damp, sweaty socks, and replacing them with dry ones. I then just hang the damp socks on my pack with large safety pins to dry and continue hiking. The boot liners cannot dry as you walk! Absorbent linings are a nuisance if you wear the boots to ford a stream because they hold lots of water to wet your socks when you put them back on. The oversocks mentioned above are handy to put on in the wet boot to keep your socks dry after crossing.

For winter use it is essential that there is plenty of room in the boots with no tight spots. Felt-lined boots are popular, but the cheapies have poor quality felt that absorbs moisture into the fibres and then ceases to insulate well. Look for a high specified percentage of wool and synthetics, and no cotton. Spare liners are useful to carry in case the others become damp. Mesh insoles between liner and boot sole work well to prevent frost melting and soaking back into the liner. The frost that forms against the inside of the boot stays in the holes in the mesh insole. You should remove them periodically and beat out the frost.

Cross-country skiers with light gear should be aware of how quickly their feet will cool down if they are immobilized for any reason. They should carry a spare pair of socks to replace sweat-soaked ones, especially as some boots breathe poorly.

Overbooties in neoprene or pile help keep feet warmer, as do gaiters and long overpants. For backcountry tourers, supergaiters are a great help, especially if insulated. With double boots, the newer foam inners insulate better than older models and do not absorb as much water. However, they are more difficult to dry than a sock on a long trip. The GoreTex waterproof-breathable oversocks could be useful if your liners get too damp and keep on wetting your dry socks. They are also useful on spring tours in wet snow.

Climbers using plastic boots need to be aware of their limitations in the extreme cold conditions of Alaska in particular. Insulated supergaiters are some help but really it is better to have extra insulation under the foot as well. It is also important to be aware of the swelling of some types of foam liner that occurs at high altitudes and that can constrict the foot. Spare liners should be carried when climbing in these areas so you have dry liners. Closed cell insulations are more effective on long trips than the absorbent types that soon get wet. Many people use vapour barriers, either made of neoprene foam or of coated nylon, to keep their boot insulation drier. "Mouse boots" are popular for cold, nontechnical terrain because of their built-in vapour barrier design that prevents the insulation from becoming wet.

Insulated camp booties with lightweight kneelength covers are great for snowcamping as you can wear the booties in your sleeping bag and put the covers on to go outside if necessary.

Gloves

If your hands become cold you can become helpless and unable to manipulate the clothes and equipment required to prevent hypothermia and possibly even death. If you let your hands get frostbitten, you are in serious trouble. Paddlers and cyclists and people in the mountains and the north should always have gloves with them, no matter what the season.

In extreme cold, mitts are of course warmer than gloves. Whatever you wear it must be big enough and not constricting, especially when the hand is clenched around a ski pole, ice axe, shovel or paddle. Windproofness and breathability are important in extreme cold, and I have had good success with GoreTex glove shells. GoreTex liners for gloves and mitts made of other materials are now much improved. Waterproof palms are important because snow tends to lodge between the palm and the tool you are holding, and then melt. A good grip is also essential. Dexterity is needed at times, and it is useful to have thick, warm gloves as well as thin liner gloves to use depending on how much dexterity is needed. Some people like fingerless gloves. For serious winter use it is essential that the gloves or mitts have a long gauntlet to overlap the sleeve cuff and form a good seal. It is also important that the gauntlet closes tight around the forearm with a snowproof and windproof seal. By far

A selection of gloves, mitts and liners.

the most effective seal is created by an elastic drawcord and tethered cordlock. It is vastly superior to Velcro and straps because it is right at the edge of the gauntlet and does not leave a place for snow to accumulate and work its way inside. Some gauntlets are not big enough to fit easily over a bulky sleeve, so be careful when you are making a purchase.

Removable glove or mitt liners that are held in place by Velcro are useful so you can carry spares to substitute when the others get wet. If you want to use a vapour barrier system with your gloves you can use surgical gloves next to your skin. Then you can even use insulated rubber work gloves if you are, say, digging in wet snow.

Glove liners are made of a number of different materials. I have had good success with fibrefills, Thinsulate, pile, fleece and of course wool. Some people recommend down for extreme cold conditions, but on a long trip you should consider using a vapour barrier with this type of insulation because it is so easily compromised by moisture. To make your liners easier and safer to hang up to dry, attach short cords or loops. Idiot strings are often used with

mitts and gloves so that they cannot blow away or fall down the mountainside or into a crevasse. They tend, however, to be attached such that snow easily falls into or is scooped into the gauntlet. Try attaching the cord to the wrist of the glove so the gauntlet flops over and closes. If you don't like idiot cords, attach snap hooks that can be clipped easily onto a ring on your jacket or pack. Make sure it is easily undone when your hands are cold and you are desperate to put the gloves back on.

Equipment

People do get away with using poorly designed, low quality or ineffective gear, but it is usually because they are lucky with the weather. They also get away with using inherently unreliable gear, perhaps because it just didn't happen to break or leak on that particular trip. These are high-stakes gambles you should not take when far from help in the real wilderness.

Minimum weight is important because of the distances you have to carry your equipment, especially because you may also be carrying a heavy load of food for a long trip. Weight can be kept down by choosing versatile gear. As a friend of mine once said, if it doesn't have at least two uses, don't carry it into the backcountry! High quality materials and construction can provide enough durability without excess weight.

Sleeping Bags and Pads

Inadequate sleep can have serious consequences by making you more accident-prone and by lowering your resistance to cold and fatigue. A cumulative lack of sleep on a long trip can be disastrous. You must therefore have a good enough sleeping bag to be certain of sleeping well. It's therefore good to have a somewhat higher performance bag than you really need. Then, when its performance is impaired by damp or when you are "sleeping cold" because the weather is bad or you are tired or malnourished or ill, you will still sleep well.

Above: Glove shells must be breathable, otherwise condensation and frost will form in the liner and you will get wet, cold hands. Below: Elastic drawcords with a tethered cordlock provide the best seal.

Manufacturers' temperature ratings of sleeping bag performance are somewhat subjective. The loft or thickness of a bag is not an infallible guide because the presence of design features such as a draft collar and a good hood can make one bag warmer than another one with similar loft but lacking the features. Also, some new materials provide far more insulation than traditional materials.

Mummy-shaped bags are far warmer for a given weight than are rectangular or barrel-shaped bags without hoods. Good down is still a better insulator than synthetic for a given weight, compressibility and durability. However, down is more costly in the beginning and loses more insulation when damp than do synthetic. The performance, durability and weight gap between down and synthetic is narrowing fast, and synthetic fill bags are a good choice for long trips and damp climates.

Down quality is only measured reliably in terms of its fill rating. The standard for quality sleeping bags is a fill rating of 550 cubic inches per ounce, and the best is 650 or even 700.

Avoid sleeping bags made with heavy external fabrics and thick cotton or flannel linings. The fabric adds no insulation, and even with lightweight fabrics, about half the weight of the bag is fabric weight.

All sleeping bags, but especially down bags, work better in winter when protected from condensing body moisture with a vapour barrier lining (VBL). VBLs virtually eliminate the inexorable buildup of moisture from your body that occurs in a sleeping bag over several successive nights. VBLs are simply a waterproof lining that goes **inside** the bag, working exactly the same way as the waterproof vapour barrier in the walls of a house. Just as the house version prevents house water vapour from entering and condensing in the insulation, so the sleeping bag version prevents body moisture entry. Learning to use these liners before a big expedition is advisable, because they take a little getting used to. They really do work, and you do not wake up in a puddle of condensation, because the barrier is on the warm side of the insulation. You may get sweaty if you overheat, in which case you must ventilate the bag.

In an experiment I recorded an overnight accumulation of as much as 110 grams of moisture (almost a half cup) in a sleeping bag without a VBL in the dry, cold environment of my garage. On the other hand, when using a VBL and a bivy bag cover, I have had only about the same accumulation after *five* successive nights in a damp snowcave.

High-tech sleeping-bag fabrics such as Gore Dry-Loft and breathable bivy bag covers do improve the temperature rating of a sleeping bag by keeping air movement out of the outer part of the insulation. Some people feel that they cause condensation, but this observation needs to be considered carefully. The condensation you see on the inside of a breathable GoreTex bag cover might in fact have occurred deep in the insulation if it were not for the improved efficiency of the bag caused by the presence of the cover. The condensation would then be invisible but would be insidiously impairing the insulation's efficiency. A GoreTex sleeping bag or sleeping bag cover also makes it much easier to keep your bag dry in a tent in really awful weather.

If you are using a double sleeping bag, a thin synthetic bag is a good overbag because the condensation will occur in the outer bag. The synthetic is less affected than down and the overbag can be removed and dried easily.

When down is dry it is fluffy, with many air spaces to form an insulator, but as soon as it becomes damp the fluffiness is destroyed along with the insulating power.

Comfortable sleeping pads are easily worth their weight. Closed-cell foam pads are absolutely reliable and still work when fire sparks fall on them, when bug repellent is spilt on them or they get abraded by being placed in an exposed place on the outside of a pack. Cheap blue foam with large bubbles visible on the edge is definitely inferior to the higher quality blue or yellow foam with smaller pores available from specialty stores.

I still remember an old Austrian guide snorting disdainfully at my new Therm-a-Rest 15 years ago, muttering, "A closed cell pad will never go down in the night." Well, after 15 years of use, from the tropics to the Arctic and from ocean beaches to the Himalayas, my Therm-a-Rest is still going strong and has never let me down. I just take care to follow the care instructions that came with it. Newer versions are thicker, lighter and less slippery. Some are as light as 350 grams. Take a Therm-a-Rest repair kit with you just in case you damage your mat.

These packs by The North Face are available with a variety of shoulder straps and hipbelts to allow you to mix and match to obtain a custom fit.

Packs

The need to be more self-sufficient means that packs for use in Canada and Alaska are usually larger than those used in Europe. Not only must you be prepared to carry more stuff, but a pack must also be big enough to put everything inside so gear is reasonably protected and cannot fall off. Try to avoid the tendency with a big pack to take too much gear! Day packs must be large as well, because on a day trip you need to carry emergency gear.

Correct fitting is essential. If you are not an average-sized person, buy only a make of pack that comes in various sizes. Do not buy a "one size adjusts to fit all" pack if you are far from a normal size and would have to adjust its harness very much. The harness may fit, but the load will be out of position and too unwieldy. Women's backs are shorter than men's, and they have a different shape to their shoulders and hips, which demands different hip belts and shoulder straps. For this reason women should buy a pack that is a women's model and is not only sized accordingly, but is also shaped accordingly. Some packs have a variety of different sizes and even more variety of shoulder strap and hip belt sizes and shapes that can be changed to suit different people.

Compression stuffsacks are useful with synthetic-fill bags, but never leave the bag tightly stuffed for longer than necessary and certainly not in a hot car trunk.

Pack fabrics are usually waterproof when new, but the seams are not. Carry a waterproof pack cover, and keep your gear in plastic bags inside the pack. You can line the entire pack with a large clear garbage bag. You cannot afford to get to the end of a hard, wet day to find that your dry clothes and sleeping bag are wet.

Tents

Again because retreat is difficult or impossible from remote trips, your tent must be capable of withstanding the weather conditions you encounter and of continuing to protect you adequately for the duration of your trip. People tend to think that only winter tents have to be the highest quality and reliability models. However, in winter at least you have the option of building a snow cave or igloo if your tent fails. It is far more difficult to improvise protection from summer rain, wind and bugs, so you need a very reliable unit in summer, too.

Insect protection is absolutely mandatory for summer use in Canada and Alaska. This means not just mosquito netting, but no-see-um-proof netting to protect against these tiny, well-named pests. Unless you can totally seal the tent while still having adequate ventilation, you are assured of sleepless nights. Zippers must be high quality, durable and reliable.

Light weight is essential, but nowadays you can get excellent protection from a two-person tent weighing less than 3.2 kilograms. However, it can be claustrophobic in these tents. Carefully consider the balance between size (and its associated comfort) and weight. If you expect to have to "live" in the tent because of bugs or bad weather, you want a bigger tent than one you will just sleep in.

Liveability is enhanced by porches or vestibules that you can leave open in a moderate storm so you still have ventilation, a view, and do not feel cooped up. The wind catches under these porches. Large ceiling vent panels also help, but if they cannot be closed they are a liability in windy weather.

Rainproofness is greatly improved by a fly sheet that extends to the ground, and the best stormproofing comes from fly sheets that extend to the ground all round. Higher quality tents will have better and more durable waterproof coatings on floors and flies, and may even have tape-sealed seams on floor and fly.

If you are camping above treeline or in exposed places such as river and ocean beaches, wind stability and resistance to noisy sleep-robbing flapping is important. All-round, to-the-ground flies shed the wind better than other types because there are no porches for wind to get up under. Lower, more streamlined

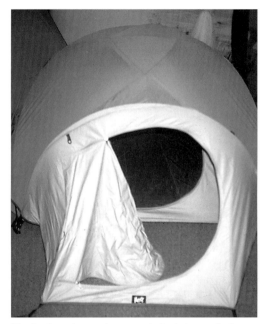

Circular door zippers give you a choice in how and where you partially open the door so you have more control over what enters with you. Note good headroom in vestibule.

The flysheet on this Sierra Designs Stretch Dome extends almost to the ground for good rain protection.

A 1.5 metre length of cord attached to peg-loops enables you to secure the floor taut so the tent sets properly, even if you cannot insert pegs in the right places.

shapes come into their own in a wind, and dome tents with a geodesic pole arrangement where the poles cross in many places are better than those where they cross just at the peak.

Look carefully at the door and fly sheet design to check that you can enter and exit without rain falling on the floor. Also look at the zipper layout. An inverted U shape means that you have to completely open the door to enter and exit, allowing all sorts of snow and bugs and rain to enter. An L or upright U or a C zipper allows you to open the door just enough at the bottom to dive in or out. Good tents will have good quality YKK #7 or 8 door zippers that do not fail if used reasonably. A zipper failure in bug country can be very serious. In sandy areas, keep the zipper out of the sand and clean it with an old toothbrush.

Ease of pitching becomes very important in a storm, when the bugs are bad, it's dark or you are tired. Hook systems, continuous sleeves, one-way sleeves and "Quick Pitch" systems all greatly speed up the process. Cheap tents with fibreglass poles with external ferrules that do not slide easily through pole sleeves are a real chore to put up.

Dark-coloured tents and opaque, aluminized fabric tents are very depressing and claustrophobic if you spend a lot of time tentbound. These dark, drab colours seem to be particularly popular in some countries outside North America. However, in those countries long trips are less common and the aesthetics of a less conspicuous tent is more important in those countries because of the intensive use of back-country areas.

Canoeing and Kayaking Gear

The water in the rivers and lakes of northern and western Canada and Alaska, and in all the oceans, is cold. An unexpected dunking can be very serious, especially as the air temperature may delude you into a false sense of security and into wearing few clothes. On wilderness trips, carrying a Farmer-John wet suit or a dry suit to be put on for running rapids or for open crossings gives you an extra margin of safety and improves your chances if you have a mishap. Make sure the knees allow you to kneel without cutting off the circulation. Wet suits are not particularly pleasant to wear day after day, though a thin suit

of synthetic underwear underneath helps. Dry suits are more comfortable, especially if you wear appropriate clothing underneath to avoid overheating and to absorb condensation. The ultimate luxury is the $700 Kokatat GoreTex dry suit in which you can be both comfortable and safe. I find I can temporarily overload the breathability and get damp if I'm unreasonable and allow myself to get ridiculously hot. However, I soon dry out again and generally I can stay very dry and comfortable in this suit. I can take it off at the end of the day and carry on wearing the same clothes—they are not wet and sticky. No leaks in four seasons.

A rain suit over your clothes slows the rate at which you lose heat when swimming in the water, but it must not have elastic wrist or ankle cuffs. They must be closed with Velcro or snaps so you can drain them when trying to get out of the water. Waterfilled rainpants can be a real hazard, especially if they get pulled down round your knees by the weight of the water.

Wet suit gloves or Pogies make life more comfortable, especially on cold, rainy days. You can improve the glove grip by smearing them with rubbery glue and letting it harden. Wet suit booties are also a boon on all types of trips. I prefer to wear booties and large, cheap running shoes or cheap, light hiking boots over them, rather than windsurfing booties with soles. Those soles are too thin to walk comfortably on anything other than beach sand, and you could of course have to scramble or portage over rough terrain. Keeping your hiking boots available can make a rough portage easier and safer. Felt-soled paddling booties are now available and provide an excellent grip on slippery rocks.

Whatever type of footwear you wear in the boat, it must stay securely on your feet if you have to swim. You don't want to get ashore with no shoes and have to hobble barefoot through the rocks and brush in pursuit of your boat. This is the big disadvantage of rubber boots for canoeing on cold northern rivers— you'll kick them off or lose them if you swim, leaving you with no footgear when you get ashore. Tighter-fitting rubbers designed for yachting generally don't have good soles for walking onshore. I still have a newspaper clipping about a canoeing accident with the heading "Barefoot man walks 80 miles through bush," so if you do wear rubbers, you may want to keep some light sandals or cheap runners in your lifejacket back pocket. I recently picked up a barefoot hitchhiker who had lost his canoe and gear in the rapids and had walked several kilometres to the road. His feet were very sore!

Rubber boot users should wear mesh insoles inside the boots, along with Bama Sokkettes if you can find them. They are marvellous at controlling condensation moisture in your rubber boots and keeping your feet dry. If you cannot find them, you can wear a large cotton sock **over** a wool or synthetic sock so the cotton absorbs condensation and keeps it from soaking into socks underneath. See photo page 143.

Personal Flotation Devices (PFDs) need to be adjustable to accommodate the extra clothing you need to wear in bad weather. Needless to say they should be safety orange, yellow or red in colour. There are manufacturers who make other colours for presumably fashion reasons, and these are thankfully not government approved. Thigh loops are a good safety feature, especially in serious whitewater, and for that type of paddling an extra-flotation jacket (24 pounds rather than the standard 15$\frac{1}{2}$ pounds buoyancy) is good insurance.

Pockets on the PFD allow you to carry essential survival items, but avoid loading them to the point that the PFD won't keep you afloat the right way up. Some extremely effective PFDs are not government approved because they have pockets that could be overloaded. A good whistle attached to the jacket is essential and most skilled whitewater paddlers have a knife attached as well. Cheapie whistles are inferior, and it's worth buying a Fox 40 real whistle.

Keeping gear dry is easier now that there is a wide variety of specialized fabric and rigid containers available to canoeists. Don't take any chances and risk not having the dry clothes and sleeping bag you need to prevent life threatening hypothermia after a capsize. I heard of a youth group leader who told his group that each morning at embarkation time he would grab someone's pack at random and throw it in the river. You should only embark on a wilderness paddling trip if you would have no worries about someone doing that to your pack!

Spray covers are a boon for canoe tripping when the weather is cold and wet. The lower body stays distinctly warmer and the boat contents stay drier. However, spray covers must be easy to attach and remove. It is also absolutely essential that in the event of a capsize the paddlers can be certain of getting free of the cover quickly. My spray cover has separate kayak-style cockpits with kayak-style break-away spray skirts.

A selection of footwear and handwear for paddling on cold waters.

The large pocket on this Serratus Expedition PFD allows you to keep survival items with you all the time in case you are separated from your boat. Don't overload!

Dry suits are great for comfort and safety on cold northern rivers and oceans, and this GoreTex waterproof-breathable suit by Kokatat is the ultimate.

It is easier to keep your gear dry with the wide selection of waterproof containers now available.

This full-length spraycover by Totem Outfitters of Calgary, Canada, provides warmth and a wider safety margin for wilderness paddlers, but should not be regarded as a substitute for paddling skill.

Various methods of attachment all have their devotees, including wide, full length Velcro, snaps, D-rings and lacing and tensioned cables.

Most people think of spray covers primarily as a means of avoiding swamping in big waves. They do a good job of this, but paddlers must avoid the trap of overconfidence that can be induced by spray covers. On remote wilderness trips a spray cover should be looked on more as something that widens your safety margin in long rapids or open crossings where you could progressively fill up with splashes. It is dangerous for you to believe that you now have a closed boat and can run bigger rapids than you would normally run. It is even more dangerous to use it to offset a lack of manoeuvring skill by allowing you to bash and crash down the river through the big waves, out of control and being taken wherever the river wants to take you. I have seen parties on very remote rivers doing just that, when a little skill would enable them to take a much safer route.

Water tends to pool on the deck, and because it is high up and sloshing around, it can make the boat very unstable. A spray deck can also make the canoe more "edgy" because the water piles on the deck on one side rather than immediately sloshing into the bottom centre. Keeping the deck tight or arched with hoops or vertical poles helps prevent this. Unfortu-

A well-outfitted canoe is more comfortable and easier and safer to paddle, but a rental canoe may be totally bare.

nately, nylon shrinks in hot sun and goes slack when cooled with cold water.

Most canoeists outfit their canoes with attachments for comfort and safety. This is time-consuming and costly, and therefore rental canoes often do not have any "outfitting" such as built-in knee pads, thigh straps, tiedowns and grab loops.

Knee pads and thigh pads can be temporarily attached to rental boats by covering the area with tape, rubbing it for a firm bond and then attaching the pads with double-sided carpet tape. An outfitter who lets out his boats without proper grab-loops may not be clued-in enough to let you drill holes and fit proper ones through the hull. You will have to remember to factor in the lack of grab loops to your risk management equations. You can't put much force on a deck plate rope attachment, and you want to retrieve the hull, not just the deck plate! Similarly, a lack of proper tiedowns can make a swamping more serious so you will have to factor that in, too. Without being properly tied down onto the bottom of the boat, the gear cannot provide buoyancy. (There are two schools of thought about tying gear into canoes. One school says tie it in firmly to provide buoyancy and minimum drag so the swamped canoe can still be paddled or dragged ashore. The other says to tie packs loosely to the boat with two-metre lanyards so you can, in theory, empty the boat, get back in and then retrieve the gear. Personally I prefer the former method, partly because I don't like to risk being tangled up in a mess of packs and ropes. I tie down my packs with quick release Fastex buckle and Velcro systems.)

Ski Touring Gear

Most ski touring in the mountains is in remote areas that, unlike the Alps, do not have a chairlift on almost every peak and dozens of people on every route. Clothing and equipment must therefore be of the highest reliability. It is essential to carry enough repair tools and materials for your ski equipment and know how to use them.

With the absence of chairlift or cable car access, approaches can be long. This is one reason why the lighter Telemark style equipment is more popular in Canada than is alpine touring equipment. Unless your alpine boots fit really well, the long approaches can be killers and blisters can be a serious problem.

Rescue is not easy to obtain, so enough first aid and survival gear must be carried on day trips to care for an injured person and to equip the party for an emergency overnight stay.

Avalanche rescue services are unlikely to arrive in time to help a buried victim, so each group member must carry an avalanche transceiver and a strong shovel. Avalanche probes or probe poles are also recommended. Single frequency, 457 kHz transceivers are now standard in North America. They are vastly superior to the old 2.275 kHz units, but despite this many people still use the old frequency. All members of a party MUST be on the same frequency. Carry spare batteries. It's also useful to have a spare unit in case someone's transceiver is not working. It is very important that all members of the group have practised transceiver search techniques and know the procedures for backcountry avalanche rescue.

Ski run-away straps are worn by many backcountry skiers, especially if they have releasable bindings, including releasable Telemark bindings. However, safety straps do mean that there is less chance that you will survive an avalanche because there is more likelihood of the skis dragging you down. One philosophy says to only wear safety straps where losing your skis would create a serious or life-threatening problem, but this could be interpreted to mean a lot of places in the Canadian and Alaskan mountains. Compromise solutions to the dilemma include safety straps that would break away in an avalanche but not in a fall or crevasse fall. Lost skis can be found using the Ortovox F1 Plus transceiver in conjunction with "Ski Maus" transmitters attached to skis.

A lower-tech system to help find a detached ski is to use five metres of flagging tape tied to the ski and inserted into the bottom of your pants or your gaiter.

Unlike in the more populated areas of Europe, you are likely to be selecting and breaking your own trail. No one is ahead of you to "test" the snowbridges! Parties must be prepared with ropes, slings, harnesses and the skills to carry out crevasse rescues by themselves. There are unlikely to be other parties around to help with a 10-person "all heave on a count of three" type rescue. Remoteness

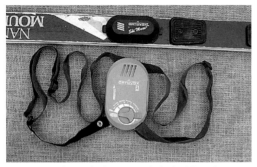
Ortovox F1 Plus with ski maus to help find lost skis.

means that loss of gear in a crevasse could have serious consequences, so glacier travellers must be equipped to secure their equipment independently to the rope system. Not many people practise crevasse rescues enough, let alone practising with a pack and skis on, or when dragging a 40-kilogram pulk.

Snowshoes

Snowshoes are the traditional means of winter foot travel in North America and were in use for thousands of years before the introduction of the ski by Europeans.

Snowshoes offer a number of advantages over skis. They are relatively simple and so equipment failure is unlikely. If a breakage occurs, repair is easy. Most importantly, snowshoes can be worn with the bulkiest of insulated nontechnical boots, whereas skis demand technical boots and bindings that hinder the use of extra insulation.

Skiing is generally more fun than snowshoeing. However, with a very heavy expedition pack it is not much fun unless you are a very good skier. It is even less fun skiing when roped for glacier travel, especially if you keep the rope tight enough to be much use. Skis have the advantage of speed and competent skiers will probably be faster over a long distance with consistent terrain and with good snow. On the other hand, snowshoers are less exposed to injury, and don't spend extra energy recovering after falls.

In some broken country such as much of the Canadian Shield, snowshoers can take a more direct route, while skiers will be detouring, putting skins on or taking them off and not really having fun on the short downhills. The looseness of the snow often means that waxes do not provide the needed climbing power for anything other than circuitous routes in this type of country. Skins are a great help for trailbreaking, even on the flats.

Expeditioners should consider the pros and cons of skis and snowshoes very carefully, especially the safety aspect. Safety is a very important consideration in the remote winter wilderness where an injury could be devastating. The speed of a party is limited to that of the slowest person anyway, and you only need one weak skier to put the party at risk and make the party as slow as snowshoers.

Snowshoes come in a wide variety of sizes, shapes and materials to suit a wide range of purposes and conditions.

Smaller sizes are suitable for compact snow, uneven or brushy terrain, and of course smaller people. Compact snow is the windpacked snow of open country, the snow encountered once the spring freeze-thaw cycle is under way and the wet snow in warmer areas. The latter soon settles to form a base and it packs quickly under the weight of the snowshoer. The Bearpaw snowshoe of the eastern regions is a typical small- to medium-size oval shape, and the Green Mountain Bearpaw is a more elongated version for better sideslope performance.

In the mountains, frequent heavy fresh snowfalls mean you may encounter deep powder. In spite of this, many mountaineers use quite small snowshoes, even though they sink more deeply, because they are easier to manoeuvre in steep and uneven ground and on sideslopes. They also look for snowshoes with little or no front turnup. Although this means they are not as easy to use for straightforward walking, the toes can at least be kicked into steep terrain.

Larger snowshoes or "trail snowshoes" are less manoeuvrable but sink in less. They therefore suit long-distance travel in deep, unconsolidated snow in unobstructed terrain or on trails. They are more popular in regions where there is little underbrush or where heavy snowfall soon buries it. They are also used in interior regions of relatively shallow snowpack where cold, dry climates cause recrystallization of the snow, making it very loose and unsettled until the spring freeze-thaw cycle.

Friends who did an ascent of Denali 20 years ago entirely on foot from the road used long (1.7 metres) "Alaskan" style snowshoes for their long trudge from the lower levels, initially ferrying loads over relatively easy terrain. The party covered an enormous distance while ferrying, so these shoes that sank in very little were a boon. They had a large turnup at the front for easy striding, and close-spaced lacing for the cold, dry snow. They were also relatively narrow so that feet did not have to swing wide with each stride. Trail snowshoes generally have a "tail," which helps stabilize them directionally as it drags in the snow while the shoe moves forward. This is a help until you get to where you need to manoeuvre. Once the climbers reached technical terrain they found big shoes to be less suitable than smaller ones.

Traditional construction is wood frames and rawhide lacing, but shoes built this way need good maintenance. Wet snow and crusty or abrasive conditions are very hard on this construction. Neoprene/nylon lacing is ugly but more durable. Modern snowshoes use metal tubing or I-section extrusions for the frame. Better quality shoes use better quality alloys. Rather than lacing, many modern designs now use sheets of neoprene-nylon material, laced or riveted to the frame around the edges. Crampons for grip on icy terrain are often built in to these designs.

Snowshoe bindings and boots are a crucial part of the system. Traditional mukluk-style footwear had no raised, built-up heel so that there was less wear on the lacing under the foot. This type of footwear is hard to find now and people often snowshoe in footwear with hard soles and built-up heels. This is hard on traditional lacing, hence the switch to synthetic lacing materials.

Traditional footwear had a moderately pointed, tapered toe that slid forward under the toe loop until the wide part jammed and stopped it going any farther forward. The foot was kept from going too far forward by this wedging effect as much as by having a tight strap over the foot. Nowadays, problems with the foot sliding too far forward often occur because people use unsuitable footwear with traditional bindings. With untapered footwear, the toe strap often has to be too tight and cuts off circulation.

The better modern bindings incorporate a cup over the toe to form a positive forward stop for any shape of boot. They therefore do not rely on tightness across the foot to stop the boot moving forward. This type of system is simple and much safer to use because there is less risk of freezing the toes. There is less constriction of blood flow, and the cup over the toes also shields them somewhat from dragging through cold or wet snow.

Other bindings incorporate a hinged sole plate with D-rings along the side and webbing lacing over the forefoot. This holds the foot snugly in place and gives excellent control. The bindings can be used with soft or hard boots, and with soft boots the pressure is well spread out rather than being localized. For people with small feet, and children especially, a toe cup binding system can be fabricated from the front part of an old rubber boot or galosh. Punch holes in the sole so you can lace it to the snowshoe with wire.

Snowshoe bindings that incorporate a cup over the toe are warmer and more comfortable than those with a strap across the forefoot.

These rugged, modern snowshoes by Sherpa have either universal or step-in bindings, monster ice crampons and great "variable rotation" bindings that adjust for hardpack or soft snow performance.

Pulks and Toboggans

For some oversnow trips it makes more sense to drag your gear behind you than to try to carry it on your back. Most people cannot carry more than about 28 kilograms safely on their backs, which greatly limits the length of your trip. The weight of winter camping gear, technical climbing or glacier travel gear, food and fuel soon adds up.

Snowshoers successfully make long toboggan-hauling trips in deep snow and wooded country with loads that include large wall tents and collapsible woodstoves. They generally use the traditional long, narrow, wooden toboggan with a curled-front. These toboggans present a full flat surface to the snow and are around 2½ metres long, but narrow enough to follow in snowshoe tracks. They are quite flexible so they "flow" along the trail rather than jumping about on the uneven surface. The load is best kept long, low and narrow and was traditionally rolled in a long "sausage" in a tarp. The toboggans are pulled with ropes rather than with rigid shafts. The long wooden or aluminum children's toboggan available from hardware and sports stores works after a fashion, but is no comparison to a handmade specialty item.

Mountaineers needing a pack for carrying gear in difficult terrain may also encounter long stretches of easier terrain with wind- and sun-hardened snow on wide, open glaciers. In these places it's nice to save your shoulders and drag the gear instead. With a large party, even deep snow travel is feasible if people take turns to break trail with a lighter toboggan. Another method of dragging your pack used with mixed success uses a children's Krazy Karpet snow slider: a piece of flexible plastic sheet about 45 centimetres by 130 centimetres, costing about $3 and weighing about 600 grams. You lash it to the pack and by attaching a rope to the pack, it is easy to drag the slippery package over hard snow. It won't track very well, but this does not matter much on wide, open glaciers. It tends to roll over unless you pack it to produce a low centre of gravity and flat underside. Some people have put the pack in a large, very heavy-duty plastic bag and pulled that behind them.

Pulks, which are shaped more like bathtubs or ski patrol toboggans than traditional toboggans, are used on many expeditions. They work in a variety of snow conditions, especially if they are raised up in the centre. They can then either behave as a sled running on narrow side runners in hard snow or as a toboggan if the runners sink into soft snow and the raised centre touches the snow.

The cheapest and simplest pulks are children's bathtub-style snow sliders. They are made of flexible polyethylene and are big enough for a full size expedition pack and a few other items as well. I've used them on a three-week glacier trip. They can be pulled with a rope or with rigid shafts. When pulled with shafts, pulks will follow a skier at speed better. However, one seasoned sled-hauler friend who is a veteran of some very long pulk trips prefers to haul heavy pulks with ropes. The best steering control is if the shafts form a rigid frame that is always in line with the direction of the pulk, as in a Ski Patrol rescue toboggan. Ski Patrol toboggans generally have metal keels that knife into hardpack to help maintain direction, especially on sideslopes. T-section metal strips can be attached to snow sliders with bolts and wingnuts inside so you can add or remove them during the trip. Without keels the cheap toboggans track poorly, especially on sideslopes.

Shafts can be made of aluminum tube or CPVC pipe, or even the cheap but heavier electrical conduit. Attach them by threading rope through the inside of the pipe and through holes in the sled.

If the pack is tied on to a pulk so its shoulder straps are uppermost, you can pick the whole assembly up if necessary and walk along looking like a turtle. My experience suggests that relatively rigid items like packs should be tied loosely to the pulk so they do not interfere with the flexibility of the unit. If the unit can flex to absorb the shock of hitting uneven spots, there seems to be less tendency to capsize. This fits in with the traditional Inuit flexible construction of their quamutiq (komatik) sleds.

On glaciers the pack should be tied independently to the rope between the travellers. If you attach a cover to the pulk, everything does not then have to be in a pack. Pulks with attached covers are also safer in the event of a crevasse fall because everything stays together and nothing can fall off. The cover can be attached with nuts and bolts or pop rivets through a reinforcing strip of metal or plastic, or by sewing through the edge of a kid's polyethylene pulk with a heavy-duty sewing machine. Sealing the seam by gluing before bolting or riveting keeps out water from sloppy spring snow.

Longer and more serious expeditions use much more sophisticated pulks costing many hundreds of dollars. The Norwegian-made Fjellpulken is a popular, well-proven but costly item with good shafts, harness, cover, etc. Some people custom-build their own units with fibre-reinforced resins. However, it requires sophisticated knowledge to come up with the right amount of shock-absorbing flexibility and the right materials in the laminate to function well at low temperatures. High-tech runner materials can be used to make pulling easier. This is particularly important with heavy loads. Dog-sled racers generally know the latest materials and sources, but generally HDPE seems better than UHMWPE at low temperatures.

If you are using pulks or sleds in the mountains, beware of three things. Firstly, a crevasse fall could be a nightmare with a 60 kilogram pulk dangling off your waist, so make sure it is attached separately to the rope. Secondly, I won't forget the sickening feeling of seeing a loaded pulk sliding by itself for a kilometre down a glacier straight toward a crevasse. Be really meticulous about tying the pulk down when you leave it. Finally, practise skiing with a loaded pulk before you go. They are miserable on a side-slope and handling them on hardpack gets interesting if you are holding them back with the shafts. They tend to want to jackknife and sneak round beside you!

Pulks can be assembled using a cheap plastic snow slider and plastic or metal piping for shafts.

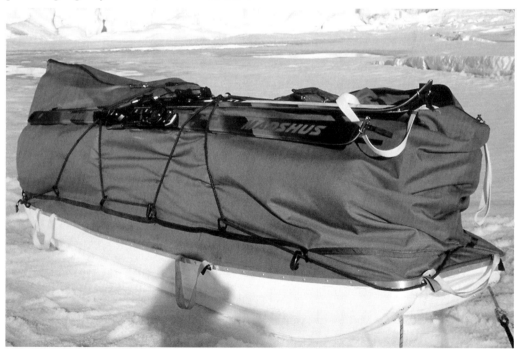

This two metre-long pulk from Arctic Light of Calgary is designed for long trips in low-angle terrain. Runners at the sides make for easy pulling on hard surfaces such as sea ice and wind-blasted snow.

Radio Equipment

Being equipped with a radio can make the difference between life and death in a serious wilderness emergency. However, there are a number of factors to consider when deciding whether to take a radio. Some people feel that the presence of a radio lessens the "wilderness feeling" and mystique. For this reason, I did not go out of the way to emphasize the existence of a radiotelephone to the clients I was wilderness guiding. I did of course make sure enough people knew where it was and how to use it if I was the subject of an emergency and unable to use it myself. Regular radio scheduled communications can spoil the atmosphere—and can create unnecessary worries if there is a breakdown in communication.

Secondly, the radio can produce a false sense of security, perhaps encouraging people to take bigger risks. This tendency is made worse by the assumption that the radio will actually work when needed, and it may not! Because of reliability problems, radio communications should be looked on as a potential bonus that will facilitate a rescue if they work, but not as a mainstay of your emergency planning. Finally, when considering whether to take a radio, you should remember that a professional organization that elected to operate without a radio might be deemed by a court to be needlessly endangering its clients.

Radios must be well protected from mechanical shock and water. Getting a rented radio wet can be an expensive error—you may find yourself compelled to buy a ruined radio for the price of a new one! Check carefully to find out the extent of your liability. If you plan on renting, take some old closed cell foam camp matting to wrap around the radio and then double-bag it in canoeist's dry bags. A truly waterproof handheld marine VHF is available. Most users of conventional handheld marine sets keep them in a sealed plastic bag such as the Sea-Tote, through which they can still work the switches and can listen and talk. Remember that for kayakers the time you will most need to use it is probably when you are swimming beside a capsized boat!

Single Sideband Radios

The workhorse of the remote areas of Canada for many years has been the HF single sideband radio (SSB), and particularly the Spillsbury SBX 11A (photo page 159). This Canadian-made radio is rugged and more reliable than most, weighs 3.6 kilograms and runs on nine "D" cells. Unlike VHF systems, HF SSBs have a long range and are not dependent on line-of-sight reception. These radios rely on the signal bouncing off the ionosphere, and the way and extent to which this occurs is highly variable. Through no fault of the design of radios themselves, they are susceptible to electrical disturbances in the ionosphere, and these are quite common, especially in the far north. Radio communication can be poor or even shut down for days or weeks at a time. Time of day, season of year, short-term solar flare activity and the long-term sunspot cycle all have a significant effect. For frequencies in the 1.6 to 8 MHz range allowed in Canada, signal propagation is generally better at night and during fall and winter rather than spring and summer. Failures are also often related to inadequate antennas. These radios work best with a long wire "dipole" aerial that needs to be stretched out, well clear of the ground and at right angles to the intended direction of transmission. This is not easy, especially in treeless areas, though I have also had good winter success with the aerial stretched out on the snow surface of glaciers.

The Spillsbury radio can be equipped with four crystals, which enables it to transmit and receive on four switchable frequencies. For example, you might have a crystal to tie in with a telephone company radio operator and the conventional telephone system. This enables you to talk to someone who only has a telephone. I was able to raise a telephone operator from the mountains of the southern Yukon and be connected with my wife on the phone in Hamilton, Ontario. I have also successfully used one equipped with a crystal for the frequency used by the air charter company that flew us into the mountains of western Yukon, as well as the "miners' frequency" in the same area. Those were notable successes, but I can recall some notable failures.

One was while sitting on the shore of Hudson Bay at the end of a wilderness canoe trip. The motor boat from the town 70 kilometres away had not come at the appointed date to take us across the treacherous waters of the bay. We were almost out of food, exposed to polar bear hazards and of course were worried in case some mishap had befallen the motor boat. With the utmost difficulty and with the help of another private radio operator who relayed our message word by word, we were barely able to converse with an operator. The operator, no doubt well fed and in a warm, dry, bug-free office in the south, was more interested in whether we had a licence for the radio and in the fact that they had no record of that licence number, than they were in our situation. (Our licence had only been issued two weeks previously.) The final gem in a performance that would have done Monty Python proud was when they asked who was paying for the emergency call anyway!

These radios are costly ($1300), but can usually be rented. In Canada, for short periods of rental they come already licensed by the lessor, and the operator needs no licence. Although rental fees tend to be higher in centres such as Yellowknife compared to say Calgary, there can be advantages to renting close to the area in which you will be operating. The local rental organizations know the most useful local frequencies and can equip the radio with frequencies to suit your purpose. For example, they may know that a telephone crystal is of little use in a particular area but that the trappers' frequency is best for getting an emergency message out. They are likely to have the crystals for the local frequencies in stock, too. Prices in 1991 were around $250 per month in Yellowknife. It is advisable to book radios two to four weeks ahead so that the unit can be fitted with the suitable crystals and of course to lay claim to a set. A deposit may not be required, but it can be a real help to ensure that you get a set.

The Spillsbury SBX 11A HF radio has been the standard for wilderness communication in Canada's north for many years. Rental unit courtesy of T D Communications, Calgary.

Marine VHF Radios

Handheld marine VHF radios are useful in coastal areas where line-of-sight communication systems are more practical. These radios are multiple channel, including the emergency channel 16 and various weather channels. Because they are line of sight only, they may not work well in areas of high relief islands and channels. The powerful coast guard radios are usually situated high up in areas of good coverage so you can hear them, but they may be too distant for your less powerful set to raise them in an emergency. The range can be greatly improved by the addition of a longer antenna.

Often the quickest initial response comes from another craft nearby that is monitoring the emergency frequency. They can act immediately and also relay a message. In the cold waters around Canada and Alaska, the rapid response by a nearby fishing boat or recreational craft to a voice mayday can mean the difference between a live rescue and a body retrieval. A voice saying who you are, where you are and what's happening obviously is more informative and is easier to respond appropriately to than is a beep from an anonymous ELT or EPIRB (see page 162) somewhere in the ocean. Unfortunately, you can't be as sure that your voice signal is going to be actually picked up as you can that an ELT or EPIRB signal will be. In some coastal mountain areas such as the Fairweather Range, marine VHF radios have been used successfully by mountaineers for emergency communications. Mountaineers with a clear line of sight to the ocean have been able to communicate with ships. In some areas there is heavy commercial and pleasure craft traffic who generally monitor the emergency channel.

Portable marine VHF sets are available for prices as low as $300. The set itself has to be

A wide selection of handheld marine VHF radios is available. Most are not waterproof, so you should keep them in an appropriate waterproof container that allows you to operate them without being opened.

UHF walkie-talkies have advantages over conventional systems, including less congestion and longer range.

licensed, and in addition, the operator must possess an operator's licence. Most users have a "maritime voluntary" licence. Obtaining an operator's licence involves studying the handbook from your local Department of Communications and taking a multiple-choice, oral and practical exam. In Canada, candidates are expected to be Canadian citizens or landed immigrants, so visitors from abroad should obtain a licence before leaving their home country. The licences are valid internationally.

Land VHF Radios

Land VHF radios have relatively short range because of the line-of-sight nature of VHF transmissions. They are only really useful on land for emergency communication in places where there is a network (usually private) of repeater stations. Outfitters, logging companies, highways' departments, mining companies, heli-ski operators, government forestry departments, parks' officials, etc., are all likely to use a VHF communication system, usually involving repeaters located on hilltops. They are obviously unwilling to have the general public use their systems, but in a serious emergency it is easily justified and legal. Some professionals in the recreation business have specific permission to use these repeaters for emergencies only.

The Denali Park Mountaineering Handbook states that on Mt. McKinley above about 4300 metres (14,000 feet) there is line-of-sight linkup possible between handheld VHF sets and 24-hour telephone operators in Fairbanks and Anchorage. Ordinary three- or five-watt Citizens Band (CB) radios are used by many climbers on the mountain, partly for communication between parties but also for emergency use. Although they are line-of-sight use only, the glacier pilots flying in the area generally monitor the emergency CB channel. Radios are highly recommended on the mountain and it is common for climbers in the Alaska Range to carry radios.

In some areas it is also possible to connect to the telephone system with some small VHF portables, and you should not dismiss portable cellular phones as an option. The cellular net is expanding all the time, and is even in some remote areas, particularly where intensive re-source exploration or extraction is being carried on. The telephone company in your area of operations will be able to provide details.

Under some circumstances an air charter operation may provide its clients with a handheld aviation frequency VHF radio, which has the advantage of size and weight compared to the HF type, but relies mainly on there being air traffic in the area. An operator's licence is also required, and the system should only be used for emergencies or to advise the company of the exact location for a pickup.

UHF Handheld Radios

The new UHF 460 MHz handheld walkie-talkie radios such as the Motorola Sport SS provide advantages over other handheld walkie-talkie type devices. The UHF band is much less congested and the sound is clearer and longer range compared to the CB 27 MHz units. Even with a short, stubby aerial I got good reception at 4.5 kilometres. However, these are still line-of-sight-only units and a hill or dense forest in the way cuts transmission range considerably. A DOC licence is needed. A coded squelch "private line" feature is available that enables you to only hear transmissions from similarly adjusted units in your talk group, though other users can hear your conversations. These units are not suitable for obtaining external assistance, but are useful for communication within the group or for coordinating a search.

Future Systems

One of the most promising systems that will soon be available is Orbcomm. The user types a message onto a small screen on the handheld device, using an alphanumeric keyboard. The digitized message is then sent as a short pulse to one of a number of satellites, from where it is relayed to a central control station. It can then be transmitted back to a similar small handheld unit or phoned or faxed to the recipient or a central emergency control centre. It uses far less power than a voice system because the pulse is so short. Obviously this system is not too suited to conversations, but for emergency messages it would be ideal. Costs will be low, in the order of $400 to purchase, plus a small annual fee for emergency-only users and

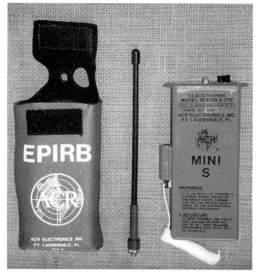

EPIRBs are intended for use on water, and use on land is technically illegal though it could save a life. These are for serious emergencies **only**.

The Satfind 406 PLB (Personal Locator Beacon) by MPR Teltech of Burnaby, B.C. is legal for use on land. Rental unit courtesy of Superior Safety, Thunder Bay.

approximately one cent per character for messages. The system also has the capability to determine the position of the sender.

By the turn of the century, two satellite mobile phone systems should be in operation. The Iridium project, which plans to involve 66 satellites by the year 2000, is already under way, and Motorola has been licensed to send up five experimental satellites in 1996. The International Maritime Satellite Organization (INMARSAT) is a similar system. However, while the Iridium system will give worldwide coverage, INMARSAT will not have good coverage of the polar regions, and the INMARSAT receiver is currently about the size of a briefcase.

EPIRBS

An entirely different type of radio to use in emergencies is the EPIRB "Emergency Position Indicating Radio Beacon." These devices do not provide voice communication, but when turned on they send an emergency signal up to various satellites orbiting the earth. The signal is also on the emergency frequency monitored by aircraft and ships. The search and rescue satellites compute the position of the beacon, then advise the appropriate search and rescue authorities. These systems are fairly reliable, and provide a good compromise system between safety in a worst-case scenario and a

radio spoiling the "wilderness feeling" for those concerned about such matters.

EPIRBs are similar to the Emergency Locator Transmitter (ELT) in aircraft, so turning one on produces a very serious response. For this reason they must only be used in dire emergencies. In a remote area with no other way to get help for a bear mauling, appendicitis, serious sepsis, heart attack or serious injuries it would be justifiable to activate the system. However, an incident just requiring you to go hungry or uncomfortable for a few days would not justify the expense that result when the signal is turned on. These units are designed for marine use and are not legal for land users. It's your decision whether to take one anyway and to argue after someone's life has been saved. Some people carry small aircraft-type ELTs, but this is not legal either.

In one recent incident, a wilderness tourist who had arrived at his remote pickup point at the mouth of an Arctic river and not been picked up, waited for six days before activating his EPIRB unit. This was a reasonable time to allow for bad weather at the base preventing the aircraft flying to meet him. In fact, arrangements had been miscommunicated, and no one knew he was to be picked up. More recently, a solo backpacker, who had failed to complete a route known to be virtually impossible, retreated to a lakeside float plane pickup point. He used the EPIRB even before his contacts at the intended end of his trip had become concerned enough to fly out and look for him. An expensive official search was triggered almost immediately, costing the taxpayer a lot of money.

EPIRBs suitable for recreationists are the type S "survival" type or the type B marine models. They are sealed units with a lithium battery inside with a shelf life of 10 years, though they should be returned to the factory for battery replacement every five years. They transmit signals for about 48 hours even at -20°C, on the emergency frequencies of 121.5 MHz and 243 MHz, which are monitored by ships and aircraft as well as by satellites. All that is required to start transmitting is to screw the flexible antenna onto the unit and turn on the switch. Some have a transmit indicator light, and some have a cord that must be pulled to turn on the unit, so read the instructions on the unit.

The newer but currently more costly Personal Locator Beacons' (PLB) units working on 406 MHz are legal for land use and are designed to be picked up by satellites in the U.S./Russian SARSAT/COSPAS system. A good example is the Satfind 406 PLB by Northern Airborne Technology of Kelowna, B.C. They offer advantages over the cheaper EPIRBs. Each unit has its own distinctive coded signal, so authorities can find out more about who and what they are looking for. Hopefully, this will also cut down on unauthorized use and the 95 per cent or so of activations that are false alarms. The latest models also emit a 121.5 MHz signal that enables searchers to zero-in quite closely without needing specialized equipment.

Do not mess around with these units! Remember that even turning the unit on for a short time could simulate a signal from an automatically activated unit being triggered by the first jolt of a crash, and then being destroyed by the final impact. If you have one of these units it is good policy to tell the authorities in the area. This is because when a search starts, a check will usually be done of who is in the area in order to help determine what is being searched for. A downed Twin Otter presents different search parameters than does a canoeist with a broken leg. In addition, make sure that a reasonable number of your group know where the beacon is and how to operate it.

Recording Your Trip

Appropriate equipment and planning will help you to keep a satisfactory record. For most people a photographic or video record is the method of choice, though some people use written or recorded words to capture the essence of the experience.

Photographic Equipment

High quality, sophisticated equipment alone will not ensure that you obtain a good collection of pictures. The great shots you see published in outdoor adventure books and magazines are likely to be the product of a considerable amount of effort made by the photographer. It takes work, knowledge and forethought to be at the right place at the right time with the right lens. You can be lucky and just happen to get some good shots, but generally you need to work at it and to think ahead and plan.

I prefer to take slides. If you want some prints it is easier to make prints from slides than it is to make slides from prints. I make up a small album of prints from selected slides of big trips.

If people are taking slides, which most of the people I know do, they sometimes agree to take two exposures of the same scene so that the subjects receive a slide of themselves. Always take far more film with you than you think you'll need. You can always use up your leftovers after you come back but you can't get more film in the bush. Don't buy all your film in one batch from one store in case there is a fault. Similarly don't take it all in to be processed on the same day in case the processor or their transport has a problem. Faulty film and faulty processing are very rare but on the two times they have happened to me the consequences have been quite upsetting. It can be difficult to find slide film in smaller communities, so buy in the larger centres.

In order to obtain good pictures you've got to have your camera handy all the time. A single-lens reflex camera is bulky and a bit awkward to keep always at the ready, so buy a good case/carrier so you don't have to keep stowing it away out of reach in your pack. Zoom "pocket" or "rangefinder" cameras are lighter and more compact alternatives that are easier to keep handy in your pocket.

As long as the light is good, I have had success with an Olympus Infinity Twin pocket camera that has two choices of focal lengths at the flick of a button—35 millimetres or 70 millimetres. This does not give you the advantages of a progressive zoom, but it is much lighter. The fixed focal length lenses do not have some of the inherent problems of zoom lenses, such as being slower and having less depth of field. The camera is very light and compact as well as being somewhat water resistant. I have managed to get good shots using one hand in the rear of a canoe in rapids as long as the light is good and from behind. I just drop it on its lanyard into my lifejacket when I have finished shooting, if I don't have a chance to immediately put it in a waterproof case. This and most other pocket cameras lack the crucial capability of manual exposure override for snowy and backlit conditions.

For many years I have used an old Pentax SP500 (similar to current K1000). It is simple and very rugged, with a minimum of sensitive electronics. I'm now using a Canon EOS Elan that definitely has advantages, not the least of which is, considering the features, its lighter weight than the Pentax, especially the lenses. The multiple metering zones give much better exposure balance and the autofocus means that in a real hurry I just point and shoot. However, it is nowhere near as rugged as the old Pentax.

I use zoom lenses—a 35-105 and a 80-200. They always say you never have the right lens on at the right time, and a zoom helps. I generally keep the longest zoom on the camera because the things you need it for are likely to be wildlife, which won't hang around while you change lenses! Scenery has been around for a while and it's not vanishing THAT fast! Because of the high level of battery dependency of this type of camera, I carry a spare battery and also keep the camera warm during winter use. Keeping a bulky SLR under your jacket to keep it warm is not easy. Also, electric rewinds are a bit harsher on cold brittle film than are a careful manual rewind, so it's a good idea to keep the whole camera warm in really cold (-25°C) weather, not just the battery. If you bring a cold camera into a warm, steamy room, place it in a plastic bag until it warms up, otherwise it will fill with condensation.

A lightweight tripod is a useful accessory, and although it won't be as rigid as a heavy professional device, it will be a lot better than nothing. Even the small units designed to be set on a rock or upturned canoe will enable you to obtain some great shots.

Many of the most pleasing shots will include your companions for "people interest" or foreground. Get to know your equipment so you can be quick and decisive and not have people hanging around, otherwise you won't have many shots where people are still smiling. (And maybe the pictures will all have a strange "blue" tinge!) Manipulating not only your position but their position as well in relation to the scenery and the sunlight direction takes time, effort and tact, but at least if everyone is taking pictures, the posing and positioning chores are shared.

Video

Good video can make a great record of a trip, especially where there is action such as skiing or whitewater. However, for scenery, albums, publications and wall pictures you should also take 35 millimetre stills. Then you get caught in the dilemma of what to shoot at any given moment! Making good video is definitely work, requiring good planning and forethought and making the effort to get into the best place from which to shoot. You also need to keep the camera handy to capture those unexpected magic moments, so the small eight millimetre units have some real advantages over the full-size models. A tripod or monopod is a great help for preventing the annoying shaking that spoils so many home videos.

Some people like to put a commentary on afterwards, but an on-the-spot commentary can have more reality and life to it. However, it takes practice to do a suitable commentary on the spot. If you start filming and interviewing people "cold" and unrehearsed you can end up with some real gems, or it can be rather banal. If the latter is likely it may be better to rehearse and at least get some sense, even if it is not very spontaneous. Also remember that things that seem inconsequential to you on the trip can be very interesting to viewers who are not well versed in the activity. For example, constructing a belay, putting up a tent in snow, loading a kayak. Carry spare batteries and keep them warm in winter. Lots of bold editing and rerecording is the key to a good finished trip video.

Protecting Your Camera

You have to make some decisions about the amount of risk to which you are prepared to expose your camera. If you keep it wrapped in three Ziploc bags and a padded bag in a Pelican box, you will certainly end up with an intact camera at the end of the trip. The trouble is you won't have any photos! In the past 20 years I have got away with one repair job and no drying-out jobs. Increasing numbers of water-resistant cameras are now on the market.

A multitude of nonwaterproof padded camera containers are available for land use. For the active person you need a system that does not allow the camera to swing around and get in the way. You should avoid having all of its weight hanging off your neck. A wide neck strap with a small amount of stretch incorporated such as the Op-Tech is much more comfortable to wear in rough terrain than a narrow or inelastic one. A bag that clips onto a backpack hipbelt is one system that works as long as you can easily unclip it for when you are not carrying the pack.

Over the years I have experimented with a variety of waterproof camera containers. The Sundog camera containers consist of a fairly conventional padded bag with a rolltop overbag of coated nylon. You can use the unit with or without the overbag and it is quite compact when not in use. Like all rolltops it is not absolutely waterproof for long-term immersion, but the inner bag protects the gear from the small amount of seepage.

The fastest access, genuinely waterproof camera containers for boaters is the Pelican rigid box, which is available in various sizes. The lid seals shut with two simple catches and the gaskets can be replaced when necessary. The boxes come with open cell cushioning foam that can be easily cut to suit the articles to be protected. In a watery environment it is better to use closed cell foam, which will not absorb splashes and dries more quickly. If you seal a camera in with damp foam and the box then gets warm you end up steaming the camera and having all sorts of condensation problems. My Pelican Mini 'S' size weighs 1.2 kilograms and has a net buoyancy of about 4.5 kilograms, which is plenty.

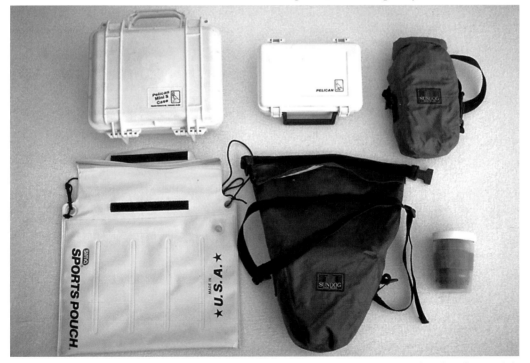

There is a wide selection of containers available to protect your camera gear. My favourites are the Pelican box, top left and Sundog bags, right.

The Basic Designs SeaSafe (top) is a great container for film, cameras, books, etc., that must be kept absolutely dry.

Double-wall camera bags are designed to be inflated for extra buoyancy and cushioning. The tops close in a variety of ways, including a Ziploc-style seal coupled with a rolltop or rigid sliding clamps. These methods tend not to be very fast and to be more finicky than a Pelican box. However, they are lighter and quiet near wildlife. Avoid bags that you inflate with your mouth after sealing if the breath goes into the compartment where the camera is. You will be blowing warm, saturated air from your lungs into the instrument and causing condensation problems.

Journals

The written word has always been a great record of trips, and the journals of some of the early explorers make fascinating reading. However, writing a journal is not everyone's forte. Waterproof notebooks are available but they are costly and quite small. Another alternative is to find a loose-leaf book of an appropriate style and to waterproof the pages. Remove them and dip them individually in a can of Canadian Tire Vinyl Silicone tent waterproofing (not the wax variety) or use Map Seal (costly for this purpose). To dry the pages, pin them to a 2x4 outdoors with thumb tacks. Use a soft pencil or a ballpoint pen to write on pages treated this way.

The days that were awful are also days one should write about in order to keep a balance, but the inclination to write is low at those times! For those reasons I have successfully used a microcassette recorder, notably on a 13-month round-the-world excursion. I'm sure there would be blank sections in a written diary from the evenings when I was lying fuming in bed after a day of fighting oriental bureaucracy and suffering from the Kathmandu Quickstep. At least I was able to lie in bed and ramble into the mike.

The disadvantage of microcassettes is the need for batteries and the weight, which is around 220 grams, as well as the need to protect the item from shock and water. A diary is much lighter and lower-tech so there is less to go wrong, though it still needs to be kept dry in a Ziploc bag or something similar.

Chapter 6

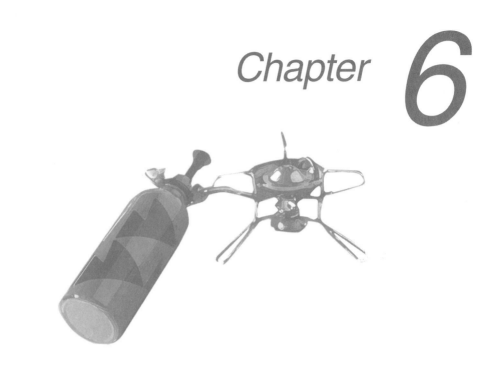

The Camp Kitchen

Good food greatly improves most people's enjoyment of the outdoors. However, in order to make high quality meals the cook needs carefully chosen, high quality equipment. Stoves, rather than camp fires, should be used by environmentally responsible campers in most regions, but they must be suitable, well understood and used properly if they are to be satisfactory. Most stove problems result from a poor choice of stove, misunderstandings and improper use. Camp cook pots must also be carefully chosen as many of the available products are of little use for anything other than boiling water. The wrong pots burn and stick easily, are difficult to clean and do not lend themselves well to cooking anything interesting. Utensils and accessories, if well chosen, make camp kitchen chores easier so cooking good food is a pleasure, not a drudgery.

Stoves

Although camp fires still have their adherents, camp stoves are used more and more widely by modern wilderness travellers. You should seriously consider the benefits of using stoves.

Advantages of Using Stoves

If you use camp stoves instead of camp fires, it is much easier to minimize your impact on the backcountry. You can also cook easily in foul weather, you do not have to forage for wood, you won't have blackened pots and all your gear won't smell of smoke. Modern stoves are light and very efficient, and are completely safe as long as they are used properly. The only disadvantages compared to using fires are having to carry the weight of the stove and fuel with you, and not being able to dry clothes easily with a stove.

Over the years I've cooked outdoors on quite a variety of stoves. One of the more memorable of these was a fearsome kerosene-burning plumber's furnace designed for melt-ing lead. Its four large burners were perched on top of a large tank in an array that looked and sounded like the tail end of a space shuttle taking off. It was great for large-expedition cooking, and also did a superb job of frightening pesky bystanders out of the camp kitchen! It certainly was intimidating, but like all stoves, all it really needed was a little love and understanding. However, without this, like many other stoves, it would do a good imitation of an oil well fire.

The best stove is one that has been well looked after by an owner-operator who loves and understands it and is using it to its full potential.

Once you choose a suitable stove, you should take the trouble to learn to use it correctly. There are some tricks of the trade that enable you to obtain much more satisfactory performance from your stove once you have learned about it and practised using it.

WELL, WE'RE TAKING A STOVE WITH US THAT WE KNOW WORKS

Modern camp stoves are in fact very reliable if used properly. *On Foot and Finger*, Jim Watson, Cicerone Press, U.K.

Types of Fuel

The range of available camp stoves burn a variety of different fuels. You should understand the advantages, disadvantages and availability of the different fuels in order to select a suitable stove.

Liquid fuels. White gas (Naptha) May be found packaged as "Coleman" or "Camp" fuel. This colourless gasoline is the most popular, economical and readily available fuel in North America for small camp stoves and for virtually all pressure lanterns. It can be obtained everywhere, in camping, hardware and sporting goods stores, campgrounds and some rural gas stations. It can be bought in one-litre (U.S. quart) and four-litre (U.S. gallon) cans. Prices are higher in remote or tourist areas. Larger containers of around 20 litres may also be obtained at bulk fuel depots. White gas stoves generally have high outputs and work well at low temperatures if they have a pump.

The only disadvantage of white gas is that the fuel is highly volatile, so care must be taken during filling and if leaks or spills occur. However, the volatility means that spills quickly evaporate without leaving a lasting smell.

Kerosene (U.K. "Paraffin") Unlike in Europe and Asia, kerosene is not easy to obtain. It is not used for camp stoves or pressure lanterns, but is occasionally used for portable wick-type household space heaters. It is usually sold in large containers or else in very small ones at exorbitant prices as coloured "lamp fuel" for decorative wick lamps. Hardware stores are often the best sources. It is rarely found at gasoline stations. Visitors with kerosene-only (nonmulti-fuel) stoves will have to be especially careful to arrange a reliable supply of this fuel. Because excellent white-gas stoves are cheap, foreign visitors should seriously consider buying a North American stove. Some kerosene stoves such as the Optimus can be fitted with the white gas jet and cleaner needle, but Optimus parts are not easy to find.

Kerosene's advantage is that it is far less volatile than white gas so it is less of a fire hazard. However, spills take a long time to evaporate and anything contaminated with the fuel will stink and be inflammable for a long time. Some kerosene is deodorized, but this is not necessarily a good thing because the leak and fire hazard is still there even though you can't smell it.

Automotive gasoline Canadian unleaded automotive gasoline currently has different additives from U.S. unleaded, and Coleman stoves that run on U.S. unleaded quickly clog with the Canadian fuel. However, as of 1992 Optimus reported no problems of this type with their stoves.

Alcohol is not commonly used as a stove fuel except on boats. It can therefore be found at marinas or as methyl hydrate (Methyl Alcohol, Methanol) in the paints department of hardware stores or as gasline antifreeze in automotive stores. They sell it in one-litre containers (service stations generally only sell it in small "single dose" containers at disproportionately high prices). It is also sold as "Fondue Fuel" but usually at high prices. Heat outputs from alcohol stoves are generally too low for winter use where snow has to be melted and where heat losses are high.

Miscellaneous liquid fuels Other liquid fuels such as diesel fuel, aviation turbine fuel, low octane aviation gasoline and barbecue starter fluid are also available and can be burned in some multi-fuel stoves. The litre or so of turbine fuel dregs from the "empty" 45 gallon barrels around remote helicopter pads can be a source of fuel in an emergency if you can remove the lids.

Propane in bulk is cheap and readily obtainable now that more vehicles use it as fuel. It is a good option for base camps if you can afford the weight of the heavy refillable cylinders. Disposable propane cylinders are heavy and a very expensive way of camp cooking. It is difficult to tell how much fuel you have left in any compressed gas cylinder, so you might want to carry a spring balance so you can use weight as a guide. The main advantage of propane is convenience and ease of lighting for people who are reluctant to read and follow the instructions of liquid fuel stoves. Coleman makes a high output burner for base camp and large group cooking, and some people make their own high output burners using old water heater burners. They

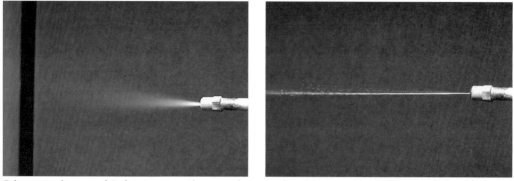

Coleman two-burner and Peak 1 stoves must be pumped up enough and the control knob (if provided) placed in the "light" position in order to produce a clean-burning spray of fuel when cold-starting (first photo). If this is not done, a jet of liquid fuel (second photo) floods the burner and flares up during lighting.

must be re-jetted for propane since they are usually jetted for natural gas (methane), and may have to be re-jetted or adjusted for use at higher altitudes.

Butane and butane-propane mixtures are used in the familiar blue Camping Gaz cylinders, but using these cylinders is a very expensive way to cook compared to using white gas. On a long trip the cost difference is significant. Camping Gaz brand is available from sporting goods stores, but is not as easily obtained as in other parts of the world. As of spring 1995, it may become more widely available through a large hardware chain, "Home Hardware." The new valved screw mount Gaz 270 and 470 cylinders are now available in Canada along with their high output 10000 BTU burners. Remember that these cylinders cannot be taken with you on public transport, so you cannot stock up in the city and then head off somewhere except in your own vehicle. Coleman is also introducing butane-propane mixture stoves and cylinders in 1996, and these should be widely available. The Coleman butane-propane stoves are, in fact, Epigas stoves and cylinders.

Butane-propane mixture rather than straight butane provides improved low temperature performance. Butane stoves using n-butane are useless in cold weather because the butane does not vaporize below about 0°C (32°F). However, at high altitudes where the low pressures assist vaporization, they work at lower temperatures. Iso-butane works down to about -10°C (14°F) and the butane-propane mixture down to about -15°C (5°F).

There is now much improved standardization of fittings and consequently much less difficulty in obtaining a compatible cylinder than in the past. However, compatibility is still a consideration. Stoves with flexible fuel hoses such as the Epigas Alpine and MSR Rapidfire are more adaptable to different cylinders than are tank-mounted burners. An adapter (from Liberty Mountain Sport, PO Box 306, Montrose, California, 91020) allows you to run a variety of stoves on the ubiquitous blue valveless Camping Gaz cylinders.

High output propane-butane mixture stoves now available in Canada are made by (l to r) Primus, Coleman/Peak 1, and Camping-Gaz. The Peak 1 units are identical to Epigas and there is interchangeability between the Primus and Peak 1 cylinders. The Piezo lighters available on many of these are a handy feature. Detached-burner models such as the Primus in the foreground lend themselves better to effective but questionable cylinder-warming techniques in cold weather!

Flaring-Up and How to Prevent It

The flaring that occurs when liquid fuel stoves are used incorrectly is what deters many people from using them. All that is needed to prevent flaring and to feel relaxed and confident around stoves is some understanding of how they work so you can operate them properly.

Flaring is caused when fuel emerges from the burner while still in a liquid state. Liquid cannot mix properly with air and so it burns slowly with a large, yellow flaring flame. Some fuels are more likely to flare than others, so if you really have problems around stoves and mechanical things you might choose your stove for its fuel's resistance to flaring.

Butane and propane and their mixtures rarely produce yellow flames and flaring. They are in a liquid state in their cylinders, but unless the tank is knocked over there is little likelihood of fuel reaching the burner without first changing to a clean-burning gas. An antiflare system is incorporated into the Epigas/Coleman stoves to prevent flaring.

White gas, kerosene and unleaded gasoline are more prone to flaring than butane or propane. Until the burner is hot, the fuel does not spontaneously emerge from the jet as a gas to mix with air and burn cleanly. Unless the stove is operated correctly, flaring will occur.

There are two ways to avoid flaring. If the stove is the type that has a preheating cup, you must preheat the burner properly by filling the cup beneath it with fuel or with lighting paste. Wait until this has almost burned away before turning the stove to the "on" position again to allow liquid into the now-hot burner. Many people do not place enough fuel in the cup to adequately preheat the burner, or else they turn

To avoid flaring-up, make sure you put enough fuel in the cup to properly preheat the burner.

Flaring-up of liquid fuel stoves is not an inherent defect of stoves and can be avoided by using the stoves correctly.

the stove to "on" again too soon. Consequently, the burner is not hot enough to vaporize the fuel, liquid fuel emerges into the burner and a flare-up ensues. If the valve is opened too far while filling the cup, fuel splashes around rather than dribbling into the cup, so there is apt to be more of a conflagration on lighting.

Stoves without preheating cups (Coleman two-burner and Peak 1) automatically avoid start-up flaring by spraying a clean-burning mixture of fuel and air into the chamber below the burner during the lighting stage. For this to work properly, the stove must be pumped the number of times specified by the instructions to generate enough pressure to form a spray. There also may be a control lever that must be put into the "light" position. If the instructions are neglected, liquid fuel dribbles into the chamber, it floods with fuel and then flares for a long time until the accumulation burns away. Even when used correctly, the stove will need to be pumped again once it is running, to restore the pressure lost during the spraying stage of operation. When using kerosene in Coleman Peak 1 multifuel models, the "generator" tube must be preheated. There is no cup so lighting paste is needed. Preheating also helps when burning white gas if the stove is very cold.

Backcountry alcohol stoves are non-pressurized, so flaring is unlikely. However, burning times are relatively short so refilling is done more often. Because the alcohol flames are invisible in daylight, care must be taken to ensure the stove is completely extinguished

before refilling. Pouring fuel into a stove that is still burning will produce a spectacular flare! These stoves are often thought to be the most suitable type for young people, but the premature refilling hazard is substantial. MSR makes a bottle cap/valve that allows safer filling.

Stove Problems and Solutions

Stove problems are generally caused by incorrect use or by dirt or water in the fuel.

Dirt or water in the fuel. Sealed retail containers of camp fuel are reliably clean. However, care must be taken to ensure that dirt is not introduced when the container is opened to transfer fuel to the stove. Make sure there is no dirt on or in the stem of the funnel and that dirt does not fall off the top of the container into the funnel when the container is tilted. Also, make sure you do not get dirt on the stove lid or pump assembly, so be careful where you put them down during the filling process.

Liquid fuel that is not from sealed retail containers must be filtered with a felt filter. The small Coleman filter funnels are ideal for this purpose. They do not, however, remove dissolved contaminants such as gasoline additives and the gum-inducing gunge in some Third World kerosene. Make sure no dirt has got into the stem of the funnel below the filter pad during storage. Once the pad has dried out after use, store the filter funnel in a plastic bag. One of the advantages of white gas over kerosene is that it evaporates quickly, so the filter pad does not stink for days as it would with kerosene.

Water can get into stove tanks when the lid is off in a rainstorm, but is more likely to enter through the pump. If the stove is left out in very heavy rain or is immersed during a canoeing accident, water can enter the pump cylinder above the piston. Unless the condition is anticipated and the pump is turned upside down to drain, the first stroke will transfer water to below the piston and then into the tank.

The easiest way to remove water from the stove is to drain off as much fuel as possible into a container in which you can see any water that comes out. Then invert and shake

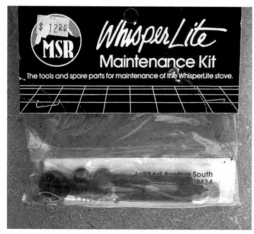

A well-maintained stove rarely lets you down in the field, but the consequences of a failure could be serious, so carry a repair kit.

Occasional lubrication will prevent many pump problems.

If the pump washer becomes dry, soak it thoroughly in neatsfoot oil or heavy gear oil. In an emergency, smear it with anything greasy.

the stove vigorously to remove as much remaining fuel and water as possible. Do this in a place where the fuel can do no harm, and don't get it on your clothes. After that, you can remove more water by adding 50-100 millilitres of alcohol, such as rubbing alcohol or automotive gasline antifreeze (methyl alcohol), into which the water will dissolve. Shake and pour out as much of this wet alcohol as possible, before refilling the stove with fuel. You can use the fuel you previously drained as long as care is taken not to pour the water back in too!

Pump failure. The other common stove problem is pump failure, usually because of inadequate lubrication. Leather pump piston cup washers lose their suppleness and sealing ability unless they are kept well soaked in oil. Any slight leakage of fuel back into the pump cylinder does a great job of washing out the lubricant. Synthetic washers and O-ring type pistons also need lubrication to seal properly. A few drops of oil through the hole (marked "oil" on many stoves) will usually suffice. If the washer is leather rather than rubber or an O-ring type, an occasional good soak in warm, heavy gear oil or neatsfoot oil in a film canister is a good preventive policy.

If your pump fails in the field, the first step is to remove the pump and smear the piston washer with any grease or oil, such as boot grease, butter, cooking oil, lip salve, vaseline or even first aid cream. Gentle finger pressure to spread the washer out wider will also help, but if the washer is really dry, it may crack and fall apart. If this happens you are in big trouble!

You should always carry a repair kit for your stove, and it will include a new piston washer.

Clogged jets. Make sure you have jet cleaners and all the tools required to dismantle and clean your stove, especially if burning suspect fuel. Manually operated wire cleaning needles are tricky to use and simply push the dirt back down into the interior of the stove, but very few stoves require these now. MSR stoves now have an internal cleaning needle that pushes dirt out through the jet. The needle is attached to a small heavy plunger below the jet, and when you invert and shake the stove the needle pushes dirt out of the jet. Coleman Peak 1 stoves have a cleaning needle built in internally, and Optimus/Primus/Svea stoves have had the feature for many years. I was very glad of the easy cleaning of the jet of my Optimus when burning highly questionable Third World kerosene. It clogged the jet often, but one twist of the control knob and the job was done. If you remove the cable from the generator tubes of a stove you must do a good job of cleaning loose particles off it and out of the tube, otherwise they will quickly block the jet. To flush it properly, attach the tube to the tank, pump up pressure then open the valve to flush the tube with fuel. Do this before reattaching the jet so you get a good flow of fuel.

Cannibalizing Parts

On long trips where stove failure could be disastrous, all the stoves in the group should be of the same type so that they can be cannibalized for parts if necessary. For example, you can pump up one stove, light it and then remove the plunger and piston to pump up another stove.

Minimizing Heating Time and Fuel Consumption

On long and remote trips you need to take special care to ensure that you have enough fuel for your trip, but without loading yourself down with an excess amount. This is especially important for winter trips above treeline, because your fuel is your only means to obtain water, but every gram of weight counts. Fuel consumption is

The Markill Stormy heat retaining system fits Coleman Peak 1 stoves. Bibler make a similar, but larger unit with a burner for propane-butane mix.

hard to gauge because there are so many variables, but it is an important consideration. I know of one small expedition that failed to reach a summit because they ran out of fuel because one member wasted fuel early on the trip.

You can measure fuel consumption and calculate a reliable average consumption for different types of trips and cooking styles. Weigh your stove before and after every trip and keep a careful record of the difference. Weighing saves emptying the stove to measure the remainder. Convert to volume by assuming white gas weighs 670 g/l (1 pound $5^1/_2$ ounces per U.S. quart).

Different stoves do have different fuel consumptions and heat outputs. However, a lower output stove being used effectively by someone who really knows how to use it can easily outperform a more powerful stove that is being used inefficiently. When people argue about one stove heating faster than another, the difference is just as likely to be because of the way the stoves are being operated as because of the design of the stoves themselves.

The main enemy of stove efficiency is wind. It blows hot flame gases away from the pot, reducing the proportion of the flame heat that actually enters the pot. Wind also takes away heat that has already entered the pot. Even if there is no wind, the pot is hotter than its surroundings, so the heat it just gained is lost by convection, conduction and radiation. This heat loss is much greater if the air temperature is low, so in winter you can waste an enormous amount of fuel unless you take steps to shield the stove and pot from wind.

Combination heat/wind shields make as much as a 50 per cent difference in fuel consumption, especially in cold weather and windy conditions. The MSR foil shield directs flame heat more effectively into the pot and keeps it there by shielding the pot from wind and by surrounding it with hot flame gases.

The MSR Heat Exchanger increases heat transfer still more, thereby saving fuel. It needs a relatively unbattered pot to fit properly and work well. The biggest savings, of around 25 per cent, occur in cold conditions and if the foil windshield is used as well. These devices should only be used for heating water, because a boil over of soup or stew would make an awful mess.

The MSR heat exchanger increases fuel efficiency significantly and is particularly useful if you have to melt snow.

The foil heat/wind shield supplied with MSR stoves is light, simple and very effective at saving fuel and cooking time.

The Markill Stormy is an effective heat retaining system that can be used hanging or on the ground. Sigg "Tourist" cooksets with heat retaining windshields are made to fit the Svea 123 stove, Coleman Peak 1 and Gaz 206. The Trangia and Sigg Traveller alcohol stoves work best if the full cook kit with windshield/heat retainer is used.

The Pot Parka heat retainer and Aluminum Tutu foil windshield from Travelling Light have been laboratory tested in a five mph wind at 20°C to produce a 51 per cent improvement in fuel economy compared to a naked stove. Improvements were of the order of 15 per cent

in a windless environment, which goes to show how even a slight breeze adversely affects stoves. The Pot Parka is similar to the heat retainer for the Outback Oven (page 182), but it is now available separately in two sizes. It is a reflective, heat resistant fabric "hat" to go over the pot. The Tutu is available in two heights, one for tank mounted burners and one for remote burners such as MSR and Coleman Peak 1 Apex. The foil sheet is connected by a stainless steel clip to make a complete circle. The metal has a slight temper so it folds up in its original manner rather than rolling at random and getting crumpled. There is also a foil collar, which instructions state MUST be attached just below the burner, to shield the tank or controls from heat.

When heating water, you should use your stove at maximum output so that heating time is reduced. This is because the pot is always losing heat to the surroundings, and if it takes, say, 15 minutes for it to boil rather than 10, the pot has been losing heat for an extra and unnecessary five minutes. That heat being lost came from the burning of fuel. If you have the stove on a really low flame you could conceivably burn an entire tankful of fuel and not get the pot to a boil because heat is leaving the pot as fast as it is entering. This effect is particularly pronounced in cold weather.

Use liquid water rather than snow or ice if you have the option, because it takes almost twice as much fuel to boil a litre of water from ice at 0°C as it does to boil it from water at 0°C. If you are making tea, only use fuel to boil half the amount of water you need, add the tea bag and let it soak for a minute or two. Then add cold (purified) water or snow to cool it to drinking temperature and increase the amount to what you need. You can do the same with soup.

A good water purifier soon saves its weight in fuel because you no longer need to boil water to sterilize it. You can also save a lot of fuel if you choose foods that require a minimum amount of cooking. Remember that at high altitudes, cooking times are greatly increased. A lightweight pressure cooker soon saves its weight in fuel because of the decreased cooking times.

Warning. With any stove enclosure it is essential to use it so that the stove tank and controls do not overheat, otherwise a fire or explosion could result. This means following directions carefully. Collars, if supplied, must be fitted correctly, and air holes must not be obstructed by snow or sand. Feel the tank periodically to ensure that overheating is not occurring. Remember also that if the pot and controls are enclosed you cannot react very quickly to a boil over by either turning down the stove or removing the pot. Removable pot handles are recommended because a conventional handle gets very hot when enclosed. If a stove enclosure causes a restricted air supply, production of very poisonous carbon monoxide can increase.

Alpine Cook Tent

The Mountain Hardwear Alpine Cook tent is a miniature tent with a transparent front and arm holes you reach through to handle your stoves and pots. In exposed, windy areas or low temperatures you enjoy enormous fuel savings and much faster cooking. The cook tent weighs 744 grams, about the same as a one litre bottle of white gas, and it doesn't take long to save this amount of fuel. The savings on extended or group trips can be dramatic. The waste stove heat can be used to dry small clothing items in a "loft" in the tent or to melt snow for water. The tent can also be used as a solar oven to melt snow as it has a transparent front and side, dark floor and reflective rear. A pot containing two litres of water in the cook tent in September afternoon sunshine in Calgary reached 39°C in two hours from 10°C. The air temperature reached 52°C inside, with outside air at 19°C! The solar heating also helps to clear frost and cooking condensation from the interior.

A further advantage of the cook tent is that there is less incentive to cook in your sleeping tent or vestibule so there is no risk of fire or of contaminating the tent with food smells that attract animals. However, the usual fire precautions are in order, particularly when lighting your stove. Even during careful priming the loft is

Alpine Cook Tent.

perilously close to the flames, though on production models it will be removable to provide more headroom. It's a good idea to carry a piece of polyethylene sheet to protect the floor from spills, and a piece of plywood or one of the new stove bases (see below). You MUST also peg it down VERY securely. The clear plastic is the same super-tough material that is used as a window in a Mountain Hardwear tent.

Stove Safety

Stoves should be regarded as friends, not as foes to be feared. People do make mistakes with stoves, especially when tired or half asleep, and these mistakes can lead to some interesting moments. The problems are most dramatic if you are disobeying a cardinal rule and are filling, lighting or changing the cylinder of a stove in tents, vehicles, cabins, etc. In a dramatic incident 30 years ago, I was returning through the mud and pouring rain of a bleak Scottish campsite to the van in which my climbing partners were cooking breakfast when I saw the doors suddenly open and several cursing bodies tumble out into the mud in their underwear. They were almost immediately followed by a stove enveloped in a ball of flame along with a stream of quaint invective and derision from the person still in the vehicle. This was aimed mostly at the clods who had bailed out, leaving him asleep in his sack beside a blazing stove, rather than having the presence of mind to kick the stove out themselves.

On another occasion some successful Everest summiters had a very close call. During their epic descent they had a gas cylinder changing problem that probably only occurred because they were in the last stages of exhaustion. The resulting fire in the tent could have cost them their lives. I have seen several episodes with two-burner gasoline stoves that were used incorrectly and allowed to flood with fuel and were then relit indoors. So—follow the rules and light and fill stoves and change cylinders outside whenever possible. It's also astounding how much better and more safely stoves operate if people read and follow the instructions!

I repeat again, if you are using any kind of heat retaining windshield on your stove, be especially careful it does not cause overheating of the tank. This could of course lead to a devastating explosion. Feel the tank periodically with your hand.

Suspend your lantern from a hook or toggle like this so it can be easily lifted down if it flares up, without having to put your hand above the lantern.

All stoves use up oxygen from the air, and this may be the oxygen you need to breathe! In an enclosed space such as a snowcave, tent or vehicle, the oxygen level goes down surprisingly quickly. This in turn leads to incomplete combustion of the fuel and the production of lethal carbon monoxide rather than carbon dioxide. Carbon monoxide is a deadly poisonous, odourless and colourless gas. The only warning of its effect is drowsiness and headache, and if you miss these signs the consequences can be fatal. To prevent this deadly loss of oxygen and buildup of carbon monoxide occurring, avoid using stoves in enclosed spaces such as small huts, tents and vehicles. If weather conditions give you no alternative but to use a stove inside, you must arrange for a throughflow of air in a tent, snowcave building or vehicle. Small amounts of carbon monoxide may be produced during normal combustion, especially if the flame impinges on a cold, wet pot such as one containing snow.

Air exchange by diffusion through a single opening is not enough—you must have a **flow** of air. I found this out the hard way in a snow cave.

Stove fires only occur as a result of incorrect use, but they do occur and it is useful to know how to control them.

It was built with a large entrance and with the sleeping platform about 50 centimetres above the top of the entrance to produce a good warm air trap. Because the entrance was so large, we did not bother with a roof vent as well. The stove started making strange noises so I shut it off and cleaned it. When I tried to relight it, only the match heads would burn because there was not enough oxygen for the wooden part to burn. I finally realized what the problem was, and my hunch was confirmed when I leaned down off the sleeping platform and successfully struck a match down in the entrance well. We were lucky to survive this episode and thankfully made a vent hole in the roof. You only need vent holes open when cooking and can plug them to retain warmth for sleeping. Your breathing does not use oxygen up as fast as does a powerful stove when burning, and you do not produce poisonous carbon monoxide. A snow cave vent can be easily plugged from inside after extinguishing the stove, by crumpling a plastic bag into a loose ball, inserting it into the hole and allowing it to expand.

One of the more dramatic types of stove mishap occurs when the valve at the bottom of the pump cylinder fails to seal and fuel comes back out of the pump. It then usually catches fire,

If leakage and a flame appears around stove control valve shafts, tighten the gland nut (arrowed), such as this one on a Peak 1 stove.

and life gets exciting. Try to prevent dirt getting into the pump because it may eventually work its way past the piston and cause this seal failure. Be especially careful in sandy areas. Usually if this trouble starts, one stroke of the flooded pump will flush the dirt through the valve and wash it clean so it reseals. Because of the risk of leakage through the pump, do not store or pack your stove with the tank pressurized—release the pressure even though you have to pump it up again to use it. With Coleman Peak 1 stoves always make sure you screw the pump knob down tight to close the valve at the bottom properly.

A startling fire can occur with some Optimus stoves such as the 8R and 111 Hiker if the pot is too big and it deflects heat onto the safety valve and the top of the tank. The safety valve blows and a jet of fuel shoots up at a 45 degree angle, usually burning. The heat may damage the safety valve seal so it does not reseal properly. This is not really a fault of the stove; some people use pots that are too big.

Small flames often occur around leaky control valves. The additional heat damages the valve and may make the problem worse. Tighten the gland nut to prevent this happening. See photo, page 178.

Extinguishing Stove Fires

A wide variety of indignities have been visited on recalcitrant or misused stoves and lanterns in efforts to extinguish unexpected infernos. The simplest method of controlling a blaze is to just turn the stove off and let it burn out, as long as it won't set the place on fire or overheat the tank and explode. A few seconds to put on your gloves can save you some grief. Blazing stoves and lanterns can often be calmly picked up at the base and held aloft at arm's length while being carried outside. Watch out that your slipstream or a gust of wind doesn't blow flames or burning liquid in your face or onto your clothes. Lanterns should always be hung on a hook, nail or toggle and never be tied, to allow instant removal without any need to put your hands above them. Don't start a forest fire with your blazing stove or lantern!

A shovelful of snow will produce an instant result on stoves. Although water is not traditionally recommended for liquid fuel fires, a well-aimed dollop of water can be very effective as long as there is not a lot of burning liquid that can be spread around. Stoves have been kicked into lakes and rivers, but this can deprive you of the use of the stove permanently! We once encountered a canoeist vainly diving into an Ontario lake to retrieve his stove. Actually, it wasn't because he wanted the stove back—he hated it—but because he felt guilty about polluting the lake! If there is a puddle of burning fuel in the stove, don't kick hard. The puddle tends to stay behind and ends up burning on your foot! Smothering with clothing works well but damages the clothing, often as much by contact with hot metal as by flame burn. Be quick and decisive and use something big enough and tightly woven enough to seal out the air. A large pot or a bailer inverted over the stove may also do the trick as long as the stove is in snow or soft ground so the edge of the pot can seal against the ground.

Burning compressed gas stoves present a dilemma. If you extinguish the flame and cannot stop the leak, the gas may build up and eventually a large amount accumulates and gets ignited again and a major explosion occurs. To reduce this danger, move the leaking stove well away into the open and away from people until all the gas has dissipated. The gas will collect in hollows, basements, etc. On the other hand, if you leave a burning leak, it may heat the tank until it explodes or the heat may melt rubber seals and cause a more serious leak.

Stove Stability

A knocked-over stove can flare up and the spilt food can cause serious burns as well as being lost. Be especially careful with tall stoves. In winter, carry a piece of plywood for a firm base. Your shovel blade will be too slippery and the projecting parts easily get knocked. MSR have finally come up with a great base for their Whisperlite and XGK stoves.

Fuel Leaks

Make sure your fuel bottles are leakproof and marked to show they contain fuel. Sigg or Nalgene brand are best. Keep stoves and food totally separate from food—the tiniest trace of fuel can render food unusable.

Cooking Utensils

Good cooking utensils make the cook's job easier and safer. Utensils that are tedious to use because they are difficult to clean or are badly shaped, or worse still, unstable and likely to deposit boiling soup on your foot, have no place in the backcountry. Worst of all are those with poor handles that do not stay cool. A scalded foot on a hiker or a burned hand on a paddler can be a big problem.

Weigh all utensils and think carefully about what you really need and what you can do without. The cumulative effect of small amounts of weight saved here and there quickly adds up, and is important with the long distances and remoteness.

Pots in particular give an erroneous impression of being light simply because of their large size. They are in fact quite heavy. Weigh yours to find out. If you can't cook your meals in one pot and its lid, you may want to consider redesigning your menu.

A cooking group of four allows you to take two pots without drastically affecting the weight being carried per person, but a light-weight party of two will probably only want to take one pot. Make sure it doesn't get blown into a crevasse or dropped into a creek if it is your only pot and you only have dried food!

Cutlery

A Lexan plastic spoon weighs 12 grams, a metal one, 50 grams. Save 38 grams or take more chocolates instead! Do you really need a fork? If you need a knife, use your penknife.

Cups and Mugs

You need a large utensil to drink from because you need to take in lots of liquid while out-doors. Large plastic mugs are hard to find, but a two-cup plastic measuring cup only weighs 75 grams and can be used for measuring, eating or drinking. Many prepared food recipes require accurate measurement of liquids so it has another use.

A collection of camp cookware and utensils. Weigh everything carefully and decide what you really need.

Plates

Do you need a plate or can you eat out of your cup and the pot and its lid? Aluminum plates weigh around 100 grams, plastic ones 100-300 grams. The aluminum one is more versatile as you can cook in it or use it as a fry pan or fry pan lid.

Pots

For efficient heating, avoid wide, shallow pots or tall, deep ones. The depth should be 2/3 of the diameter and should be large enough to allow approximately one litre per person. In winter, the size must be increased considerably to melt snow for water.

Aluminum pots are much lighter than stainless steel ones. Stainless steel pots are very thin to save weight, but the thinness, coupled with the poor conductivity of stainless steel compared to aluminum, means that heat spreads poorly across the bottom of the pan. Localized heating and burning results. Poor quality stainless steel can have impurities that act as focal points for pitting and a pit can pierce a thin pot. The same can happen with aluminum pots, especially if food is left sitting in them. However, the aluminum is often thicker and is soft enough to be peened between two rocks to block a leak. If in an emergency you have to use a fire, a bail handle allows the pot to be suspended over the flames. The Coleman bail handles lock in the up position to stay clear of stove heat and to allow easy pouring.

Sigg Brand stainless steel-lined aluminum pots give you the best of both worlds with the easy cleaning steel inside and the heat-spreading aluminum outside, but are a little heavier than other pots. They are the ultimate luxury camp cookware. The new Evolution pot from Travelling Light is heavyweight aluminum with a durable nonstick coating. It weighs the same as a stainless steel pot but spreads the heat very well. The nonstick coating prevents aluminum entering your food, though this is not a serious concern anymore. (Apparently there is no relationship between aluminum cookware use and Alzheimer's disease.)

Although it weighs 100 grams, a pot lid is essential to keep heat in and reduce fuel consumption. It must be usable as a plate or better still as a fry pan if it has a side handle. Sauce-

pan-style lids with a central button handle are only any use as a lid, and an aluminum foil pie plate weighing much less at only 10 grams will do the same job.

A lightweight pressure cooker saves lots of cooking time and fuel. It is well worth the weight on longer trips and at higher altitude because its weight is compensated for by fuel savings. My wife and I carried one while trek-

The Sigg brand stainless steel pots with aluminum exteriors are very nice to cook with because the aluminum spreads the heat well and the steel is easy to clean.

A lightweight pressure cooker saves a lot of cooking time and fuel, especially at high altitudes.

king in Nepal and it was worth the weight even for just two of us because it made cooking so much quicker and meant we had to carry less fuel. I also used it on a three-week ski tour on the icefields of the St. Elias Range where altitude and the need for fuel economy were important factors.

Fry Pans

A good fry pan has a fairly thick base to spread the heat evenly and will weigh at least 450 grams (one pound). It may not be worth its weight and may be redundant with a few small changes to your menu. A fry pan lid made from a piece of heavyweight foil or a plate will enable you to cook a wider range of dishes such as bush pizzas, cakes and bannocks as well as frying food. A good nonstick surface is a big help. Domestic fry pans are generally cheaper and have better nonstick coatings than many camping ones with folding handles. You can easily remove and replace the handle of a domestic fry pan with a Swiss Army knife screwdriver for travelling, but don't lose the screw.

Ovens

Dutch ovens are usually made of cast iron and are too heavy except if you are boating with no portages. However, they enable you to do some creative baking as well as bean pots, casseroles, etc. Some people have used cast iron pots as moulds to have an identical but lighter item cast by their local aluminum foundry.

The Outback Oven's main component is a heat retaining cover that enables you to use an ordinary pot or the specially provided nonstick pan as an oven. It also includes a very effective heat spreader to dissipate the heat of a stove evenly across the bottom of a pot to reduce the chance of burning. Folding ovens to use on Coleman camp stoves, and reflector ovens are other options.

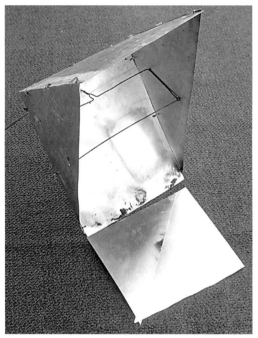

A reflector oven for use with camp fires can be bought or made from aluminum flashing, which you join together with twist ties.

The Outback Oven is light, easy to use and very effective for camp baking. Its pan can be used for frying, too.

Hot-Smoker

This enables you to quickly cook fish by hot-smoking. Lightweight ones are hard to find nowadays, but it is basically a tin box such as a cake tin with the paint removed and a wire rack inside. You place a tablespoon of hardwood sawdust (from a fishing or BBQ supplier) on the bottom, place the fish on the rack, close the lid and put the closed tin on coals or a stove for 10 minutes or so until the sawdust is charred and the fish is cooked by being baked in the smoke. It is quite light to carry.

Water Bottles

A water bottle for each individual is a crucial item to ensure everyone can drink enough liquids to avoid dehydration. I prefer to use a Sigg aluminum one-litre bottle weighing about 130 grams (4-1/2 ounces). The Sigg bottles designed for drinks have a coating on the inside to prevent drink acids from attacking the aluminum, but this is absent from those designed for fuel. Plastic one-litre bottles weigh about the same but many do not have a good seal. Nalgene brand are good and are available in a wide variety of sizes and shapes for food and beverages.

The big advantage of an aluminum bottle is that if it freezes, you can always thaw it out on a stove or fire, but you cannot do that with a frozen plastic bottle. I have seen people carrying around a kilogram of useless ice in their bottle and trying to thaw it out in their sleeping bag! I have also heard of two incidents where parties lost their only cook pot, and only one group had a metal water bottle to use to cook their dried food for the rest of the trip. One was a canoe party where they were committing the sin of washing the pot in the river, the other was a ski party where they were dipping for water through a hole in the ice on a creek. I once saw a pot blow away down a crevassed glacier, and pots obscured by snow have been trodden on with crampons, too.

People will cite the risk of freezing your lips to the aluminum bottle. This is only a risk if the bottle is frozen, and there is no point in putting it to your mouth if that is the case. If it is not frozen and you can shake liquid around in it, it cannot be at a temperature below freezing, and the shaking will bring the metal near the neck up to freezing. A touch of butter or other grease will prevent the stopper freezing in the neck, and holding the neck in your hand will quickly thaw it anyway.

Water carriers and basins are convenient and enable you to camp with less impact.

Water Carrier

It is undesirable to camp right on the edge of the water, and in many parks you are required to be 50 or even 100 metres back from the water. You therefore need something for carrying water from a creek or lake to your campsite for cooking and washing and maybe putting out your fire if you have one. It is not for carrying water while you travel.

Also, a good-sized water carrier is convenient and more environmentally friendly because you aren't submitting the site to the wear and tear of traipsing back and forth with a small pot. In addition, if you have a big enough container you are more likely to follow the rule of washing yourself and dishes back somewhere in the bush and not in the watercourse.

The aluminized plastic liner from a four-litre cardboard wine cask makes a good, lightweight water carrier for use around camp. The buff-coloured valve comes off with a twist and an oblique pull, or can be pried off. The bag holds much more than four litres and they are surprisingly strong as long as you do not put them down on sharp rocks or sticks. They are also useful as water carriers for sea kayakers because they mould well to the bottom of the boat, especially collapsible kayaks. Simple water buckets made of lightweight nylon are also available. Reliance Products of Winnipeg have produced collapsible five- and 20-litre plastic water bottles with taps for many years, though these are not as compact when empty. Ortlieb makes canoeist's rolltop dry bags with a tap in the bottom for use as a water carrier. Ortlieb also makes a convenient lightweight water bag in several sizes with a screw cap/valve. MSR Dromedary bags are easier to fill than most bags because of a large diameter filler cap. They have a convenient pourer spout. The shower hose attachment can also be used to direct water into a cook pot by pressing on the bag.

Wash Basins

The availability of a wash basin ensures that pots and people are not washed in the creek or lake. Ortlieb makes an excellent lightweight collapsible vinyl basin. Containers similar to the Reliance 20-litre collapsible bottle are sometimes used for chemicals such as pool chlorine. One of these with the top cut off makes a good basin and is self-supporting as long as it is fairly full of water.

Ordinary rectangular, rigid, plastic wash basins are light, especially the cheap ones. They can be packed with other items when travelling, and in a boat they keep items out of the bilge water.

Plastic basins seem to have a strong attraction for the black off pots used on fires, and they stain horribly. If you have blackened pots, don't put them in the basin.

Pot Cleaners

Knitted nylon-type pot cleaners are boilable to sterilize them and they dry fast so bacteria don't grow much. They are fairly easy to keep clean because residue such as porridge or cream soup rinses easily. The more abrasive but denser green "Scotchbrite" types of pads are great for stubborn residue, but can harbour a lot of the softer porridge gunge. J-cloths have the advantage of being thin and easily rinsed and dried and eventually burned if too badly soiled. Dish drying towels are unhygienic unless boiled often, and even more so with a group of people. It is much better to just let things drip and air dry.

Whatever type of cleaner you use, don't leave it damp, rotting and culturing bacteria in a plastic bag.

Dish Soap or Detergent

Liquid can be packed in a well-cleaned empty insect repellent bottle that is clearly labelled. Some liquid soaps are described as being "biodegradable," but this term is somewhat vague and the product is not necessarily very benign. Do not contaminate streams or lakes with used water. Scatter it onto the ground, well away from camp, creeks or lakes. Remove food scraps first and place in the garbage bag or fire.

Gloves or Pot Lifters

Hand injuries are particularly serious for paddlers, but can spoil anyone's trip. A pair of leather gloves can save the cook from injuries from hot pot handles and while gathering wood. A filleting board and clamp and fish-gripping gloves reduces the risks when filleting fish.

Chapter 7

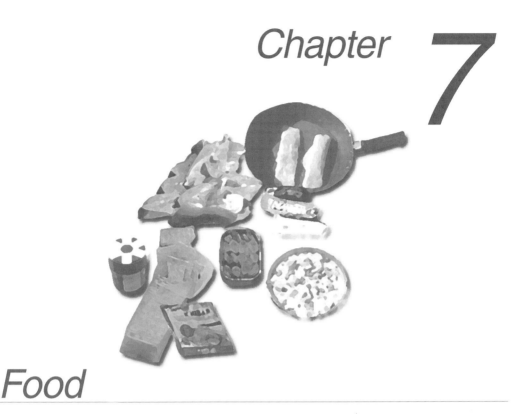

Food

Food can have a big influence on the success of a trip. Appropriate types and quantities of food are required to provide the energy and nutrition needed to meet the physical demands. Although you can meet these demands with some very mundane meals, food that is attractive and pleasant to eat will go down easier and be better for morale. Wilderness trips in Canada and Alaska often require you to go for long periods without resupply, so provisioning must be done meticulously. It can be a lot of work, but with appropriate "systems" it is easier, and the time and effort put into selecting and organizing the food pays dividends in less work in the field.

Food for the Backcountry

There is a saying that "you are what you eat." There is a lot of truth in that, though not to the point where you should avoid eating flaked, boneless turkey! The amount and quality of food you eat has a significant effect on you even on short trips, but particularly during long wilderness trips. On a day trip, your performance can be considerably affected simply by what you ate for breakfast. However, you can probably get by on inadequate food by using your body reserves if the day is not too strenuous. On a weekend trip, the consequences of insufficient or inadequate food can be more serious. If you consume less food than you need, you will use up body reserves and deplete your insurance against unexpected demands. A sign that you have probably not been balancing energy output with food energy intake is if you head for the nearest "greasy spoon" restaurant as soon as you get back to the car! On multi-day trips, there will be a significant decline in your performance if you are using your body energy reserves instead of your daily food intake to supply energy needs. Your ability to cope with emergency conditions will be much eroded.

In Canada and Alaska, you are likely to be away from sources of supply for extended periods because towns with stores and restaurants are few and far between, unlike in Europe where the mountains are well supplied with eating and drinking establishments. Many is the time I have looked across a Canadian mountain vista and commented that if it were Europe there would be cows, not grizzlies, in the meadows, and there would be a source of cold beer, fresh bread and sausage over the next hill. Backcountry travellers therefore need to plan, pack and organize food and drink with great care, especially when food weight must be kept to a minimum.

Not only are food stores few and far between, but lightweight foods suitable for serious outdoor pursuits are rare in remote areas. Also consider that some remote stores are only stocked once or twice a year, during favourable water or ice-road transportation times. You should never rely on being able to resupply in them, especially those accessible only by air or water. You may be lucky and find a well-stocked store, you may only find staples such as flour and rice, or you may find bare shelves. There may be little that is of any appeal, and it will probably be in cans and expensive. Also remember that a large group's purchases could

Attractive and nutritious meals can be produced under primitive conditions and will pay dividends in morale.

Variety and choice make food more enjoyable, and even on a three-week glacier trip it was possible to have a choice of cheeses, a variety of crackers, candy bars and goodies like smoked oysters.

adversely affect the availability of supplies to villagers who have no hope of resupply for months. It is not always simply a matter of "more business for the store owner."

To avoid these difficulties, some groups mail extra food ahead to a remote post office. Check that it has arrived before starting the trip and advise the postmaster when you will pick it up so that it is not "returned to sender" before you arrive. You can sometimes make arrangements with "expediters," "bush order specialists" and air charter operators to fly packages to remote locations. Their addresses can be found in the Yellow Pages and by making local inquiries. Some advertise in tourist brochures. You need to be sure they will keep your food where it will stay cool and protected from animals.

Food weight must be carefully controlled because you are already carrying a lot of gear to be self-sufficient. Weight control is especially necessary on long trips, although there is more latitude on canoe trips if there are no portages. If food weighs too much, you create a vicious circle where carrying its extra weight expends extra energy, which in turn requires you to eat more food, which in turn requires more energy for carrying, and so on. On the other hand, too little food may keep the weight down and allow rapid travel, but the trip will not be any fun if you are hungry all the time. I recently talked to someone who did a 15-day crossing of the Greenland Icecap. They travelled very fast and very light, but regretted their 4000 kcal/day food supply, which should have been at least 5000 kcal/day to satisfy their needs.

The keeping quality of food is important on longer trips. Remember that food has to keep longer than the actual trip; you may be transporting it in a hot vehicle for a considerable distance even before you get to the start of the trip. If you have to discard spoiled food in places where resupply is impossible, you are going to go hungry. Food poisoning from spoiled food is unpleasant and potentially serious anywhere, but more so in a place remote from assistance. Even just a mild attack can weaken you and make you accident-prone. Choose foods that are well packaged and that don't leak or smell during storage and cooking, to prevent both spoilage and conflicts with animals.

Meals must be attractive and must taste and smell good. To quote Elton Jesup (*Camp Grub*, E. P. Dutton Co., NY, 1924), "You can't enjoy the most entrancing view or even be sociable with your fellow men if your stomach is full of, say, burnt beans." No matter how well planned for light weight and nutritional efficiency the food is, if people can't force enough of it down it won't supply their daily nutritional needs on a hard trip. Also, if your rations are a monotonous repetition of white glop for breakfast, hard tack for lunch and brown glop for dinner, some of the best aspects of tripping will be missed.

Variety helps make food appealing. On one 24-day trip we had a different menu for each evening meal. There were two couples, each responsible for a meal for four on alternate nights. You can eat well on a trip if you are imaginative and make an effort. Friends told of a time they sat on a gravel bar on a remote northern river eating their hors d'oeuvres of Camembert and olives, while clams linguine simmered on the stove and cheesecake cooled at the water's edge. Another party showed up who had been living on beans, bannock and "boiled birdseed" and not much else for a week. They gaped in amazement before fleeing out of reach of the tantalizing sights and smells. Our friends felt quite smug and knew their considerable preparation before the trip had been well worthwhile.

You won't always be on trips where you can do exotic cooking. Winter trips in particular generally dictate maximum simplicity, though I have presented my wife with crepes suzette in a snowstorm at 3000 metres on a glacier. Even on more luxurious trips, always have a "floater" or "emergency" meal available that can be cooked easily in foul conditions after a rough day. If you're horribly hungry, hypothermic and harassed by bugs, you don't want to cook a complex and time consuming dinner.

Fundamental Principles of Nutrition

The most important function of food during a trip is to provide the energy you need to carry on your activity. Energy is obtained primarily from carbohydrates and fats, so these are the most important foods for you to carry.

Carbohydrates are categorized as "complex" or "simple." Complex carbohydrates are the main constituents of starchy foods such as pasta, rice, couscous, potato, oatmeal, flour, bread, crackers and pancakes. Simple carbohydrates are found in sugary foods such as honey, candy, jam, sweetened foods and of course in common sugar.

Fats are contained in fatty meats such as bacon, dairy products such as butter and cheese, and plant products such as peanut butter, margarine and cooking oil. Fats contain twice as much energy per kilogram as do carbohydrates, so at first sight it would seem that they are the most efficient foods to carry in order to minimize weight. However, it is not that simple. For one thing, releasing energy from fatty foods requires a large initial input of energy. In fact, close to 40 per cent of fat energy is used up in the releasing process, leaving just 60 per cent to fuel our activity. When you compare that with carbohydrates where only about seven per cent of the energy is used in the release process, fats don't look so much better. Digesting and metabolizing fats requires substantial amounts of oxygen, which your body will be unwilling to spare at high altitudes. Many people cannot tolerate fatty foods at high altitude. One mitigating consideration is that more heat is released during the metabolism of fats than of carbohydrates, and this heat can be useful to the body in cold environments. People have reported a fat craving when exposed to intense cold for long periods, and revulsion at high altitude.

Studies of how the body actually uses energy from the two sources indicate that for strenuous exercise over long periods, the diet should actually contain somewhat larger amounts of carbohydrates and lower amounts of fats than a normal North American diet. The energy from carbohydrates should increase by about 10-15 per cent to around 55-65 per cent of the total, and the energy from fats should drop by 10-15 per cent to 25-30 per cent. This increased intake of energy (calories) from carbohydrates has the effect of better maintaining or replenishing the body's energy stores, which consist of an energy-rich substance called glycogen, in the muscles and liver. If these stores are not maintained, the body quickly becomes fatigued.

Complex carbohydrates are better body fuels than are simple carbohydrates for a number of reasons. They digest slowly and provide a steady stream of glucose to the body. This is preferable to the sudden heavy doses of glucose that enter the body shortly after consuming sugary foods. The body reacts to these heavy doses of glucose by producing insulin to reduce the blood sugar level. This results in swings in blood glucose levels, which can actually hinder performance. Also, complex carbohydrates often contain fibre that helps maintain bowel function at a reasonable level. Constipation is no fun where the bugs are bad or the wind and snow blow!

Proteins, the other main food group, are not primary energy sources, although they can be broken down to release energy if necessary. The main function of proteins is to supply the "building blocks" from which materials required by the body can be assembled. These include materials for growth and repair, and enzymes and hormones required for normal body functioning. Proteins are found in foods such as meats, fish, cheese, peas, beans and whole grains. Very strenuous "to the limit" exercise can result in increased loss of body protein and greater need to replace it from food protein sources.

Vitamins and minerals are only required in trace amounts. Symptoms of vitamin deficiency might develop as a result of long-term use of preserved and highly processed expedition foods, so daily multiple vitamin supplements are useful on longer trips. Generally, the required minerals are obtained from the food, but if the rate of mineral loss is large because of heavy sweating, electrolyte replacement drinks may be beneficial.

Some Foods and Their Nutritional Content

Food item	Water %	Carbo, Fat, Protein	Energy kcal/kg
Apples, fresh	85	C	580
Apples, dried	25	C	2750
Apples, dehydrated	2.5	C	3530
Bacon, packaged	60	FP	2160
Bacon, cured, dry	19	FP	6650
Beans, dry	1	CP	3400
Beans, canned	70	CP	1220
Beef, canned, corned	60	PF	2930
Beef, fresh	50-70	PF	2500
Beef stew, canned	83	PF	890
Beef, dried	10 approx.	PF	3500
Bread	35	C	2630
Butter	15	F	7160
Butter oil	0.2	F	8760
Cake	20-30	CF	3000
Cereals	10	CP	3800
Cheese	40	PF	3800
Chocolate	2	CF	5280
Cod, dried salted	52	P	1300
Cod, dehydrated	12	P	3750
Cookies	2-3	CF	4800
Crackers	2-6	CF	4500
Dates	22	C	2740
Eggs, dried	4	PF	5920
Flour	12	CP	3640
Ham, dry-cured	40	FP	3890
Ham, regular	56	FP	3080
Honey	17	C	3040
Jams	30	C	2720
Luncheon meat	55-60	FP	2950
Macaroni	10	C	3690
Margarine	15	F	7200
Milk powder	2	PC	3600
Muffins	38	CF	2900
Noodles	10	C	3880
Oatmeal	8	CP	3900
Onion, dried	4	C	3500
Pancake mix	8	CPF	3560
Peanuts	2	FPC	5820
Peanut butter	1-2	FPC	5810
Peas, dry	10	CP	3400
Potatoes, raw	80	CP	760
Potato flakes	5	CP	3640
Puddings, canned	65-75	CF	1400
Prepared dinners	65-75	CPF	1060
Pudding mixes	1-2	CF	3600
Raisins	18	C	2890
Rice	10-12	CP	3630
Rolls	30	C	2980
Sardines	60	FP	1600
Sausage	50-60	FPC	3450
Salami, dry	30	FP	4500
Soups, dried	3-10	CPF	3700
Spaghetti, dry	10	CP	3690
Tuna, in oil	52	PF	2880
Tuna, in broth	70	P	1270
Turkey, canned	65	FP	2020

Minimizing the Weight of Food

There are four ways to keep down the weight of needed food supplies.

- minimize the water content of the food
- maximize energy (calorie) content per kg
- minimize the weight of packaging materials
- take the correct amount in order to eliminate waste.

Minimizing Water Content

Water contains no energy whatsoever, and since the reason for carrying food is primarily to provide energy, it makes no sense to carry food with water in it (assuming you have plentiful water at your campsites, which you generally do).

The previous table shows just how much the amount of water in food influences the amount of energy present per kilogram. For example, a kilogram of fresh apples, which contain 85 per cent water, provides only 580 calories of energy, but a kilogram of dried apples containing 25 per cent water provides 2750 calories (4-1/2 times as much). If the rubbery "dried" apples are fully dehydrated to about 2.5 per cent water they provide 3530 calories per kilogram (six times as much as fresh apples).

As another example, bread contains about 35 per cent water, so the energy in a kilogram of bread is far less than in a kilogram of dry flour from which you can make bannock. A wide variety of dried foods are available from supermarkets, whole food stores and stores catering to the food storage needs of Mormons.

Maximizing the Energy Content per kilogram

Having minimized the water content, you still want to choose foods with as high energy content as possible. Fats contain twice as much energy as the same weight of carbohydrates. If you just ate butter, a half kilogram of butter per day would contain enough calories (8760/2 = 4380 kcal) to fuel some strenuous activity, whereas about a kilogram of carbohydrates would be needed. However, as was pointed out earlier, too much fat in your rations is not necessarily a good thing, and the fat content must be kept within reasonable levels compared to carbohydrates.

Usable foods with the most energy per kilogram are therefore those that are dry and that contain a proportion of fats with the carbohydrates and/or proteins. For example, cookies contain much more energy than bread because of their fat content and low water content. Bacon, which is fatty, contains far more energy than does lean beef, which is not fatty.

Minimizing the Weight of Packaging Materials

Packaging materials have a significant weight—we once returned from a three-day backpack for two people and weighed the packaging to find the plastic bags, cardboard boxes, foil pouches and an empty tuna can weighed 250 grams (over nine ounces)! The key is to decide how much packaging is really needed. In winter you can make do with less packaging because you are less concerned about smells attracting bears and about the food becoming wet. For the Footsteps of Scott expedition to the South Pole, they removed the packaging from the chocolate bars and packed them loose in the toboggans to save weight. Where bags are only needed as organizers, I use the really thin supermarket vegetable bags to save weight. Do not take the cardboard boxes when the contents are in a pouch or bag inside. See discussion on food packaging later in this chapter. On long trips better packaging is needed to not only exclude water and keep smells in, but also to be strong enough to withstand the rigours of repeated handling.

Canned goods are viewed by many people as being "too heavy." However, it's not so much the can itself that is heavy—a 400 millilitre size can only weighs 50 grams, and a tuna can is only about 40 grams. The superfluous weight is more likely to be the water that the food in the can contains. You can therefore avoid most of the problem by selecting the drier types of canned foods. Canned corned beef, which has no gravy or juice, is 2930 kcal/kg, but canned beef stew is only 890 kcal/kg, largely because of the watery gravy. Tuna in oil is 2880 kcal/kg, which is reasonable, but in broth it is only 1270 kcal/kg, so choose carefully. Tuna in oil is now hard to find in Canada.

The tasty part of many meals is the meat and fish in them. Unfortunately, meat and fish must often be canned, otherwise they are too attractive to animals or too perishable. Taste is a very important function if it helps you enjoy your food and to eat enough, and the protein is important on longer trips. You can perhaps afford the slightly greater weight of cans if other parts of your meal are light. Some products are available in light aluminum cans, for example, Maple Leaf ham, some canned fish and some types of Brie or Camembert cheese.

Calculating the Correct Amount

The correct amount of food will keep the weight down by avoiding carrying unnecessary excess. When calculating how much food to take, you must consider a number of factors. These include:

- the demands of the trip—how strenuous it is, time spent daily in travelling, weight of loads being carried, etc.

- the skill of the participants. Inefficient skiers, paddlers or climbers are likely to expend considerable energy picking themselves up after falling, swimming rapids, making speed-robbing correction strokes, repeatedly trying and failing the same move and just by being tense or frightened.

- the expected temperatures—cold weather increases energy demands

- the gender of the participants—most females eat less than most males

- the build and metabolism of the participants. Small or lanky people cool down more quickly than large, plump people, and generally as a result need more food just to keep warm.

Because of all these variables, you cannot generalize how many calories to provide per person per day, though it is likely to be between 3500 and 5000 kcal for an active outdoor trip. Really strenuous activity such as sled-hauling in polar regions could require as much as 6000 kcal per day. Actually, it would be difficult to consume enough food to re-

plenish a 6000 kcal/day expenditure, and even taking in 4000-5000 kcal/day requires some fairly serious eating sessions.

To gain a clearer understanding of your requirements, probably the best thing to do is to keep personal records of how much and what foods you take and use on each trip, how much you bring back, and the type and length of each trip. If you then calculate the energy content of your foods, in time you will obtain a reasonable picture of your daily energy expenditure under different conditions. Weigh your food with a kitchen scale, and use data from the table on page 192 to calculate the calories in the food. For dry carbohydrates use 4000 kcal/kg, fats 8000 kcal/kg and dry proteins 4000 kcal/kg as approximate figures.

You can't expect to be spot-on with your calculations, because for one thing you can't predict the weather and its demands on your body. To cover the extremes of energy demands, take extra flour for bannock or extra pasta or rice, and use more or less as dictated by the conditions actually encountered. The excess doesn't take up much room and is cheap enough to be discarded if weight is a real problem and if you can handle the questionable ethics of discarding excess food.

The weight of dry food required to supply a given number of calories per day in an appropriately balanced way can be calculated. First of all, decide on the daily calorie requirement for the activity and the weather conditions. As a guide, assume that long, strenuous days in cold weather require around 5000 kcal/day, less strenuous days in warm temperatures need around 4000 kcal/day. The energy sources are appropriately apportioned among carbohydrates, fats and proteins.

The example on the next page shows how to calculate the weight of dry food needed to supply a theoretical diet of 4000 kcal/day. It also shows how a different fat content affects the weight of dried food required.

If this is getting a bit technical, a reasonable rule of thumb for outfitting a trip is around 900 grams (two pounds) per person per day if it is fairly dry food. If you include apples, oranges, canned beans or stew, the weight will rise dramatically or else you will have insufficient calories.

Calculating the Weight of Food Needed to Supply 4000 kcal

Example 1, Minimum fat content (20% energy from fat)

65% of the energy from carbohydrate   (65% of 4000) =   2600 kcal
15% of the energy from protein   (15% of 4000) =   600 kcal
20% of the energy from fat   (20% of 4000) =   800 kcal

Assuming carbohydrates contain approximately 4000 kcal/kg, proteins contain approximately 3500 kcal/kg and fats contain approximately 8000 kcal/kg:

2600 kcal requires   2600/4000 = 0.65 kg of carbohydrate
600 kcal requires   600/3500 = 0.17 kg of protein
800 kcal requires   800/8000 = 0.10 kg of fat
          Total   **0.92 kg**

Therefore, assuming that the food is completely dry, we can obtain our 4000 kcal per day with 0.92 kg (2 lb.) of food.

Example 2, Maximum fat content (35% energy from fat)

If the ratio of fat to carbohydrate is raised, the total required is as follows:

50% of the energy from carbohydrate   (50% of 4000) =   2000 kcal
15% of the energy from protein   (15% of 4000) =   600 kcal
35% of the energy from fat   (35% of 4000) =   1400 kcal

2000 kcal requires   2000/4000 = 0.50 kg of carbohydrate
600 kcal requires   600/3500 = 0.17 kg of protein
1400 kcal requires   1400/8000 = 0.17 kg of fat
          Total   **0.84 kg**

So the energy requirement is met with 0.84 kg of food instead of 0.92 kg when the fat amount is raised. This is a saving of 0.08 kg or nearly 3 oz.

Measuring Food by Weight

Notice that at no time have I mentioned measuring food by volume such as litres, cups, etc. This is because the energy content of food is related to how much actual material there is, not how much space it takes up. Buy a kitchen scale and weigh your rations.

The following comparisons of "airy" and compact foods should clarify the point: two cups (500 millilitres) of macaroni contains only 270 grams of carbohydrate, whereas two cups of rice contains 420 grams and two cups of flour contains 320 grams of carbohydrate.

If you use volume to measure your food, you will have some rather thin meals some days and will be a bit bloated on others. If space is at a premium you should consider only dense foods that have very little air in them.

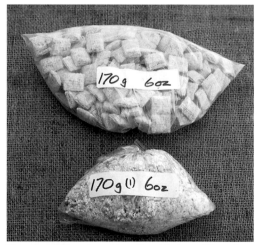

These two different samples of breakfast cereal have the same weight and therefore approximately the same energy content, but they take up very different amounts of space because the upper one is mostly air.

Food Organization and Packaging

Careful organizing and packaging of food before you set off will allow you to reap numerous benefits once you are on the trip. The most important packaging processes are making up meal-size and day-size packages of food.

The Benefits of Careful Packaging

Packaging or repackaging into meal-size packages serves four purposes:

- it keeps the food consumption controlled so you don't run out of food

- it allows you to premix your ingredients at home for ease of cooking in the field

- it keeps the food dry and uncontaminated so it will keep better

- it helps keep odours in, so there is less problem with animals

But—remember that packaging materials **do** have significant weight!

If you further organize your meal-sized food packages into day bags, each containing all the food for one day, there are even more benefits:

- you save a lot of packing and unpacking and wondering how much food you have left once you are on the trip.

- all but your current day's food can be kept sealed up from weather and dirt and can be placed in an animalproof cache immediately on arriving at camp. You don't want a bear wandering off with all your food for the entire trip while you pitch the tent!

- you don't have to decide what to eat, how much to eat or where everything you need is. It's all there in a day bag, premeasured, preseasoned and with all the necessary instructions. You can get on with cooking the meal quickly and efficiently.

Meal bags and day bags are great for the main components of the meals, but it does not make sense to try to package a few tea bags, a few tablespoons of coffee, etc. in meal or even single day quantities. A better plan is to have a multi-day "Drinks and Condiments" bag with tea, sugar, salt, etc., in small plastic screwtop containers or bags so they are readily available for every meal. Plastic containers are best be-

Keep frequently-used foods in screwtop plastic containers. Set up lunch bags with a variety of items to last several days.

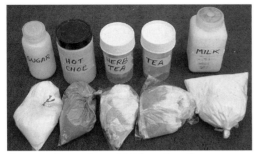

Keep your frequently-used drinks and condiments in plastic containers and refill them with a plastic bagful, say, every six days.

Food bagging do's and don'ts. Left: too much air, bursting likely, space wasted. Centre: tied tight against food, cannot change shape during packing without bursting. Right: correct, no air, food loose to allow packing without bursting.

Knotting a plastic bag correctly makes it easy to undo without destroying the bag.

The correct way to seal a bag effectively with a twist tie.

cause they are easily opened and closed and kept clean. Baggies become wet and dirty above the twist tie.

On long trips, screwtop drink and condiment containers can be replenished periodically from "fill-up" bags that are in, say, every fifth day bag. That way you do not need large screwtop containers, and you can keep reasonable track and control of how much you are using.

You may also consider packing a three-day "lunch bag" with honey, peanut butter, etc.— you can keep adequate track of how much to use each day over that short period.

Food Packaging Methods

Some food comes already excessively pre-packaged, adding weight and taking up additional space. For example, packet soups are often in foil/plastic envelopes inside cardboard boxes. Discard the boxes, except for the part with the instructions! However, the inner envelopes may not be very robust and will need to be protected from folding and puncturing from outside or from within by sharp noodles, etc., so pack them carefully. Fold or clip sharp corners so they do not puncture other bags. Some interior bags are inflated, either with preservative gas or because of reduced external air pressure at your altitude. Take a clean pin and deflate the bag to take up less room, and reseal with tape. If you subsequently gain even more altitude and the bag inflates, just pull the tape back to expose the hole, deflate and reseal.

Packaging of individual premixed meals can be done using lightweight sandwich baggies for most items. However, freezer bags are stronger and more smellproof, but heavier. Knotting the bag produces the best seal, and when knotting, twist it into a "rope" and then double the end back on itself before pulling it through the knot loop. You can undo the knot by pulling on the loose end and you can reuse the bag for a lunch bag or to store unused food. Knots can also be more easily undone without fingernail damage to the bag by twisting the material to a hard "rope" that can then be pushed **in** to the knot. If you are using twist ties, twist the bag into a rope as before, double it back on itself and fasten the tie around so as to maintain the loop of rope. Roll the ends of the tie so they cannot puncture adjacent bags.

When sealing any type of bag, squeeze the air out or suck it out with a straw, but do not apply the seal (knot, tape or twist tie) tight against the food. The bag contents should be free to move around so the bag can change shape without bursting for easier packing into odd corners of your pack, into pots or bearproof containers.

Food bags for long trips should also be packed tightly in rigid or semirigid containers. This protects the bags from abrasion and reduces the tendency for macaroni, noodles, hash browns, etc., to puncture their own bags from within with frequent bending and handling. Suitable containers to provide both abrasion resistance and waterproofing are plastic olive barrels, lard pails and rectangular ice cream or fruit pails. Olive barrels can be scrounged from Greek specialty food stores, and ice cream pails or square fruit pails from ice cream stores and restaurants. The cafeteria at work or a friendly local res-

taurant may also have suitable containers. Attach tie down loops/handles made of webbing using small bolts and washers, sealed on the inside with glue or tape. Markill makes a plastic pack box with a large gasketted screw top that is an ideal food container. A disadvantage of rigid containers is that they do not fold to take up less space when empty. However, for canoeists, the empties continue to be useful because if they are properly closed and tied down in the boat, they provide buoyancy in the event of a capsize.

Ordinary cardboard boxes can be sealed in polyethylene sheet or bags with duct tape, and then placed in fabric bags to protect the poly from puncturing. A rafting company I worked for used waxed cardboard boxes lined with a garbage bag. The waxed cardboard material was waterproof and held its strength quite well.

Another packaging option for food is to use a medium size rolltop PVC canoeist's portage pack, lined with a stiffener made of Coroplast, a plastic material that looks exactly like cardboard box material. It is available from handyman suppliers and hardware stores and is often used for outdoor temporary signboards. Make a rectangular tube of the material to fit inside the pack. Join the vertical seam with tabs and slots or string stitching

Organizing and premeasuring your food supplies has numerous advantages once you are on the trip.

through punched holes. Alternatively, make smaller boxes from Coroplast and lift them out of the pack when needed. You then have a reasonably rigid, waterproof container that seals well to keep food smells in.

When the box is empty, it can be dismantled to save space. The material then makes a good camp kitchen work surface as well as insulation under a tent floor, and can even be used to make splints. For water sports enthusiasts, the empty pack held in shape by the boxes will also provide buoyancy for a swamped boat.

I have successfully used a plastic kitchen tote box and lid that slides nicely into a rolltop waterproof portage pack. It's just the right size for the entire camp kitchen and food for a five-day trip. Basically, it's a small wannigan in a waterproof pack. Rubbermaid 53-litre Rough Totes just slide nicely into 115-litre Cascade Designs' portage packs if you treat them with Armour-All or a silicone car wax. Make up some webbing straps to keep the lid on in the pack.

If you use any kind of rigid container such as an olive barrel or ice cream pail, it is always best to line it with a large plastic bag, which is sealed before attaching the lid. The reason for this additional precaution is that when a warm rigid container is immersed in cold water, a partial vacuum forms inside, which draws water in through the slightest leak.

Always be careful not to contaminate the outside of otherwise sealed and smellproof

These waxed cardboard boxes lined with a plastic bag were great for a long trip. Note the labels for the days and trip numbers.

food containers with food residue that could attract animals.

In areas where squirrels have learned to leap considerable distances onto suspended food packs, smooth-surfaced plastic containers, or even thin metal containers if you can still find them, may be required for protection.

Large plastic totes inside waterproof canoe packs are handy for food and camp kitchens.

Food Organizing Made Easy

All that organizing sounds like work, but the following system can help make it easier. It is a methodical system that at first sight looks complex. It will save you a vast amount of time in the long run, whether you are planning food for two people for 20 days, for 20 people for two days or 20 people for a month. It generates a shopping list so that you don't waste time traipsing to and from the supermarket. When you get down to the nitty gritty of packaging, the column with "meal package sizes" makes the job go more smoothly. If you have a computer and a spreadsheet program you could computerize the whole process very easily.

1. Prepare your menu for each day of the trip as in the example below.
2. Draw up a table with column headings as below.
3. Take the first item on the menu (pita bread) and write it in the first space in column **A**.
4. Read through the menu and cross out the word pita each time it occurs and count the number of times it occurs (or use the "find" function on your word processor). Enter the number in the first space in column **B**.
5. Take the next item, butter, write it in column A, and read through, crossing out and counting as in step 4. Enter the number in column **B**.
6. Repeat until all items are crossed out and counted.
7. Calculate and fill in each of the remaining columns.

Use column **F** as your shopping list and **G** as your package size list. Buy all the food you need and then take each item in turn and make up all the meal packages you need using column G for the size, column B for the number needed. Once all the packages are made up, refer back to the menu and select the packages needed for each day bag and pack the day bags.

Menu for Four People

Friday
Breakfast: At home, campground or hotel

Lunch: Pita, butter, cheese, salami, cookies, juice crystals

Dinner: Soup, rice, surprise peas, cooked dried ground beef, fruit, tea

Saturday
Breakfast: Granola, bacon, English muffins, jam, tea

Lunch: Pita, butter, cheese, salami, cake, juice crystals

Dinner: Soup, mashed potato flakes, canned corned beef fried in butter with tomato powder and dried onion, stewed dried fruit, tea

Sunday
Breakfast: Granola, pancakes, honey, butter, jam, tea

Lunch: Crispbread crackers, butter, canned tuna, cookies, juice crystals

Dinner: Civilization. Emergency food if delayed: macaroni cheese packet

Generating a Shopping List and Packing List

A Item	B # of times item occurs	C Servings each time	D Total servings Col BxC	E Quantity per serving	F Total quantity to buy DxE	G Meal package size Col CxE
Pita	2	4	8	2 rounds	16 rounds	8 rounds
Butter	5	4	20	15 g	300g	60 g
Cheese	2	4	8	30 g	240 g	120 g
Salami	2	4	8	30 g	240 g	120 g

How Well Food Keeps

"Good Old Days on the trail...when the coffee pot was upset...and the sugar and salt got wet and sometimes the beans went sour and the bacon musty and the wind blew smoke in your eyes...how I wish I could live them all over again!" Tom Wilson, Banff Crag & Canyon, May 1, 1925

The keeping quality of food is important because of the distances from sources of supply, and the seriousness of food poisoning in remote places.

Food goes bad because of bacteria or other microorganisms decomposing it and producing toxic substances. Some types of organisms can enter your body and survive to multiply in your gut and cause illness. Others render the food toxic with their chemical waste products. Food preservation works on one or other of two basic principles:

The first principle is that if the organisms in the food are killed and no new ones can enter to replace the dead ones, then the food will keep. Cans and the foil pouches used for wet foods such as Freddy Chef meals are sealed with the food and probably organisms as well inside, but are then heat treated to kill all the organisms. Nothing can enter the sealed container to start the decomposition process again. In some parks such as Algonquin in Ontario where there is a can and bottle ban, some people transfer food from cans to bags or plastic jars at the trailhead. It is almost impossible to do this without contaminating the food

HELP! THE RAIN'S GOT INTO THE DEHYDRATED FOOD!

Jim Watson, *On Foot and Finger*, Cicerone Press, U.K.

and it will go bad in time. This contamination is especially likely if the outside of the can was not cleaned first, if the can opener was not scrupulously clean, and if the new container and spoon were not sterile. In warm weather, the introduced organisms will grow fast.

The second preservation principle is to make the conditions in the food inhospitable to the organisms. That way, even though they are alive, they cannot grow and multiply and produce their toxins. This can be done by depriving them of warmth or moisture. In winter, conditions are usually cold enough to keep food frozen so the organisms are dormant. As soon as frozen food thaws, the organisms become active and the food starts to go bad, so it must be cooked before that happens. Once it is cooked it will keep for a while because all the organisms are killed by cooking. It will go bad as soon as more organisms contaminate it and start growing. However, do not count on cold conditions—we spent a week in February at 2300 metres (7000 feet) in the western mountains and the precooked casseroles and other food did not stay frozen! While guiding two-week raft trips in the N.W.T., we kept meat frozen by packing in dry ice in insulated chests with seven-centimetre thick walls.

Moisture is absent from dry foods such as flour, rice, potato powder, milk powder, pancake mix, soup mixes and pasta, and they all keep well as long as they are kept dry. A trace of moisture and they will spoil. I can still remember the scene when, one week into a five-week kayak trip, we discovered that the pasta and a number of other dry foods had become wet and were starting to spoil. The hard and sharp pasta had made tiny holes in the plastic bags and the sharp corners of the soup packets had perforated other bags. Luckily it was a hot day and we were able to lay the food out in the sun to dry! We still had to discard some, though.

Preserved meats are a traditional good source of protein on trips: *"I have a profound respect for bacon,"* remarked a thoughtful citizen. *"Did it ever occur to you that we are indebted primarily to bacon for the opening up and development and civilization of this great*

and glorious West? Without bacon, this grand country, with all its wonderful evidences of progress and prosperity would probably be a howling wilderness at the present moment!"
Bacon and Civilization, Banff Crag & Canyon, Feb. 18, 1901

Preserved meats keep partly because of the low moisture level. Good double-smoked ham, bacon, sausage and schinken speck keep better than the cheaper varieties that contain large amounts of water. The good stuff is available from specialty smokehouses and European delicatessens, especially if you pay for an advance order to be double smoked. Some stores in places like Whitehorse cater to the needs of camps and outfitters and supply particularly well-preserved products. The real stuff is costly because a lot of pork goes into one kilogram of dry product. The cheaper, more moist products labelled "keep refrigerated" are not appropriate—you want the stuff that is hanging up in the air behind the counter.

Chemical preservatives that inhibit microorganism growth in other ways are also used in cured meats and sausage, but the amounts used have been considerably reduced in recent years. Preserved meats must not be kept in plastic or other sealed containers, even though they are smelly and attractive to animals. In these containers, warmth causes moisture to move to the surface of the meat and condense on the inside of impermeable packaging. This "sweating" causes a rise in the moisture level at the surface, which can then be enough to allow microorganisms to grow. These meats must be kept wrapped in breathable paper and cloth.

Food is nowadays pickled for flavour rather than for preservation, so the pickling agents are often not strong enough to prevent the growth of organisms that enter the container once it is opened. For this reason most pickles are labelled "keep refrigerated after opening." They will go bad if organisms are introduced and the temperature is too warm.

Contrary to what many people believe, you cannot stop food from going bad by sealing it to exclude air or by vacuum packaging. In fact, the most dangerous organisms thrive in an airless environment. The only useful thing that sealing does is exclude organisms such as mold spores that are in the air, but if the food is already contaminated before sealing, the food will still go bad in a sealed container.

Lightweight Food Suggestions

There are plenty of outdoor cookbooks to peruse for recipes. What follows are general ideas to help your overall food planning and to help you develop a way of thinking so you can develop your own menus.

Breakfasts

Granola is nutritious, compact, keeps well, is available in a variety of flavours and makes no messy pots. A large serving, 200 grams for example, of good granola is probably all you need for breakfast. If you premix it with milk powder at home, all you have to do is add water. If you want 250 millilitres (one cup) of milk with your portion, add 80 millilitres (1/3 cup) of milk powder to each serving of granola as you package it. If you want the granola hot, just add hot water. Fortify your backcountry granola with extra nuts, raisins, dried apple, etc., to make it more appealing.

Oatmeal is not as filling as granola and is messy to cook and clean up after. It doesn't keep you going all morning like granola will, for two reasons. The first is that although you can probably eat 200 grams of granola quite easily, you are unlikely to be able to force down the amount of oatmeal porridge made up from 200 grams of oats. To obtain the same calories, you would have to eat all that porridge. The second reason is that porridge digests much more quickly than does granola, so you are left with an empty feeling an hour or so after breakfast.

Other hot cereals requiring cooking and messy cleanup include Red River Cereal, Cream of Wheat, millet, bulgur and couscous. "Instant" hot cereals often come expensively packaged as individual sparrow-size portions, so they are an expensive way to eat. They generally digest too fast to provide lasting satisfaction for the morning even if you eat two or three packets.

When cooking hot cereals you will have quicker cooking and fewer problems with burning and sticking if you bring the water to a boil and then add the cereal. You then only need a very low heat to keep it simmering or you may be able to simply remove the pot from the stove and let it sit, perhaps wrapped in a jacket, for a while. To prevent lumps forming, pour the cereal into the water in a fine stream while stirring vigorously.

Bacon and eggs is a traditional camp breakfast food, and I must admit to being partial to a good piece of bacon, fried eggs and the aroma of fresh coffee. However, the same tantalizing smells we enjoy can waft downwind for long distances into the nostrils of a bear. Although you are cooking shortly before leaving your site and the bear may arrive too late, the smells linger, so a bear may come back when the next campers are using the site. The bacon smells also linger in your clothing and hair, which is a disadvantage when you are asleep in your next camp. In the old days when bacon was a key camp food, people often had dogs to warn of bears and travelled armed. They thought little of shooting the poor, unfortunate bear who was simply attracted by the smells.

I remember one winter trip where the grease was regarded as a delicacy. A packet of bacon was cut into bite-sized pieces and lightly fried in a pot lid. The lid was passed around the group of us, each taking a piece until all were gone, at which time it went around again with us each taking a spoonful of tasty liquid grease! At least we were not participating in the appalling waste associated with overcooking bacon and then discarding the grease.

Bacon does not keep well unless you can obtain the good dry smoked stuff, and, like the eggs, it contains quite a lot of nonnutritious water. You can usually find a good European delicatessen in larger centres who will double-smoke the bacon for you so it keeps better. Keep it in a breathable container or it will go bad. Occasionally you can find Hungarian or Danish canned bacon, though usually it has a large amount of fat packed with it. Plan on saving the fat for hash browns or pancakes. Ham is available in cans and is good for breakfast if you are not using it for lunches.

Eggs, of course, present transportation problems in the backcountry. Some people crack their eggs into a screwtop jar to transport them as liquid. However, egg is a great medium for bacterial growth, so this is not advisable for more than a few days except in cold weather. Yolks that have been frozen stay rubbery after thawing and don't fry well. Traditionally, eggs were carried buried in the flour sack or in the bag of horse feed. They were well cushioned and if they broke in the flour sack you simply got a slightly richer pancake, maybe with some crunchy bits! I have used a similar method except using a rigid plastic container for the pancake mix. I had good success carrying eggs on raft trips by cutting discs from square egg tray flats to fit inside a plastic pail. As long as one only used complete egg pockets to hold eggs and treated the well-labelled pail with respect, few eggs broke.

Egg omelette mixes are available from specialty outdoor stores and are much improved over earlier versions, but they are quite costly. I have yet to see anyone concoct a really satisfactory homemade omelette mix from bulk dried egg powder. The Young's Modulus of elasticity tends to be a bit high!

The other thing to remember is that frying bacon, and particularly eggs, requires a good frying pan, which will probably be heavy.

A good compromise if you really must have your bacon and eggs is to make an egg and bacon sandwich at home, wrap it in foil and warm it up on your stove before eating. Alternatively, seal the sandwich in a home vacuum bag sealer or freezer bag and heat it up in your tea water while you eat your granola. This method works well for winter trips when the sandwich will not go bad.

Pancakes are another breakfast favourite, but it takes a long time to cook enough for a group, and you need a good, probably heavy, fry pan. If you plan to replace granola with pancakes, 200 grams of pancake mix, which has approximately the same energy content as 200 grams of granola, makes a vast number of pancakes that will take ages to cook and eat. The pancakes digest very quickly, too, so you don't stay satisfied all morning. They are not very inspired unless slathered with syrup, which is heavy to carry and needs an absolutely leakproof container. You can make a syrup from brown sugar and maple flavouring. You may want to thicken it with cornstarch, because a lot of sugar dissolves in a very small amount of water to make not much syrup.

Lunches

Lunches need to be fairly high in carbohydrate. Unfortunately, many people's lunches are higher in protein and fat because they are using generous meat and cheese fillings in sandwiches made of airy bread and crackers.

Keeping the carbohydrate proportion high without too much bulk is difficult as most breads and crackers are largely air. For serious trips I make up dense crackers that do not take up much room, are strong and are very satisfying. I grind porridge oats up dry in the blender, add about 30 per cent of whole wheat flour and then water to make a very stiff dough. I knead it and roll it out to four millimetres (1/8 inch), cut it into five-centimetre (two inch) squares and fry gently both sides in a lightly greased pan to brown. I then dry them in the oven between wire grills to stop them curling. You can do the same thing by adding whole wheat flour to porridge to make a stiff, rollable dough.

On multi-day canoe trips we make a bannock at breakfast time for our lunch, using about 230 grams of bannock mix for two people (Bisquick tea biscuit mix and whole wheat flour 50:50 and one tablespoon baking powder per 500 millilitres of flour). That amount (230 grams) of dry mix would make a huge number of bread sandwiches and commercial crackers, so it is a real meal! Cheaper, too.

The drier and denser breads such as pumpernickel and pita are better than the usual white bread. Rolls provide a better ratio between carbohydrate and the fatty or protein fill than does bread because of the greater thickness. One outfitter I worked for used to supply sweet breads that were more like cakes for lunch. They were dense and satisfying and were much easier to produce than sandwiches for the guests.

A wide variety of high energy meal replacement bars are available, but are expensive for what they are. I use some of them as survival kit food because I think they taste ghastly. There is no risk of finding that I've already raided the emergency food, because I won't touch the things until a real emergency arises!

My mum's old standby bars that fuelled me through the shorts-clad cold and damp of the U.K. winters continue to fuel me in the mountains and rivers of Canada at a tiny fraction of the cost of commercial bars:

One cup each of brown sugar, golden syrup, and margarine or butter melted together. Stir in quick cooking oats until you can't "wet" any more oats. Press the mixture one centimetre thick on a greased cookie sheet with wet hands. Bake at 180°C (350°F) for 30 minutes. Cut while warm into squares.

If you have the time you can have a treat and make pita bread over a fire. Form a skin on the dry, thin dough in the fry pan, then place it over HOT coals (left) so that steam inside inflates it to a hollow ball.

Tabouli makes an excellent high carbohydrate lunch in pita bread. You need a reliable container for soaking the bulgur during the morning while you travel. Tabouli mixes are available.

If you like sausage and salami in your lunches, you will have to find dry products that will keep without refrigeration. This is the type of sausage you find hanging behind the counter in delicatessens. Inquire carefully of the staff about its keeping qualities and explain what you want it for. It must be kept in a breathable container such as a cloth bag to prevent it sweating, so it is capable of contaminating other articles with food smells and of being an animal attractant. A safer way to carry meats for lunches is to use the huge variety of canned meats, canned fish and canned pâtés available.

Cheese is a popular lunch item. Real cheese is the real thing, and keeps adequately for a few weeks at moderate temperatures. I buy it in 225 grams (1/2 pound) sticks sealed in plastic. That way it is eaten very soon after the packet is opened and becomes contaminated, so it does not have time to go bad. The packets are not completely sterile inside, but it is surprising how well the contents keep if unopened. The aged cheddars seem to go bad quicker than the younger ones. The other advantage of these packets is that if the cheese does get warm and starts oozing grease, they don't leak if unopened. Exotic cheeses such as Brie and Camembert are available in aluminum cans and they keep well for the later part of your trip.

The individually wrapped portions of processed cheese keep adequately. "Process cheese," "cheese food" and other synthetic cheese substitutes are usually loaded with chemicals and will keep.

Tahini and hummus mixes make a pleasant change for lunch.

Dinners

Dinners are often the camp meals that least resemble the appetizing meals of home. They are the meals that can most easily degenerate into an amorphous brown glop. If you can present separate carbohydrate, protein and vegetable components on the plate, your dinners will be far more appetizing.

Carbohydrates. There is a wide choice of dry carbohydrate products available so you can have lots of variety. They are light and keep well if kept dry. To save fuel weight, choose quicker cooking products, especially at higher altitudes where cooking time is longer. Quick-cooking suggestions are: instant rice, quick-cooking macaroni (Creamettes), potato flakes, fine egg noodles, oriental noodles and couscous.

Slower-cooking products are the larger noodles and pasta, bulgur, kasha, hashed browns, scalloped potatoes and ordinary rice. If you can afford the time and fuel, Kashi is a very pleasant mixture of grains that takes 20 minutes to cook, even at sea level.

Protein. Some of the worst food poisoning organisms flourish in meats and fish, so choose carefully products that will not spoil. Canned products are safest and the weight is not excessive if you choose those with minimum juice and gravy in the can and eat reasonable sized portions. The average North American eats far bigger portions of meat than needed.

Possibilities are canned corned beef, canned tuna in oil if you can still find this type, canned luncheon meat, canned ham, canned turkey and chicken. These are all absolutely reliable keepers for long summer trips. The weight of the can and the water content make them somewhat inefficient, but the scope for tasty meals they provide is often worth it.

Some parks have a can and bottle ban that makes it illegal to take such containers into the backcountry. The contents of cans may be transferred to a plastic bag or screwtop plastic jar immediately before starting a trip. Unfortunately, the moment you open a can the sterile food will become contaminated and start going bad. You can minimize the risk by sterilizing the outside of the can, the spoon and the can opener in boiling water and using a clean,

Rolling out a tortilla with a kayak paddle shaft on the bottom of a pot. Tortillas are somewhat time-consuming but make a pleasant change. Photo Mary Enright.

unopened plastic bag. The procedure is still quite risky and you should keep the food cool and not keep it for more than a couple of days.

Extra-lean ground beef can be cooked and dried easily and rehydrates quite readily if you follow this procedure: cook the meat gently in its own juice and possibly a little water. Do **not** brown it, otherwise it will be more difficult to rehydrate. If you have a pressure cooker, use it. The key is to break the meat up as much as possible because lumps dry slowly and rehydrate even more slowly. Once the meat is well cooked, drain or skim off the fat from the surface of the liquid. Carefully evaporate off most of the liquid and then spread the meat evenly on a cookie sheet. Dry gently in an oven at about 80°C (170°F) or in a food dryer. Stir it around occasionally and use a rolling pin to break up lumps once it gets crisper. Make absolutely sure it is bone dry before packaging and keep it dry. It is not sterile so if it gets at all damp it will spoil. The small remaining fat content can also go rancid, so do not keep it for too long before your trip.

You can also grind the dried ground beef in a blender into a fine powder that instantly rehydrates to form a meaty gravy. Another variation is to cook a curry or tomato-flavoured ground beef stew and dry it the same way. Chunky dried meats such as jerky do not rehy-

drate effectively, but dried fish and shrimp can be used if you have the skill and the time to soak them.

Adequate protein intake can of course be achieved on a totally vegetarian diet. However, you have to learn how to combine the various types of plant proteins so that they complement each other to provide all the necessary protein components you need. Generally this means using a mixture of whole grains and legumes in your diet. Traditions like eating brown bread with baked beans were based on good science, even if people didn't know it! Refer to vegetarian cookbooks for more information and recipe ideas.

Peas, beans and lentils generally require soaking and long, slow cooking, so they have limitations unless you can afford the weight of a pressure cooker. This usually means you are a large group or a canoe party. If you are in a remote place, you may be able to offset the weight of the pressure cooker with savings in the weight of fuel to be carried because of quicker cooking. These foods can sometimes be obtained in "flour" form, which can then be used in soups. They can also be precooked, and then dried whole or ground up in a blender to form a powder that will cook quickly. Quick-cooking split peas and lentils are also available in some supermarkets.

A selection of carbohydrates suitable for camping.

A selection of canned and preserved meats for tripping.

Fresh-caught fish is a wonderful treat if you are a good enough fisherman to catch some. However, it is best not to rely on catching any and it is better to look on it more as a bonus if you are successful. Plan flexible meals so you can substitute fresh fish for the preserved stuff you brought.

Vegetables. "Surprise" brand freeze-dried peas are no longer available from supermarkets, but similar products are available in camping stores. Unlike many dried vegetables they cook up into a vegetable that is fine to serve as a vegetable rather than needing to be camouflaged in a glop mixture. Peas provide colour, flavour and texture to your food.

Freeze-dried corn, green beans and carrots are available in specialist camping stores at a high price. They are well worth it if you use them in quantities to provide some essential colour, texture and taste, or "palatability factors" rather than being an essential nutritive part of the meal. Other commercial dried vegetables such as dried soup greens are okay in soups and stews, but not as separate vegetables.

Dried onion is readily available, but there is nothing like a sliver off a small fresh onion to liven up a sandwich. Onions keep reasonably well.

Tomato powder can be bought or can be made by spreading tomato paste thinly on a lightly greased cookie sheet and drying it carefully in the oven at 80°C. Peel off the sheet of tomato "paper" and grind it to powder in the blender.

Many vegetables can be dried in a home dryer, so it is worth obtaining a book such as *Dry It—You'll Like It*. Fresh carrots, zucchini and celery will keep fresh enough to make pleasant additions to your meal in "garnish" quantities.

Fruits and desserts. *"To give the trail breakers a welcome, a bright idea popped into my head. 'They shall have pudding'. I made the pudding and we all tasted it and it was a good pudding, that is if it had been intended for a cannon ball."* Mary T. Schäffer, *Old Indian Trails of the Canadian Rockies*, NY, Knickerbocker Press, 1911.

Fruit and desserts round out a meal with a bit more feeling of "home." Some desserts provide a significant number of calories, making it easier to keep up a 4000 or 5000 kcal daily intake without having to eat ridiculous quantities of starchy stodge with your first course.

Dried fruit (apples, apricots, pears, pineapple, etc.) are pleasant snacks and can be stewed to form a compote-type dessert. Custard is a pleasant addition to a dried fruit dessert or can be poured over a piece of rich fruit cake. Premix the custard powder, milk powder and sugar in a baggie at home. Commercial dried apple can be dried out more in the oven at home to bring the water content down from 25 per cent to about five per cent to save weight.

A few apricots, figs and prunes ("CPR Strawberries") in your compote can be useful to keep everyone "moving." This is especially useful if cold conditions or insects make defecating unpleasant so people keep putting it off and become constipated. The problem is exacerbated by dehydration, especially at high altitude. A common medical problem among troops building the Alaska Highway was constipation brought on by their unwillingness to use the frigid "facilities" in -40°C weather!

Cake mixes and oatmeal cookie mixes can be cooked in the backcountry! If cake mixes are mixed with about 30 per cent by volume of pancake mix they are much less fussy and less

A feed of fresh fish, especially if it is this Arctic char, is a real treat, but you should not rely on being able to live off fish.

You can do a lot of food drying in your oven, but you may want to build a dryer or buy a commercial one.

The green of some freeze-dried peas adds colour and appeal to an otherwise amorphous pot of glop.

prone to collapse. If made a little drier than the recipe, they can be spooned on top of cooked dried fruit in a pot (minimum liquid), which is then simmered gently for half an hour or so. You greatly increase the calories in the fruit dessert that way. Cake mixes with about 30 per cent pancake mix added can also be cooked in a double boiler made by putting a small pot inside a larger one, or even in a boilable bag. Dutch ovens or the Outback Oven also enable you to bake good cakes.

Oatmeal cookie mix can be cooked slowly in a fry pan, moved around over the stove and fitted with a tight foil cover. You can use it as a pie shell for instant puddings or cooked dried fruit. Instant puddings work fine with powdered milk as long as you dissolve the milk fully before adding the pudding mix. You end up with a source of protein (dried milk) and the 100 or so grams of carbohydrate in the pudding.

Fruit leathers are readily available fruity snacks or can be made at home from pureed fruits in the same manner as tomato powder (above), but don't overdry, and roll rather than grind when a leathery consistency is achieved.

Prepared Foods

Packet soups are available in a wide variety of flavours. Choose the five-minute ones. Ichiban-type oriental noodle soups are very easy to cook, and when overdiluted provide a reviving drink/snack. They can even be eaten dry in an emergency. Packet soups can be used as a base for "gloup," which is a cross between glop and soup. You add to the soup instant rice, noodles, couscous or even potato powder to provide more "body," along with pieces of sausage, chicken or ham and a dollop of butter. These are great when you need lots of liquid as well as some filler. A tripping partner once made up a hideous-looking brew of soup, potato powder and fragments of dried Swiss chard leaves. We almost convinced the rest of

MAKE SAUCE USING 1 CUP, NOT 1-1/2C WATER
BRING TO A BOIL AND SIMMER TO THICKEN.

MIX CAKE MIXTURE USING JUST ENOUGH LIQUID
TO MAKE A STIFF BATTER WHICH WILL BARELY
DROP FROM A SPOON. ONE SMALL EGG WOULD BE
PLENTY IF USING EGG AS IN INSTRUCTIONS.
TRANSFER TO TOP OF SIMMERING SAUCE,
COVER TIGHTLY, SIMMER 15-20 MINS OR UNTIL
KNIFE COMES OUT CLEAN

This pudding was easily made by simmering over low heat on a stove, despite what the recipe suggested.

the party it was the contents of a caribou's stomach I had brought back from the Arctic, and that it was a northern delicacy!

Numerous prepacked carbohydrate-in-sauce products are available. These include Hamburger Helper, scalloped potato mix, a wide range of pastas in seasoned sauces, maca-roni cheese, seasoned rice, etc. They are tasty, usually easy to prepare, but very expensive for what you get—usually a few cents' worth of pasta and a packet of sauce mix. The serving sizes are a joke unless you are feeding mice at a fat farm. They will say things like "makes four 1/2 cup servings." Each person on a moderately cold or strenuous trip will probably eat two cups at least. The way to judge though is to bear in mind that the calorie content is related to the **dry** weight of the food before you cook it. You probably want at least 150 grams (five ounces) dry weight per person. Calculate energy content assuming it is mostly carbohydrate. You can make up your own sauce mix from milk powder, grated parmesan, a few seasonings, some flour and maybe an Oxo cube, all put together at home in a baggie. You can put a dollop of butter in the baggie, too, in cool weather—even if it

A fruit sponge desert is easily made with dried fruit, cake mix and pancake mix in a pot without an oven. Oatmeal cookie mix can make a shell for an instant pudding.

melts, the other ingredients will soak it up before it leaks. Use finely grated parmesan or grind it up finer in a blender.

Some of the prepared foods burn easily on a camp stove because of the thickening agents included. If you stir continuously you break up the pasta or potatoes. You are often better off to boil the pasta or potatoes in water alone until nearly cooked. About halfway through cooking, drain off some liquid into a cup and mix it thoroughly with the sauce powder. Let it soak

You can make a pie shell from oatmeal cookie mix or shortbread mix in a fry pan or Outback Oven and can then fill it with a conventional starch pudding mix.

The Gourmet Touch

On a long trip the quality, variety and appeal of the food becomes very important for morale as well as for keeping up the energy supply for action. In the Canadian and Alaskan backcountry you won't find little mountain top restaurants to slip into for a change from your dull camp glop!

On one long canoe trip with another couple, each couple was responsible for producing a meal for four people on alternate nights. There was a certain amount of competition to produce the most exotic grub, so coupled with the variety, we ate like royalty. Another group we ski with at a hut is organized so that each person produces a dinner for 15 or a breakfast and lunch for 15. Again, there is a certain amount of competition to feed everyone really well.

Remember that food costs are likely to be a minor proportion of your trip costs so you might as well buy good food and eat well. Also, if you are making the effort to carry food you might as well carry what you enjoy. Providing variety is also an important part of making food attractive, and can be as simple as varying the type of crackers or cheeses or sausage.

Often you can make a mundane meal into something special by the inclusion of just a very small quantity of a treat or delicacy. **You** know what **your** special weaknesses are! Even though the delicacy is perhaps heavy for what it is, its actual weight may be a small price to pay relative to its value in making the meal special. You will rarely be in a situation where you cannot spare an extra 50 or 100 grams for something decadent to liven up your meal times. If it's a multi-day trip, look at your average daily food weight— maybe you were light one day and can splurge the next.

Remember that an apparently complex recipe may be easy to cook outdoors if you take the time to premix most of the ingredients in the comfort of your home. Put them into labelled baggies and use Nalgene bottles for items such as fresh lemon juice, vinegar, sherry, etc. Small quantities of liquids such as Worcestershire sauce, Tabasco or Marmite can be put into the baggie with dry ingredients such as rice, pasta, herbs, thickeners, etc. They get soaked up by the dry materials so they cannot leak.

before placing the sauce in the pot for the last few minutes of gentle cooking.

Boil-in-the-bag meals such as Freddy Chef are convenient for a short trip where weight and expense are not such major concerns, but usually need a carbohydrate "filler" to go with them. For example, you can decant some of the juicier ones into a pot and add dumplings made of bannock mix and simmer gently, perhaps adding a little more water. If the bag is clean you can use the boiling water afterwards to make mashed potato or couscous.

For short trips, where sterility and keeping are not major concerns, you can make your own meals and seal them in boilable bags with a home vacuum bag sealer. Store them in the freezer at home.

Biscuit dough mixes such as Bisquick can be used to make either bannock or pancakes. For bannock, mix to a **stiff** dough, form into a cake about 1/2 centimetre thick, dust the surface with dry mix and cook dry (without grease) over medium heat in a floured aluminum plate or fry pan with a tight foil lid. Cheese can be mixed into the dough before cooking. For the best bannock, make up a mix of four cups 100 per cent whole wheat bread flour with two tbsp. baking powder and three or four cups of Bisquick. Use 200 gram portions to make a fairly dry dough and cook slowly in a covered pan or wrapped around a stick over coals.

Pancake mixes are only really good for making pancakes. This requires a good fry pan, which you may not want to carry because of the extra weight.

The cook's job is much easier in the dark if they have a headlight. Petzl left, Streamlight with Liston headband right.

With a little imagination you can make exotica like crepes suzette with dry ingredients in the backcountry.

If you are using powdered milk for puddings, dissolve it in water BEFORE you add it to the pudding mix powder. If you mix everything together the milk won't dissolve and you end up with a rather diseased-looking dessert!

Look through your favourite recipes and examine them critically to see if there are ways to make them portable for backcountry use. You'll probably find plenty that can be adapted. Think which ingredients are available in dry form, which ones can be mixed together at home, what type of containers are needed, what the keeping qualities are and how much water unavoidably has to be carried around in the food. Also consider the number of pots required and cooking time, especially at higher altitudes. These may make the item impractical.

Hors d'oeuvres Ideas

- Small canned pâtés—lobster, crab, liver.
- Canned escargots (packet escargot sauces are available).
- Canned smoked oysters, caviar and miscellaneous seafood snacks.
- Exotic cheeses, some available in cans.
- Cocktail onions, dill pickles, etc. Cut to pack tightly in a Nalgene bottle with juice. Keep cool and not too long if package says "refrigerate after opening."

- Gorp made with top quality, **fresh** whole nuts and good dried fruits.
- Exotic or different crackers.
- Good mustard (from dry powder).
- Relishes (in Nalgene bottle).
- Mayonnaise in a tube. Check if it needs refrigeration.
- Fresh carrot sticks, zucchini, bunching onion. Don't cut or peel until needed.
- Dips made from sour cream powder mix or certain Mayacamas brand soups.
- Made en route. For example, raw, thin Arctic char fillets marinated 24-36 hours in lemon juice and dill in a plastic bag kept cool on the bottom of your canoe. Other fish will do.
- The one small trout you caught can make a great hors d'oeuvre or a skimpy meal!
- Miscellaneous exotic soups, especially some Mayacamas brand. Lemon juice or sherry in Nalgene bottle for the special touch.
- Fish poached in Knorr Fines Herbes soup.
- Fondue—although in a packet, needs to be kept fairly cool. Sticks to pot. Serve with bannock pieces, cocktail onions.

A wide variety of sauces is available to help you make your meals more interesting.

Spices and condiments can add lots more appeal to a meal. The pouch is by Outdoor Research.

Seasonings

These can make all the difference. Experiment! Save film canisters for use as seasoning containers or premix when you make up your meal bags. "California herb rice" seasoning in the water livens up rice, as does bouillon. A few slivers of fresh onion improves most casseroles, cheese dishes, sandwiches and especially quiches made with scrambled egg mixes and ham in pastry or bannock shells.

Lots of commercial packaged sauces are available. Knorr Bearnaise and Hollandaise sauces are great. However, you can put ingredients for some sauces together yourself for a fraction of the cost—a lump of butter, some milk powder, some Veloutine (doesn't go lumpy) and seasonings in a baggie.

Garnishes

Bacon bits, croutons, parmesan and premixed herb garnishes. Real butter adds something— look for it in cans for long trips—NADP is one brand that I found in the north. In summer, keep butter and margarine in Nalgene jars or other containers with a totally reliable seal. Margarine containers are not reliable in warm weather, nor are some so-called camping butter containers.

Desserts

- A few glace cherries makes even a mundane packet whip-type dessert look more appealing. They keep well and can be packed in a baggie.
- Exotic cookies or wafers buried in custard or stuck in a whip-type dessert add some je-ne-sais-quoi.

- Maple syrup. A little of the real thing is the real thing on a crepe, cake, etc.
- Fruit syrups. Available in a variety of flavours. Nalgene bottle again.
- Canned cream. Unfortunately, needs to be kept cool, no good in coffee.
- Cream substitute mixes. Remember that things you wouldn't use at home can be appealing in the backcountry.
- A few flavoured chocolate chips or slivered almonds can work wonders.
- Fresh fruit is heavy, but even just a few fresh orange segments can be the touch that greatly improves a packet dessert.
- Icing sugar. A dusting over thin crepes rolled around wild or reconstituted dried fruit adds something.
- A lump of Toblerone sitting on top of your dessert!
- Make up your own dried fruit mix—you have control over the proportion of CPR strawberries (prunes) that way!
- Even the ingredients for exotic items such as bananas flambé or crepes suzette are quite portable in small Nalgene bottles.

Emergency Meals

As mentioned earlier, always have an "emergency" meal available that can be cooked very easily and in foul conditions after a rough day. A couple of packets of Ichiban with some dried ground beef or a can of ham flakes is delicious and very quick, even at high altitude. Add couscous for extra carbos. You can even eat the ham uncooked, the beef as jerky powder and the crushed Ichiban dry like chips, sprinkled with the contents of the seasoning packet!

Chapter 8

Getting There

Getting to the start of your trip with all your gear can be a major logistical headache, especially if you do not have your own vehicle. Public transport by land, water or air will get you to many remote communities, but using public transport can present problems because of a prohibition on carrying items such as stove fuel, bear repellent and flares. The final stage from the community to the trailhead can be difficult to arrange from a distance, so it is useful to know some of the options available to you. Chartered vehicles, boats and particularly aircraft are commonly used to reach the trailhead. Although backroads provide access to many remote areas, travelling on them is hard on vehicles. Winter driving on remote northern roads and in extreme cold requires vehicles to be properly prepared and operators experienced in northern operations. One advantage of going on a fully organized trip with an outfitter is that the transport and logistics are taken care of by someone else.

Transportation

Virtually every transportation mode known to man has been used at some time to reach the start of wilderness trips. The following are some of the factors you have to consider when selecting a particular mode of transport. Getting there may well be the riskiest part of the whole trip! By far the closest call on a recent Arctic trip was the late night taxi ride home from Calgary airport with sleepy but maniacal drivers carrying on a feud!

Prohibited Baggage

A significant problem for travellers using public transport, and using airlines in particular, is that items such as camp fuel, gas cylinders, emergency flares and aerosols such as bear sprays are prohibited. Even items such as matches, particularly windproof matches, are frowned upon by airlines.

Gas cylinders for small stoves are not easy to obtain in the north. You can avoid transportation problems by switching to liquid fuel stoves and buying fuel at your destination. Overseas visitors using small propane and butane stoves should be aware that liquid fuel stoves are comparatively cheap in North America, especially when bought in the larger centres. The savings in fuel costs on a long trip will quickly pay for the stove. Liquid fuel stoves can be transported empty, and you can reduce your concerns about being able to obtain the correct type of liquid fuel if you have multi-fuel stoves. In the unlikely event that you are unable to buy white gasoline, you could then use other available fuels such as diesel, kerosene, aircraft turbine fuel or motor gasoline.

Coastal ferries may want to know if you have white gas camp fuel in your vehicle and people have been told there is a one-litre limit. If you obey that you will be faced with buying higher priced fuel at your destination. Railroad operators seem to be resigned that people they are transporting to backcountry halts will have camp fuel, outboard motors and fuel. These items must be stowed in the baggage area.

The most serious problem is the restriction on transporting your emergency flares from home. However, when flares are part of a complete sealed survival kit they may be viewed more favourably. They are not very likely to be available in a remote community, so don't assume you can buy them at your destination. They are costly, too. EPIRBs and PLBs are also regarded as hazardous due to the lithium battery.

Because of the air transport restriction, the only way to fly prohibited goods to your destination airport is as air cargo. This is only possible after due inspection, proper packaging and documentation by certified person-

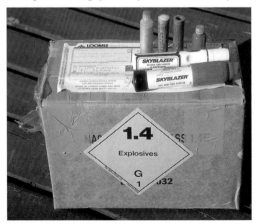

Flares, bear bangers and aerosol bear sprays are not allowed in your baggage. They should be sent by ground or air cargo after appropriate compliance packaging. You may not be able to send them to some places that are served only by cargo-passenger "combi" aircraft.

Air freight compliance packaging for these bear sprays entailed sealing in plastic, packing in a box of vermiculite, which in turn was packed in styrofoam pellets in a bigger box, duly labelled as "explosive." Special documents were also supplied.

Air travel is the way to reach many remote places with your gear.

nel, usually by a specialist compliance packaging contractor. It is unlikely the materials will arrive at the same time as you, so send them well ahead. Some points in northern Canada, such as Resolute, are served on a regular basis by "combi"—cargo-passenger aircraft that cannot carry some hazardous goods even as cargo. Allow time to track down a cargo-only flight.

You may find it easier to use ground transportation by bus, courier service or trucklines. Of the courier services, Loomis seems to be the one most often mentioned. Flares and similar items are given a rating; those rated 1.4S are generally more acceptable and 1.4G items are a problem. Check with the manufacturer or supplier for the rating. One source of transportation information is the retailer who will probably know how the item is transported to his premises.

Strobe emergency lights may be a good alternative because they are not hazardous to transport, though lithium batteries may be frowned on. They are quite a good substitute for handheld flares for sea kayakers, canoeists and travellers in open areas and above treeline. See Signalling, page 365.

If you wear a belt knife, don't forget to put it into your checked baggage. You won't be allowed on the plane with it in hand baggage!

Air Travel

Air travel is the norm in many parts of the north, whether by scheduled, private or chartered plane. Savings in time and aggravation frequently make flying the best option. Visitors from overseas should realize that costs are more reasonable than one might think, especially considering the distances involved.

Check when booking interconnecting flights to remote northern areas that the baggage limits and excess baggage fees for all flights are the same. You may find that there is a lower load limit on small regional connectors than on the major airlines. Airlines tell me this does not occur if they are actual subsidiaries of the majors and have the major's flight numbers. One reason for the different limits is that people tend to stock up to the limit with food and supplies when returning home to the remote communities. Excess baggage fees can be high on expedition food, skis and hardware or a folding kayak. Even if there are no extra charges or you are happy to pay, some of the smaller aircraft used simply do not have room for a lot of baggage. It may not accompany you and it could be a day or two before it arrives.

Some scheduled aircraft used in the north are capable of carrying canoes and kayaks. These are airliners with some seats removed and a large part of the passenger compartment partitioned off. Access is through a wide door. Lockheed Electra and HS 748 Turboprops, and Boeing 737 jets are used in this configuration. Planes going north tend to be full and prices to be high, but coming back south they are more likely to be empty so boat transport is easier to arrange, and you may even be lucky and have your boats on the same plane with you. Details are best obtained from the local agent at the remote community. Booking agents in a head office are unlikely to be fully aware of obscure practices in distant outposts, so spend the money on a phone call to Coppermine or Tuktoyaktuk or wherever to speak to the person who's actually there. The freight depot may not be at the airport so be prepared to suggest that you will get the boat to the airport yourself if you think that will increase your chances of getting it out on the flight you want.

Rail Travel

Passenger rail service in Canada is a shadow of its former self, but there are still some gems that provide access to wild country. Some you can even prearrange to stop at spots in the middle of nowhere. The Via Rail "Bud Car" still winds its way through the northern Ontario wilds from Sudbury to White River three days a week with reasonable charges for canoes in the baggage car. Via also runs the service between Winnipeg and Churchill. The Black Bear Express (Algoma Central RR) between Sault Ste. Marie and Hearst is yet another of these handy services I have used over the years as part of my trip logistics. The Polar Bear Express (Ontario Northland), the British Columbia Railway and Quebec North Shore RR are other possibilities along with other Via Rail services and of course the Alaska Railroad. You can obtain Via Rail information from toll free numbers anywhere in Canada and you can obtain a timetable from your travel agent. See page 374 for the addresses of these rail services.

Travel on these routes is not necessarily the high-speed luxury travel foreign visitors associate with trains, but if you want to see some wild countryside and absorb the local scene, the experience can be unforgettable. Check whether there are freight restrictions. My experience has been that they do not ask about well-sealed containers with reasonable quantities of fuel if it is in the baggage car. If fuel is leaking and your gear stinks of white gas, you deserve to be given a hard time.

Bus

Bus travel in Canada and Alaska is reasonably cheap and quite fast, certainly faster than many trains. Luggage allowances are usually gener-

Passenger rail service is much reduced in Canada, but a train trip through the wilds is a special experience.

ous and excess baggage charges are reasonable. Buses also provide a fast, reliable parcel service between depots, which are often simply restaurants or gas stations. Hazardous goods restrictions apply on fuel, flares, etc.

Ferries

Many communities on both east and west coasts are accessible only by ferry. Some of these ferries are quite small and infrequent, but the services do exist. The smaller and quainter, the richer the experience if you are in the mood. Don't forget your seasickness pills and keep your warm clothes and waterproofs handy so you can take refuge on deck from stuffy saloons. In areas where sea kayaking is popular, ferries are usually able to carry rigid kayaks, sometimes perched in odd places. A folding kayak has the advantage of being packable along with regular baggage. Some of these ferries have a crane for a "wet launch"—the loaded kayak and its occupant are lifted into or out of the ocean if there is no dock to tie up to (see page 222).

Time Factors

If you do not have your own vehicle or if there is no road access to the start of the trip, you will have to rely on other people. You must therefore allow plenty of time for making and executing the arrangements with them. Most urban people are used to a very regimented, clock-dominated daily regime, where things generally happen quickly and on a tight schedule. However, when you get to remote rural areas, things are often very different. Even if you think you have made a "booking," people may not have made major scheduling arrangements until you actually arrive on the scene. They may have been inconvenienced too many times before, making their arrangements and then waiting in vain for people who don't arrive. Paying a deposit in advance may help, because it indicates your commitment. A phone call as you get nearer the place, to confirm the arrangements and that you are on your way, is a good idea.

When you are trying to arrange transport, be flexible in your timing. For example, someone with a minibus used for work or tourist trips may be glad of an opportunity for more work

but only in the evening or other "off" hours. On several occasions I have been flown in to remote northern locations to arrive by the light of the midnight sun. Who really cares, unless of course it's the pilot's unofficial 18th hour of flying that day!

Also remember that the people you are dealing with understand the local laws of nature and are content to live much more in tune with them. If it's foggy or windy or the tide is flowing the wrong way, they are content to sit and wait. Even if it looks okay where you are, they may know things you don't about conditions at the destination. "Hurry up and wait" all too often sums up the situation. You scramble to be ready at the appointed hour but then have to hang around for hours, days or even weeks, always ready to leave at a moment's notice when the weather clears. If you "push" your operator against their will into making an unsuccessful attempt, expect to pay for this extra trip.

Unfortunately, the reason for a delay is often poorly communicated. You are left pacing in frustration, wondering whether your tardy transporter is in league with the local motel and bar owner! You have little option but to be patient and not aggravate them.

Taxis

There is usually someone providing some sort of taxi service around remote communities. I remember a ride from the airport to one northern community in a decrepit old sedan full of dust purporting to be a taxi. It was expensive but there were no alternatives other than a long walk. Twelve-seat vans are also used, and for a party of people with gear they may be more satisfactory. They may also have a roofbox in which you can put baggage or on which you can carry a canoe, but just like in the city you can expect drivers to complain about handling baggage. Roofboxes may be a wire mesh box so it is useful to have large garbage bags handy to protect gear from dust, mud and wet. In some tourist areas there are small sightseeing tour operators with minibuses and you may be able to make an arrangement with one of them for transport to and from your starting point. They might like a chance to make extra money early or late in the day when regular clients are not being carried.

Be imaginative and resourceful when it comes to organizing local transport for your gear.

Contacts and Unofficial Taxis

If you are using the services of hotels and air and boat charter organizations, they usually have some sort of vehicle or they will make arrangements for you. For example, one air charter organization actually expected to automatically pick us up at the airport and take us to the float plane base from which they would fly us to the river. Do not be afraid to ask anyone from whom you are purchasing services about these logistical connections. Even if they cannot themselves help, they will be highly likely to tell you who can.

Contacts can be a local afficionado of your activity, tracked down through a national recreation organization such as the Alpine Club or Recreational Canoeing Association. In rural areas these people may be particularly happy to talk to kindred spirits and help with logistical support and information. Local recreation supplies stores can also be a great source of information and help.

Don't be shy, make and use contacts! The most tenuous of connections can be used. Maybe you are a member of a church, hobby club, conservation group, service club or professional association and can make a contact through these organizations. On one occasion, through an international youth organization I belonged to, I enlisted the help of a member across the continent to provide a small but crucial link in trip logistics. I contacted him with some trepidation, but in fact he was only too pleased to meet someone from another part of the world. He helped with a car shuttle and provided a secure place to store our vehicle.

Compared to European and particularly British attitudes, people are generally more generous with the use of their vehicles in North America. However, one way to enlist help without putting the contact people out too much is to offer to rent a vehicle that they will drive back to the town after dropping you off. That way they don't need to use their own vehicle. Similarly, your rented vehicle is not sitting unused in the bush for days or weeks, particularly if your trip is not a round trip. Purchase no-deductible insurance and set up some system whereby you are certain the vehicle is returned immediately and not driven around for weeks at your expense!

On the three occasions when I have needed road transport, some local inquiries soon produced people willing to help out. On one occasion we arrived in Whitehorse by public transport and wanted to get to a village 500 kilometres away with canoes and people. This was in the days long before there were outfitters in Whitehorse specializing in providing logistical support. My very first inquiry of the campsite operator as to whether he knew someone with a truck who would do the job for $100 (yes, it was a long time ago!) produced a positive result. On another occasion a similar request in a restaurant in a small northern Ontario river town produced the desired ride for us and our canoe to the railhead, for a cash fee. On a trip in B.C., a request of an air charter company produced a driver to return our vehicle to a float plane base.

It is useful to have a generous amount of cash or traveller's cheques and to mention it early in the negotiations. Your time and aggravation have a cost, so be prepared to pay well to reduce them. Even if someone wants a ridiculous fee to help, the cost as a percentage of your overall trip is probably quite small. Be careful how you make the arrangements because if an insurance company can prove a private vehicle owner received payment, they can refuse to pay an insurance claim.

Chartering Aircraft

Visitors should be aware that chartering aircraft is not the activity of the super-rich like it would be in Europe and that prices are not prohibitive except for very long flights. Some of the best locations are most easily reached using chartered fixed wing aircraft or helicopters. In fact, in Alaska there are so few roads that air is often the only access. Costs can look

high at first, but savings in time or in vehicle wear and tear can more than offset the higher cost. You might gain an interesting aerial perspective of the terrain of your trip, too, so keep your maps handy and a pencil to annotate them. Maybe a Polaroid camera, too, so you have instant air photos to use on the trip.

For example, the South Nahanni watershed can be reached by road, but the necessary vehicle shuttle would take a very long time. By the time you add in the true cost of wear and tear of motoring on northern roads and your time, flying is an appealing option. Similarly, I have used both train and air access to paddle a certain river in northern Ontario. The additional cost of flying to the headwaters from a lake on the river was well worth it. We were not tied to a train schedule, we saved a lot of time and we paddled right back to our vehicle. We didn't need a shuttle to the station and were much less concerned about security of our vehicle left at a float plane base than at a station. Remember that flight costs don't look so high when you amortize them over the number of days when you will be living at no cost in the backcountry. Camping in "civilization" incurs campsite fees, gasoline and perhaps eating-out and beer, which soon add up.

Air transportation is not always quicker than land. You must be prepared for delays caused by weather, especially if you are flying into or out of the mountains. Always have extra food in case you have to sit around and wait to be picked up.

With a large enough group, even chartering large aircraft can be a cost-effective way to reach the start of your trip.

A chartered aircraft is often the best way to reach the start of your trip and can be surprisingly cost-effective.

Canoes can be carried externally on the float struts of floatplanes. Mary Enright photo.

Helicopters have better capabilities than fixed wing aircraft in the mountains because they can land in much worse visibility. Fixed wing landings on open glaciers and snowfields are notorious for dangerous flat light conditions with no horizon. In the clearings in trees or rocky areas usable by helicopters there are usually reference points even in poor visibility. Although fixed wing flying is cheaper, helicopters are more likely to be able to land just where you want them to. In winter, fixed wing travel is more practical in wooded lake country than above treeline. This is because on frozen lakes in wooded areas, the trees provide perspective and a horizon for gauging height for landing.

Fixed wing aircraft. Float plane charters are available in many road-accessible remote communities in Canada and Alaska. This is especially so on the coasts and where there are plenty of lakes. They cater to the summer tourist, fishing and hunting. They are also used for general transportation and for industrial uses such as mineral exploration and transporting high-value seafoods. These aircraft are often converted to operate on skis or ski-wheels for winter operation between airports and snow or ice runways.

There are numerous small, rough airstrips in the north, especially in Alaska. There are about 200 rough airstrips in the Wrangell-St. Elias Park in Alaska. Charter companies will know where they are, so ask if there is one in the area you wish to visit.

In some areas aircraft are equipped with "tundra tires" for landing on beaches, river gravel bars and tundra. Operating an aircraft on wheels is cheaper than operating on floats or skis. On two occasions I have used a DC-3 (Dakota) on wheels to transport people and canoes to an airstrip near the river. For 10 people with five canoes the price was very reasonable.

I have used a wide range of aircraft for wilderness access. Each trip had different requirements depending on distance, the gear we were carrying, the size of the party and what performance characteristics were needed to fly into the area in question. The cost of flying is very dependent on how closely you can match your requirements to the capabilities of the aircraft available. Having some knowledge of aircraft capabilities can help you obtain the best ratio of cost per mile to number of passengers. We used a Single Otter on ski-wheels at the start of our trip to carry eight people and three weeks' ski-mountaineering food and gear, but needed three flights with a smaller Helio-Courier small STOL aircraft to fly out.

Canoes can be carried tied to the float struts of aircraft. They cause fuel-robbing drag and turbulence over the tail so you will be charged more for external loads. How many can be carried seems to depend on the operator. One canoe can be carried by Cessna 185s and Beavers, and usually one each side on a Single Otter. If you remove the thwarts, seats and deck plates of two different sized canoes, they may nest completely one inside the other. Then you may be able to carry two of them externally, but counting as one canoe. New Canadian regulations (1996) will affect the carrying of passengers in planes with external loads. In many cases this will mean paying for two flights instead of one and a doubling of cost.

Some aircraft can carry canoes inside the cabin, particularly if they are nested inside each other. Check that you can remove the appropriate parts and that the boats really will nest before you show up at the charter base and are committed. Don't forget to take appropriate tools and some spare nuts and bolts and washers.

To carry canoes in a Twin Otter, the row of double seats is removed, leaving just six single seats along one side. If you have more than six people, you could fill the Twin Otter with canoes, gear and six people and use a smaller aircraft to ferry the remaining passengers. A Twin Otter will carry 12 people and two weeks' rafting gear, depending on the distance and fuel load required.

When carrying canoes in a DC-3, one complete row of double seats is removed leaving seven double seats on the other side. One of these has to be occupied by a flight attendant, so you can carry 12 people and their six canoes nested inside each other.

Helicopters. Helicopters are most useful to mountaineers and skiers because of their capabilities in rugged terrain where there is nowhere to land a fixed wing plane. They have also been used by kayakers for access to some wild rivers. Costs are high at around $800/hr in Canada for a four-seat Jet Ranger (Bell 206), but you can do a tremendous amount in one hour.

If you are using one of the smaller helicopters such as the ubiquitous Bell Jet Ranger or a Hughes 500 or an A-Star, package your gear in relatively small containers rather than big packs for more efficient packing in the machine. When flying in to ski huts, we usually pack the food in liquor store boxes, tied and sealed with tape to exclude spindrift. In recent years I have noticed that the companies I fly with no longer let you get in the machine and then put a pack in on top of you. That practice certainly was dangerous in that it hindered a rapid exit in an emergency. With a large group the cost of an extra flight just for baggage is not prohibitively expensive.

On several occasions we have transported the gear in a net suspended below the machine. This is quick and easy and the load limit was higher than when carrying passengers. If the weather is wet it is a good idea to have bags ready to waterproof your gear. Large, light articles such as canoes are not suitable for carrying suspended below helicopters because of their tendency to "sail," but I know people who have transported river kayaks weighted with gear in this way. Flying speeds will likely be lower so you will pay for more flying time.

Some machines are equipped with a ski rack akin to a car roof rack, but wire basket racks are better because they are quicker to use and parts cannot fall out. The underbelly compartment of a Hughes 500 is ideally shaped for skis though it is not quick to load and unload.

Loads can be carried in a net slung under helicopters.

Minimizing air charter costs. Fixed wing is cheaper than helicopter by a large amount. Fixed wing charters are billed as a rate per mile or kilometre, helicopters on a rate per hour in the air. The rate is the same whether the machine is full or empty so you can halve your costs by "dovetailing" with another group that wants to come out from where you are going to. This is relatively straightforward to arrange if you are, say, going in to a hut to ski or climb. The charter companies would obviously prefer to do the maximum amount of billable flying, so don't necessarily expect them to go out of their way to set up dovetails. We set up a dovetail once through a charter operator, but it was a case partly of good connections and also the probability that neither party would go unless there was a dovetail. Do it yourself through the hut operator or seek out groups through the grapevine or ads in club magazines.

A major expense is the cost of the "deadhead" or flight from the aircraft's base to where you will start your flight. If you can track down another group to cooperate with on this cost you will save. Generally, it will be cheaper to use a small machine if the deadhead is long, provided that it can carry enough fuel or that there is a fuel cache already at the place from where you wish to fly.

If you have local contacts in a remote community where you plan to end a trip, you could find out if anyone is chartering a flight to bring in supplies and ask if you might use it on its homeward leg.

Unfortunately, the most economical aircraft may not be available at the time you actually show up to do the trip. I have heard of people getting a quote for one flight in a Twin Otter or the more expensive option of two flights with a single Otter. They assume the Twin Otter will be available, but when they arrive it isn't. Sometimes a quote is given for the aircraft the operator is certain will be available, but on arrival there may be an aircraft available that offers a cheaper option. Check what aircraft actually are around when you arrive and be prepared to negotiate.

Loading and unloading aircraft. Loading an aircraft at a dock, airport or helipad is relatively easy. Usually you can get a vehicle close to the aircraft. However, be prepared for some interesting antics when it comes to unloading in the backcountry. When using float planes keep your rubber boots or wading shoes handy—it may simply not be feasible to land precisely where you want to. If there is a sand beach, you may be able to beach the aircraft for unloading and step ashore or wade in shallows.

One friend of mine was flying in to a remote northern river and the pilot misjudged his speed and overdid the beaching process by about seven metres. It took several hours of hard work to relaunch a small Cessna 185! If the shore is rocky (particularly with sharp rocks rather than round boulders) the pilot may not want to approach at all, and even less if there is an onshore wind or the water is choppy. On one flight the water was so rough when we arrived that the pilot kept the plane well offshore and told my wife and I to unload straight into the canoe. We had to stand on the floats, untie the canoe from the float struts, unload our gear into it and paddle ashore. Our raingear wasn't handy enough, so by the time we had loaded the boat from the wave-washed floats we were soaked. We were thankful that our gear was already fully packed for paddling rather than having many loose items in the plane, because there were a few centimetres of water sloshing around in the canoe.

You never know what weather and conditions you will disembark from the plane into, so dress accordingly. Don't be lulled into a false sense of security by the conditions where you get into the plane and have any preconceived expectations about conditions where you will be put down. I saw one person who was dressed to be back in his car in 10 minutes, get unceremoniously unloaded from a helicopter into three metres of snow on a remote mountainside. The pilot had realized after leaving the mountain top that he was overloaded and made an emergency landing in the first available clearing farther down the mountain to unload some "weight."

Friends being flown out from a mountain hut and expecting to be getting out of the ski-wheel plane at an airport were instead left on a remote lakeshore down in a valley while the pilot returned for the rest of the party. He felt that if he took the time to go all the way out to the airport with the first party the weather would have deteriorated too much to be able to

The DeHavilland Twin Otter is a northern workhorse that can operate on skis, tundra tires or floats.

get the rest of the group down from high up. The ferrying idea did work and he got everyone down to the lake before the cloud came down on the heights. He then completed the job, ferrying the group from the low-level lake along the valley to the airport. However, they still spent a lot of time hanging around in the cold, and those who were not well dressed suffered most. Usually problems arise on the way in, where you take off from a dry springtime valley floor and in 10 minutes are jumping out into deep snow with a blizzard whipped up by the rotor downwash.

Regulations concerning load limits and passenger seating seem to be more carefully followed than in the past. I remember flights where the aircraft was obviously overloaded. When making arrangements with a charter company, be sure you give a truthful estimate of your total weight, including people, gear and boats. You can increasingly expect you and your gear to be weighed. Remember, pilots have to factor in the weight of fuel needed for the distance in question, too. Published load capacities may not apply to your trip because of fuel weight.

Safety around aircraft. Whirling propellers and rotors, and hot turbine exhausts kill and maim with monotonous regularity. Fixed wing operators will shut off the engines before unloading and loading but occasionally high winds or fast water may mean that it is safer to start a float plane engine before casting off from shore. Extreme caution must be used when doing this.

Helicopters are the greater danger because they often do not shut off the engines and they keep the rotors turning while loading and unloading.

- **Always** watch for signals from the pilot before approaching or exiting a helicopter.
- **Never** walk behind a helicopter.
- **Keep your head low**, especially when the rotor is slowing down. At slower speeds it is more subject to wind, and it droops down under its own weight, too.
- **Never** carry anything above waist level around helicopters.
- **Always make sure** gear cannot blow around, especially packs and sleeping bags, which can roll easily in the downdraft.

Ingenious methods are used by some boat skippers to launch kayaks and kayakers without docking. Wilf Cameron photo.

Chartering Boats

Motor boats with a skipper can often be chartered to take you to or from a dropoff point. Sometimes these boats are operated by people who make a living by fishing and whale watching charters, other times it may be someone who just happens to have a suitable boat. These can be quite small, open boats with outboard motors such as are common anywhere there is a large body of water. We travelled 60 kilometres across Hudson Bay from the mouth of the Seal River to Churchill with four 17-foot canoes. They were inverted and tied in pairs over two big 22-foot "freight canoes," which are proportioned like a regular open utility dinghy but built in traditional cedar-canvas style. With a large outboard motor we made rapid but cold and spray-blown progress, with the native boat-owners steering surprisingly accurately on what appeared to be instinct. The Churchill grain elevator was close to dead ahead when it appeared over the horizon. Another group we know of bought an old scow and with their own (reliable) outboard motor used it to transport themselves and their canoes 800 kilometres down a big river from the road end. They did this in two days of almost nonstop travelling, and then flew by chartered plane to the start of the trip proper. This saved them enormous transportation charges for the canoes, but it was a noisy, smelly, cold trip.

Other Mechanical Transport

Ski touring parties have used snowmobiles pulling sleds to transport themselves and gear to a base camp. Hikers have used motorcycles and "quads" on old logging roads to gain access to good hiking country. Canoeists have even used "quads" to pull canoes and gear on light trailers over washed-out, abandoned industrial roads. Fitted with proper mufflers and used in a sensible manner, these vehicles can be acceptable tools. However, you will have to leave them somewhere. Lock and hide them well because they are especially appealing to the criminal element. You will also need to stash helmets and other protective garb.

Getting to the Right Place

Be certain your transporter understands exactly where you want to go and drops you at the right place. It's all too easy to go along with your local "guide" and not keep a close enough check on the map. On one occasion a local dropped us off on a lake he assured us was the headwaters of the Little Nahanni in the N.W.T. We foolishly took his word for it without checking our map. Only after he had departed with our vehicle back to Watson Lake in the Yukon did we realize that we were on the wrong side of the height of land. We were in the Flat River drainage and had to do an unplanned portage over the divide!

I recently heard of a party of canoeists who were left by an air charter company on the wrong river in a very remote part of the northern N.W.T. mainland. Luckily, the river was navigable and they reached the coast. They were then able to paddle the shoreline to reach the scheduled pickup point at the mouth of the intended river some distance away. Although this incident was a navigation error, there can also be problems related to the use of local rather than official names

for places. Minimize the chance for error by pointing exactly to where you want to go on the map or provide grid references. Air navigation maps only have latitude and longitude, not UTM grids, so you have to specify a location with air charter operators in terms of latitude and longitude.

Ideally you should have maps that cover a wide area around your intended access route so you can keep a close check on where you are being dropped off.

Once you've reached your starting point, check carefully that you have all the gear out of the vehicle. Do a final check that you have everything you need—now's your last contact with civilization! (Matches?!) Even after this check you may be worried you've forgotten something until after the first night when you have had to use everything. Then revel in the silence and the prospect of no more contact with the infernal combustion engine for a while. Savour the great feeling of freedom and independence that comes from living out of your pack, canoe or pulk in the wilderness.

Although some backroads are excellent gravel and can be driven at 80 km/h, others are steep and winding and with washouts. Read the signboards (inset) on backroads and beware! Truckers who know the road, and are using radio traffic control, drive fast and often do not expect recreational traffic, especially on weekdays.

Road Access

Canada and Alaska have roads leading deep into the wilderness from the major highways and they provide excellent access. However, unlike the rural backroads of many other countries, these roads do not necessarily take you through scenes of pastoral serenity. Most of the roads were built for resource extraction so they are likely to take you through areas that have been mined or logged. We have to realize that these roads provide us with access we would not otherwise have. Also, we must be aware that they provide access to motorized recreationists, trophy hunters, etc.

Backroad Conditions

The backroads are often rough, loose, steep, winding, dusty, slippery when wet and poorly or infrequently maintained in winter, if they are maintained at all. Roads can be blocked by fallen trees, high water at fords, washouts, absent bridges or early snowfalls. Hazard warning signs are usually absent, as are crash barriers. Even on main roads, vehicles have gone off the road and down the embankment and been found days later. Driving these backroads therefore makes heavy demands on vehicles and drivers. Directional signposting is usually absent, so becoming lost is a distinct possibility. Maps are often not up-to-date and you definitely need a navigator to keep track of landmarks and distances using the odometer. Fuel consumption is usually high so fill up before you enter the backcountry. Fuel consumption becomes even higher in cold conditions and snow.

Overseas visitors especially must take special care to adjust to this type of driving, which can go on for 100 kilometres or more and can prove to be very draining both physically and mentally. People used to driving on the left have to be particularly careful because on single-track roads with no centre line and no other vehicles for reference it is easy to instinctively turn the wrong way when suddenly confronted by an oncoming vehicle.

Stop and read signs that pertain to use by the public. Industrial roads are used by mining or logging trucks driven by people who know the road and drive fast. Truck drivers are not thrilled at being held up by travellers, so get out of the way as quickly as possible. Be very wary of one-way systems and roads where vehicle movement is radio controlled. Radio controlling allows trucks to move fast with less concern about the possibility of meeting oncoming traffic on blind curves.

Dirt and gravel roads are hard on vehicles so breakdowns and punctures are more likely. There may be very little traffic, so if you have a mishap or breakdown it could be days before anyone else arrives to help. You might have to go a very long way on foot for assistance.

Vehicle breakdowns and mishaps in the backcountry are more serious if you have only one vehicle, especially if no one knows where you are. Friends of ours recounted an incident where their route ahead was blocked and they were concerned about getting back up a steep hill they had previously descended. No one knew where they were, and it was a 50-kilometre walk to any assistance. Luckily, they were able with much effort to get back up the hill. In winter where inability to start a vehicle could mean you are stranded in the middle of nowhere at -30°C with insufficient gear, the situation could be life-threatening.

Rental Vehicles

Renting vehicles in Canada and Alaska is far cheaper than in Europe, especially for long periods, but it is costlier in northern areas because of short seasons and the high cost of everything in the north. It may be well worth the cost to have the freedom to go where and when you want and the peace of mind of having a good vehicle to use. This is especially the case if the cost can be split among several people.

Unfortunately, full coverage for damage to the rented vehicle is an extra cost and very expensive at around $12-$15 per day. Although some "gold" credit cards cover this extra premium, it may be cheaper to add a rider to your own vehicle policy. Be aware that your deductible will apply.

Depending on the company, unlimited kilometre rates may limit you to a certain geographic area around the rental point. You may need to select a rate with a kilometre charge to allow more freedom. Don't forget that distances are large in North America and you will quickly clock up a large number of kilometres.

Restrictions may apply in some places as to where you can drive a rental vehicle. Generally, you are limited to paved roads and graded (maintained) public gravel roads. Some agreements may refer to "government maintained" roads. Some backroads are technically private roads, which may make them off limits to rented vehicles. Check the small print of rental agreements. However, if the roads are open to the public the insurance requirements may be satisfied. Gravel road and remote road use limitations may apply even for rentals from major centres, especially for recreational vehicles. Very specific restrictions may also exist. For example, I was informed in 1992 that in Goose Bay, Labrador you cannot use rental vehicles outside town. A party requiring transport from Goose Bay to a river was caught off guard by these restrictions once they arrived. When planning to rent vehicles, especially in the more remote areas, **check** carefully about possible restrictions before you arrive. Worldwide reservation offices may not be aware of restrictions so contact the local office.

If you are planning to transport canoes or other roof loads, you must check if there are any restrictions in your rental agreement about attaching a roof rack or about carrying anything on the roof. Even if there are no restrictions, be very careful not to mar the vehicle and lose your damage deposit. If you are using rubber pad types of racks or canoe carriers, dust from dirt roads tends to get under loose pads or dusty ropes and chafe against the vehicle. Protect vulnerable places with duct tape, and remove duct tape residue with gasoline if necessary afterward. You may be liable for stone chip damage, even if the rental agreement allows you to use gravel roads. It may be worth covering vulnerable areas with tape, plastic or self-adhesive plastic film such as is used for shelf linings. Make sure that it will not leave a baked-on adhesive residue after a few days in the sun—check a small area occasionally.

Rental companies generally only give you one key and travellers need at least two for safety. It is legal to have a duplicate key cut at your own expense. Get several people listed as drivers on the rental agreement, too.

Renting a cargo van without seats in the back when you need to transport more than two people is not a good idea. Most provinces have seatbelt laws making it illegal for people to travel loose in vans and pickup trucks.

If you are used to driving a well-equipped vehicle, remember that rental vehicles are unlikely to have snowscrapers, shovels, jumper cables, a tow rope, chains, tools and other crucial items.

Bringing Vehicles from Abroad

Whenever I see foreign-made vans and campervans with European licence plates in remote areas, I wonder if they know how to fix them and if they carry enough spare parts. Certainly these vehicles (apart from Volkswagens) are very unfamiliar to local mechanics and you stand no chance of buying parts, either new or used, locally. Make sure you carry a complete workshop manual, preferably in English, though the diagrams are a help in any language. Also, remember that vehicles built for European conditions tend to be lighter and less able to stand up to the rigours of rough North American backroads and cold winter temperatures.

Buying Beaters and Bangers

Visitors from abroad might consider buying a cheap second-hand vehicle when staying for a long period. However, the days of the crude, simple, easy-to-fix North American vehicle are fading fast as vehicles become more complex. North Americans don't seem to buy new cars as often as they used to, and are hanging onto them, so it's more difficult to find good used vehicles at a bargain price. However, visitors with sufficient time and mechanical knowledge can still purchase cheap vehicles that will last them the summer.

The dilemma is always whether to buy something really cheap, which you just discard if it needs expensive repairs, or whether to invest more money in the first place for a more reliable vehicle, but be prepared to put money into repairs if you are unlucky. The extra outlay on repairs then would make it imperative that you spend the time to sell the vehicle advantageously at the end of your trip, whereas a real heap can be written-off and junked.

Good vehicle preparation will reduce problems on roads like this.

Using Vehicles in Remote Areas

The road journey to or from the start of your trip is likely to be the riskiest part of the whole adventure. Backcountry driving is more of a calculated risk than highway driving because there is less traffic, so you are less at the mercy of other drivers. However, the conditions place heavy demands on your skill, and the consequences of mishaps are more serious. Telling people where you are going and when to expect your return is a vital aspect of your survival.

Vehicles and Driving Skill

You don't have to have an expensive four-wheel drive vehicle to get a long way into the backcountry, though it helps. Old beaters have amazing capabilities if you know a few tricks, and they are easier to fix, too! Our canoeing group regularly uses very rough backroads for access to mountain rivers, and with care, patience and ingenuity everything from 4x4s to vans and pickups and small Hondas gets in and out again. If you have good driving skill, prepare well, take your time and if you carry some basic equipment, you can greatly reduce the risk of running into the sort of backcountry driving difficulties from which you cannot extricate yourself.

Vehicle Preparation

Good tires are crucial to your safety, so don't skimp on quality. I remember one nail-biting ride on bald tires over 200 kilometres of remote road in the Yukon. The ancient vehicle was heavily loaded, and to lessen the strain on the worn-out treads, we all rose up off our seats at every bump, like jockeys rising in the saddle! Tires take a lot of abuse on backroads, so make sure you have at least one good spare. For extensive backroad travel, carry two spares, especially in summer and if you are one vehicle travelling alone. Take along one of your winter tires, or better still take both winter tires, one in the place of the regular spare. Then you have two really grippy tires available if you encounter slippery conditions. I always carry a tire pump and a puncture plugging kit. However, these are useless if you let the tire go so flat that the bead comes off the rim. The only way to get the tire bead back on the rim without a high pressure and high volume hose is to insert an inner tube as a temporary repair. Remember that radial tire sidewalls are very fragile. We destroyed a $150 tire, 50 kilometres up a remote logging road simply by driving over a branch that snapped and pierced the tire wall.

Fuel tanks can be protected from rocks by using rubber matting or even old truck inner tubes attached to the front and undersides with wire. It's an awkward task, and beware of harbouring mud and moisture that will accelerate tank rusting. Oil pan and transmission protectors are available for some sport utility vehicles but will probably have to be custom-made for cars. Be careful not to impede the cooling airflow over oil pans, transmissions and catalytic converters with these protectors.

You can expect considerable stone-chipping of the vehicle's paint work, and if you are driving a rented vehicle you may be charged for this damage. Good, big mud flaps on the front wheels are reasonably cheap and easy to attach and go a long way to help preserve the body work. Some attach with clamps and require no drilling. You might even consider taping plastic sheeting over vulnerable areas temporarily, or using an adhesive plastic film such as Mactac. North American windshields do not disintegrate into thousands of pieces like some European varieties when hit by a rock. Many vehicles have custom-made headlights, which are now extremely expensive, so fit them with wire or plastic stone guards. It's also worth attaching a piece of household bug screen mesh or a homemade shield over the front of the radiator grill to deflect rocks and keep the radiator from clogging with insects. Large screens that cover the entire front and provide some protection to the windshield are available and easy to attach, but make sure you protect paint work with tape or foam where the screen touches.

Coping with Dust

Dust is a significant hazard on many backroads because it obstructs visibility. Always drive with your lights on and within safe visibility and stopping distances. Clean your lights frequently. This means **inside** the tail-lights as well because an amazing amount of dust gets inside to reduce the brightness. If you are not driving in someone else's dust cloud, close your windows and operate your fan to pressurize the interior of your vehicle and prevent dust entry. Keep food and equipment protected in packs or plastic bags.

Driving on Slippery Surfaces

The surfaces of many roads are loose gravel or just whatever soil there happens to be at the particular location. You have less control and cornering and braking ability than on a hard-surfaced road. Some surfaces are very greasy and slick when wet. If the road is bumpy or "washboard," contact between tires and the road is diminished and this reduces adhesion. If the shock absorbers are in poor shape the adhesion is worse still and this kind of surface can become very dangerous. Unfortunately,

Dust on backroads is unpleasant and can impose dangerous visibility restrictions.

the worst washboard exists where vehicles brake, accelerate or corner, and these are the places you need the best adhesion.

Ground Clearance

Low ground clearance is probably the biggest drawback of small vehicles, especially when loaded down with gear. Mudholes, through which you need to maintain some speed to avoid becoming stuck, can be a menace if protruding rocks are hidden under the water. Poke around in the mud with a stick to check for rocks first. Drivers of low vehicles must take great care to keep their eyes open for projecting rocks and stumps and for holes and ditches across roads. Unfortunately, these low vehicles that are most affected by such road hazards also provide a poor view of the road surface ahead. With any vehicle, if you brake hard to slow down before hitting a hole or bump, take your foot off the brake immediately

Dust infiltrates everywhere! Clean inside your tail-lights to maintain brightness for safety.

before you hit the hole. This allows the front of the vehicle to rise up again and take some of the load off the front suspension so it is better able to absorb the impact.

Leaks

With any vehicle, if you hear a loud thud underneath, get out to investigate. If it has caused an oil, fuel or transmission leak, at least you can collect the fluid in pots, hubcaps, etc. Then you can fix the leak with epoxy or proprietary products made for the purpose, reinsert the fluid through a cloth as a filter and go on your way. Waiting for hot smells and knocking noises or gas gauges reading "empty" is a poor way to identify a leak! Even small loose rocks on the road hit at 30 kilometres per hour can do considerable damage. A friend had the oil pan drainplug partly sheared by such an object on a very remote road in northern B.C.

Traction Traps

Being unable to retrace your route is a real possibility if the hill you easily descended later becomes slick and slimy after a rainfall or snowfall. We regularly use a steep river access road that is just clay and is a nightmare when wet. It has been the scene of a number of epics, trying to get vehicles the two kilometres up the hill in the rain. Tire chains have saved the day on several occasions, and I never go anywhere, winter or summer, without this cheap insurance against getting stuck. In some conditions such as this slick, slimy clay, four-wheel drive is not an infallible answer unless you have really aggressive (and noisy) tire tread patterns. In some conditions two-wheel drive with chains is better than four-wheel drive without.

Washouts

During heavy rain or spring melt, be particularly aware of the possibility of washouts that can block your route behind you. My wife and I were marooned for three days on a very remote road in the Yukon when the spring melt washed out a culvert in front of us and then an entire bridge behind us. If you see a culvert being blocked with debris or by beavers, stop to clear it—you might be glad later!

An emergency tire sealer may quickly solve a minor leak and get you home.

Fords and Flooded Areas

If you do decide to risk driving through a flooded area, stop and think carefully first. Getting stuck with your vehicle and all your gear in the middle of a rising stream puts you in a serious predicament! The risk may not be worth the potential benefit.

Washouts do not have to be as big as this one to cut you off. This one in the Yukon marooned us for three days.

You can see the depth of water in regular fords if the water is clear, but washouts and dangerous depths usually occur during floods when the water is likely to be muddy and you can't tell what the depth is. Remember also that what appears to be a ford, with wheelmarks each side, could be a winter-only crossing, and besides, you don't know what sort of vehicle made the marks. Taking meaningful soundings from the shore is tricky, and doing it from the hood of a moving vehicle is dangerous, especially if the line you are dangling gets wound up around a spinning wheel and pulls you in. A long horizontal pole with a vertical pole or line and weight attached provides a bit more scope.

It is essential to drive through slowly to avoid stirring up silt, and thereby harming fish habitat. It is also important to go slowly to prevent swamping the engine. Removing the fan belt will prevent the fan from throwing water all over the engine, but will also disable the water pump so the engine will soon overheat. The task is easier with electric cooling fans since all you need to do is disconnect the power to the cooling fan, perhaps simply by removing its fuse. Don't forget to replace it. Check where the air intake to the fuel injection is—it is much lower on my new car than it was on my previous, carburetor-equipped vehicles.

Fording washouts must be done carefully, because getting stuck is a very serious occurrence.

If you are uncertain about the likelihood of crossing successfully, anchor one end of a rope on the shore and pay it out as you proceed. Then if you get stuck you have a means of getting ashore without being washed away. If the rope is long enough, loop it round a tree so you can pull on one end to retrieve the rope. If you do get stuck, the swirling water around the wheels tends to undermine them, making matters worse because the vehicle becomes more firmly stuck and unstable.

Winter Starting Problems

A significant winter hazard is not being able to start your vehicle at a remote trailhead at -25°C. To improve your chances of starting a cold engine, use thin, 5W-30 oil rather than 10W-30. Ether sprays such as Quickstart can usually be used with older vehicles with carburetors and with some single-point fuel injection systems, but check the instruction manual very carefully. Complex computerized ignition and multi-point injector systems provide no scope for fiddling, so your only option may be to warm the engine and battery.

When starting, depress the clutch so that the starter does not have to turn the gearbox as well. Even in neutral the cold oil provides an incredible amount of drag. It was enough to stall my five-litre van engine when I released the clutch at -35°C before the engine was warmed up.

A vehicle will be easier to pushstart if you park facing the right way at the top of a hill. Preferably also park so the sun shines on the hood. If you do have to push start, it will be much easier in third gear, especially on slippery surfaces. However, you must be quick to depress the clutch as soon as the engine fires because it can't "drive away" in third. You cannot push start an automatic transmission. You can also damage automatics by towing.

Leave the vehicle in gear and don't apply the parking brake, which may freeze up. I remember one morning when I had to grovel in the snow at -25°C with a propane torch to thaw the parking brake cables.

A camp stove under the oil pan will eventually warm things up enough to help, especially with smaller engines. Make absolutely sure there are no dripping fluids or caked-on oil and dirt to catch fire, and be careful not to overheat rubber hoses. Bank some snow to keep wind away. A standard technique for heating engines in northern areas is to insert a propane Tiger Torch into the end of a metre or so of stovepipe lying on the ground. A flow of hot air comes out of the end, and a chimney elbow piece directs the heat up onto the engine. Alternatively, build a fire and shovel hot rocks and coals under the engine. Friends reported doing this to their VW van at -35°C. They said they waited until they heard "deep-frying sounds" from the oil pan and then it started instantly!

Battery power is much reduced at low temperatures. Always carry tools so that you can remove it and warm it carefully in front of a fire. Creeks continue to flow with water at 0°C even when air temperatures are very low, so you can place the battery in a flowing creek and the 0°C water flowing around (not over) it will slowly bring its temperature up from air temperature to zero. You can also swap batteries with a vehicle that is started and warmed up if you don't have jumper cables (but you never get caught out without cables, do you?!). Re-start the warmed vehicle with your weak battery **before** you exhaust the other battery trying perhaps unsuccessfully to start your vehicle!

Even modern engine oil becomes sticky like molasses in winter temperatures, so use a thin grade such as 5W-30 to be certain of trailhead starts.

If You Get Stuck

If you do get stuck in snow, take the time to dress properly before you start digging, so you stay dry. After all, you cannot be sure you will be able to get unstuck. You may have to stay there, in which case you need as much of your clothing as possible to be dry and warm. Don't try to drive out until you have evaluated the situation carefully. If you spin the wheels, all you achieve is hot tires and polished snow, making matters worse. Evaluate whether you should try to get out the way you went in or whether you will do better continuing in the same direction. If you are in a ditch on a hill, you may do better driving downhill along the ditch to get up enough speed to pop up onto the road again. Whatever you decide to do, prepare the route with lots of digging. Take the trouble to put your chains on **now** rather than after messing up your preparation with a failed attempt to get out. You must also dig the compacted snow out from under the vehicle so its wheels can press properly on the ground to grip. Be patient and do enough digging to be certain of getting out on the first try. In mud and loose sand or gravel, the same rules apply about good preparation of your route out. In some situations chains will just cause you to dig in, so don't spin the wheels. In mud you'll be glad of a coverall, rubber boots and gloves.

A selection of equipment for getting vehicles unstuck. The old bumper jack has holes drilled so it can be used as a winch.

The Spanish Windlass is a very powerful winch system. The magnification is the ratio of the lever length to the vertical spool diameter. It is more stable and manageable if both ropes are kept in a direct line. Stepping over a tensioned line is **very** dangerous, so you need two people. It works best with wire or chain.

Pulling Systems

Various pulling systems can be used to get out of trouble. A tow is the simplest if there are other people around and if they have a suitable vehicle. A tow has the advantage of moving fairly fast so the stuck vehicle can be driven to provide assistance. Winches and similar pulling systems are slow, and trying to drive the stuck vehicle to help will result in wheelspin or a burned clutch. These situations are easier to handle with an automatic transmission, but it too can overheat. The elasticity of rope as opposed to chain pulling systems is helpful if you are driving the vehicle out while pulling at the same time.

There is a serious risk to people and property if winches and other pulling systems involving tensioned wires and particularly tensioned synthetic ropes are used incorrectly. If the line breaks or comes untied, it springs back with incredible force like a slingshot, and people have been badly hurt. During a canoe rescue, a tensioned rope broke and a friend was hit on the head by a pulley attached to the rope end as it

A chain nailed to a frozen road is an effective anchor.

kicked back. He would have been seriously injured or even killed had he not been wearing a helmet. In another incident I heard about, a hitch ball became detached from a vehicle and flew back on the end of the tow wire. To guard against the danger of a line breaking, stay clear and drape car mats, branches, etc., over the line to reduce the scope of a devastating kickback.

Anchors for Pulling Systems

The usefulness of a winch or pulling system presupposes that you have an adequate anchor, and the convenient tree you see in the pictures isn't always there in real life. A "deadman" is a relatively easy type of anchor to build in snow, sand, gravel, or loose soil and bog. Basically, it is simply a buried object with the rope attached to its middle. A log behind a snowbank will hold an incredible force, and a spare wheel will also work well. The key with any kind of deadman is to ensure that the rope goes down a slot to the deadman in such a direction as to not lift the deadman out of its hole.

You can also pile rocks on a log, but use some finer material as well to add friction with the ground and to prevent the rocks moving

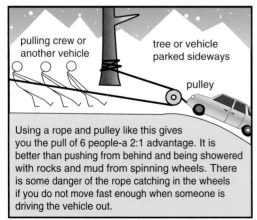

pulling crew or another vehicle

tree or vehicle parked sideways

pulley

Using a rope and pulley like this gives you the pull of 6 people-a 2:1 advantage. It is better than pushing from behind and being showered with rocks and mud from spinning wheels. There is some danger of the rope catching in the wheels if you do not move fast enough when someone is driving the vehicle out.

independently. You can even build a pile of snow to use with a deadman as an anchor. Mix and trample it to make it set up more quickly.

The advantage of deadmen is that they require no equipment other than your shovel. Everyone should have a shovel in their vehicle. (A strong snowshovel in winter and a dirt shovel or trenching tool in summer.) Anchors involving pegs and spikes require the use of an axe or maul to drive them. You may carry an axe, but a folding saw is lighter and more compact, and is certainly better for cutting away fallen trees from across roads.

Some people carry 60-centimetre metal spikes for use as anchors, but your chances of driving one far enough in to firm enough ground without hitting a rock are a bit slim, and you need a substantial hammer, axe or maul. If you do succeed in driving it you will have difficulty removing it unless you have a bumper jack and a piece of chain. An amazingly effective anchor is a length of tow-chain nailed to frozen ground or to a packed dirt road with at least six 15-centimetre nails. The pull must be reasonably parallel with the ground. You won't strike lucky with every nail and not hit a rock, but they are easy to remove and retry. Make sure that the chain is taut between nails so that the load comes on to them simultaneously. It is easy to remove the whole rig one nail at a time after use.

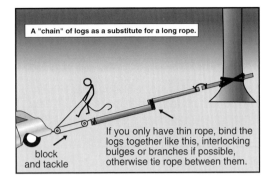

A "chain" of logs as a substitute for a long rope.

If you only have thin rope, bind the logs together like this, interlocking bulges or branches if possible, otherwise tie rope between them.

block and tackle

If you use improvised stakes driven in to the ground or are tying to a tree that is a bit suspect, the anchor will be much stronger if you brace it as in the diagram.

You might find a good anchor, such as a tree, that is beyond the reach of your rope. If you tie fallen tree trunks end to end in a line with short pieces of rope, you will have all the length you need. A big advantage of this over a long rope is that it does not stretch.

Improvised pulling systems have an advantage over a winch for self-rescue in that they can be attached to either end of a vehicle. A winch on the front of a vehicle is not much use for pulling yourself out the way you went in!

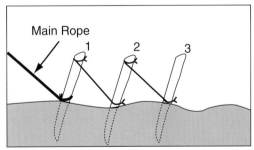

A strong anchor if you can drive pegs into the ground. Rope between pegs must be tied tightly and go from the top of the forward pegs to the ground level at rear pegs.

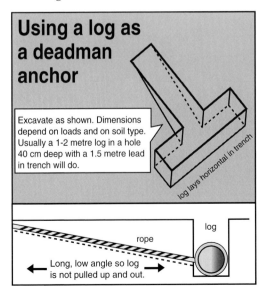

Using a log as a deadman anchor

Excavate as shown. Dimensions depend on loads and on soil type. Usually a 1-2 metre log in a hole 40 cm deep with a 1.5 metre lead in trench will do.

log lays horizontal in trench

log

rope

Long, low angle so log is not pulled up and out.

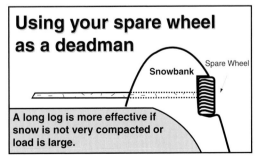

Using your spare wheel as a deadman

Snowbank

Spare Wheel

A long log is more effective if snow is not very compacted or load is large.

Carrying Equipment On Your Vehicle

I've often seen thousands of dollars worth of gear attached precariously to the roof of a vehicle barrelling down the highway at 100 km/h. The airstream and wind forces on the gear at highway speeds are surprisingly large. Add to that the vibration and jolting from backcountry roads, and it's not surprising that you occasionally see pieces of mangled equipment strewn across the highway. Canoe repair shops tell me that the majority of the damage they fix occurs on the road, not the river. If a rack or load comes off, you risk damage to your vehicle as well as loss or damage to the gear. Also, consider the hazard to other vehicles and the risk of prosecution of the driver for having an insecure load. If you get into an accident, an insecure roof load can become a missile capable of causing a great deal of injury and damage. You can't afford to take these risks, so obtain a good rack and attach it and its load properly.

You must have a strong enough rack to resist upward and backward forces as well as to support the weight. In addition to choosing a good quality rack, you must choose the correct rack for your vehicle and adjust and attach it properly. If you are used to the heavy load-carrying ability of gutter mounts, beware of overloading any rack that rests on the roof. Also, be very wary

of decorative pseudo-gutters, which are weak. You should carefully heed the vehicle and rack manufacturers' load limits. Many factory luggage rack rails are not designed to support loads, only to stop them sliding off.

You must attach the gear properly to the rack, and with long loads, tie the ends of the gear directly to the vehicle as well. If you are mounting a canoe with rubber gunwale pads instead of a rack, try to position the pads near the edges or front and rear of the roof where it is more curved and therefore stronger.

If you frequently carry large items, you should seriously consider the long-term convenience and peace of mind that comes from permanently fitting a rack attachment plate to the roof or side of the vehicle. These are reasonably unobtrusive and could save your vehicle from damage. They can be attached without removing vehicle headlinings and are also useful on truck cabs when suitably reinforced inside.

It is well worth attaching tiedown ringbolts to your vehicle to make it easier to tie down the front and rear of long loads. Locate them so that the tiedown rope is not in the driver's primary line of sight and where loose rope ends are well clear of moving parts, particularly with front wheel drive vehicles.

Don't overload your vehicle! Clayton Roth photo.

Even if you have a very strong rack, you must consider the effect of a high-placed load on vehicle handling. When carrying items that extend far beyond the rack crossbars, such as canoes, kayaks and hang-gliders, beware of the teeter-totter motion caused by wind, slipstream and bumps in the road. The resulting leverage causes large upward and downward forces on the rack and roof, particularly if the rack bars are placed close together. You must tie the load to the car at front and rear and tension the lines so that no rocking can occur. Bending forces on the item are large, too, if it is not tied at the ends.

Chafing and surface wear of all equipment will happen if it is not cushioned and attached absolutely rigidly to prevent it oscillating in the turbulence. Even slight oscillation between equipment and the rack or tiedowns will soon mar surfaces, especially when grit, dust and road dirt get in between to act as an abrasive scouring compound. Put your tiedowns in the washing machine occasionally.

For tiedowns, use slightly stretchy white nylon utility rope from a hardware store or better still some six millimetre nylon kernmantel rope from a climbing equipment supplier. The stretchiness means that it maintains its tension even after the knots slip a little. Nylon costs more than cheap yellow polypropylene, but is easier to handle, less harsh and more durable. Learn the Packer's hitch, which acts as a 3:1 winch and helps you put precisely the right amount of tension on your rope to hold a load without crushing.

If you don't want to use knots and ropes, straps with locking buckles are available from most rack suppliers. Ratchet webbing tiedowns from hardware stores and automotive suppliers also work well. You should also pad your rack or use the special cradling and cushioning clamps and fittings specifically designed to fit different outdoor equipment.

Roof boxes are a popular way of carrying skis, backpacks and miscellaneous gear. Once the box is attached, the equipment can be easily and quickly loaded, even in the dark, rain or a howling blizzard when you are tired at the end of the day. Gear is well protected from dirt, water and road salt, and more secure hidden from prying eyes in the locked box. Most roof boxes are reasonably aerodynamic so

The Packer's hitch enables you to tension tiedowns strongly and precisely. For clarity, it is shown with much thicker rope than you should use. Note the ringbolts that make it easy to secure your load.

Ratchet webbing tiedowns enable you to securely attach your load with precise control over tension and without the need to know how to tie knots. Packer's hitch shown on right.

they are quieter than an untidy bundle of gear. They are subject to considerable windlift, especially if they project in front of the windshield. Because of this windlift, some rack systems are not recommended by the manufacturers for use with roof boxes. The cheaper boxes that sit directly on the roof and attach with web straps and hooks look insecure, but at least the wind can't get under them to cause lift. The attachment buckles must be threaded correctly to tighten and lock properly.

The better quality boxes that have close-fitting lids and gaskets keep water out, but it is advisable to have everything in water-resistant bags of some kind. Short boxes that do not extend forward of the windshield may be more prone to leakage because the front is hit by the full force of the water blowing up over the top of the windshield.

Ribbing on the bottom of boxes keeps gear off the bottom where melting snow, boot mud and water seepage tend to accumulate. On the other hand, smooth-bottom boxes are easier to clean out and you can put removable perforated mats in them to keep gear off the bottom. The Seattle Sports Sherpak is a collapsible roof box made of heavyweight vinyl. It protects gear well and folds up small for storage when not needed. You can also use large canoeist's drybags to protect your baggage.

Surviving in Your Stranded Vehicle

If you become stranded you are faced with surviving for an unknown period; possibly hours, days or even weeks, depending on where you are and whether anyone is likely to come looking for you. Hopefully, you have told someone where you are going and when you expect to be back.

Clothing to Keep In the Vehicle

If you were out recreating you will likely have good outdoor clothing with you, but you may be wet and need a change of clothes when you get to the vehicle. You will probably get out of the vehicle to try to fix it, push it, pull it, dig it out, dig out another vehicle or reconnoitre. The weather may well be very cold, snowing or wet. The insects may be horrible, making any attempts to fix the vehicle purgatory. Do **not** **assume** that you will be able to solve the problem and warm up or dry out soon. Dress to stay warm and dry from the **beginning**.

Keep the following items in your car if you are driving backcountry roads. Remember, in many areas it can snow in any month of the year.

- Waterproof clothing. Preferably a type that won't get too stiff when cold, and large enough to go on over extra clothes.
- Breathable, windproof, water-repellent shell for cold conditions. A ski coverall shell suit, insulated ski suit or snowmobile suit is good.
- Wool toque or balaclava
- Several pairs of gloves, including insulated rubber work gloves or mitts for shovelling and pushing, and thin gloves for manipulating tools.
- Insulated boots—mukluks or snowmobile boots in winter, rubber boots in summer
- Wool socks
- Insulating clothing—an old ski jacket, warmup pants, pile jacket, etc.
- Coverall
- Safety orange vest
- Swiss army knife
- A sleeping bag, preferably with full length zipper, that remains in the vehicle.

Keep these miscellaneous vehicle survival items in your car when going into remote areas:

- Cookies, chocolate, crackers. Mark your calendar and replace every four months or so.
- Small camp stove, pot, matches, fuel
- Quick soups, tea, coffee, juice crystals
- Piece of material to form a flag on your aerial if vehicle is getting buried in snow
- Flashlight with alkaline batteries
- Candles for light and warmth in vehicle.
- Matches or lighter or both!
- Pocket handwarmers
- Snowshoes
- Long book to read
- Flares
- Head net and insect repellent
- Large orange garbage bags
- Large ice cream pail to use as a toilet to save going outside the vehicle.
- Paper towels, Kleenex
- First aid kit

Vehicle Survival Procedures

Carbon monoxide, which causes drowsiness and eventually death, has poisoned many stranded motorists who have left their engines running for heat. It happens especially when the vehicle is partly buried in snow and the exhaust cannot readily escape.

If you must run the engine occasionally to stay warm, to recharge the battery or to prevent the engine from freezing up, clear snow away from the exhaust pipe and the underside of the vehicle first. Listen for any sounds of damage-induced leaks (snow muffles sounds—be careful). If you can move the vehicle, park crosswise to the wind so that the exhaust is blown away but you do not have snow blowing into the radiator. If you have a recirculating setting on the heater, consider setting it to recirculate because the vehicle will heat up quicker. However, if there are any exhaust leaks, setting it to bring in fresh air from in front of the windshield will pressurize the vehicle and keep out exhaust trying to enter from other points. If there is any doubt, use the fresh air setting. Open a window in a location that will minimize risk of exhaust entry. Unfortunately, car windows open from the top, which means that the warm air will convect out.

Camp stoves, lanterns and catalytic heaters are **extremely dangerous** in vehicles because they very quickly use up oxygen and start producing carbon monoxide. Good ventilation is essential so keep two windows open to produce cross-ventilation.

A winter storm can quickly bury your car.

Be especially alert to any feeling of drowsiness or headache as these are the only warnings you will get of the presence of lethal, colourless, odourless carbon monoxide.

Vehicles tend to be cold unless insulated or well plastered with an insulating layer of snow, so do not worry if snow builds up on and around the vehicle, unless you want to start the engine. If fuel is short and you aren't going to start the engine anyway, you could consider piling snow on and around the vehicle. The first time I slept in a snowcovered vehicle was at a ski area parking lot. At that time I was not aware of the insulating properties of snow, and I woke up in my sleeping bag during the night drenched in sweat. Tie a flag of some kind to the aerial so you don't get hit by a snowplow! The light from a candle or the interior light will show through a considerable thickness of snow. Remove the bulbs from all but one interior light to save the battery.

A snow shelter such as a snow cave or quinzee near the vehicle is less appealing but may well be warmer. The big danger is that you cannot hear approaching rescuers or snowplows. They can't see you unless you mark the shelter well. Being in a snowhouse when a snowblower arrives is not a nice scenario—if it doesn't grind you up it may bury you deeper.

Insulating materials within the vehicle that you can use as additional clothing include carpets and sound deadening materials that can be wrapped around you. Newspapers, cardboard, plastic spare tire bags, spare tire covers, tents, etc., will all help if used carefully and ingeniously to make a small, warm nest in a corner of the vehicle.

Huddle close to your companion(s) to change the immediate environment of your body from "cold air" to "warm body," so less body heat is lost. Keep your feet up out of the cold air that sinks to the floor. The advantage of a sleeping bag with full zipper is that you can wrap it around two people or use it as a cloak.

Deciding Whether or Not to Leave your Vehicle

Factors to consider:

Does it really matter if you get home today instead of tomorrow if you may die or be permanently injured in today's attempt? There is a wealth of survival material and good shelter in the vehicle. A vehicle is easier to find than a person. IF someone will miss you and come looking **in the right place**, then you will be better off staying in the vehicle.

Do you know where you are, where you should go and how to get there? Do you have the means to leave a message concerning your plans if you leave? Do you have the energy, fitness and equipment needed to travel the distance in the conditions? Will conditions get worse or better? If conditions are worse than you expected, will you be able to reach or find your vehicle again if you have to retreat back to it? Can you survive long enough away from the shelter of the vehicle? Is that light over there a single bulb 300 metres away or a picture window two kilometres away on the other side of a creek or irrigation ditch?

What will happen if visibility deteriorates? Do you have a compass and know how to use it? Do you have the means to carry survival equipment with you from the vehicle? What will happen if the snow gets deeper? Did you make snowshoes from saplings, hubcaps, air filter lids, masonite spare wheel covers, etc., in the comfort of the vehicle **before** you left it?

If you do leave the vehicle in winter conditions, your shovel is your #1 survival tool, so take it with you. Do you have the means to make a fire once you are away from the vehicle? (You had gasoline and a battery to make a big spark at the vehicle.)

Can you take your spare gasoline or oil or flares? Can you take along floor mats or carpets so you have insulation for the floor of a snowhouse if you have to bivouac?

If you can't answer "yes" to most of these questions you should stay put!

Chapter 9

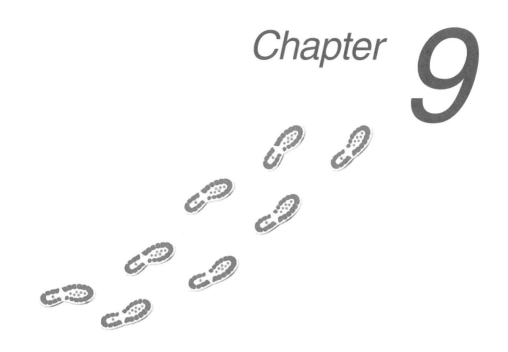

Reducing Your Impact

One of the attractions of outdoor recreation in Canada and Alaska is that you can still find pristine places where there is no sign that man has been before. However, the number of these special places is fast dwindling, and travellers must take care to preserve them by leaving no trace of their visits. Even heavily used areas that clearly show wear and tear should be treated carefully, because careful use can slow down their degradation. Everything we do in the backcountry has some impact, especially in the more fragile areas that are often of interest, so minimum impact techniques must be used whenever possible. This includes choice of campsites, use of stoves and fires, and dealing with human waste and garbage. It is also important to minimize wear and tear on the trails and to avoid adverse effects on local cultures, cultural relics and wildlife.

Is Your Impact Necessary?

An important factor in reducing impact is to decide whether you really need to use a particular area at all. I was appalled recently to read the itinerary of an ocean cruise during which a well-known financial advisor would be giving lectures. The ship would visit Glacier Bay and while there the speaker would be giving an afternoon investment seminar. The ship would have an adverse impact on the place and spoil the scenery for others, and people on board would not even be receiving any benefit from being in that particular location. I have attended a number of courses and conferences in national or provincial parks or in recreation areas, usually in resorts or hotels. In the majority of cases it was not necessary to use those facilities at all, and the event could just as easily (and for many people, more conveniently and cheaply) have been held in the city. Certainly the surroundings were congenial, but I don't feel the impact of our presence was justified.

The impact is subtle and more far-reaching than most people realize. First, there is the obvious contribution we make to the local pollution levels simply by "being there." The degradation of water quality in the Bow River downstream from the resorts of Banff and Lake Louise is a case in point. What is more significant in the long run is that by using facilities, we help make them profitable and help create an indication of demand. This means more people will want to build more developments to cash in on the perceived demand, and the amount of development increases. Eventually the facilities themselves become the attraction. You then have an area being overrun and degraded by the impact of thousands of people who would not be there at all without the attraction of the facilities. Urban Banff rather than Banff Park is the attraction for a disturbingly large proportion of visitors, who in turn degrade the environment over a wider and wider area.

On the other hand, maybe we should patronize organizations providing services that enhance visitors' appreciation of the true values of the area. These include outdoor schools teaching about environmental awareness, nature and environmentally appropriate activities, equipment rental organizations and outfitters, and the providers of unobtrusive low impact basic accommodation and essential food. Then at least the wilderness areas have a "constituency" and some economic basis for their continued existence. The need for the latter is an unfortunate reality.

It could be argued that the wilderness would do better without any organized activity and that the fewer people who go there, the better. The

Although nonmotorized recreation doesn't do as much damage as driving ORVs has done here, we mustn't become complacent and think we do no damage at all.

This "hardened" backcountry tentsite does not have much of a wilderness atmosphere, but this type of hardening is preferable to the erosion that would occur without it.

flaw in this argument is that the wilderness then has no constituency of defenders when someone comes along to clearcut it or build a copper mine in the middle of it and pollute the watershed with acid rock drainage.

Since some impact is inevitable no matter how you travel, people should make sure they obtain the maximum legitimate benefit from being in an area. I question the legitimacy of canoeing the South Nahanni, for example, if the skill level is such that all the energy goes into surviving the challenges of navigating the river. People who have no energy left to appreciate the other values of the river, are like a diner at a good restaurant who takes up a place and dirties the tablecloth but only eats the bread rolls. Should the West Coast Trail be subjected to the impact of unskilled backpackers (who occupy a quota space, too) if they are too taxed by the hiking to pay any attention to the surroundings? My feeling is that one should develop skills in less fragile and less popular areas first.

Minimizing Your Impact

The destruction wrought by motorized recreation is serious. Motorized summer recreation causes ground erosion and scarring as well as wildlife disturbance. Winter use by snowmobilers disturbs wildlife when they are in a fragile state, and compacts the snow into convenient pathways for predators. However, nonmotorized use can also have an adverse effect. There are many ways you can damage the backcountry. This section will outline how to plan and how to behave to minimize your impact and help slow the inevitable degradation of the backcountry. Perhaps a few more generations will then be able to experience quality recreation in unspoiled areas.

The Impact of Being There

Even careful backcountry users can end up "loving to death" their favourite recreation areas. This happens particularly easily in northern and alpine areas where the vegetation is very fragile and quite small disturbances impair its chances of survival. The scars left by people being there and walking around take many years to heal. In areas such as the Canadian Shield, where campsites are relatively scarce, heavy foot traffic results in soil compaction and loss of moisture-retaining duff. This in turn leads to soil erosion, root exposure and the death or ill health of the trees that once made the site pleasant.

I once helped in some research into the effect of foot travel on alpine vegetation. I was the person who did the "prescribed tramples," walking back and forth a set number of times. It was surprising how few tramples were needed to do a lot of harm, though the damage did not become really apparent until later. The bruising and breaking caused a dramatic appearance change after a few days. Once a mat of vegetation is broken by foot traffic, erosion can start, particularly when the vegetation is underlain by permafrost. The resulting inexorable cycle of destruction is much the same as in the south where damage to vegetation by overgrazing leads to soil destruction and erosion, and the formation of an environment that plants can no longer colonize. In warmer and wetter environments, the land heals more quickly because of the high rate of growth under these more favourable conditions. However, we still need to go lightly in those places, too.

The Impact of Camping

Many parks now prohibit random camping, and you are required to use specifically designated campsites. This is the best way to preserve the more heavily used areas of the backcountry. Camping in designated areas with other people can be a little tedious after a day of hiking or paddling through pristine terrain. However, the environmental advantages of these designated sites easily outweigh the personal disadvantages. Campsite establishment is based on sound environmental reasons, and failure to use these sites is an offence that can incur substantial fines. See page 124.

Note how the tent is pitched so that the heavy-wear zone outside the door is on gravel rather than on fragile vegetation.

Often the level of use of these campsites and the fragility of the terrain is such that even if everyone practised no-trace camping, the mere trampling of feet would cause major damage. To overcome the problem, designated campsites may be "hardened" with tent platforms and gravel walkways, and even provided with picnic tables. The latter may seem unnecessary, but people tend to sit down on banks and shuffle their feet while they eat, contributing to slope erosion. Heavy, stiff hiking and climbing boots are very hard on fragile vegetation and soft ground, so the sooner you remove your boots in camp the better. Soft running shoes, sandals, slippers or insulated booties are comfortable and don't cause anywhere near as much damage. If you want to use the booties in your sleeping bag, wear bootie covers outside to keep the bootie clean. Tent platforms are often hard, so bring a good sleeping mat such as a Therm-a-Rest.

Campsites may also be provided with a pit toilet, which is highly desirable in heavily used sites. In the northern climate, toilet paper and faeces decompose slowly because of the low temperatures that prevail for much of the year. Even if everyone buried their waste in proper cat-holes, the area would become a health hazard, especially as animals like to excavate the holes.

Designated campsites tend to be off the main trail and hidden in the forest, so they may not have the magnificent view provided by a site you would choose if you were random camping. Designated campsites do not provide the private experience you may wish, and the company of other campers may not be to your liking. You can minimize this problem by only sleeping in the site. Find a rocky, nonfragile place somewhere distant from the campsite and spend the evening there, cooking dinner on a stove. Similarly, you can leave before breakfast and stop somewhere on the trail to eat. This has the added advantage of keeping your food smells away from camp.

One of the more detrimental effects backcountry campers can have is to intentionally or unintentionally feed bears. In parks, a bearproof cache may be provided at designated campsites for your food. By insisting on people camping at designated spots with a prebuilt cache, the authorities ensure there is a better chance of people bearproofing their food properly than if they random camp and use an improvised cache. The official site cache may be a steel shed, a pole and hook system, a cable hoist device or a hoisting frame for which you need your own rope.

As much as you may dislike the presence of other people in these designated camping areas, you might sleep better knowing other people are around. Statistics show that there have been no fatal bear attacks involving groups of six or more people. Also, if you cooked away from the site and they did not, their campsites will be smellier than yours and the bear will visit them first! Unfortunately, you may be camped in a place that is reeking of food from the previous occupant or that a bear has learned to visit regularly. This is always a worry when camping in frequently used locations.

Random camping is allowed in some of the more remote parts of parks, and of course outside the parks on public land. There are, however, areas of public land leased to special interest groups for purposes such as ranching. As a result of the impact and bad behaviour of certain users, some leaseholders are now hostile to use by any travellers and are treating their leases as private land. If you behave discreetly and practise no-trace camping, they are unlikely to know you are there or have even been there, but a chance encounter with a leaseholder may be unpleasant. If your site looks like a dump during your stay, you can expect leaseholders or landowners to be far more concerned than if you operate a tidy low-impact site and look as though you will leave no mess behind.

Your tent should really be placed on a nonvegetated site, but a suitable flat place will probably have plants growing on it. As long as the tent is only pitched for one night, the impact of the tent on plants may be a lot less than that of heavy boots in a vegetated cooking/living area. However, it is better to pitch the tent on gravel or sand and use a good sleeping pad as cushioning. If you are concerned about wear and tear on the floor of your tent on rocky ground, use a piece of plastic or nylon under the tent floor. It is easy to fold the dirty side to dirty side, and plastic sheets are particularly easy to wipe or wash clean on the lawn at home with a hose and broom.

You can choose a less fragile place for your cooking/living area where you will probably do more clumping around in heavy boots. Replace your boots with camp sandals or shoes as soon as possible, and organize the site so you can just sit down in one place and reach every-

Designated backcountry campsites often have a prebuilt food cache to protect bears from obtaining human food.

Huts have the advantage of concentrating use into a small area, which can be preferable to having lighter, but still significant impacts spread over a wide area.

thing. A cooking/living area will probably be more comfortable anyway if it is rocky and gravelly or has logs strewn around and if it slopes. There are then ledges to put things down on without bending, and to sit on and use as back rests. Your tenting area and your cooking area need to be separated by a considerable distance anyway, to keep food smells well away from the sleeping area.

The more resilient sites where you'll have least impact are nonvegetated river and ocean beaches. There are no plants to damage and your footprints are eradicated by the next flood or ocean storm. The main problem is sand getting into everything, but care can eliminate that problem. Some outfitters use rakes to eradicate the footprints of their clients before leaving sandbar campsites, and rakes can be used to make flat tent sites on beaches. However, do not break the roots and horizontal spreading roots of beach grasses because these plants are essential for maintaining the stability of the sand.

To Use a Hut or Tent?

Large public huts are not as common in Canada and Alaska as they are in the mountains in Europe. Huts concentrate use into limited areas, ideally into areas that are not too fragile.

One argument in favour of this is that it is better to have small limited areas of overuse with miles of relatively pristine country between them, than it is to have an endless succession of moderately scarred and overused campsites throughout the backcountry.

This is all well and good in theory, but there is a snag. Although the huts are usually small and primitive by European standards, they still act as an attraction and bring people into areas where they would not otherwise travel. This has the double disadvantage of both increasing overall impact and bringing into an area people who may not be skilled enough to cope properly with the demands of the terrain and weather. The problem is particularly acute if people fail to find the hut! Also, many people do not know how to function in a public hut with due consideration for other users. Some even bring radios and stereos!

Fires

Camp fires are a tradition that dies hard, but their impact is unacceptable in many areas. However, they do have their uses, particularly during bad weather. It is useful to know how to minimize their impact if you must use them.

Impact of fires. A camp fire's impact on the environment is through the use of the dead wood and scarring of the ground at the actual fire site. Dead wood burned in camp fires is wood that would otherwise provide habitat for small mammals, birds and insects and would help prevent erosion and gradually enrich the soil. When it is gathered for firewood it is no longer available as habitat, and when it is burned the nutrients are released all at once and are usually concentrated at one place. There are consequently many places where using a small stove is the only acceptable option.

However, there are places where fires can be legitimately used if done so for good reasons and in an appropriate manner. A fire can serve a vital function for drying gear in wet weather. However, this does not mean it is acceptable to go into the backcountry with inadequate clothing and to make a bonfire whenever you are cold or wet. Fires can be used for cooking if you are travelling very lightweight for an extended period and cannot afford the weight of a stove and fuel. A fire for an hour or two for atmosphere is justifiable, but not the mindless blaze some people keep burning day and night.

In parks and campsites, fireplaces are probably provided to reduce the proliferation of fire scars, and it may be an offence to build fires other than in the firepits or fireboxes provided. This can be frustrating because the firepits are often very inefficient from the point of view of radiating heat or providing an efficient cooking fire, though they may be efficient as containers to reduce forest fire hazard.

Firewood may be supplied in an effort to reduce the depredation on the local forest. Foraging may be illegal and there may a fee for wood. Campsite firewood is often rather wet and green, which helps to reduce consumption. It usually has to be split, so a splitting axe or a small splitting wedge is useful (but heavier than a stove!). Regular axes with a sharp edge and narrow taper, designed for cutting across the grain, are not very useful for splitting. They penetrate and jam long before they produce a significant splitting force. Blunt, fat splitting axes are much better. They tend to be heavy, but you can grind down an old, lighter axe head to make it split better, and carry a folding saw for cross-grain cutting. A plastic chain-saw wedge is light to carry and enables the careful and ingenious user to exploit existing splits using a log as a mallet.

Driftwood is a fuel supply that is replenished relatively frequently, and its use in moderation has little impact. However, the use of dead standing wood around frequently used campsites soon results in total denudation of the area. I remember one northern camping spot that was an obvious site in a stunning location. Stark, silvery grey and brownish gold dead tree skeletons added colour and contrast to the greenness of the arctic landscape. I visited it over a number of years and noticed the gradual loss of these features as they were used for firewood. If you are canoeing and know you are about to camp in a heavily used and denuded spot, you might consider picking up a load of driftwood a kilometre or so before you reach the site.

Even dead trees have a more important function in the environment than just becoming firewood. They provide homes for many animals as well as enriching the soil and preventing erosion.

These Swedish visitors built efficient, minimum-impact fires, burning small, neatly cut and split pieces of wood.

A selection of fireboxes, including the Horizons Unlimited Bill Mason model (front), two made from four-litre Coleman fuel cans (rear) and one from a paint can (left). These all reduce the impact of fires and conserve wood.

Firetrays eliminate the need to make a firepit, and the inevitable damage that results. A firetray is simply a thin, sheet metal tray of a size to suit your purpose, on which the fire is built. You can make a fire tray quite easily from thin, galvanized steel sold for flashing at builders' supply stores. If you look around, you might find a perfectly serviceable item, such as a metal garbage-can lid, the bottom liner from an oven, a fridge freezer compartment door, a large cookie sheet, the lid off a 45-gallon drum, etc. However, when you first get it hot enough to burn off the galvanizing, enamel or paint, you generate some nasty fumes. Use plain steel if you can find it. The tray needs low sides to stop burning sticks falling off onto the ground, and a few rocks hold it off the ground to prevent charring of the duff. A thin tray is lighter, and will suffice if the bottom is supported with plenty of rocks. You can even use two Coleman fuel cans opened out flat and wired together. Thin material is easily battered and bent, but this does not impair its function, and it is equally easy to straighten out again. It will rust through eventually, how soon depending on whether you leave it full of ashes in the rain. Aluminum such as aluminum flashing will work if you add a layer of sand to stop it burning through and if air can get underneath to keep it cooler.

Folding fireboxes. A firebox is better than a firetray for reducing the impact of fires. It contains the fire better and directs the heat upward onto your pots, and it incorporates a grill support for your pot. The effectiveness is particularly pronounced in places where strong winds tend to blow the flames sideways away from your pots. Since many people select windy places to camp to get away from the bugs, this is a significant problem. Because the fire is better contained in a box than a tray, there are also fewer sparks and embers blowing around, so there is less chance of starting a forest fire.

Fireboxes ensure that you use less firewood, since more of the heat is directed up into the pots. This is particularly important where wood is very scarce or slow to regenerate, such as on the tundra. If all you have available is willow twigs, labouriously gathered from a bush here and a bush there, you want to use every bit of heat.

Commercially made fireboxes on the Bill Mason pattern are available from Horizons Unlimited in La Ronge, Saskatchewan. These are quite heavy at around 3-1/2 kilograms but are robust enough for long-term use. Lighter ones for occasional use can be made from scrap cans. Four-litre Coleman fuel cans may be cut and opened out flat to make a tray. Sides can be made from four-litre paint tins or from cut-down Coleman cans and held in place with twist ties or wire. Kebab skewers make good pot supports.

The paint can stove is particularly efficient because the flames are directed onto the sides of the pot as well as the bottom. A handful of twigs and even dry grass will boil a pot of water very quickly, particularly if you fan it with a plate or hat. However, maintaining a simmer is more difficult.

The paint can stove is simply a four-litre paint tin with the top rim removed with a can opener. The rectangular hole is easily cut with snips or by scoring with the tip of a sharp knife and then cutting with an old but sharp knife along the weakened score lines. You'll probably have to sharpen your knife again afterward. The pot rests are cut from a wire coat hanger, which is strong enough as long as there is only about a one- or two-centimetre gap between the pot and the can.

Disposing of ashes. Although fireboxes and trays can eliminate ground scarring, there is still the problem of what to do with ashes and particularly with charcoal. As any archaeologist will tell you, charcoal never decomposes, and remains as a tell-tale sign for ever. On the other hand, the white powdery ash is largely soluble and will dissipate into the ground eventually, providing plants with nutrients as it does so. The main thing then, is to use only small sticks for your morning fire, which will quickly burn away to white ash. Tend the fire so there are no blackened twig ends left, then extinguish and cool the ashes with water. Stir them around in the water in the tray to ensure all are wetted and then bury the ashes. You may want to use several holes to spread the nutrients around, and of course you must be absolutely certain the ashes are extinguished and cold. You should also wet down the ground that was under the tray, as a precaution.

Firepits. If you decide you really must light a fire and do not have a tray, box or pre-existing firepit, you should build a proper firepit. Select a location where there will be the least damage. This means a place where there is no vegetation or organic (peaty) soil. A beach on a river, lake or ocean is a good choice. Exposed

If you know you will be camping at a heavily used site you might consider gathering firewood before you get there.

sandy areas of eskers are another possibility, and scree is good if it happens to be adjacent to a supply of firewood. Bare rock is very safe from the fire hazard point of view, but is subject to scarring. Also, strong winds may roll bits of glowing charcoal across a slab of rock and off into the duff at the edge. You might find a slab you can turn over to build your fire on and then return it to its original position to cover the ashes and blackened rock after the fire is properly extinguished.

Whenever your fire is heating stones or solid rock, there is the risk of flying fragments when the rock shatters with the heat. This is particularly likely with rocks that have been immersed in water and are porous sedimentary (layered) types. A self-supporting metal grill and sheet metal windshields make it unnecessary to build a rock fireplace and blacken any rocks.

If you have absolutely no option but to build a fire where there is organic soil and roots, you must be aware that fires can live and spread unnoticed under and in the duff, even after you think you have extinguished the fire. Starting a forest fire is a guaranteed way to have a big impact on the environment! The key is to remove the duff and dark peaty soil down to "mineral" soil, which is sand, gravel and usually light-coloured soil. This should be done over a wide area, at least a metre across so that the heat does not char the duff and vegetation around the edges. If you have a small trowel that is strong enough and sharp enough, you can remove turf with much less damage so it will regrow better. Place the turf to one side, root side down, and water it occasionally. A covering of leaves or duff will slow the rate of damage caused by drying.

When it comes time to leave, allow the fire to burn away as completely as possible to ashes so there is a minimum of charcoal left. Thoroughly wet down the entire area, including the duff and turf well back around the edges. Stir and dig up the ashes and underlying soil to allow the water to penetrate properly. Use a pointed stick to make holes to assist penetration. Feel with your hand to check if the area is cold before replacing the turf and duff, and then water it thoroughly. You will need several gallons of water to do this, so you need a good water bag or water carrier that is easily filled.

Human Waste Disposal

Human waste can pose a serious aesthetic and public health problem in the backcountry, especially as it does not decompose well in northern climates. It is important to understand how to dispose of it in the most effective way.

General considerations. The solutions are threefold and simple.

First of all, if there is a biffy, use it! **Never** put disinfectants, chloride of lime or bleaching powder into a biffy—you poison the decomposition process so it fills up more quickly.

Secondly, if there is no biffy, walk a considerable distance from the campsite to "do your thing"—perhaps during an evening stroll or after you leave camp next morning. That way the deposit will probably be where it will not be encountered again by other people. It should of course be a considerable distance from any ponds or creeks and not in dried-up creekbeds or gullies.

Thirdly, bury the faecal matter properly so that it will remain covered and will decompose reasonably quickly. A log or rock may help discourage excavation by animals.

Contrary to popular belief, deep burial is not necessarily the best answer. With deep burial, deeply buried faeces will remain just that, deeply buried faeces, and for a long time. This is because the biological processes that normally break down the paper and faeces into carbon dioxide, water and a few minerals do not proceed well in the oxygen-starved, biologically inactive deeper subsoil. Shallow burial, 15-20 centimetres, and preferably no deeper than the limit of the active organic topsoil, promotes faster decomposition, but on the other hand the material is more readily uncovered by animals.

With group toilets, the problem is premature filling of a shallow hole. This is often carried out for aesthetic reasons or fly control by users who do not understand the principles that govern its use. A long trench helps alleviate this difficulty, but you may have to resort to a hole that is deeper than ideal. At least you have better control over the situation than if everyone had to go off and make their own hole.

Used sanitary pads and tampons are a problem because of their attractiveness to animals, especially bears. Even deep burial is not enough to prevent the strong scents from permeating up through the ground. Burning in a hot fire is a good solution. A supply of thin baggies (which create minimum fumes from combustion) and paper bags allows this to be done discreetly. Some authors advocate transporting used sanitary pads and tampons with you, but this requires very careful sealing, otherwise you will have bears digging in your pack, not just in the ground! Sandwich baggies are not thick enough to prevent smell permeation (even humans can smell things such as onion through the thin plastic). Double and triple bagging is advisable, or the bags can be placed in a screw-top plastic jar carried for the purpose. An empty plastic peanut butter jar or an empty bulk pill bottle from your pharmacist will do, and can be placed intact with its contents in the domestic garbage.

In winter conditions it is all too easy to take the "out of sight out of mind" approach, with insufficient thought for what will happen in spring. This is somewhat mitigated by the fact that summer and winter campsites are usually very different places. Obviously, even if you can dig down to the ground you can't dig into it while it is frozen, so whatever you leave in the snow will be revealed in spring. Toilet paper should be burned or bagged and brought out. Alternatively, use chunks of snow or snowballs. This sounds a bit Spartan but actually isn't as unpleasant as you might think, and of course the superior cleansing effect is useful on long winter trips. In heavily used areas such as some glaciers and climbing routes, and particularly on Denali, one should take more elaborate steps. A hole lined with a good quality garbage bag pegged open with pieces of wands makes a serviceable latrine that can then be sealed and disposed of. It is easy to drag and of course the contents will usually be frozen. It can be taken out to the trailhead or dumped in a deep crevasse.

Another approach is to use a kovik (Inuit name for a block of snow on which you do your thing). It can be situated near a crevasse and pitched in with a shovel. You may want to let it freeze before doing so in case your throw doesn't work well! In a storm and if your tentmates or cavemates are good friends, you can use the same system in the shelter and throw it outside—in a place where you won't confuse it with a block dug for a water supply! On steep routes with limited camping spots that will be heavily used you can hurl it off the route, preferably after it has had time to freeze hard and only if you are sure no one is below.

Faeces are broken down rapidly in sea water (but not in fresh water), so disposal in the ocean is acceptable and in some cases better than on land. Preferably make disposals at low tide to minimize exposure. Alternatively, put a layer of sand on a paddle blade, do your thing and then pitch the sand and faeces into deep water.

Bag-it-and-bring-it. The bag-it-and-bring-it approach to faecal matter disposal is becoming more the norm in some areas of the U.S., and I can think of a number of places in Canada where it is appropriate. It is certainly useful for winter use at cabins and cottages that do not have winterized sewage systems. Fairly large plastic bags are needed, and of course they must be reliable quality. Steps should be taken to not urinate in the bag because transporting a mix-

A plastic pail lined with plastic bags can be used for bag-it-and-bring-it toilet systems.

ture of urine and solids is much more difficult than transporting solids alone. Urine is sterile and is generally regarded as being a fairly benign waste that can be left in the backcountry.

I remember one incident where I was skiing down a slope dragging a bag of toilet waste behind me on a length of rope. The weather was warm and I knew the contents were not frozen. I wiped out with a tremendous faceplant at the bottom of a steep drop, lost my glasses (temporarily) and couldn't see anything. I was face down and afraid to move because I had no idea where the bag had ended up and I didn't want to roll on it or poke a ski or pole through it. To make matters worse, my companions were howling with laughter and were decidedly unhelpful!

One system for use by several people or a small group is a plastic pail with a good quality snap-on lid such as can be obtained from restaurants and bulk food dealers. Line it with two good quality garbage bags and fold the tops of the bags down over the outside of the pail. Maybe even perch a seat on top. When it is time to move on, close the inner bag permanently with a knot, making sure there is as little air trapped inside as possible. Then close the outer bag in a manner that allows it to be re-opened at the next stop, and replace the lid. At the next stop, insert a new inner bag above the sealed bag and fold it out over the edge of the pail as before. Eventually the pail and liner bag will be full of individual daily "parcels." The disadvantage is the number of plastic bags used. In hot weather the bags may inflate, too.

When you come to dispose of the waste, remember there are likely to be regulations about where and how you can dispose of such items. These regulations are mostly for the health and well being of the public and of garbage handlers. If you discard in domestic garbage the entire pail or the entire parcel still properly wrapped so it will not burst open, you are probably within the spirit and intent of the regulations, even if not the letter. In theory, the most desirable action is to open the containers and flush the contents down the toilet. However, this exposes you to unpleasantness and maybe health risks, and you are still left with contaminated containers to deal with. Never put bags of faecal matter into campsite vault toilets because they clog the pumps used to empty the tank.

The Ortlieb folding washbasin and water carrier/drybag make it easier to wash people and dishes away from the water source.

Other Human Impact

Besides the impact of fires, human waste and camping, or just "being" in an area, there are a number of other ways in which we can adversely affect the backcountry.

Washing pots and people. All too often you go from a campsite to the edge of a lake or creek to fill a water bottle and find specks of rice and macaroni on the bottom from the previous residents. This is unsightly and very discouraging, especially if the water is not flowing. Carrying a proper water carrier and a folding basin makes it much easier to follow one of the rules of camping, which is to not wash oneself or utensils directly in bodies of water. Ortlieb makes an excellent lightweight folding basin, or you can use the bottom half of a collapsible four-gallon plastic water carrier. Similar containers are used for bleach for swimming pools and can be scrounged. They are self-supporting as soon as there is enough water in them.

Cheap quality semirigid plastic basins are quite light and can form part of a kitchen box when canoe camping. All plastic basins are readily stained with carbon from pots used over fires, so do not place the blackened pot in the basin. Instead, pour water into the pot to wash its inside.

A wide-mouthed water bucket or bag is easily filled and helps you carry water from the water source to the place in the bush where the basin is being used.

Garbage left around this backcountry hunt-camp site encourages bear problems as well as being slovenly and an insult to the environment. A. Zybach photo.

Most people use far more detergent than is necessary to get pots clean, and it is a good idea to minimize the amount of this contaminant being introduced into the backcountry. Soap-filled scouring pads are a particularly bad offender. They are not as effective as a knitted nylon pad or Scotchbrite for removing most types of food anyway. They are reasonably good for removing black from the outside of pots, but there is no point in doing that in the field, and little point in doing it at all if you have a plastic supermarket bag or a cloth bag for each pot. Some cleaning agents are described as being "biodegradable" and you may wish to use these, especially if you use larger quantities in heavily used areas.

The dirty water should be scattered on land in a place chosen so as to produce minimum aesthetic disturbance. Because of the animal-attracting smells in the water, this should be done distant from camp. Food particles should be removed before scattering the water, and should then be burned or packed out with the rest of your garbage. In some areas where there are many bears, and where decomposition is slow, it may be less hazardous to dump the water in a big, fast river. This seems sacrilegious, but does sometimes make more sense.

Garbage. The general rule is that if you can carry it in, you can carry it out, particularly once it is empty. The problems arise when you have food scraps or containers such as cans that will become smelly and attractive to animals once opened. Rinse the cans into the pot and wash them out before placing them in your garbage bag. Burn them out, along with any food scraps and nonplastic wastes in your fire if you have one. If you use plastic bags for your food, seal them with a twist tie or a knot as shown on page 194 so they can be reused to seal up garbage.

Leftover cooked food, and particularly porridge, is a problem to carry. Be careful to cook only the amount you need. Burn leftovers if possible. Porridge is difficult to burn, so you may have to carry it all day and burn it in the evening when you will have more time—or fry it up for supper!

On long trips where you may have fuel in four-litre cans, you can make a garbage burner from an empty can. Cut a seven centimetre-high hole at the bottom of a narrow side and cut the top loose on three sides. Orient the bottom hole into the wind, fill the container (perhaps include a few twigs) and ignite.

Fish guts and scraps. Fish guts and scraps are a real animal attractant, especially to bears, and their incorrect disposal is a hazard. Generally, the safest place to put guts is back in the river. If it is a large river they will be carried away, but this is rather an "out of sight out of mind" approach and is undesirable on smaller streams. We once fed a pile of guts from several grayling, a handful at a time, to a large lake trout lurking in a northern river just off our campsite. However, guts will not necessarily be eaten. Throwing guts back into a lake is less desirable, especially if it is small or if decomposition will be slow because the water is cold. Burying on land is also not very desirable because animals are likely to dig them up again, but doing so a long way (several hundred metres) from campsites may be a workable option. If there is a hovering flock (or even just one or two) gulls, they will clean things up fast. The trouble with that is they soon learn to hang around people and campsites and can start to be a nuisance or leave too many obnoxious calling-cards behind. In the ocean, put guts in deep water where they will not be exposed when the tide goes out.

Other scavengers may clean up for you, too. On one sea kayak trip we were eating fresh fish for lunch on a beach, and a mink showed up and made off with the heads and backbones that were at the water's edge awaiting deep-water disposal from the kayak after lunch. Burning guts requires a very hot fire and the smells may attract animals.

Preserving the trail. Impact on the trail is reduced by lighter and more flexible boots, and some even have sole patterns touted as being less damaging to the terrain. Try to avoid walking when the trails and ground are at their most fragile, which is usually in spring when the frost is coming out of the ground. If a trail is soft and muddy, squelching through the mud and puddles on the trail itself does much less harm than trying to detour, which simply widens the damage and the mudhole. Wear adequate boots and gaiters so that squelching is no problem. "Rocky" brand GoreTex socks are useful items to carry so you can squelch even if you have nonwaterproof light hiking boots.

If a trail is a zig-zag, never cut across the corners because this promotes erosion. If you see that a drainage structure has become blocked, take a few moments to clear it. Where there is a choice, avoid walking on soft vegetation and walk instead on gravelly and rocky areas. However, if these areas have tenuous vegetation that is barely surviving, it may be better to walk in more dense vegetation areas. The scattered and tenuous vegetation may be all that is holding the land in place, particularly on dunes and eskers, so trampling it may be very harmful. If you must walk in fragile areas, it is often best to walk in a line abreast rather than single file. That way less damage is done to the vegetation because no one plant is subjected to repeated foot contact.

Cultural impact. As well as influencing the physical environment, we can also affect the cultural environment in adverse ways. You must take care in how you interact with the local people. They can easily get annoyed with having cameras pointed at them as though they are zoo curiosities, and the presence of inquisitive tourists can be very intrusive in a quiet remote village. Just because someone is living in the northern bush does not mean they feel any better about strangers walking up to their front door or into their home territory than you would at *your* home. Some people are living in remote places precisely because they want to avoid other people. On the other hand, some people are keen for new human contact and will be very glad to talk to you and invite you in. If you make a point of being aware, you can soon tell if you are welcome or not.

Enjoy cultural and historic features such as these pictographs, but do not touch, deface or disturb.

Make sure you do lots of listening and not too much questioning and no lecturing or moralizing. Generally, it is best to avoid discussions about environmental concerns and the ethics of hunting and trapping. This is particularly the case if you wear leather goods, eat meat and have never visited an abattoir! It is usually inadvisable to share your alcohol with locals, and in fact it may be illegal to even possess alcohol in some northern communities. See Regulations section.

Do not interfere with cultural history. It is illegal to deface or disturb historic and prehistoric artifacts. See Regulations section.

Group size. Group size has a big influence on the impact we have on the backcountry, and many parks impose group size restrictions. Organized groups must be particularly careful to inquire specifically about group size regulations beforehand. Limits as low as six have been proposed for some areas.

It is particularly important that organizers of group camps and trips choose reasonably resilient areas for large groups because many people gathering in one spot causes considerable ground compaction and vegetation trampling. They also tend to cook on fires and to have larger fires as well. It is also more difficult to supervise everyone in a large group to ensure that they all practise low-impact disposal of human wastes and washing water. Kitchen/eating/meeting/fireplace areas should be located on a well-drained, nonvegetated area, perhaps a gravel bar, a moraine, bare ground or a rocky area so that vegetation trampling is kept to a minimum. Construction of a latrine may be considered, or else toilet and washing areas could be designated in appropriate spots.

Climbing paraphernalia. Part of the appeal of climbing in Canada and Alaska is the wilderness feeling engendered by trails that are not broken, rappel points that are not festooned with ancient slings and routes where you are not tripping over dozens of old fixed ropes. There are exceptions of course, but every effort should be made to keep things clean and to remove all of your unwanted items within the dictates of safety. This also includes removing your unwanted cached materials. If you do abandon cached materials, try to leave a note

indicating whether or not they are up for grabs, and preferably your name and the date. In some areas it's a good idea to do that anyway so someone doesn't think your vital cache was abandoned! Avoid the temptation to leave stuff that is really garbage in a "cache" for others—the food you can't stand is probably food others can't stand either, but fuel is always useful. Ice-climbers' conduit rappel anchors melt out in the spring and remain at the foot of the falls, but ice bollards and ice tunnel anchors (Abalakov anchors) disappear totally. Crush and carry out empty Gaz cylinders and empty Coleman fuel cans. The one-litre cans weigh only 20 grams more than a one-litre Sigg fuel bottle that you would carry out anyway.

Winter recreation. You can certainly damage the vegetation beneath the snow by skiing too early in the season when the snow is too shallow. In fact, in Banff National Park some popular early season skiing spots are closed to skiing until there is enough snowcover. People have been fined heavily for disobeying the closures. On winter trails the compacted snow is less effective as an insulator and so the ground freezes to a greater depth. The compacted snow takes longer to melt in the spring, too. Consequently, a trail used in winter will take longer to thaw and dry out in spring than will the surrounding ground or other trails. Compaction of a shallow snowpack can also interfere with the activities of voles and other rodents that burrow in the snow at the ground surface.

Although some impact is inevitable from your activities, you can usually keep it to acceptable levels. To keep a clear conscience you should make great efforts to minimize your impact.

Interacting with wildlife. Seeing wildlife is one of the pleasures of the Canadian and Alaskan backcountry. Most of us would rather see wildlife behaving naturally, not disrupted by our presence, so there are some things to consider about how to behave in the outdoors. Sure it is fascinating to try and get close to animals, but the attempt invariably ends in one of two ways, both of which are unacceptable. The animal may respond with aggression, which is a waste of its energy and resources and might result in injury to you that

Keep your distance from wildlife so as not to disturb them, and view them through binoculars or a telephoto lens.

you may deserve. Or the animal is distracted or driven from its feeding area and flees. Usually, once the animal is disturbed it keeps moving for a considerable distance. This kind of disturbance can have a significant effect on the amount of time an animal can spend feeding and therefore on its state of nutrition. In some areas, the numbers of people walking the shoreline disrupt feeding migratory shore birds enough to hinder them from gaining sufficient food to properly fuel the next leg of their journey.

Many animals lead a precarious existence in winter, barely balancing their energy expenditure with energy from their fat reserves and from their meagre winter food intake. Unnecessary disturbance causing them to flee uses up energy they may be unable to spare from the equation. Even when not deliberately harassing wildlife, snowmobiles cause considerable stress, and the effect of skiers and snowshoers, although quieter, must not be discounted. "Disturbing or harassing" wildlife is an offence in many jurisdictions.

A good pair of lightweight binoculars allows you to watch animals and birds without disturbing them. "Outdoor adventureproof" bin-

oculars are light, well sealed or even waterproof, and padded with a rubber housing. The resilient stretch lanyards from Op Tech make carrying your binoculars at the ready much

Seeing wildlife is one of the pleasures of the wilderness.
Ken Ellison photo.

more comfortable when hiking. Op Tech also makes a case that stops the binoculars from banging against your body. A spotting-scope and a tripod enable you to really get a close look from a distance. If you want to photograph animals, buy a decent telephoto lens, some fast film and a small tripod.

Feeding mammals and birds is one of the worst things you can do, either deliberately or by accidentally allowing them access to your food or garbage. They do not know when to stop and can be a real nuisance around camp once the novelty wears off. They may also turn nasty and become a hazard. The main thing, though, is that human food is bad for them. Also, remember that animals learn to see the humans of summer as harmless providers of food and no threat to their safety. Suddenly these humans are replaced at the opening of hunting season by people whose express purpose is to kill them.

If you arrive at your intended campsite and find a bird persistently making anxious noises or attracting attention to itself, it probably means there is a nest nearby. It will contain eggs or young that cannot be neglected for long without dying, so you should move on. I have been "terned back" by nesting terns from several appealing campsites in the north, and their divebombing gives you little option. I was once mortified to find the neglected nest of a small bird in the low bank that sheltered our mountain camp in the Yukon.

For some reason, fish are not often accorded the status of a protected or protection-worthy organism in the psyche of many outdoors people. People who would not dream of interfering with wildlife that flies or walks often seem quite happy to decimate the fish stocks of a small alpine lake or arctic stream. Canadian national parks, which are some of the best protected areas against hunting, do permit fishing. Laws on daily limits and sizes exist everywhere, but a party of keen fishermen can have a significant impact if they keep and eat all they catch. This is particularly the case with cold northern waters where fish grow slowly. I enjoy a feed of arctic char or arctic grayling just as much as the next person, but you should fish in moderation.

Animalproofing Your Food

Allowing animals access to your food has a serious environmental impact because of the adverse effect on the animals concerned. There can also be serious consequences for your trip if animals are allowed to steal, damage or destroy your crucial food supplies. You should take appropriate precautions to prevent this type of disaster.

General considerations and ethics. The consequences of damage to equipment and loss of food can be very serious in the backcountry because it will probably not be possible to replace lost or damaged items. On a long, remote trip, loss of food could obviously be catastrophic because it could lead to actual starvation, not just being hungry. Even on a shorter trip, loss of food can be one event in a chain of events leading to an accident or a survival situation. A person who is low on energy is more likely to make mistakes that lead to injury or other problems. Then, if an emergency arises, the hungry person is also less able to handle the situation effectively, and is more susceptible to hypothermia and frostbite. Damage to equipment is serious, too. If a tent is destroyed by a bear, it will not protect you from the elements, and an inflatable sleeping pad nibbled or torn by teeth or claws will not provide a good night's rest.

Bears are the most dramatic and serious food stealers, though mice, rats, raccoons, martens, porcupines, foxes, wolverines, ravens and squirrels can seriously deplete or damage your supplies. What they don't actually eat is likely to be scattered about or fouled and rendered inedible, and the damage they cause while trying to get at the food may be serious.

Seeking human food and garbage is often a learned behaviour. A nuisance bear or other animal is not born, it is made, usually as a result of human carelessness or irresponsibility. Once an animal has had a taste, it learns fast, becomes conditioned and develops into a confirmed "nuisance animal." These animals associate humans with food and deliberately approach campsites and travellers.

A nuisance animal is not only a hazard to people, but also to itself. Becoming conditioned to human food or garbage may result in it being inadequately nourished, relocated or destroyed by parks authorities, or shot in so-called "self defence."

All backcountry users have the responsibility to prevent animals from gaining access to human food or garbage.

If animals are to obtain human food, they have to be able to detect its presence and then gain access to it. Animals detect food primarily by using the sense of smell, which is particularly keen in the case of bears. You should therefore reduce or preferably eliminate food and garbage smells. If you also keep food in a place inaccessible to animals, you have used two lines of defence. This is enough to virtually eliminate the problem, and even using one line of defence will greatly reduce it.

Preventing animals from detecting the presence of the food is always the first step. Even if you make the food inaccessible, you don't want to go to your food cache to find a troop of frustrated, angry bears pacing around while tantalizing scents waft down from it! Highly scented foods (and other products) are therefore best avoided, especially if they are not packed in odourproof containers. Bacon and other meat, fish, cheese, condiments and scented soaps, toothpaste and cosmetics are some of the worst offenders. Avoid foods that are heavily spiced and that require long cooking time because they send enticing smells wafting downwind for a long time.

In one incident on a remote canoe trip, my wife and I had taken great pains to cache our remaining two weeks' canoeing food while we did a five-day side trip on foot into the mountains. Our companions were rather complacent, and simply left their food under their canoe. We returned from the mountains to find their food packs had been torn open by a bear. Luckily, the bear had only eaten the really smelly items, which were fire starters and scented dish detergent. It had hardly touched the freeze-dried food in sealed packets that had no smell.

Ziploc-type closures seal well until the closure channels become clogged with powders such as salt, sugar, coffee and flour. Do not use them for foods that can cause this clogging.

The sealed foil/plastic laminate pouches in which soups and prepared foods are packaged are usually made to be smellproof. This is

A bear will not bother to unzip the door to go inside if it smells food in the tent.

because taste and smell are closely related functions, and leakage of smells would probably mean leakage and loss of flavour, too. They are adequate for use in bear country as long as they do not become punctured. Screw-top polyethylene jars, especially the Nalgene brand, are also satisfactory as long as the outside is kept clean. Some smells pass through thin polyethylene such as is used for sandwich bags, but the heavier freezer bags are better. Home heat-sealers such as the "Decosonic" use relatively light plastic through which you can eventually smell strong scents such as onion, but the seal is otherwise very good.

Plastic bags that are repeatedly opened and closed soon become contaminated with smelly food outside the closure point, so they attract animals. Reduce the problems caused by these smelly half-used food containers by packaging and sealing food in meal-size units. You eat the entire contents of the bag in one meal and seal the empty bag up in your garbage bag. All the rest of your food is then still in clean, sealed containers producing minimum odour.

The waterproof packs used by canoeists, and especially the food barrels, are smellproof. As long as they are kept closed and clean on the outside they are not attractive to animals.

If the meal bags for each day are then grouped together and packaged in a plastic, sealed "day bag," you have a second line of defence. However, I remember from my student days a friend's attempt to bring a donkey's head back to England from Turkey as a biological specimen. Three layers of polyethylene were not enough to prevent a certain "aura" emanating from the package on the truck roof!

The food bag is pulled well away from the tree and out over a drop to increase the height above the ground.

Some backcountry sites provide a bearproofing device.

The other advantage of having "day bags" is that immediately on arrival at your campsite, you can cache most of the day bags out of the reach of animals. Then if a bear wanders into camp while you are cooking dinner it could only obtain the current day's food. You can't put the food in the cache too soon—I remember one occasion when a friend had unloaded a food pack from a canoe and carried it up the bank, and returned with the next pack to see a bear making off with the first!

Don't forget that you should keep the really smelly contaminated utensils, opened containers, garbage and clothes worn while cooking in a cache too, perhaps a separate one made later. Don't take smelly clothes, especially if you've been frying bacon or fish, into the tent at night—if you don't want a furry visitor.

Empty containers should be sealed up in the garbage bag or be totally burned away to ash in a hot fire. This should be done preferably shortly before vacating the site, because burning garbage smells may attract bears.

Preventing animals from reaching your food. Once you have taken these first steps to reduce the likelihood of an animal sensing the presence of your food or garbage, you must take steps to make the food inaccessible even if the animal does find out where it is. If you have a vehicle, keep food locked inside, preferably in the trunk. In backcountry campgrounds in parks you may find bearproofing facilities already built. These can take the form of a steel shed or lockers or various structures to help you hoist food high off the ground.

In the absence of prebuilt structures, you supposedly hoist the food up a tree, 4 metres above the ground, 2.5 metres out from the trunk, and 1.5 metres below the branch. That's what most books tell you, and they have illustrations of just the right kind of tree.

Possible ways to hoist food in the wilderness

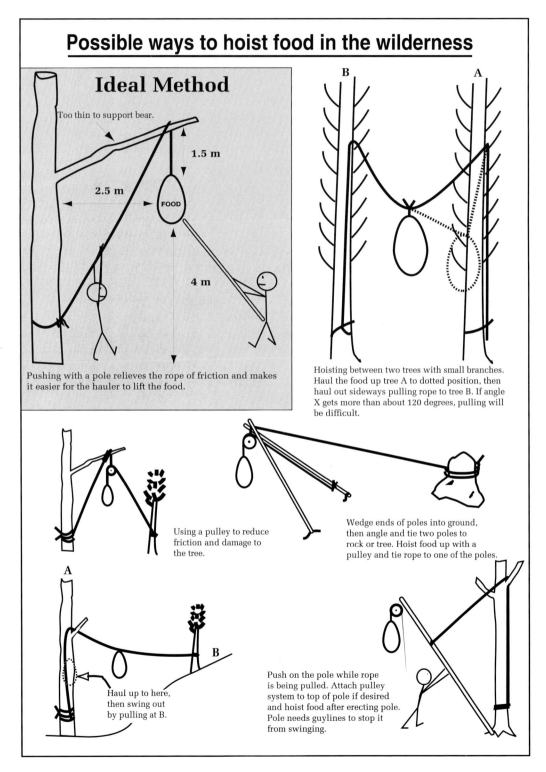

Ideal Method

Too thin to support bear.

1.5 m

2.5 m

FOOD

4 m

Pushing with a pole relieves the rope of friction and makes it easier for the hauler to lift the food.

Hoisting between two trees with small branches. Haul the food up tree A to dotted position, then haul out sideways pulling rope to tree B. If angle X gets more than about 120 degrees, pulling will be difficult.

Using a pulley to reduce friction and damage to the tree.

Wedge ends of poles into ground, then angle and tie two poles to rock or tree. Hoist food up with a pulley and tie rope to one of the poles.

Haul up to here, then swing out by pulling at B.

Push on the pole while rope is being pulled. Attach pulley system to top of pole if desired and hoist food after erecting pole. Pole needs guylines to stop it from swinging.

Unfortunately, you rarely see a tree like that in the right place, and certainly not in a coniferous forest! The reality of the thick foliage around it probably makes it very difficult to get a line up over the branch in the first place. Even when you do get a line over, hauling more than five kilograms, let alone 50 kilograms, of food up there without a winch may be difficult. You risk girdling the branch or covering your rope and hands with sticky resin. The more food you have, the harder it is to bearproof it in this way. However, the more food you have, the longer the trip probably is so the worse the consequences of food loss. It is therefore doubly important to make the effort to set up a good cache when you have a heavy load of food.

There are some tricks of the trade that make caching your food easier. The first step is to find a suitable location and to decide which type of cache to build. Practice, engineering imagination and developing an "eye" for a suitable site are all a help here. Whatever method you choose, the cache, like your "kitchen," needs to be at least 100 metres downwind from your tent. Resist the temptation to have it closer "so we can keep an eye on it or we will hear if anything tries to get into it." Having chosen your location and style of cache, the next step is to throw your weighted rope over the branch. A stick is easier to tie on to than a rock, but it is more likely to hang up and be irretrievable. Rocks are more satisfactory if you are good at knotting because they are less likely to hang up, and they penetrate foliage better. Be very careful if the rock snags and you pull to retrieve it. When the rock comes loose the stretch in your line acts like a slingshot and flings the rock directly toward you.

A major factor in making it difficult to haul a bag of food up into a tree is rope friction over the branch. Friction may require that you pull with a force of 50 kilograms just to lift 10 kilograms of food. One effect of this is that to take the strain, a much thicker rope than expected may be needed. Also, the friction and cutting caused by the rope may girdle the branch, which is obviously undesirable, especially in heavily used areas. To withstand your heaving, you may also have to use a branch that would actually be strong enough to support a bear.

This friction problem can be reduced in a number of ways. A twisted, polypropylene rope with a "laid" structure slides better than the braided "parachute" utility cord because the surface strands are almost parallel with the axis of the laid rope.

If you pull from directly below the branch there is a large amount of friction. However, if

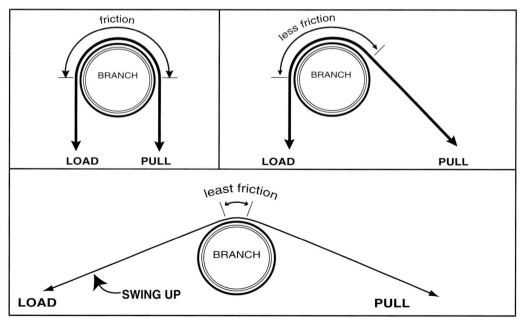

When hauling a food cache up a tree, pull from the side rather than from directly below the branch to reduce friction.

The Bear Necessity, by Expedition Leader in Hamilton, is a pulley device that greatly facilitates hoisting your food by producing a 3:1 pull magnification.

In the mountains you can lower the food over a cliff to keep it away from bears.

the rope is long enough or there is raised ground nearby, pull so that the rope passes around little more than one quarter of the circumference of the branch to reduce friction. Swing the load and time your pull for the top of the swing.

Another way to reduce friction is by using a pulley. The first rope is thrown over the branch and a pulley (awning pulley or climbers' crevasse rescue pulley) is attached to its end. A second rope is threaded to its middle through the pulley and its ends are tied together. The first rope is then used to hoist the pulley up to the branch, and is then tied off. The second rope, which is through the pulley, is used to haul the food up to the pulley. The "Bear Necessity" pulley system by Expedition Leader in Hamilton greatly facilitates food hoisting.

If you do not have access to a suitable branch, or if squirrels jumping down onto the pack are likely to be a major problem, you may have to string the food between two trees. Unfortunately, as the food is raised you have to pull harder and harder and often further hoisting becomes impossible before the food is far enough off the ground.

Suspension in a clear gap between two trees is preferred in some heavily used areas where acrobatic and enterprising squirrels are a problem. To prevent them walking along the rope, use about five metres of wire with rope attached to each end, and suspend the food bag from the middle of the wire. Where squirrels have learned to jump across and down onto packs, a slippery cone over the pack made from a foil cookie sheet or oven liner may prevent them from obtaining a toehold. A tightly packed smooth nylon food bag rather than a pack with pockets and straps may be more difficult for pesky jumpers to land on.

I remember one backpacking trip in a heavily used area where the squirrels were so conditioned to raiding hoisted food packs that it seemed the food was at less risk (from squirrels at least) if it was on the ground! I remember looking up at a suspended food bag with a hole gnawed in its side and seeing a squirrel poke its head out of the hole!

If there are no trees, you have more serious problems. You may be able to find a rock crevice that is too small for a bear to reach into. Lower the food in or push it in with a stick. (Attach a retrieval cord first!) However, this sort of place is likely to be home to smaller but still very destructive animals!

Most people are better rock climbers than bears, and a few pleasant moves may give access to a suitable ledge for a cache. The food could also be tied to the centre of a rope and lowered down a cliff. If it is then pulled away from the wall using the other end of the rope, it will be effectively protected from other animals as well, whereas it would be exposed to smaller animals on a ledge.

In the absence of these solutions, a number of caches of totally externally clean, sealed containers could be well distributed on the ground, downwind away from the camp, and perhaps covered by rocks. Then perhaps only one (if any) would be found by an animal, and you would not lose everything.

Animalproof containers. Another solution is to use bearproof or animalproof containers. The bearproof containers made by Garcia Machine of Visalia, California are made of ABS with animalproof lid locks, and weigh around 1.3 kilograms for a capacity of 10 litres or 2.3 kilograms for the 15-litre heavy duty model. Cost is approximately $75 US, $16 for the carrying bag. They are available from the manufacturer, Garcia Machine. See Appendix for address. Lighter models are scheduled for 1997.

The smooth, hard plastic container is sized and shaped so a bear cannot obtain a crushing grip with its jaws or hold the container with its claws. The lid locking arrangement is simple, requiring a coin to turn the two flush-fitting catches. Even park bears don't carry money yet! As well as being tested in zoos, they have been successfully tested by rangers, bears and the public in Denali, Glacier Bay and Sequoia parks in the U.S. Although heavy, they have

Bearproof containers have been well proven in numerous experiments with bears. Photos courtesy Garcia Machine.

been quite well accepted, especially by back-packers in Denali Park. In some U.S. parks their use is mandatory.

Some people fear that bears thwarted in their attempts to obtain food would turn their frustration onto people or their equipment. However, initial data from Denali Park indicated an overall reduction in aggressiveness toward people and their food.

If you plan to leave food supplies in a cabin, they must be proofed against mice, rats, martens and wolverines. Don't forget that it is not uncommon for bears to break in to cabins. Hanging the food from a beam is a partial solution, but ideally the building will be equipped with a good metal food container. It may be a steel cabinet, a 45-gallon barrel with clamp lid system or a metal garbage can (clearly labelled!). Tie the lid onto the garbage can with wire. I have cached food in huts in tin lard pails with the lid duct taped and wired in place. Some people use large plastic bulk ice cream or margarine containers, but these are not rodentproof unless you line them with aluminum mesh insect screening material. There is less incentive for animals to start gnawing if the container is spotlessly clean. Also, if it is well sealed, perhaps by lining with a garbage bag, animals are less likely to be interested in starting to gnaw. Light, collapsible rodentproof containers for caches can be quite easily fabricated from aluminum flashing material (from builders' supply store) sewn together with snare wire. They take a little time to put together and dismantle, but they can be folded flat or rolled up for reuse.

If a bear gets into a building, nothing much less than a safe will save your supplies—even canned goods are not immune to their destructive attentions. One of the better ways to deter bears from breaking in through windows and doors is to lay a four foot by eight foot piece of plywood with 10-centimetre (four inch) nails protruding through it on the ground below doors and windows—a common practice around Churchill on Hudson Bay, where polar bears are a problem. You must keep it clear of snow.

Food drops or caches are quite often used by ski-touring parties. They are usually buried in the snow and marked with a tall wand with a flag. Although the location is usually high up above treeline in a remote place, this type of cache is not immune to the attentions of mammals and birds.

An effective way to prevent bears breaking into cabins is to place boards with protruding nails on the ground around the building so the bear cannot approach without stepping on a nail. Note: nails in door, too.

I have also seen photographs of caches uncovered by snowmelt and wind erosion. A food dump we left overnight in the heart of the St. Elias Range was investigated by ravens but luckily not damaged. People touring in the Coast Mountains have often seen the tracks of grizzly bears through the high glaciated passes. Take care that the package is well sealed to keep smells in, and that it is well buried in snow or under rocks.

The nearer you are to habitation, frequently used campsites and cabins, etc., the more the potential for animal problems because the animals are more likely used to scrounging from man. "Civilization ravens," more used to humans and their gear, would certainly have destroyed our food in the St. Elias. We recently skied past someone's tent in a fairly well-used area of Banff National Park, and saw ravens finishing off a major feast on a food bag left in the snow outside a tent.

So, be on your guard against pesky nibblers and munchers. As the Roman philosopher Horace said in 50 BC, "Man drives out nature with a pitchfork but she always returns in stealth to triumph over his foolish contempt." However, if we all take a little bit of extra care, we may break the habituation cycle and minimize the number of nuisance animals. The backcountry would then be a better place for all of us, and particularly for its four-legged residents.

Chapter 10

Health Concerns

You should be aware of health concerns that can seriously influence the success of wilderness trips in Canada and Alaska. Some are common to recreation everywhere, but others are specific to Canadian and Alaskan conditions. Most of them can be avoided or dealt with by effective planning and carrying suitable supplies and equipment. Avoidance is the key because in remote areas you will not have easy access to medical assistance. Cold injuries are a concern at any time of year. They are easier to avoid than to treat, so take special care to choose suitable equipment and to conduct activities appropriately. You can attain some degree of physiological adaptation and increase your resistance to the cold by exposing yourself to cold over an extended period, as often happens to travellers who are active through the fall season. Visitors who have not had a chance to acclimatize must be careful, especially if their companions are acclimatized.

Hypothermia

Hypothermia is a significant concern for all recreational travellers and is the actual cause of death in a high proportion of wilderness fatalities. Hypothermia is a progressive lowering of body temperature, which causes gradually increasing impairment of body functions, eventually ending in death if not treated. The usual reasons people become hypothermic are immersion in cold water or inadequate protection from the weather. Treatment of hypothermia in the outdoors is difficult, and proper recovery, even from fairly mild hypothermia, can take 24 hours or more.

Avoiding Hypothermia

Body temperature will drop whenever conditions cause us to lose heat faster than we can produce it. To keep a balance between heat loss and heat production, you must be aware of how the surrounding conditions and your activity are affecting your heat production and your heat loss.

The body loses heat quickly if any of the following conditions exist:

- Air temperatures are low
- Clothing provides inadequate insulation
- Clothing is wet and especially if it is made of cotton
- Weather is windy
- Clothing is not windproof
- Victim is immersed in water

The body produces heat slowly if the person is:

- immobile because of bad weather, an accident or an equipment problem
- tired
- hungry
- ill or injured

If more than one of these conditions exists, especially if one or more from each list exists, you must be really on the lookout for hypothermia. It is very important to monitor each party member carefully and to recognize when a person or the party is at risk. If there is a risk of hypothermia, you must address the problem before hypothermia sets in.

A change over a few hours from pleasant, dry fall weather to wet snow and rain could have easily caused hypothermia if these teenagers were unprepared.

Minimizing heat loss from the body. "Low air temperatures" means temperatures are lower than you expected, so you have ended up inadequately equipped and are getting cold. "Low" can mean entirely different temperature ranges depending on whether you are engaged in winter or summer activities. Summer temperatures of +1°C can present as much or more risk than winter temperatures of -20°C because they may be associated with wet conditions and may be unexpected. The much colder winter temperatures of -20°C could in fact present much less danger because you have winter gear and can keep dry and probably can dig snow caves for shelter. The key in any season is to always carry a reserve of warm gear and to keep it dry in a properly sealed plastic bag for emergency use. If you have the option, travel in the warmer parts of the day and by a sunny route, and camp where you will have sun at least at one end of the day.

When planning your clothing make sure the outside layer is windproof and that it seals against air penetration as much as possible by effective overlapping. Design your insulation layers in the correct sequence so that each successive layer is larger than the one underneath and doesn't compact the insulation. Make sure that all layers can be pulled down to the wrists and ankles and do not ride up from these high heat loss areas.

If you get cold, raise the collars of all layers to protect your neck, which loses lots of heat, and of course wear a sensible hat and do up the hood. Spare socks can be used as gloves, and if you are walking you may be better off with the jacket cuffs undone and your hands withdrawn into the sleeve. A PFD is a good insulator, especially if you can put something windproof over it such as a rain suit or even a large garbage bag with head and arm holes. However, make sure the overgarment cannot hinder swimming. Some garments will ride up and act like a straitjacket making swimming impossible, so ensure that the waist drawstring is tight.

If clothing is wet, its efficiency as an insulator is diminished. If it is made of cotton, its insulation value will be virtually nonexistent, hence the references to "killer cotton" at hypothermia inquests. By contrast, polyester fleece and pile still insulate quite well when wet. Look at the labels and avoid cotton like the plague. Change out of wet cotton clothes if you have the chance, and certainly try to separate them from the skin with clothes that are not cotton.

If the clothing is drying out while you wear it, considerable evaporative cooling of your body will occur. This is in addition to the cooling from the loss of insulation efficiency of wet clothes. The result can be rapid heat loss, possibly leading to hypothermia. Remove as much water as possible from the clothes by wringing, wrapping in a towel and wringing, shaking them as if cracking a whip or beating against a dry smooth rock or upturned canoe. After putting the damp clothing back on, you may benefit by wearing tightly closed rain wear over it to prevent evaporation and evaporative heat loss. If the clothing is synthetic fibre, a lot of water will simply drain out, and it doesn't cause cooling as it does so. You may want to squeeze out the lower hems periodically.

If you cannot stay warm and have some dry clothing available, you should change into it. However, if you use up all your dry clothing you are now in a risky position if another mishap occurs. You should stop and dry out properly as soon as possible. If you do not have a full set of dry clothing, put whatever dry items you have next to your body and put the wrung-out wet clothing on the outside. You may be able to separate the wet and dry with a rain jacket or pants or a plastic garbage bag so the layer next to your skin stays dry.

If the weather is windy, especially if other cooling factors exist, you must keep the wind out of your insulation. This is essential to prevent the wind from disturbing the insulating dead air in the clothing and to reduce evaporative heat loss as the wind dries out the clothing. Wear your windproofs or even your waterproofs, and close them up to prevent wind penetration. This may be awkward to do if your hands are already cold—help each other with hood drawstrings, etc. Improvise clothing using a tarp or tent fly or space blanket as a cloak, use garbage bags with head and arm holes as a waistcoat and another as a skirt. Seek a more sheltered route or campsite, build a windbreak from your canoe, raft, tarp, or simply get in the tent.

If the victim is losing heat from being immersed in water, get them as far out of the water as quickly as possible. Heat loss from the body into water is about 27 times quicker than heat loss into air at the same temperature. Two victims, one each side of an upturned canoe or kayak, can support each other up out of the water onto the bottom of the canoe. Hold crossed hands (crossing makes the arms effectively shorter and pulls you farther out) or hold the shoulders of PFDs.

Swimming and general thrashing are not helpful because they greatly increase the movement of water past the skin, thereby increasing the heat loss. The HELP position (Heat Escape Lessening Posture) with arms pressed to sides and legs pressed together works if you have to stay put. Close any shell clothing tightly at wrists, neck and ankles to reduce water flow-through.

Maintaining body heat production. The main steps you can take to keep up your body heat production are to eat and drink plenty during your trip and to keep moving. However, keeping moving if you are hungry or tired is not a good idea because your body may not have enough "fuel" to both keep you warm **and** keep you moving. If you use up too much body fuel you can become hypothermic very quickly. Unfortunately, conditions that are likely to make you susceptible to hypothermia tend to hinder movement, cooking and eating good meals, and making a good hot drink.

Any time where you are relying solely on keeping moving to produce heat and stay warm, you are at enormous risk. If you suddenly have to stop because of bad weather, nightfall, equipment failure or injury to you or someone else in your party, you will cool down rapidly and probably become hypothermic.

An injured person's heat production is likely to be low because they are no longer moving. If they are suffering from shock they will be even more likely to become hypothermic. Little can be done to boost heat production in an immobilized person unless their level of consciousness and degree of injury allow them to eat and drink, so concentrate on controlling heat loss. Don't forget that they may be losing heat fast because they are sitting or lying on the ground, so insulate underneath them. Consider whether the injured person can move slowly back to civilization without risk of worsening the injury, per-

haps with assistance and support from other members of the party. You must also consider the location and the conditions. If you are on a windswept, bare hillside in a driving rainstorm, the victim and the party are at far more risk than if they are under some thick spruce trees with a huge pile of driftwood or avalanche debris nearby for fuel.

Heat-producing ability is also reduced in someone who is tired after a bad night of sleep, or debilitated from the rigours of the trip. Make sure that people do get adequate sleep, and plan for recuperative rest days on a long trip. Be particularly careful if someone is ill, as their heat-producing ability and their resistance to hypothermia will be low.

Recognizing

A simple tool for remembering the progression of hypothermia is the "Four -umblings":

Gr-umbling—mild hypothermia

F-umbling—mild hypothermia

St-umbling—mild and severe hypothermia

M-umbling—severe hypothermia

The progression is also divided into the mild, or field-treatable hypothermia, which extends down to the stumbling stage, and severe hypothermia, which is very difficult to treat in the field and which includes the serious stumbling and collapse stage through the mumbling stage to coma and death.

Severe hypothermia is an extremely serious condition and victims have a poor chance of survival in a wilderness setting, so **concentrate on avoiding hypothermia**.

Mild Hypothermia

The following is a general progression of symptoms of mild hypothermia. They actually correspond to specific core temperature ranges, but few recreationists carry or use low-reading clinical thermometers. If you wish, you can read up on those specifics in a specialty first aid book.

Gr-umbling. If you are alert, you can see that the person is cold and miserable. The victim is not necessarily actually grumbling, because it is quite common for people to be stoic and say nothing or even deny that they are having a problem. The person is cold, maybe shivering, their performance is diminishing and they are probably lagging behind, just at a time when they need to be monitored by the rest of the group. Hopefully the other members are not becoming hypothermic, too, and are alert enough to detect the signs in their companions. However, all too often conditions are bad for everyone and they become too absorbed in their own discomfort to notice their companions' problems.

F-umbling. Fingers are clumsy and ineffective at just the time it would be advantageous for them to be dexterous for doing up zippers, lighting a stove, tying a hood drawstring or pitching a tent. The body is responding to being cold by sending less blood out to the extremities where it would be cooled down. It does this to preserve a warm circulation in the "core" of the body where the vital heart, lungs and brain are located. Although vital organ functions are preserved, the function of the fingers is sacrificed. Shivering continues. If the entire group is in this condition, there is a big problem because you can't help each other much.

St-umbling (beginning). As the body cools down it reacts by further restricting blood flow to the limbs to maintain warm core circulation. As the supply of blood in the limbs diminishes and they get colder they become less controllable, hence the stumbling or clumsy skiing or paddling. Slow thought and speech is starting to make the situation worse. Shivering continues, but if it stops this could be a sign of a *worsening* condition.

Treating mild hypothermia. As with all emergencies, someone must take charge. Women may have to take the leader role in handling hypothermia because women tend to be more resistant to hypothermia than men and are more likely to be still functioning well.

In the earlier stages of mild hypothermia people have some chance of rewarming themselves and recovering. The first course of action could be to redouble your efforts to reduce heat loss and increase heat production as previously described. Monitor the victim carefully and often for signs of improvement or worsening. Then if further travel with the vic-

Working around an injured or hypothermic victim in deep snow is difficult and it takes skill and practice to keep them protected from the snow.

tim appears dangerous and likely to lead to a worsening of the condition, you must stop travelling. If the victim does not improve, you have a more serious problem requiring more drastic measures.

You must stop in the nearest available area sheltered from the weather. Delegate some of your party to set up tents or tarps, build a shelter and get a fire going so they keep warm, feel useful and don't become hypothermic, too. Remove all wet clothing from the victim and put the person in whatever dry clothing you can obtain. Get organized with at least a tarp as a rainbreak and windbreak so you can keep the clothing dry during the change process.

If you are working around a victim in deep snow, take a few moments to prepare the site by packing the snow down for a metre or so around the victim so there is less loose snow. If the victim is going to be sitting or lying on a tarp while you work on them, it will be easier to keep snow out of everything if the victim is on a raised snow plinth. Loose snow can be more easily pushed off the sides of the tarp if you are pushing downward away from the victim. However, they will be more exposed to wind, so once you have them well wrapped and dry you may want to drag them to a lower and more sheltered area. Alternatively, have your party build a snow wall or a quinzee.

If you have a sleeping bag or preferably two, place the hypothermic victim in the bag naked with a warm, naked party member. If you have a couple sleeping bag it is much easier and you may be able to put the victim between two rescuers. If you are using a tent you may heat it with hot rocks but not a stove because of the risk of carbon monoxide poisoning. Hot water bottles may be applied to the trunk area only, suitably wrapped in socks or clothes to avoid burning the victim. Take care, the skin of the hypothermic person is very easily burned. Cessation of shivering is **only** a good sign **if** the general condition is also **improving**.

When the victim recovers they may seem and feel okay, but they will be weak and susceptible to a relapse for a day or so. If you have camping gear for the whole party, abandon travel and stay put at least overnight. Monitor the victim carefully over the next few days. Never give alcohol to a hypothermia victim. The "warm" feeling is caused by the alcohol overriding the body's cold defences and sending warm blood out to the extremities. It gets cooled in the cold flesh and comes back to cool the core, with serious results.

Severe Hypothermia

If you have not detected and arrested hypothermia in its milder stages, the victim may regress into severe hypothermia. This is a very serious situation that will require skill and resources if the victim is to survive.

St-umbling and m-umbling. At this stage the victim's St-umbling worsens to the point of collapse. The core temperature has dropped, so brain function is more seriously affected, leading to slurred speech (M-umbling), lack of coordination and irrational behaviour or comments. The irrationality often manifests itself in carelessness about doing up clothing, closing the sleeping bag, etc. **The body gives up on shivering as a means of generating heat and shivering stops. Do not confuse this cessation of shivering with the cessation of shivering characteristic of the recovering victim—the worsening victim will have a low level of consciousness and mobility.** The victim's consciousness level continues to get lower and they become unresponsive. At this stage it is quite common for the victim to experience a feeling of extreme warmth and to undo clothing or open their sleeping bags.

Respiration and heartbeat diminish to the point of being undetectable, which has led to some premature pronouncements of death. "Do not consider a victim cold and dead until they have been warm and dead" is an oft-quoted maxim. This is particularly the case with victims of cold water immersion and drowning.

Treating severe hypothermia. The serious hypothermia victim must be handled very carefully because jolts can easily trigger fatal ventricular fibrillation (ineffective heartbeat). For this reason an evacuation with improvised methods is hazardous and evacuation by helicopter or some other smooth vehicle is really required. If a ground evacuation is your only option and you can get the person out to a proper medical facility in five hours or less, you might consider trying it if you have enough personnel. Even if the rough travel causes ventricular fibrillation, the really cold victim may survive several hours of severely impaired circulation because of the "metabolic icebox" effect.

It is extremely difficult to rewarm the severe hypothermia victim in the field. Incorrect rewarming procedures can stimulate the return to the core of large amounts of the stagnant, cold, waste-laden blood from the limbs, resulting in sudden cooling of the core, and death. Warm the core with heated and well-insulated rocks or water bottles applied to the neck and trunk, being very careful not to burn the patient. Treatment should focus on preventing further heat loss by keeping the victim in a warm sleeping bag, preferably in a warm tent. The victim's own minimal heat production may then very gradually result in rewarming. Placing another person in the bag with the victim at this stage of hypothermia is not a good method of heat transfer in that it tends to warm the entire body rather than the trunk. Try to arrange for the victim to breathe warm, moist air to minimize evaporative heat loss and cooling of the lungs. Rebreathing exhaled air through a hat over their face helps, or breathing the air in the sleeping bag. Monitor the victim especially carefully if their face is covered.

Frostbite

Frostbite is a cold injury caused by freezing of tissue. It occurs whenever the temperature is below freezing, especially in hypothermia victims and people with impaired circulation. There is not enough warm blood going to the extremities so they cool and freezing occurs. The areas most affected are the hands and feet (including heels) because they are distant from the source of warm blood, and also the nose, cheeks and ears because they are exposed. Frostbite is serious so concentrate on avoiding it rather than treating it. It is incapacitating and can result in loss of tissue and appendages, though with modern treatment amputation is not as common as in the past. Damaged areas remain cold-sensitive for life.

Avoiding Frostbite

Avoiding frostbite requires you to maintain good circulation to the extremities, and to keep normally exposed flesh covered. To maintain the blood flow to the extremities you must:

- Consume enough nondiuretic drinks to maintain blood volume and prevent dehydration.
- Maintain overall body warmth and certainly avoid becoming hypothermic.
- Avoid tight and constricting clothing and footwear. Elastic at the wrists and particularly elastic tops on socks can restrict circulation. Never add an extra pair of socks "because it's cold," as they will almost certainly restrict circulation when jammed into your boots. Make sure that children's feet have not grown to the point where boots have become too tight. Traditional soft mukluks are very warm because there are no stiff parts to create pressure points, unlike in a stiff climbing or hiking boot. They also breathe well to keep the socks or liners dry. Avoid smoking because it causes constriction of peripheral blood vessels that would otherwise bring warm blood to the extremities. Be especially aware of feet swelling causing boot tightness, which in turn constricts blood flow. Be aware that some closed-cell foam liners of double boots can swell with increased altitude.

Other things to bear in mind for avoiding frostbite are:

- Thick mitts and a hat that covers your ears are essential. Mitts are warmer than gloves, but a glove you can keep on to do tasks is warmer than a mitt you have to take off!
- Liner gloves protect you from freezing your flesh against metal objects.
- Keep the insulation of socks and gloves as dry as possible so that even if circulation is diminished, the insulation will still be good enough to slow down the freezing process. Keep insulation from becoming wet with sweat using vapour barrier socks, neoprene closed-cell foam socks and latex medical gloves. Mesh insoles keep your socks out of the frost that may form on the boot sole and then melt to wet your socks.

Symptoms of Frostbite

The successive stages of frostbite are:

- The area feels cold.
- The area may feel painful.
- The area turns pale. You cannot of course see this on hands and feet.
- Tissues begin to turn white and freeze. Pain diminishes and sensation is lost as a result of the freezing.
- As the frostbite extends deeper, the tissues become hard and usually turn purplish rather than white.

Treatment of Frostbite

Superficial "frost nip" is where deep-tissue freezing has not occurred. It can be treated by rewarming with a bare hand. Do **not** rub the afflicted area or you will damage the tissues. You will be grinding the cells up with the sharp ice crystals that have formed in and around them! Feet can be warmed bare against the bare skin of a (good) friend's belly, under a good covering of clothing. To prevent recurrence, adjust either the clothing or the activity.

Deeper frostbite is much more serious and is very difficult to treat properly in the backcountry. Field treatment is frequently inadvisable beyond taking steps to prevent a worsening of the situation. Proper treatment involves rapid rewarming in a large water bath at a carefully controlled and maintained temperature of 38-42°C. The victim must be warm and definitely not hypothermic when this is done. There must be absolutely no risk of refreezing the thawed area. The process is extremely painful and the thawed area cannot be walked on or used, otherwise severe damage will be done. Thawing large areas poses the risk of cardiac problems when large amounts of toxins and wastes from the frozen part are mobilized on thawing. Preventing infection over the weeks or months of healing is virtually impossible unless you have access to proper antibiotic therapy. It is highly unlikely that you will be able to do the job properly in the field and care for the victim and their pain afterward. Consequently, the least harmful option is often to walk out on a frozen foot or travel with frozen fingers and not thaw the affected area until a hospital is reached.

You may be inclined to fly directly to a hospital at home, but remember that staff in a hospital in the cold region where you suffered the injury may be more familiar with treating frostbite. I was appalled to hear of a case where a person had immediate amputation treatment for frostbite in a hospital where frostbite was not commonly seen.

Other Health Concerns

Although hypothermia and frostbite are the outdoor health concerns that come immediately to most people's minds, there are others that can be quite serious in a remote location.

Dehydration

A dehydrated person is likely to become fatigued more quickly and is also susceptible to hypothermia and frostbite and shock from an injury. If the rest of the party are also dehydrated and fatigued, they may not be able to deal with the incident effectively and may also become casualties. Dehydration is more serious than a shortage of food. It is therefore essential to make sure that you and your group are adequately hydrated at all times. This requires an awareness of water intake and particularly of water loss so you can maintain an adequate balance.

Water is lost from the body not only by sweating and urination, but also in ways that are less obvious. Even without sweating, there is continuous loss of water by evaporation through the skin. This is known as "insensible perspiration." Water is also lost by evaporation from the lungs because exhaled air has been moistened with water from the lungs. It is therefore possible for the unwary person to lose a considerable amount of water without realizing they are doing so. This unnoticed loss is significant in winter and at high altitude when one is breathing heavily in cold, dry air.

Water loss by sweating is not always apparent. In very dry climates sweat evaporates instantaneously so you are less aware of the water loss. On a dry, windy Alberta summer day you could be losing a large amount of moisture, but your skin may not even be wet. On the other hand, on a high-humidity summer day in southern Ontario, the sweat does not evaporate. It becomes very obvious from the squelching in your shoes and the sweat running into your eyes that you are losing significant amounts of water.

The simplest way to check whether you are drinking enough is to monitor the colour and volume of urine. A dark colour and less than 0.5 litres of urine per day indicates dehydration. However, this 0.5 litre guideline can be misleading if people are drinking diuretic drinks such as coffee, tea, cola, pop containing caffeine, and alcohol. These fluids cause the production of a large amount of urine even though the body is not really properly hydrated. The best drinks for travellers are water, weak juices, herb teas and bouillon-type soups, especially as the latter may contain vital minerals or "electrolytes." Powdered juices and soups are best served at less than full strength.

It is sometimes difficult to get people to drink enough in the evenings as they do not want to get up in the night to urinate. I find that if I drink nondiuretic drinks I can rehydrate myself fairly well without waking up in the middle of the night with a full bladder. I really notice a big difference in my performance if in the morning I make a conscious effort to drink plenty of nondiuretic drinks. Strong coffee in the morning does taste and smell good, but it is really counterproductive! Daily intake may have to be four to six litres total, including food.

Unfortunately, dehydrated persons do not necessarily feel thirsty enough to drink sufficient fluids even if they are available. Be systematic and make regular stops to drink— every half hour or hour, timed by your watch. A smaller quantity at frequent intervals is better than larger quantities infrequently. Keep your water bottle handy—perhaps use a small one in an outside pocket of your pack. Refill it from a larger bottle inside where it is better positioned for carrying. I like the excuse to stop and take my pack off, but many people like the hydration systems with a hose.

Salt tablets are generally thought to be of questionable value, especially as they only contain sodium chloride and therefore they do not replace potassium. Many people find electrolyte replacement drinks and juice crystal drinks more palatable if they are over-diluted. Water is the safest drink to give a dehydrated person.

Safe Water Supplies

Providing a plentiful supply of safe drinking water will help to ensure that the common problem of dehydration and gut disturbances are avoided.

Water quality. Canada and Alaska are often portrayed as places where there are still plenty of drinkable lakes and rivers. Although this is still true in some areas, man's influence coupled with some naturally occurring contamination makes it necessary to be careful. Many major river systems are polluted with industrial effluent (particularly from pulp and paper mills), as well as with municipal sewage and agricultural runoff.

If you are travelling a river downstream of industrial activity or human habitation, you may want to consider taking a large water container to fill from safe sources. If you do take your water from the main river, it is advisable to fill your containers for the morning during the evening when pollution levels are likely to be less. I have heard reports from canoeists

Although there are still places where you can safely drink from creeks and lakes, they are diminishing in number and in most locations you should treat water before drinking it.

about "mysterious" increases in the pollution level at night, presumably from dumping of effluent when it is less likely to be seen!

Sewage contamination from human and agricultural activities, as opposed to chemical contamination, is a significant concern in many streams, rivers and lakes. The dilution factor helps reduce the risk, but there is still a chance of ingesting enough organisms to start an infection. Consequently, you should treat water near or downstream of habitation with some degree of suspicion. This also applies, of course, to water downstream of campsites, mountain huts, ski resorts, hunting or fishing camps, logging camps and mining exploration sites.

Natural contamination of water with harmful organisms is something one must also be aware of. Probably the most troublesome of these organisms is one called *Giardia lamblia*, which causes an unpleasant and debilitating gut disturbance known as Giardiasis or Beaver Fever. As the name suggests, this organism is carried by beavers and so one needs to be particularly careful with water downstream of beaver ponds. However, the organism is also carried by a number of other animals including dogs, cattle, horses and muskrats. It is also carried by man and is the organism of greatest concern around remote communities and backcountry facilities. The infective cysts of *Giardia* are thought to survive better in cold water, so that clear, cold mountain stream is not necessarily better than that warm, dark Shield country river. Cryptosporidum from faecal contamination is also becoming a serious concern.

Effective water purification is therefore advisable for virtually all sources except melted snow—and in some areas of heavy use, even that is contaminated. High mountain streams can be contaminated. Just because it comes out of the ground as a spring does not mean it is pure. Flowing underground through fractured rocky materials doesn't do much filtering!

Warning—water purification vs. filtration. Be aware of the difference between filtration and purification. Many devices filter water but do not purify it. That is, they do not guarantee to remove or kill all organisms. You can only be sure that the water is safe to drink if you use a device or system that is a "purifier" and it is used properly. Many filters remove *Giardia* and they are adequate as long as *Giardia* is all that must be removed from the water. However, if bacteria or viruses are present, and this is less likely in Canada and Alaska than in many countries, filters will not necessarily make the water safe.

Prefiltration. Prefiltration, or settling, is an important first step in making any cloudy water drinkable. This is because suspended materials impair the effectiveness of chemical purifiers. Also, harmful organisms are somewhat more likely to be associated with the settled particles, though the clear water above will not be free of them just because it is clear. Even sterile silt can have a serious irritating effect on the intestine.

Many rivers are naturally silty, for example, the Nahanni or Alsek. Other rivers may be un-naturally silty because their watersheds have been logged, mined or farmed and are eroding more as a result. High in the mountains, rivers may be bacteriologically pure but heavily laden with silt from glaciers. Silt can be removed by simply allowing silty water to settle. A quicker method is to filter the water through several layers of tightly woven fabric. Hats, especially felt ones, were traditionally used as filters, but your friends may not appreciate water that has gone through YOUR hat! A bag of tightly woven cotton cambric or good quality light canvas is easy to make and if equipped with a handle can be filled and hung from a branch over your pot. If you use a flat cloth, mark one side "top" so you don't wash the residue of the last use into your next sample of clear water! A good quality handkerchief works okay.

Once the water is clear of suspended materials, it must be treated in such a way as to either kill or remove the minute disease-causing organisms that will have passed through all but the finest of filters.

Boiling. Boiling is a reasonably effective method of sterilizing water at sea level, but its effectiveness is reduced at high altitude. This is because the boiling temperature drops with increasing altitude at a rate of approximately 1 C degree per 300 metres/1000 feet. At 3000 metres/10,000 feet altitude, boiling point is 10 C/18 F degrees lower, i.e. at about 90°C/194°F. This temperature is less effective at killing some disease-causing organisms.

There seems to be some dissent about the required boiling times and temperatures. To be on the safe side, follow the old guideline of a 10 minute rolling boil. Boiling as a water treatment method requires considerable extra fuel to be carried.

Water purifying tablets. Iodine water purifying tablets (tetraglycine hyperiodide) are useful as long as they are fresh. They lose their potency when exposed to air and especially to damp air, so the containers must be kept tightly closed. For safety you may want to discard the remaining tablets after each season. However, keep the bottle and transfer a dozen or so tablets from your next season's fresh purchase to this bottle that you will use as your "field use," frequently opened bottle.

Leave the stock bottle tightly closed at home where it will keep better.

These tablets are much less effective in cold water and longer contact times are required, especially against *Giardia* cysts. Position the water bottle in your pack where the sun or warmth from your back will raise its temperature, and allow at least half an hour if the water is below 10°C before drinking. Prefiltering is really important because many contaminants reduce the effectiveness of chemicals, especially chlorine. The chemicals get used up by reacting with the contaminants rather than with the microorganisms. If in doubt, increase the dosage of the chemical. **Do not** add flavourings until after the tablets have had time to work, because they too will react with the purifying chemicals and nullify their effect. If you are using chemicals in your water bottle, wait until they have dissolved and then invert the bottle with the cap loose and allow a little of the water containing chemicals to flush untreated water from the cap threads. Then close the lid and allow to stand.

Iodine. Tincture of iodine, which is iodine and sodium iodide dissolved in alcohol, is a reasonably reliable sterilizer for water. The taste is noticeable and iodine may cause a thyroid disturbance in some susceptible individuals. Effects are more pronounced with long-term use, and it should not be used by pregnant women.

The recommended dosage for 2.5 per cent tincture of iodine (not iodides) is:

- four drops/litre for 1/2 hr if water is clear
- eight drops/litre for 1/2 hr if water is cloudy.

Contact times should be increased if the water is very cold. Iodine seems to be effective against *Giardia* cysts except at low temperatures. Iodine needs to be carried in a glass bottle with a Bakelite or hard plastic lid, and there is some risk of breaking the bottle and damaging whatever the corrosive iodine leaks into. You may want to carry the glass bottle inside a small plastic bottle or at least wrap it in duct tape to make it less susceptible to shattering.

Another well-tried and proven method is to use crystalline iodine in what is known as the Kahn-Visscher system. You will have to special-order the iodine from a drugstore, and will probably have to buy 30 grams, which is much more than you need. Put approximately four grams in a 30-millilitre clear glass bottle with paper-lined Bakelite cap (from drugstore), and fill with water. The iodine is sparingly soluble in water and a tiny amount dissolves to form a saturated but weak solution the colour of tea. When you need to purify some water, allow the crystals to settle and then decant 15 millilitres or approximately half the tea-coloured solution into one litre of water in your water bottle. Shake and allow to stand for 30 minutes. Refill the small bottle ready for the next time. The iodine is so sparingly soluble that four grams will pro-

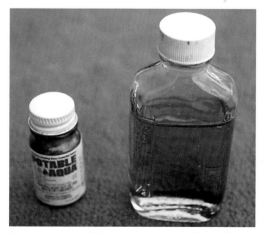

A simple way of purifying water is by using purifying tablets or iodine crystals and water in a glass bottle. See text.

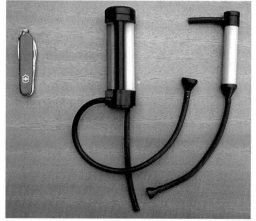

The Travel Well iodine resin units are very small and compact for day trips and emergencies.

duce enough 15-millilitre doses to treat about 500 litres of water. Iodine in quantity is poisonous, but it seems unlikely that even ingesting the whole four grams at once would be seriously harmful. Avoid pouring the crystals into your water bottle.

Some outdoor stores carry a kit called Polar Pure, designed for this system with the iodine already in a bottle and a filter in the top to keep the iodine crystals inside. Be careful not to crack the lids on these—the sample I saw broke easily.

Iodine resin purifiers. Another way of using iodine is by incorporating it into resin beads in a water purifier cartridge through which the water flows. The iodine is in either the Penta-iodine form or the Tri-iodine form. As the organisms in the water pass between the beads, their electrical charges cause them to attract a lethal dose of iodine onto themselves. The organisms are killed and relatively little iodine ends up dissolved in the water, though the actual amount varies between manufacturers. Various models also incorporate a carbon filter to remove the residual iodine taste from the water. Some residual iodine is actually useful to prevent recontamination of the water. Higher levels of residual iodine are also useful if the water will be used for washing vegetables that will be eaten raw. Some people feel that you should let the water stand for a few minutes in

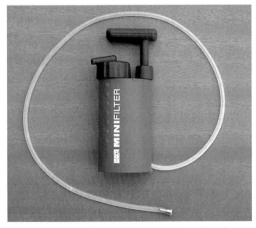

The Katadyn Mini-filter uses the time-proven Katadyn silver-impregnated ceramic filter in a light, compact unit.

order to be certain the residual iodine has killed the resistant *Giardia* cysts. These iodine resins can also be used in conjunction with filtration in combination devices, see below. The iodine resin device alone does not filter out particles.

Water filters. A wide range of water filters is available to backcountry users. Their effectiveness in making water safe to drink varies considerably. Some are only capable of removing the relatively large cysts of *Giardia*, while others will remove the much smaller bacteria. None are capable, on the basis of their pore size at least, of removing viruses. Water that is contaminated may contain all three types of organisms, so filters that just remove the large *Giardia* cysts are of limited value.

The Katadyn brand of ceramic filter is a time-proven and reliable device, and will filter out most disease-causing organisms except viruses. Even these seem to be moderately well filtered because they tend to be on the surface of larger filterable particles. This Swiss-made tool is costly at about $280 CDN but is very effective and causes no chemical tastes or chemical-induced health disturbances. The newer Katadyn mini-filter is small and handy to carry and costs around $150. Both filters are impregnated with silver to prevent bacterial growth on the filter itself.

The problem with ultra-fine filters is that considerable pressure is needed to force water through them and they clog easily. The built-in backwash on the PUR Explorer purifier is really convenient when using silty water.

Allowing water to settle and using an inlet pre-filter and hose-end filter saves a lot of aggravation. Suspend the hose-end filter clear of the sediment and below the surface scum using a stick as a float or with the attached float on some models.

Filtering followed by chemical treatment is a good approach to actually purifying water to make it fit to drink. This is because the small organisms that are difficult to remove by filtering are generally readily killed by quite low doses of iodine.

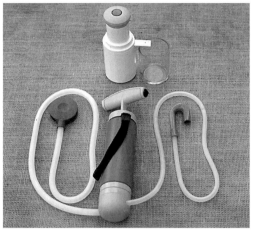

The PUR Explorer (lower) is a true purifier, having a filtration stage and an iodination stage. A carbon stage to remove taste is optional. It has the big advantage of a built-in backwash.

Water purifying devices. There are a number of purifying systems available that incorporate a filter to remove large organisms and that then treat the water with tri-iodine or tetra-iodine resins as described above. The coarser filter is less prone to clogging so you have the best of both worlds. The Pur Traveller, Scout and Explorer are units I have used with great success. Do not confuse these units that combine a filtering action and iodination with devices that iodinate without significant filtration. A carbon filter is available for the Explorer and Scout to remove iodine taste and for the sweetwater guardian. The slight trace of iodine it accumulates helps prevent bacterial growth on the carbon filter when not in use. This bacterial growth can be a problem with some types of filters, especially carbon ones.

With all water purifying devices, you must maintain the unit according to instructions and try to keep the inlet and outlet hoses separated from each other.

Whatever method of purification is used, do not contaminate containers used for purified water with unpurified water.

Altitude Problems

The effects of altitude are well known and well documented in mountaineering medicine and first aid books, yet people still push their luck and get into trouble. Denali (McKinley) seems to have large numbers of altitude-related medical problems. Temperatures and atmospheric composition in northern areas worsen altitude illness and cause problems at lower altitudes than in, for example, the Himalayas. It is therefore essential to allow plenty of time for proper acclimatization. Be particularly careful to avoid the trap of neglecting an appropriate pace for acclimatization to "take advantage of good weather," or to make up for the time spent waiting out bad weather. Be aware that some people, even though they are very fit, simply do not acclimatize well no matter what they do. Also, some people start to feel the effect of altitudes as low as 2000 metres, so hiking parties need to take this into account in many areas.

The treatment for most altitude-related medical problems is immediate descent. Arctic conditions make this more difficult. With the exception of crowded Denali and a few other popular peaks, there are unlikely to be other climbers on hand to help evacuate the patient.

Exposure to Sunlight

Compared to many parts of the world, the atmosphere in most parts of Canada and Alaska is very clear. This allows the penetration of more sunlight with its damaging UV (ultraviolet) rays. The depletion of the ozone in the atmosphere makes the problem more serious, and many weather forecasts now include an ultraviolet warning index:

- Low—skin burns in 60 minutes
- Moderate—skin burns in 30 minutes
- High—skin burns in 20 minutes
- Extreme—skin burns in 15 minutes.

Sunlight-related problems such as sunburn, eye irritation or worse still, snow blindness, can put your trip in jeopardy. Sunburned shoulders are not conducive to carrying a pack, and of course snow blindness is very unpleasant and can prevent you from travelling for several days. Burned lips can be very unpleasant and make eating a nasty experience, especially as UV exposure triggers cold sores. As everywhere, the higher the altitude, the worse the burning effects can be, and the burning rays can still be very strong through overcast and fog. Halving the thickness of sunscreen can reduce the protection to one seventh. The worst lip burns I ever suffered happened on an icefield weekend at 3000 metres when we saw no sun at all.

Careful and systematic use of high SPF sunscreens, good quality sunglasses with sidepieces and nose protectors, and appropriate clothing will protect you. On one northern spring glacier tour several of our party brought long, white nightdresses for cool protection from the intense sunlight. The images of nightdress-clad figures with Foreign Legion headgear, pulling sleds and telemarking down the vast glaciers with Mount Logan as a backdrop were unforgettable. It looked ridiculous but it worked, even though such fabrics have quite low SPF ratings. Large, old white cotton dress shirts are commonly used but the SPF is only around 8-15. Unlike sunscreens, they are not subject to washing off, uneven application or deterioration with time. New regulations have been introduced in the U.S. to govern "sun protective" fabrics. So far none are as comfortable as cotton in the heat.

Long Days

In the northern spring and summer, the long hours of daylight have significant effects. One of these is that the length of time you are exposed to sunburning rays is greater than farther south, so sunburn is more likely to be a problem.

Another common problem is the tendency for people to put in days that are too long. Rather than sitting around the camp fire after dinner or retiring to bed, they go off for a hike or a ski and stay active right up to bedtime. This is permissible on a short trip, but after a few days people get overtired, cranky and out of sorts. I have seen this happen many times on northern trips, especially with less experienced people.

A solution is to follow a regular routine of meal times and bedtimes. If you don't keep a regular schedule you will eat and sleep at all times of the day and night and different people will be on different schedules. Their internal biological clocks will get out of order, they won't eat properly and they will generally perform below par. I remember meeting vehement resistance to keeping a regular eating and sleeping schedule on a northern summer trip from one so-called guide. It was just another symptom of his inexperience and ineptitude.

Keeping cool with adequate sun protection can be a problem on spring ski tours. These skiers near Mount Logan are using unconventional garb, but these light fabrics (SPF 8-15) are not a total protection from ultraviolet rays.

The northern spring evening light can tempt you into putting in days that are so long that you become overtired.

Of course, it may occasionally be necessary to alter the daily schedule. For example, you may have to travel at night on skis when the snow is firmer, by canoe when there is less wind or at times dictated by tides. When this happens, plan your time carefully so you still leave time to eat and rest. Do not let yourself become overtired and accident-prone.

Exhaustion

The large scale and long distances of the back-country require the carrying of heavier packs than in more populated areas. This makes bigger demands on people's fitness and stamina. To make sure that you get a good night's sleep every night, don't stint on the quality of your sleeping bag and mattress. Inadequate rest can detract from your ability to function competently and safely, and re-duces your resistance to hypothermia and infection. A night of inadequate sleep in a noisy storm, perhaps coupled with long-term cold and wet is significantly debilitating.

Know your limits and don't "overdo it" and injure yourself by overloading or trying to prove something.

Make sure you provide for rest days when planning your schedule for a long trip. Most people are not used to continuing recreational activity for more than the few days of a long weekend. The long trip in Canada or Alaska may be the first time you have an opportunity to continue day after day for a week or a month, and most people don't have the stamina to keep going in this fashion for more than a few days without a break.

If you have had a long journey to the start of the trip, perhaps coupled with jet lag, make your first rest day very early in your trip. Maybe even spend two nights at your first camp. Approximately every sixth day should be a rest day during which you stay put. It could be used as a reserve travel day if you lose a day due to bad weather. Beware of guide-books that say you can do a trip in, say, 12 days using a schedule indicating hard travel each day. Most people can't stand that sort of pace, particularly if the weather is bad.

Constipation

The provision of adequate fluids helps reduce the likelihood of constipation occurring, but you may also wish to provide plenty of rough-age and mildly laxative foods such as prunes and apricots in the rations. This will be par-ticularly useful in serious bug country. Def-ecating is doubly unpleasant in a cloud of mosquitoes when constipated, and even peo-ple who are not yet constipated may delay defecating and end up becoming constipated.

Flatulence

Some people experience serious flatulence on outdoor trips, usually in response to the unfa-miliar foods and exercise. In the close quarters of a tent or snow cave it can get beyond a joking matter. The problem is legendary if eating a lot of beans, cheese and legumes, but can be alle-viated by using Beano drops on the food. You can obtain Beano from health food stores. Simethecone pills such as Ovol-80 also help.

Transmission of Infection

Colds and flu spread easily in a party, and can devastate a trip. Other more obscure infections can also be spread, including gastrointestinal diseases. Upsets can occur simply from expo-sure to unfamiliar but not necessarily patho-genic gut flora. Spreading of infections is par-ticularly likely to happen if water bottles and cups are shared. My feeling is that this should be avoided, and if you have a community water filter readily available at all times there should be no reason for anyone to drink from other people's bottles or cups.

Cooking and handling food with unwashed hands is another common way infection is spread, and all groups should have at least one collapsible wash basin to facilitate hand wash-ing. Keep it in a prominent place and make sure the cooks use it.

Communal dishwashing is another potential route of infection. If fuel is in plentiful supply, a simple solution is to immerse everything in a large pot and heat it. If you raise it to a tempera-ture that is much too hot to remove the items by hand, most disease-causing organisms will be deactivated. Use barbecue tongs to stir the uten-sils around and to lift them out. Rinse and air dry. Do not use dishtowels for drying unless you boil or bleach them frequently.

If you do not have fuel for a really hot wash, wash the utensils first and then rinse them in new water with bleach added. Do not add bleach to the first wash water because it will react with all the dirt and be deactivated before attacking the bacteria. Carry bleach in a good leakproof container such as a Nalgene bottle.

Rubber gloves are light and easy to carry and enable you to wash items with much hotter water than with bare hands.

Dishcloths and scourers are a great environ-ment for the growth of bacteria. Bleach or boil them often, and do not keep them in plastic bags where they would stay damp and culture bacteria. Squeeze or shake them dry and hang in the sun and wind.

Food Quantity and Quality

Health can only be maintained if you provide enough appealing and satisfying food to meet the energy demands of the trip and the particular conditions under which you are doing it. You must also make sure that the food will still be safe to eat by the time you are several days into the trip, and certainly by the end of a long trip, so choose and pack it carefully. If the food is suspect, don't risk a serious attack of food poisoning in a remote place by eating it anyway. Always inspect it carefully before eating. I remember an incident where a can of green furry corned beef nearly ended up in a super-hot curry when cooking in the dark. The curry would have masked the taste but not destroyed the bacteria and toxins.

Pre-existing Health Conditions

Pre-existing conditions are usually influenced for the worse by exertion, adverse weather conditions, unfamiliar foods and routines, altitude and disturbed sleep. Some of the ailments that can create a serious problem in the outdoors include allergies, diabetes, heart disease, tooth problems and asthma. Sufferers must be realistic in their personal expectations, must get a medical checkup before the trip and must carry appropriate medications on the trip. A *duplicate* set of any crucial medications must be carried by someone else in a different pack or canoe in case gear is lost in an accident. People with food allergies must be involved in the trip food planning so that they will be able to eat enough of the group food to remain adequately nourished. The whole group should be made aware in the planning stage of any pre-existing medical conditions so they act appropriately.

Mental Health

The incessant buzzing, probing and biting of insects is just one of the many factors that can affect mental health on a wilderness expedition. Like so many other stresses related to being outdoors and especially to being with a group, it can increase impatience, friction among group members, carelessness, accidents, etc. The vastness and remoteness of the wilderness can also prey on some people's minds with strange results.

Insect Bites

Blackfly bites often cause swelling and infection in the bitten areas, and swollen lymph nodes in adjacent node areas. This general infection can be quite miserable and is to be avoided as much as possible by using protective clothing and repellents. The associated itching can lead to scratching and more infection, so antihistamine creams are useful to reduce the itching and the incentive to scratch.

Mosquito bites generally produce local allergic responses rather than infections. The associated swelling and itching can be unpleasant for susceptible people (visitors especially), so topical antihistamines can be helpful. See Chapter Eleven, Bugs, Bears and Other Hazards, page 283.

Sanitation

Unburied faecal matter around a campsite presents a health hazard if flies are present to transport bacteria to your food. It may also contaminate your water supply. Make sure that your group members defecate a considerable distance from camp and that they bury the faecal matter properly. Sometimes you arrive in a site that has been used by people who have not been careful enough, so there is a hazard. Burying that material does not immediately solve the problem of the flies that have already been contaminated, so you may want to choose another site. See section on Low Impact Camping, page 248.

Foot Problems

Wet feet Canoeists and kayakers may have wet, cold feet for extended periods. Avoid wearing wet suit booties for any longer than necessary during the day, and make sure you have dry socks and footgear to wear in camp. Turn your booties inside out to dry in the sun and for the ultraviolet light to help discourage bacterial growth.

If you have to wear dry socks with your wet boots around camp, cover the socks with a plastic bag to prevent the boots wetting them. Try not to wet the socks from inside by working up a sweat if you do this. Rocky GoreTex socks work better because they are breathable.

Trench foot. Prolonged periods with cold, wet feet can cause constriction of blood supply, which over days or weeks leads to permanent painful nerve and other damage, as well as to a permanent sensitivity to cold. If wet feet are inevitable, at least keep them warm by keeping active or wearing neoprene socks. Always keep one pair of dry socks or some camp booties to wear in camp and in your sleeping bag.

Athlete's foot can really spoil any holiday but particularly a hiking trip. It is caused by a fungal growth that tends to flare up in hot, sweaty boots and when a person's defences are reduced because of the debilitating effects of prolonged exertion. The extent of the problem can be controlled by washing the feet often, keeping them dry, changing to clean socks as often as possible and using a fungicidal foot powder. Breathable boots are a big help. Wear-

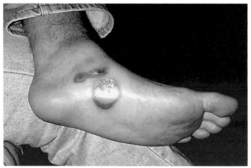
Blisters can really spoil your trip so break your boots in before a big trip and treat hot spots immediately with Moleskin, Compeed or Second Skin.

Keeping your feet healthy by keeping them clean and changing into dry socks at the end of the day.

ing a polypropylene or polyester moisture-transporting liner sock with an absorbent sock over it also helps keep the skin dry. Change socks often and hang them to dry on your pack inside out in the sun. Better still, wash socks out between changes and try not to put an infected sock on a healthy foot. If you are using vapour barrier socks, it is particularly important to remove them as soon as you get into the tent to allow your feet to breathe and dry out.

Blisters can really spoil your trip or even bring it to a standstill. If you need new boots for your trip, obtain them well in advance so you can break them in properly. Do not skimp on money to buy good quality socks. They must fit well and have smooth seams. Close-fitting, stretchy wicking liner socks with a thicker wool sock over them should minimize any problems. The new Merino wool socks seem to be better than many of the old heavyweight ragg socks. Avoid socks containing cotton for all except the hottest summer conditions. Keep your Moleskin, Compeed or Second Skin handy rather than buried in your first-aid kit. It will be easy to stop

This sock has a poorly made toe seam that forms lumps at the side, and its high cotton content results in it being not sufficiently elastic to fit without wrinkling.

Apply Moleskin before the trip if you think you will have blister problems, or apply at the first sign of a "hot spot."

and take some preventive measures at the first sign of a "hot spot." The key is to fix it as soon as it starts to make its presence felt, not when the blister is fully formed. Broken blisters are a serious infection risk, so wash them carefully and apply antiseptic cream.

Foot infections are less likely to occur if you keep your feet and socks clean. A folding basin makes it easy to wash your feet using soap without contaminating a creek. A soft nailbrush makes it easier to clean the crevices around the nails where nasty nail infections can start. Carry nail clippers on long trips to trim your toenails so they don't get driven against the end of your boot. At the least sign of redness or soreness around a nail, wash thoroughly and apply an antiseptic. Soak in hot water. The salt in seawater soaks has a "drawing" effect when the swelling prevents access of antiseptics to the root of the infection. I've had success using salt on a damp dressing for "drawing" infected wounds. Carry several pairs of liner socks so you can change them frequently during your trip.

Skin Problems

Sunburn has already been mentioned. Canoeists' and kayakers' hands often become chapped, dried and cracked, and the same happens when anyone washes dishes. Rubber gloves for doing dishes help reduce the problem, but wind, water and sun exposure still induce cracked and dry skin. I keep a small Nalgene bottle of hand cream such as Vaseline Intensive Care or zinc oxide cream (Zincofax) handy in my lifejacket pocket for use during the day. I also use it at night. If your hands get really badly dried and cracked, slather them with the grease at night and wear an old pair of thin liner gloves to keep your sleeping bag clean.

Personal Hygiene

Contrary to what many North Americans seem to believe, going for more than 24 hours without a shower is not terminal. However, it does feel nice to get clean if conditions allow. There is a No Rinse shampoo and Body bath available (800-410-9653 for nearest retailer) that makes washing with a limited amount of water easy.

Unfortunately, you rub the dirt off onto your towel rather than rinsing it off, so the towel gets pretty revolting. However, it is often much easier to rinse your towel than to rinse your hair. Changes of briefs are certainly desirable, especially for women because susceptibility to bladder infections is higher. On winter trips, using lumps of snow rather than toilet paper seems to keep the anal region cleaner. If food preparation and eating involve contact between food and the hands, hand washing is important. Remember that the inside of your gloves may be a seething repository of bacteria. Regular soap does not work in sea water so you need to take a special sea-water soap. Some of these are all-purpose dish soap/body soap/shampoo products. You will find them in specialty outdoor stores, especially those in coastal towns.

Motion Sickness

Some ocean kayakers experience seasickness, and it can significantly impair their ability to perform. This is doubly inconvenient because the rough seas causing it are probably demanding maximum performance. Make sure you have appropriate medications, preferably ones that do not cause drowsiness. Flying in light planes can also cause considerable sickness. One whiff of turboprop exhaust and my stomach starts to churn. Every time I've been in a Twin Otter fumes have got into the cabin before takeoff. Take your pills and carry some plastic bags.

Tularemia

This disease is carried by snowshoe hares in Alaska and occasionally by beavers. It can be transmitted to humans handling or skinning them. If you have to handle these animals in a survival situation, avoid squashing any ticks and avoid contaminating any cuts or scratches on your skin with the animals' body fluids.

Lyme Disease

This potentially serious and debilitating disease is spread by ticks. It tends to go unrecognized as its early symptoms mimic influenza, with headache, fatigue, stiff neck, stomach problems and sore throat. If recognized it can be cured with antibiotics such as tetracycline. However, recognition is not easy. At the stage of the tick's lifecycle that it is thought to infect most people the tick is very small and the bite is unlikely to be felt. A circular red skin rash is an indicator in about three cases in four and occurs within a few days of infection. The flu-like symptoms take up to three weeks to develop. Blood tests are not yet very reliable. If untreated, Lyme Disease progresses to cause serious arthritis-like symptoms, headaches and even heart problems.

The extent of the risk is unclear because of inconsistencies in reporting the disease and of difficulties in making an absolutely positive diagnosis.

Precautions include wearing long sleeves and pants tucked into socks and doing a full body check for ticks at the end of the day. It is easier to see ticks against pale-coloured clothing and underwear. If you find one, remove it as described on page 291 and keep it, along with some grass, in a baggie or film canister for testing. If you are lucky to spot the rash it is a good indicator that you have been infected and must see a doctor. Since not all doctors are familiar with Lyme Disease, you should tactfully indicate to your doctor that Lyme Disease may be something to consider as a cause of your symptoms.

Animal Bites and Rabies

Rabies is common in many animals in Canada, (see section on Other Problem Animals, page 299) and is an extremely serious and likely fatal disease. A bite from any wild animal, especially if the animal is behaving strangely or the bite is unprovoked, should be looked on as a very serious occurrence. Any animal capable of carrying rabies that bites a human should be presumed to be rabid until it has been killed, tested and proven otherwise. The wounds must be washed out as thoroughly as possible and medical aid sought immediately. You can pressure-irrigate the deep wounds with a #19 needle and syringe using clean water with a little salt added. Past medical treatment for suspected rabies infection was so unpleasant that people were almost as

scared to seek preventive treatment as they were of the disease. However, a new human serum makes precautionary treatment much less unpleasant. If available, antibiotics should be taken to control infection, and antihistamines administered in the case of allergic reactions to bites and stings.

Tetanus

Most types of outdoor injuries, especially deep puncture wounds, expose a person to tetanus (lockjaw). Make sure you keep your immunization up to date. Many people neglect this precaution because we usually get a routine tetanus shot at the hospital any time we are injured, but this won't be available in the wilderness.

Hantavirus

This virus is carried by deer mice and affects humans with a serious flu-like ailment, sometimes known as "Navajo Flu." If untreated it leads to serious pneumonia-like symptoms with large amounts of fluid in the lungs. Death can occur, especially if the disease is not recognized and treated promptly. In spring 1994, it has spread north to Montana and into western Canada. The virus is spread through faeces, urine and saliva of the deer mouse, and infection of humans is often by inhaling contaminated dust. Avoid handling deer mouse nests and make sure your food does not become contaminated by nibblers. Be careful around buildings such as cabins and outhouses if there are faecal pellets present, which indicate these mice are around.

Chapter 11

Bugs, Bears and Other Hazards

The wild, untamed Canadian and Alaskan backcountry has many potential hazards for the unwary traveller. Most untoward incidents are not accidents, but are the predictable results of the actions or omissions of the unprepared or uninformed victim. Problems can be avoided by being well informed about potential hazards and being prepared to avoid or deal with them effectively.

Bugs

Insects are the bane of the outdoors in many parts of Canada and Alaska. At certain times of the year they can transform an idyllic holiday location into a miserable buzzing, biting, itching hell. They can also add significant stress to the day-to-day operations of a trip, making it difficult to relax until you finally retire to the tent and exterminate the last of the buzzers that entered with you. If the trip is already stressful for other reasons such as unsatisfactory group dynamics, poor weather or difficult travelling, bugs can be the final irritant, leading to major problems. The worst pests include mosquitoes, blackflies and no-see-ums, but horseflies/deerflies, wasps, hornets and ticks are also cause for concern.

Different people react to insects in different ways, showing varying degrees of psychological and physiological adaptation. When I first immigrated to Canada, mosquito bites produced skin welts one centimetre across. However, within a year or so I had adapted physiologically and subsequently experienced much less discomfort. As for psychological adaptation, some people allow the bugs to "get to them" much more than others. Once, after a summer spent guiding on the Coppermine River in the bug-infested N.W.T., I was revelling in the almost bug-free camping at home in the Rockies. However, our camping friends were swatting and slapping and complaining about too many (at least three) mosquitoes!

Visitors to this country need to be especially wary if they are not used to biting insect pests, particularly as they may experience the same welts and irritation I had in my first year in Canada. I remember guiding a foreign client who was very psychologically sensitive to bugs. We never saw him without his head net on, so I hardly know what he looked like! No one should underestimate the influence these tiny pests can have on the success of your trip. You must take good preventive measures in the form of insect repellents, suitable clothing and bugproof tents. Unfortunately, these methods are not 100 per cent effective so you should also have an adequate supply of medications to at least relieve the post-bite discomfort. Topical antihistamines such as Caladryl or topical anaesthetics containing benzocaine and even a nonprescription oral antihistamine are useful medications to carry, especially for sensitive individuals.

The most significant insect pests are mosquitoes, blackflies and no-see-ums, largely because of their numbers. Mosquitoes are annoying and the bites can be very itchy. Occasionally they spread serious disease—equine encephalitis—but it is not common. Blackfly bites are much more unpleasant than mosquito

Bugs are present in enormous numbers in some regions and make life miserable unless you are well protected. Ken Ellison photo.

Equipped for serious bug country—head net, pale-coloured clothes, gloves and a gun to shoot down the mosquitoes!

bites in that they bleed, itch, produce lumps and easily become infected. Swollen glands and general malaise can result, and large numbers of bites around the eyes may cause swelling and hindered vision. No-see-um bites are unpleasant and also frustrating because the insects are so small, hence the name.

Defence Against Insects

There are four main defences against insect problems—avoiding buggy times, avoiding buggy places, using insect repellents and using suitable clothing and tents.

Avoiding buggy times. Some times of the year are much less buggy than others, and that does not mean you can only camp bug free in winter! You should therefore definitely make inquiries locally about the timing of the bug season in the area you wish to visit, because a few weeks can make a big difference to the enjoyment of your trip. However, be wary of local perspectives on bug seasons. Everything is relative, and the "no bugs to worry about" season for locals in a buggy area can be rather grim for those from elsewhere. The start and finish of seasons is not fixed and fluctuates with the weather. A cold spring delays the hatch, a hot, dry spell finishes the blackflies and mosquitoes off, but they can be encountered in October even in north-central Ontario after a wet summer.

When we lived in southern Ontario and wanted to avoid the worst part of the blackfly season in the central Ontario Canadian Shield canoeing country, we stayed at home during late May and June and tended the garden and hiked. For a canoe trip on the end of May long weekend we would go a long way north to where the bugs would not yet have hatched. It recently took me all of three milliseconds to decide to turn down an invitation for a late June (high bug season) canoe trip on the Canadian Shield! In Alaska the bugs can be avoided by staying above treeline in June and July. If you want to travel at lower levels, May and August are better. The bugs are either not out yet or else they have finished their lifecycle.

Blackflies breed in moving water, and when the water temperature reaches the key temperature for the species in question, they emerge in millions. The critical temperature varies from 4°C to around 18°C. As runoff dries up through the summer, the population diminishes. In the north, the blackfly season tends to be later than in southern parts of the country because it takes longer for the water to warm up. The northern varieties of mosquitoes have adaptations to enable them to function at surprisingly low temperatures.

Avoiding buggy locations. The second defence against insect problems is to avoid places where the bugs are likely to be really bad. Mosquitoes breed in standing water and in damp vegetation, but different species have different requirements. The mountainous, well-drained Nahanni River has been relatively bug free on the three occasions I have run it. Certainly it's been bug free compared to the low-lying plain of the Liard into which it runs or with the boggy tundra Coppermine River, which I have run many times and which has always been buggy. The rivers of the Rockies and the coastline of B.C. in September have provided us with relatively bug-free paddling compared to, say, the rivers of the Canadian Shield where there is more standing water and poor drainage. Even within a region there will be areas where the bugs are less of a problem. We recently paddled a big river in the Alaska/Yukon border area in late July and did not use any insect repellents for 11 days. It is a heavily glaciated region with large areas of well-drained fluvial and glacial deposits so there was little in the way of breeding grounds for bugs. It was also a dry year.

One of the best defences against insects is to camp in places where there are fewer insects in the first place. Dry places devoid of vegetation are therefore desirable, though sandflies and no-see-ums may be a problem. Windy places are also desirable because wind disturbs the various insect attractants around people, making it more difficult for the insects to home in. If the wind is really strong it just makes flying difficult. You should therefore seek out moraines, eskers, river gravel bars, ridge tops, promontories, islands and other exposed places devoid of standing water and damp vegetation. However, you generally require a good wind-resistant and free-standing tent to camp in these locations. You should be cooking well away from your tent to minimize bear problems, so you could set up camp using an exposed location for living, cooking and eating, and a sheltered place back in the bush for sleeping.

Insect repellents. The third defence is to use effective insect repellents. Insects locate their warm-blooded prey partly by detecting water vapour, carbon dioxide, scents, chemical attractants and infrared radiation. The chemicals are present in larger amounts around you, and insects zero-in toward increasing concentrations.

Insect repellents usually work by emitting a vapour that interferes with the ability of the insect to home in on the attractants. There is no doubt that they do work, especially those based on DEET. A small plastic bottle of DEET repellent is a permanent fixture in my lifejacket survival pocket and in my summer survival kit. The various products have varying proportions of DEET. Higher proportions are needed in highly infested areas or by individuals who are badly affected by bugs.

However, repellents are unpleasant to use and have a damaging effect on a number of plastic materials and synthetic fabrics. Most of the spray-on repellents have an annoying scent, too. Any scent is undesirable in bear country because it can arouse curiosity, especially among young grizzlies exploring the world alone for the first time. Worse than this is the irritating effect sometimes caused by frequent use of repellents on the skin. Skin effects are particularly noticeable when people use highly concentrated products and apply them liberally from the bottle to limited areas of skin. Saturation and frequent reapplication is not necessary anyway. A better way is to sprinkle the repellent on a 15-centimetre square of J-cloth or rag kept in a plastic bag, and then wipe the rag over larger areas of skin or the hair. The only problem with this is that the repellent is a great cleanser, and the rag soon becomes very dirty-looking! Sprays are another solution, but they are heavy and expensive. You can apply a spray to an old white cotton shirt and wear that next to your skin or over your other clothes to obtain a repellent effect without putting the chemical on your skin. The U.S. Environmental Protection Agency recommends washing repellent off your skin when it is no longer needed, and particularly when you go to bed.

You must be careful not to allow repellent to come in contact with rubber, synthetic fabrics and many plastics. This means latex seals of canoeist's dry suits, plastic spectacle lenses and watch glasses, cameras, paddle handles, fishing rod handles, compasses, clothing, etc. I have seen people spray the insect netting of their tent with insect repellents and then wonder why it falls apart next time it becomes stressed!

While repellents work better against mosquitoes, insecticides like Permanone are more effective against ticks, blackflies and other crawlers.

An **insecticide** spray is also useful to have if you are vehicle-camping, to rid the vehicle of bugs before retiring. It can also be used in tents for the same purpose. The main thing is to cover all food and utensils, use a bare minimum of spray and to vacate the tent or vehicle while the spray does its job. A quick spray can save a lot of ill will and acrimony when someone has left the door open.

Some people burn mosquito coils in their tent or cabin. These flat coils, about 12 centimetres in diameter, are made of materials that smoulder when lit to release an insecticidal and insect repellent smoke. The idea of breathing the toxic smoke is not very appealing though. I remember being incensed when people in the next campsite used an insecticide fogger and the toxic fog drifted over me. They were surprised that I was concerned about the potential toxicity of the fog. They seemed to think they were doing me a favour, protecting me from a few mosquito bites.

A selection of bug repellents and insecticides.

Insect protection clothing. Clothing that keeps you cool so that you sweat less is advantageous because you produce less water vapour and scent for the insects to home in on. Light cotton is good for this purpose. We use old white cotton dress shirts, not only because they are cool but also because white is not as attractive to the insects as are dark colours. This is because white is a poor emitter of the infrared radiation that insects use for homing, and is a good reflector of the entirely different visible wavelengths of light emitted by the sun. The fluorescent whitening additives left in the fabric by detergents possibly produce wavelengths that are still more confusing to the insects. We sew up the sleeve slits and front opening to prevent entry by crawling blackflies. However, in serious blackfly country, you really need cuff and neck elastics, so a knitted cotton T-neck with good resilient, tightfitting cuffs works if it is long enough to tuck reliably in to the waist with a good overlap. An elastic waistband on your pants is most effective at excluding these persistent crawlers.

Dark colours are much more attractive to insects, and even more so if the surface is rough. Dark jeans, which are of little use for

Special mesh jackets impregnated with bug repellent are among the most effective insect repellent devices.

any serious outdoor activity anyway, are particularly bad in this respect. My old brown felt hat sometimes appears furry because of the thousands of mosquitoes probing and prodding at it. I prefer them up there wasting their time than prodding at me, though!

You must certainly make sure that you have clothing that covers as much of the body as possible. This means sleeves long enough to overlap gloves, clothes that overlap reliably at the waist and thick socks long enough to tuck pants into without coming untucked when you sit down.

Unfortunately, blackflies crawl in through the smallest opening, for example, the small channel formed where pants are puckered when tucked into socks. Good elastic tops on the socks and a long overlap are needed to seal this opening. Some people even seal wrist and ankles with tape. Blackflies do not bite through fabric, but mosquitoes easily penetrate breathable fabrics. However, they are discouraged if the garment is baggy, because the fabric slides around over the skin and disturbs their aim. The old Norwegian-style string underwear helps add clearance between the shirt and skin without adding too much insulation, and this helps against mosquitoes. You can still find these garments occasionally in Nordic ski stores with strong Norwegian connections.

There are a number of "bug jackets" on the market, which are impregnated with repellent to produce a powerful shielding "aura" around the wearer. They are made of a special loose mesh, which you periodically reimpregnate by sprinkling the jacket with repellent and rolling it tightly in a plastic bag for a few hours or overnight. They look awful, and are costly at around $40, but they really work and are the answer to making life bearable in serious bug country. Depending on conditions they last several days between reimpregnations. When not in use, the jacket is kept wrapped in a plastic bag to prevent unnecessary evaporation of the repellent. This also prevents it coming in contact with items that could be damaged by the repellent. I heard one case where a jacket was left in contact with the lower plastic window of a helicopter and damaged it so it had to be replaced. There are also bug jackets that use no chemicals.

The Canadian Skeeter Guard mesh bug jacket with integral hood has fabric that is specially

The Skeeter Guard jacket uses no chemicals and is specially constructed so it stands clear of your skin (top).

The Original Bug Shirt (Trout Creek, Ont.) is a good combination of breathable white cotton and mesh with an attached head net for effective insect protection.

Head nets can be a great help in serious bug country. Some have stiffening rings, but the Lynn Valley head net (lower) needs none, and has a dark mesh one side and pale mesh the other so you can rotate the net for best vision in the prevailing light.

"puckered" to make it stand away from your skin to discourage mosquitoes. Other jacket/hood combinations are made of mesh and rip-stop nylon, which is much less breathable but is reasonably proof against a probing proboscis. These are not breathable enough for strenuous activity but are satisfactory for fishing, bird-watching and around camp.

Another Canadian jacket, from the Original Bug Shirt Company in Trout Creek, Ontario, is made of tightly woven white cotton cambric that is mosquitoproof and more breathable than the ripstop nylon versions, especially as it has mesh panel inserts in places where the mosquitoes are less likely to land. It comes complete with an attached head net and is very effective. Matching pants have special cuffs to protect the vulnerable ankle region.

Head nets can be a godsend, producing an immediate sensation of relief and relaxation, once you get used to accepting that the frenzied buzzing is on the outside. However, they are hot and a bit tedious to wear. They also need to be sealed at the neck to exclude blackflies, so you need a tall T-neck shirt collar to roll up. The nets with a shoulder yoke held down by elastics under the armpits seal well. Some have built-in stiffening rings and a suspension system that keeps the net away from the face, but others have to be worn over a wide-brimmed hat, which may be aggravating on a hot day. The Canadian-made Lynn Valley bug hats have a Lycra neck seal and black mesh one side and pale mesh the other so you can rotate it to suit the prevailing light conditions.

Tents for insect protection. It is absolutely essential to have a tent equipped with no-see-um-proof mesh screens for the door and window. This allows you to sleep or just seek refuge in a bug-free environment while maintaining ventilation and a view. My first camping trip in Canada, with a British tent with no bug net, convinced me of the folly of trying to do without! Lighting a mosquito coil in your open tent and sleeping with it burning is an unhealthy and unsatisfactory substitute.

The design of the door zipper significantly affects the number of insects that can enter with you. The common "inverted U" zipper arrangement requires you to have a very large area open for a significant amount of time

while you enter. On the other hand, doors that unzip along the bottom and one side or the middle, hang in the closed position until you actually dive in. The fabric brushes insects off your back as you get in, too. Circular zippers also give more options on how much you need to open the door.

In bad bug country you may want to consider taking a larger tent than usual. It will be more "liveable" since you might want to use it as a haven to spend time in rather than just as a place to sleep. Large windows at both ends provide a good view and airiness, and a number of tents are now available with large screened panels in the roof or walls. They can be used without the fly sheet until it rains, although this exposes the tent to destructive ultraviolet radiation.

Blackflies generally do not bite when inside a tent or building, but mosquitoes are persistent pests, and just a few can really disturb your sleep. I remember a night spent in a cabin where, to escape the mosquitoes, we slept in our tent, pitched on the bed! If you are expecting to spend time in cabins in serious bug country, I suggest you take a tropical-style mosquito net to sleep under. Some of these nets hang from a beam or light fixture and drape over the bed, others have their own frame. You can buy them or make them from no-see-um netting or coarser netting. Be aware that they may not be fireproof, so care must be taken if using a stove or lantern under them.

If your tent accumulates a large number of unwanted visitors during the day, a quick puff of insecticide (not insect repellent) spray, some time before retiring, can be useful. If you must resort to swatting, avoid grinding mosquitoes into the tent fabric and causing blood-staining and an unsightly mess. I find that using the flat of my hand over the mosquito against the fabric and then moving the hand sideways over the fabric kills or disables them without really squashing them. Similarly, when taking down a tent containing well-fed, blood-bloated mosquitoes, I let the tent down flat to disable them, then shake the mosquitoes out of the tent before rolling it tightly.

Toilet tents. Defecating can be an excruciating experience in bug country, leading to "Mad Crapper Syndrome." A quick shot with spray repellent on the exposed areas is a partial solution. However, a toilet tent is worth considering with a larger group on a canoe or vehicle trip where weight is not a major concern. A cheap department store dome tent with the floor cut out to within 30 centimetres of the wall works very well. Be careful with the poor quality zipper, and if the poles have external ferrules, round off the corners of the ferrules with a file or grinder to make the poles easier to slide into the pole sleeves. The same tent can be used as a sweat lodge or sauna (in a different location, of course).

Cook tents. With larger groups on canoe trips or horse packing, it may be feasible to take a large mosquito net cook shelter to use as an eating/cooking/socializing centre. They can be purchased for as low as $70 and in bush country you can do without the heavy poles if you take lots of rope. Smaller mosquito net tents are light and allow two people to sunbathe, cook or admire the view from a sitting position. Spray with insecticide before occupying these shelters since they have no floor, and mosquitoes may otherwise erupt from ground vegetation.

Bug nets can be used in a buggy cabin or outside for sunbathing or cooking.

Other Problem Insects
Although blackflies and mosquitoes are the chief villains, other insects and members of the spider family can also make life unpleasant unless you are prepared.

Deerflies/horseflies. Deerflies or horseflies are annoying because of their large size and painful bite. They appear from nowhere and can be a considerable annoyance to hikers, especially on horse trails. Repellents seem less effective than with other insects unless they actually cover the entire skin surface. These pests are persistent, so it is no good just waving them away. However, their numbers can be small enough that you can exterminate your tormentors, especially if they are following your canoe. I wait until they settle and then wallop them, just before they bite. Tightly woven light fabric seems to discourage them.

Snipe flies are found in the southern half of Alaska in some mountain areas. They are active in the daytime and can bite through thin clothing if it is not loose fitting and tightly woven. Bites are painful for a while but unlike mosquito and blackfly bites, there is no visible sign of the bite.

Ticks. These members of the spider family are a problem because they may carry a disease. Rocky Mountain Spotted Fever, Tick Paralysis, Relapsing Fever, Eastern Equine Encephalitis and now Lyme Disease are all carried by ticks. Lyme disease is an increasingly serious concern in eastern Canada and Alaska. See Health section, page 281. Tick season is from spring through to fall. They are found in grass, brush and shrubbery in places inhabited by sheep, deer and other ungulates and will attach to people walking through or sitting in the vegetation.

The ticks require a blood meal from people or another passing animal to produce eggs. Luckily, ticks do not immediately attach to the skin, so you have time at the end of the day to remove all clothes and examine them and your body for ticks. The back of the neck, scalp and other hairy areas are common locations. Don't forget to check under your watch strap. The tick nymph is very small, about the size of a pinhead. The adult is larger and both can bite and transmit infection.

Light-coloured clothing that makes the ticks easier to see is a help, and pants should be tucked into socks. Ticks must be removed carefully. If the tick's head is not deeply embedded, it can be extracted by gentle pulling with tweezers, taking care not to crush the animal and force body contents out through its mouth and in under your skin. Special "tick pliers" and tick forceps reduce the risk of crushing the body. Whatever you do, do not pull so hard as to remove the body and leave the head embedded. Some people feel that it is better to encourage a more firmly attached tick to withdraw by itself by touching it with a still-hot extinguished match or with a Q-tip soaked in camp fuel (but not lit). However, when ticks release voluntarily they regurgitate a highly infectious brew of the disease-causing organisms into your body. Whatever method you use, the resulting wound should be carefully cleansed with antiseptic. Prompt removal (12-24 hours) of ticks makes Lyme Disease unlikely.

Bees, wasps and hornets. Problems with these insects can occur anywhere, but I have seen most cases associated with people bushwhacking, portaging, looking for secluded spots to attend to calls of nature, or foraging for firewood.

Anyone blundering into a nest or into a sapling or stump with a nest in it usually provokes a dramatically violent response from the inmates. The stings are very unpleasant, and are potentially life threatening in large numbers and even in small numbers to those who are allergic. You must cover the head and eyes as much as possible and vacate the area quickly, possibly into a creek or lake. Antihistamines are useful to relieve the pain and to reduce the extent of the allergic reaction. Topical analgesics are of some help, too.

If you are allergic you should carry an "Anakit" containing injectable epinephrine and a strong oral antihistamine, and you should receive training from your physician in how to self-administer the drug. Party members can assist in the administration but should avoid doing the actual injection unless they are medically trained or the victim is so severely affected as to be incapable. Adrenaline inhalers are now available so the drug can be administered in a less invasive manner.

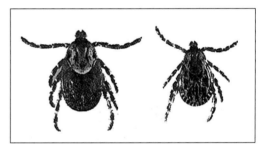

Wood tick. Female left, male right. Actual size about 1/4 inch long.

A selection of tick-removing devices. Tick removal must be done carefully and without squashing the tick. Left Ticklicker, centre Sawyer tick plier, right pointed tweezers.

Bears

The chances of ever seeing a bear on your trip are quite small, and the likelihood of having a problem are smaller still if you take certain basic precautions. Although a bear "incident" may be dramatic and something you'll never forget, the far less dramatic, but insidious, nonstop niggling of bugs is far more likely to adversely affect your trip. The three types of bears present different potential problems, and your reactions to them must be appropriate to the species involved.

Polar Bears

Polar bears are very different from black bears and grizzly bears because they are almost exclusively carnivorous and live by hunting and killing other animals. Man may be seen as food and therefore may be hunted by a bear with a meal in mind. (And they almost always do have a meal in mind!) Whatever you do, do not underestimate the seriousness of an encounter with a polar bear. Even if you are armed you need to be very much alert all the time for these cunning and tenacious hunters. Polar bears are definitely active at night (and you have to sleep sometime), and you will be very vulnerable at that time. In areas where the bears are likely to be encountered, extreme caution and a good lookout for bears must be maintained.

Polar bears are found along the coasts from Anticosti Island in the St. Lawrence to the mouth of the Yukon River, including all the coasts of Hudson and James bays and of the Arctic islands as far north as the northern tip of Ellesmere Island. Although that is their range, they are most common around the Arctic islands and around Southampton Island in the north end of Hudson Bay. They are also common along the Alaska coast north of Bering Strait, and in Amundsen Gulf and the Beaufort Sea. They are less common from Coronation Gulf east to the Boothia Peninsula.

In summer when the pack-ice melts and these white bears are on land, they are moderately conspicuous against the dark background of land devoid of snow, but are much less conspicuous on patchy snow or an all-snow background. They cannot hunt seals at this time, so they are likely to be very hungry.

Polar bears are expert hunters and when stalking humans, are capable of coming very close before you are aware of their presence. Special care must be taken not to send cooking smells wafting downwind because of the bears' excellent sense of smell. A friend who was involved in polar bear research told me that they could attract suitable study subjects seemingly from nowhere by just frying a piece of seal blubber and letting the smell drift downwind for awhile. Once a polar bear has found you, it is likely to stalk and hunt you. It may not attack, but if it has you in mind as prey it will probably continue until either it is successful, it is killed or you are able to leave the area in a manner such that the bear cannot follow. In some areas the bears are wary of man, but you have no way of knowing if a particular bear is wary or hungry. Friends have had very close encounters with polar bears where the bear was extremely close and they had to have the gun cocked and ready. Luckily, they were able to discourage the bear without shooting it.

Remember that you will probably not have the early warning provided to traditional travellers by their dogs. Think carefully before you deliberately plan recreational activities in an area known to have a high population of polar bears because it is quite possible that a conflict will occur that will require you to shoot a bear. Bear sprays have proven effective in two documented cases up to 1995.

Black Bears and Grizzly Bears

Grizzly "brown" bears are found in Alaska, the Yukon, the N.W.T., British Columbia and western Alberta. In the Northwest Territories they are found in the western mountains and in the Barren Grounds north of a line approximately from the Mackenzie Delta passing south of Great Bear Lake to Ennadai Lake in the southeast, then north to the mouth of the Back River. Black bears are found everywhere except western and Arctic coastal areas of Alaska, and areas north of the treeline in Canada.

Black bears and grizzly bears are omnivores, depending to a large extent on plants and carrion for their food. The number of incidents

Diggings where grizzly bears have been excavating ground squirrels are an impressive testament to the power of these animals. Fresh diggings for ground squirrels or roots are a clear warning of the proximity of a bear!

where black or grizzly bears have actually hunted people and attacked them to eat is very small and limited usually to old, injured and the occasional rogue bear. When blacks and grizzlies do attack humans it is usually because the bear has been surprised by the person's arrival in their territory and feels threatened or cornered. This is especially serious if the bear has young. The bear will also respond vigorously if it has food such as a carcass nearby that it wishes to defend. Sow grizzlies with cubs are particularly aggressive because, unlike black bears, they cannot send their cubs to safety up a tree. They don't climb well, nor do they live in places where there is as likely to be a suitable tree anyway. If a bear has stolen your food, it will guard it against your attempts at repossessing it.

How to Avoid Bear Problems

Because black bears and grizzly bears very rarely hunt and approach humans, there is much less risk than with polar bears. Incidents usually involve bears that were actually just minding their own business and were forced into a con-frontation they would have preferred to avoid, had they been given the chance. The best defence is to avoid close or provocative encounters, and there are a number of ways to do this.

The first precaution is to find out where bears are likely to be and to avoid those places at appropriate times of the year. Examples would be berry patches in late summer, creeks during salmon migration runs and lush alpine meadows and avalanche slopes colonized by plants such as hedysarum, which appeal to bears in summer. Although bears can travel considerable distances in a

Following some simple rules goes a long way to preventing bears from becoming a nuisance.

short time, park authorities will often have information about bear sightings so they can warn area users.

Secondly, you should give bears some warning of your approach so they have time to vacate the area. This entails making sufficient noise for the bear to know well in advance that you are coming. There is much less of a problem with large groups, partly because they inherently make more noise, but also because they look more threatening and the bear is more likely to flee even when surprised at close range. Statistics show no incidents where bears have attacked groups of six or more. There are proposals in some parks to impose a minimum party size rule to reduce the danger to park users.

Noisemaking may require systematic yoo-hooing in a singsong voice, especially near noisy creeks where there is a lot of background noise that would drown out the regular sounds of your approach. Some people, especially solo hikers, carry "bear bells" that make noise as they walk, but these devices can get on your nerves and bear bells are not very effective so you still need to yell frequently.

It is also important to make more noise if you are travelling into the wind, because both noise and smell are being carried away from the bear. All that's left to warn of your approach is the bear's mediocre eyesight, which it tends not to rely on as much as its sense of smell. You need to be even more careful if visibility is poor because of dense brush. Mountain bike riders need to be very alert because they travel fast and quietly. They are less likely to see signs of bear activity as they travel, and park authorities just recently issued a special warning to riders after a mountain biker surprised and was mauled by a bear.

Thirdly, you should learn to recognize a potentially hazardous area and make an appropriate detour. The area near a carcass or near offal left by hunters should be vacated immediately. Fresh diggings of plants in alpine meadows or of marmot burrows are also a warning to be very careful. A fresh, steaming bear scat on the trail means there is a fresh, steaming bear nearby! If there is any sign of garbage such as plastic bag fragments in the scat, be especially careful. And, as some joker once said, be even more careful if you see rings and watches in the

scat! Bears, like man, prefer to follow trails, so never camp on a trail, and be particularly wary when hiking on trails. If finding food has been difficult for bears, such as during a dry summer with a poor berry crop, they may well be driven by hunger into more populated areas in search of food. The combination of their boldness caused by hunger and proximity to people increases the likelihood of hazardous interactions between man and bear.

Any campsites with garbage are risky, particularly campsites used by hunters and fisherpeople because of the smells of fish and animal parts. You should ensure that your own camp and equipment do not attract bears looking for food or garbage. See section in Chapter Nine, page 255, on animalproofing food supplies. Avoid carrying smelly substances. Bears may approach man closely in response to food smells and other "unidentified but intriguing" smells.

Bear attacks on humans are complex events with many factors making each one different. For detailed information, read *Bear Attacks—Their Causes and Avoidance* by Stephen Herrero. You should "bear" in mind that:

- Bears generally want to avoid humans, so give them a chance to do so.

- If the bear obviously sees you as a threat, make yourself as unthreatening as possible by backing off, talking in a soft monotone and avoiding eye contact. Curling into a ball and playing dead also makes you appear less threatening, but it takes a lot of nerve to lie still and not fight back.

- If it is clear the bear has predation rather than self-defence on its mind, because it has stalked you or attacked at night, playing dead is useless. In this case be as threatening as possible by looking it in the eye, yelling, banging pots and fighting with anything and everything—axes, knives, rocks or sticks.

- Black bears climb trees easily and grizzlies have been known to pursue people part way up trees, so climbing a tree is not a guaranteed escape.

- Some close encounters are "curious investigation" rather than "attack" or "defence," and often involve young bears. These animals may be discouraged by noise, hostile activity or be distracted by a dropped pack.

This bear scarer pistol uses starter pistol blanks to fire either bang shells or screamer shells. Six rounds can be fired in quick succession and they are cheap.

Bear repellents. From left—foghorn, two capsicum sprays and a pencil flare gun with a bear banger round and a round attached.

Bearsprays do not project very far, especially against the wind. You must have the nerve to wait until the bear is very close.

Bear Repellents and Guns

None of these devices is any use unless it is handy for instant deployment and you know how to use it with certainty under stress.

"Bear bangers" or "crack shells" are pyrotechnics that throw an explosive projectile for about 100 metres. It then explodes up in the air with a very loud report. They come in various forms. Some attach to pencil-type flare projectors, others come as 12-gauge rounds for use in a flare gun or in a shotgun. Others are fired from an adaptor on a starter's pistol. Their effectiveness is quite variable, and depends on the bear's motivation and familiarity with man and such sounds. Flare guns have been used successfully against polar bears. You need plenty of shells to lay a pattern of flares in front of (not behind!) an approaching animal.

Pressurized gas foghorns that make a piercing sound have been effective in warding off some bears. These devices, which are designed for small boat use, are handy and light. They are readily available in marine goods' stores for use as foghorns.

Bear repellent sprays containing capsicum (the hot stuff in hot peppers) are generally felt to be very effective on black and grizzly bears if used in time and used correctly. The irritant effect on the eyes and nose causes the bear to retreat immediately, but causes no permanent harm. You must have the spray handy in a quick-draw holster, especially in dense bush where a bear can be on you in seconds. You must, however, hold fire until the animal is well within range, about six metres or less. My experience with one brand of these items is that the claimed range of four metres was a maximum because the spray is very easily deflected by wind. Four metres is **very** close to a bear! Remember that a bear encounter is more likely if you are approaching upwind or crosswind, and these circumstances do not favour use of the spray. The sprays only allow a few bursts, so you must hold your fire until certain of a hit. Unlike with crack shells, the bear is discouraged for a long time and usually won't return for at least 1/2 hour, if at all. The efficacy of capsicum spray bear repellents against polar bears has not been established experimentally, but some actual use reports indicate good success.

Some authorities may lead you to believe that capsicum sprays are illegal. They certainly are a prohibited weapon if used against humans or carried in "civilization." You should not experience problems if you have a bona fide reason to carry a capsicum bear spray. Mace is illegal in Canada and in a recent well-publicized case an elderly American visitor with mace in her purse was prosecuted vigorously.

Guns

Shooting a bear is fraught with practical, moral and legal difficulties. You should only shoot a bear as a last resort and if all the other precautions have failed to protect you.

Shooting is not an action open to visitors to Canada because they cannot obtain the firearm acquisition certificate needed to purchase a firearm. Firearms cannot be imported into Canada by a nonresident for purposes other than a sanctioned competition or an organized prebooked hunt. The legal owner of a firearm is unlikely to risk lending a firearm to a visitor. U.S. visitors to Alaska cannot transport a handgun through Canada, but can mail the unit to Alaska through the U.S. postal service. Americans can transport long-barrelled guns, if not of a prohibited type such as an assault weapon, through Canada to Alaska after suitable customs declaration. You can avoid the hassles by sending the item in bond. Canadians must allow plenty of time to obtain a Firearms Acquisition certificate and take the required training course, even for a shotgun.

It is also illegal to carry a firearm in Canadian national parks and in Denali, Glacier Bay and Katmai national parks in Alaska. Guns must be sealed for transport through Canadian national parks. They are discouraged on the Chilkoot Trail. In the rest of Alaska, guns may be carried, but generally they must be kept in view. If they are handy enough they are in view anyway.

Firearms are not a total panacea because like other devices they must be kept handy at all times, and particularly because they require considerable skill to be used effectively. Shooting at a charging bear demands skill and coolness, which are only really acquired with the combat-style type of practice most people don't obtain. Users must be practised enough to be able to shoot quickly and accurately when scared. A bear injured by a poorly aimed shot can be very dangerous.

A short-barrelled pump action 12-gauge shotgun such as a Winchester Defender is a common choice for bear defence. It has heavy hitting power at the close range at which you would be using it. To return the magazine capacity from three to five rounds, most people remove the plug that is normally fitted. There is usually less concern from the authorities about possessing a shotgun and shooting a bear with it than about using a rifle. If a person did shoot a bear with a shotgun it would have to have been close enough to have probably meant trouble. Nevertheless, it is unfortunate that bluff charges are a common occurrence and bluffing bears have probably been killed unnecessarily.

There are differing opinions regarding ammunition. Rifled slugs are heavy lead slugs of around 1 to 1-1/4 ounces that have enormous impact. On the other hand, heavy gauge buckshot (#00) gives some spread and more chance of hitting the target, but has poorer penetration and therefore must be used at close range. Some people load the magazine with alternating shot and slug. Ammunition of this type may not be readily available in the south, especially outside hunting season.

Bears are difficult to kill quickly. Their physiology is such that they are able to continue their intentions and do considerable damage for some time even after major circulatory system destruction, so a heart/lung shot is not quick enough. A shoulder shot can be effective at disabling the bear and stopping its charge while a second shot does the killing. A side neck shot may prove effective because the impact can break the neck even if the projectile misses the spine.

If using a rifle, it must be capable of firing a heavy bullet, for example, a 30-06 with softnose bullets in excess of 200 grains. Lighter loads simply do not have the necessary stopping power.

Heavy pistols such as .44 Magnums have been used for protection from polar and grizzly bears in the Canadian north by industrial workers operating with special permits and training. Handguns are generally illegal in Canada, though they are readily available in Alaska. At close range these heavy pistols do have the stopping power needed for bears. However, an inherent problem is whether the operator can shoot the first shot straight enough, let alone the subsequent shots after the recoil. Although handier than a shotgun or rifle to carry and have with you at all times, a weapon of this type is still a nasty, heavy lump to lug around and requires lots of expensive practice if you are to use it effectively.

If you do kill any animal in a defence situation, it is not yours to keep. The authorities require you to salvage and hand over the meat and in the case of bears, the hide and claws.

The vast majority of serious wilderness travellers, in Canada at least, travel unarmed. They rely more on keeping a clean camp and using their brains to avoid problems with bruins.

Bears are not a problem to get paranoid about—paranoia can be unconstructive in that it tends to cloud judgement and impinges adversely on your ability to take rational precautions. Learn about bears and keep your eyes and ears open and your brain in gear.

Even though the inhabitants of this filthy camp are gone, the hazard remains in the form of garbage-habituated animals, broken glass, nails and general filth.

Other Problem Animals

In addition to the more well-known bugs and bears, there are many other animals in the backcountry that can cause problems for travellers. Although their depredations are less dramatic and spectacular than those of bears, they can nevertheless create havoc. Be on your guard!

Man

A dangerous denizen of the outdoors is Homo sapiens. Worse still is the subspecies Homo nonsapiens, especially Homo nonsapiens intoxicatus. He is an even bigger hazard when equipped with motorized toys and firearms. See also the section in Chapter Four, Security.

Remember that nowadays not everyone in remote places is there for serious recreational purposes, and there are too many people who simply drive a 4x4 into the backcountry and sit and drink all weekend and then drive back in an impaired state. Substance abuse is common among local residents as well. Idyllic northern areas are not necessarily the paradise they seem to be.

Recreational motorboaters are another cause for concern, particularly because of drinking but often simply because of their carelessness, irresponsibility, bad manners, lack of consideration or plain stupidity. Even if he is looking, the vision of the steersman of an outboard motor craft is often obstructed by the raised bow. If you are in a low craft such as a kayak or canoe and cannot see the steersman of an approaching motorboat, that means they cannot see you, so be ready to take avoiding action. Bright-coloured clothing and paddle blades that you can wave are a big advantage over some of the dull, decorative or otherwise impractical fashion colours and patterns so often used. My white paddle blades are adorned with a fluorescent orange paint stripe to make them into a signalling device as well as to make them easier to find. Attaching a tall, flexible flag mast and fluorescent flag such as is used by cyclists is useful in some heavy use areas. Be particularly careful if you are directly into the sun from the motorboat and are therefore even more difficult to see. In fog, be aware that plastic kayaks and canoes do not reflect radar and do not produce a good radar image for other boat operators. A proper radar reflector is useful, but you can improvise one with a couple of foil space blankets loosely crumpled in a big garbage bag (preferably orange), inflated by mouth and tied onto your deck.

Jet boaters and jet skiers are an increasing menace on many of the larger rivers and on lakes. Be very wary around these individuals as too often their behaviour is irresponsible and inconsiderate toward wildlife and other river users. The large amount of noise made by most of their machines at least gives you some warning of their approach. A rapid retreat to the shore is often prudent, but their wake may then pound your boat on the rocks.

Rafters can be a hazard to other river users in canoes and kayaks. Rafts are often out of control and even in skilled hands lack the manoeuvrability of kayaks and canoes.

Irresponsible users can create hazards that remain long after their departure. In any location showing signs of use, be especially on the lookout for broken glass, nails and garbage that attracts animals. Sites accessible to motorized access, hunting and fishing sites are particularly likely to have these hazards.

Be very wary of recreational snowmobilers. Apart from the noise and smell of their machines, their behaviour can make life unpleasant or hazardous to others in the vicinity. Be especially careful in avalanche terrain because they can quickly get into a position where they can trigger an avalanche that buries you.

The hunting season is a time of year to be particularly cautious in the backcountry. It is absolutely essential to wear clothing that cannot be mistaken for wildlife. Orange is not safe unless it is fluorescent or is well on the red side of orange. I have somewhat faded orange life jackets and an anorak that are definitely too close to the colour of a deer for use in the fall, especially considering the effect a hunter's sunglasses can have on colours. Small white items, especially handkerchiefs, can be mistaken for the white tail "flag" of deer. I have black tights and a black fleece jacket that could be mistaken for a bear (remember, there is a spring bear hunting season, too).

In hunting season wear bright colours and make lots of human-type noise. Orange vests are available for a few dollars from hardware and hunting-fishing stores. They are useful to keep in your car to wear at accident scenes, etc.

Be very wary of hunters if you are in the woods during hunting season. They are not always careful enough about what they are really shooting at.

Moose, Elk and Buffalo

All of these animals can inflict serious injury with hooves as well as horns. Females are very protective of their calves, and you may not be aware of the presence of a calf because it is hidden, so you unwittingly come between mother and calf, provoking an attack. This is more likely to be a problem in parks where animals have become bold and are present in areas heavily used by man. I recently found myself about 10 metres from a moose calf while

I was canoeing a small creek. The calf on the bank was only a few days old and it was an enchanting sight. It was also quite scary realizing the cow could have been on me in seconds in the shallow water.

During the rutting season, moose, elk and bison bulls are particularly irritable and ornery and should be avoided. They are known to investigate and attack on sight anything that seems to be invading their territory. You can occasionally find small trees that have been stripped and mangled and these are innocent bystanders that have been beaten up by ornery bulls. Climbing a tree or cliff provides protection if you are quick enough.

Domestic Cattle

You may encounter cattle running free on public land, especially in the foothills of the Rockies and in parts of B.C. My experience has been that they are fairly skittish and usually move away, rather than being inquisitive nuisances around camp like English cattle. Presumably this is because they associate people with being chased, roped, branded, injected, dosed and with the loss of various bits of their anatomy. Bulls are sometimes encountered but they do not usually behave like the potentially deadly dairy bulls or rodeo bulls. Keep reasonably clear anyway and plan an escape route just in case.

Cougar

These animals are reclusive forest residents and it's a rare privilege to see one in the wild. However, they have been known to be driven by hunger, injury or old age to seek the easy prey of humans and their pets and livestock. Incidents of small children being attacked do occur, but they are rare. Children are exposed to many hazards in the outdoors, and this is just one more that parents should be aware of when providing for adequate control and supervision of small children outdoors. An approaching cougar has a meal on its mind, so fighting back, threatening it and appearing as large as possible are appropriate responses.

Wolves

Again, it's a privilege to see these magnificent animals in the wild. The wolf species has been badly treated by man, and it is much to their credit that there are so few documented cases of actual attacks on humans in North America. This is in contrast to European and Asian wolves, which have been responsible for attacks on humans. Certainly the risk is so slight as to be a nonissue. However, like a number of animals in the dog family, wolves can be infected by rabies and therefore behave totally out of character. A friend of mine was approached on the tundra by a wolf that later proved to be rabid. She was driven back to her helicopter, fending the beast off with packs and items of equipment. I was once approached to within about 30 metres by a wolf on an arctic tundra hilltop, and my thrill and excitement at this unusual honour was, I admit, tempered with thoughts as to whether this wolf was rabid, too. And I didn't have a helicopter equipped with a survival gun to retreat into. For a few magic moments we looked at each other before the wolf went on its way. They will prey on domestic dogs, eating them off their chains in some cases. They will also use a female in heat as a "bait bitch" to lure domestic dogs away from humans to become the main attraction at a feast. If you do see a wolf or a den, savour the privilege but be careful who you tell about it, and be vague about the location. There are plenty of people around still who will kill wolves on sight. Often this is simply because they view wolves as competitors that feed on ungulates they want to kill for themselves.

Coyotes

These animals are generally fearful of man, though in some areas they will come close to farms and homes in search of food. In some urban areas they have adapted to life in ravines and other wooded natural park areas and can do well on a diet of cats and small dogs. Friends with a house abutting on one of these areas known to be inhabited by these bold urban coyotes were warned not to leave their infant child in the yard unsupervised. Coyotes can carry rabies, and also use the bait bitch technique.

Foxes

Like coyotes, these animals are becoming increasingly habituated to man and urbanization, so there is probably more chance of encountering them at close range in more civilized areas than in the wilderness. They are also commonly affected by rabies, and any fox getting too close, behaving oddly or erratically or obviously sick must be avoided because of the possibility of becoming infected. Arctic foxes are bold and inquisitive, and after the novelty of their presence wears off, they can be a real nuisance around camps.

Porcupines

These slow, lumbering animals can create major problems for outdoors people in two ways. The obvious problem is injury from their quills, but a far more likely and serious problem is that they are destructive gnawers of gear. Although there is little risk of humans becoming impaled with porcupine quills, domestic dogs frequently run afoul of the spiky defences. Even intelligent dogs don't learn to avoid porcupines, so the fact that your dog has had one run-in doesn't mean he won't have another. Removing the barbed quills with pliers from a frightened, angry and confused pet without anaesthetic (for the dog, though you will probably feel

Porcupine. Photo courtesy Primrose Wilderness Encounters, Whitehorse.

Porcupines can do a lot of damage to vehicles by chewing on rubber hoses, etc., and in some areas it is essential to place chicken wire around your vehicle when leaving it. Prop it up with sticks or logs.

you want one, too!) is a thoroughly unpleasant experience. Broken or incompletely removed quills are a serious problem because the barbs cause them to work their way in deeper. The dog will almost certainly have to be evacuated even if only for suitable antibiotic therapy.

More serious and common problems stem from the porcupine's propensity for gnawing on anything that tastes salty. This means anything contaminated with sweat, urine or road salt. Porcupines will gnaw on the rubber hoses and wiring on the underside of parked vehicles. This can obviously have quite serious results, and in some areas it is enough of a problem to warrant wrapping chicken wire around the parked vehicle.

I have encountered the problem myself near Hyder, Alaska where we were awoken by the sounds of gnawing underneath the van in which we were sleeping. The beast was not discouraged and we had to move to another location. The locals were not at all surprised and asked whether we had seen the gnawed plywood road signs. The parking lot at the trailhead for the Bugaboos and Conrad Kain hut is so notorious that everyone fences their vehicles. Last time I was there in 1992 other users of the parking lot had left a vast supply of mesh.

Porcupines will also gnaw shoes and boots left outside the tent. Sweat-contaminated bike saddles, helmets, paddles, life jackets, packs, etc., are all at risk. If you stash them in the bush for any reason you may wish to suspend them out of reach of the porcupines (who do climb trees, so dangle the items clear of the tree).

Raccoons

These animals are bold, strong and equipped with powerful teeth and jaws. They can be a real pest in urban areas as well as in campgrounds in some parts of the country where they will approach campers and enter tents in search of food and garbage. They are quite dexterous and can manipulate latches and other closures. Like most animals they can be vicious if cornered or thwarted. Their offspring are cute to most people's way of thinking, but should never be handled. It is too easy to do something the mother sees as a threat, eliciting a dangerous response, especially to the small children who are at-

Porcupines will gnaw anything sweaty, particularly boots and shoes, so do not leave equipment accessible to these pests, especially at night.

tracted by animal young. Raccoons can carry rabies. Although they are primarily residents of the eastern woodlands, they are now increasing in number in southern Alberta.

Skunks

Skunks have a famous propensity for spraying people and dogs with a foul-smelling liquid when frightened or cornered. The smell of the butyl mercaptan in the spray is pervasive and lingering and can make the contaminated article unusable. A sprayed dog will be an unwelcome member of the party for a week, and just when you think the smell has gone it will be revived when the dog gets wet! The mercaptan is broken down by oxidation with bleach, and a 1:5 or 1:10 solution of household bleach will do the job. Unfortunately, this sort of strength of bleach will damage many fabrics, and needless to say should not be used on a dog! The traditional standby is washing with tomato juice. Skunks are also affected by rabies so don't try to make friends with them. You occasionally hear the nightmare story of the small child playing with the "strange cat." Do not allow children to approach or play with any wild animal.

Squirrels, Chipmunks, Ground Squirrels

These denizens of many a campsite are often regarded as being cute and part of the scene. They are generally harmless, but are capable of administering a painful bite if hurt or cornered. They also carry a good population of fleas that can carry disease. It is best not to feed or encourage these animals for their own sake, and it is illegal to feed any wildlife in national parks anyway.

Packrats

These animals can be a real pest around huts and cabins. Their tendency to collect and hide small shiny objects can result in the loss of a vital item of gear.

Martens and Wolverines

These animals are generally shy except near cabins and camps where they can be a nuisance rather than a danger. Their depredations on the food supply are the biggest risk, though when cornered they can be vicious and tenacious fighters. Attempts to repossess your food can elicit an incredibly vicious response. They also tend to leave a foul smell, and this coupled with damage can render a cabin uninhabitable. They have been known to descend chimneys or tear out stovepipes to gain entry.

Mice

Although small, these animals can play havoc with food supplies and gear by nibbling holes in food bags and contaminating the food. They are likely to be a problem around huts if there is not a resident weasel around. They also get into parked vehicles through the tiniest of holes, including heater ducts. We have twice had mice enter our van at night and start nibbling our supplies.

The Hantavirus, which is carried in Deer Mouse saliva, faeces and urine, has spread into southwestern Canada and causes a serious, often fatal, disease in man. See Health section.

Snakes

There are a few rattlesnakes in some areas of Canada, including the hot, dry interior of B.C., the badlands of Alberta and Saskatchewan, and a few areas around southern Georgian Bay in Ontario where the Massasauga rattlesnake is occasionally found.

Given the chance, snakes will move out of your way, but if trodden on or otherwise provoked they will quite understandably bite.

Keeping your eyes open and listening for the rattle is a good defence. Small children should not be allowed to crawl around until the area has been thoroughly checked for snakes. Wearing pants or gaiters is a sensible precaution, and special care should be taken if climbing or scrambling on rocks not to put your hand on a dozing rattler who then strikes at your face!

Bites are painful and serious for weak individuals and children, but rarely fatal. Antidotes are usually available at a local hospital, but evacuation times may be long so the situation can become more serious. Carrying a snake bite kit and knowing how to use it would be a good idea in areas where these snakes are found. There are differing opinions about the advisability of some of the traditional methods of treating snakebite, so read an up-to-date first aid manual.

Birds

Ravens can be very destructive to food supplies, including food suspended in a cache or insufficiently buried in snow. Their powerful beaks will break through plastic containers such as margarine tubs. They are generally more trouble closer to civilization where they are more used to humans, but they are also a pest high on Denali, and we came close to losing food to ravens deep in the St. Elias Range. Arctic terns will press their divebombing attacks on people walking close to nest sites and can inflict a painful, infection-prone wound on unprotected heads. I also wandered into an area where a large hawk must have had its nest, because it dived at me and let me know in no uncertain terms that I was not wanted. I was very glad it did not make contact.

Shellfish

Paralytic shellfish ("red tide") poisoning from eating contaminated shellfish is a real risk. Filter-feeding molluscs such as clams and mussels become contaminated with potent toxins absorbed from the plankton they feed on. These toxins can have serious effects on humans, so be sure to heed any posted warning signs and to inquire locally from fisheries or coastguard officials before setting out. Some people feel that warnings are maintained to minimize tourist depredations on the local shellfish, but it would be unwise to make any assumptions about this. The butter clam of the west coast can retain a toxic residue in the siphon and gills for a long time, possibly as much as two years after a red tide outbreak. Remove these parts before cooking so as not to transfer the poison to the edible portions.

Scorpions

Scorpions are found in the dry badlands of southern Alberta and Saskatchewan, and also in the Okanagan Valley of British Columbia. They look like the dangerous scorpions of tropical countries, but in fact their sting is no more serious than a bee sting. However, like the bee sting it could bring on a serious or fatal allergic reaction in susceptible individuals.

Fish

Some easily caught sea fish such as some of the rockfish and sculpin of the Pacific coast are quite spiny, and puncture wounds from these spines can be painful and easily become infected. I always use leather gloves when landing these fish in a kayak. A hook remover or pliers can also prevent painful injuries when trying to unhook fish in the confines of a kayak. I carry a short stick to club fish in the landing net before bringing them into the kayak. This is particularly important if the fish is still hooked—you don't want a fish with two barbs of a treble hook dangling from its mouth thrashing about between your legs while you head for shore to get sorted out! Of course, you must always have a knife handy in case you have to cut loose a fish that is dangerously big to bring into a kayak. Trying to stab a thrashing fish is likely to be hazardous. Large fish, especially halibut, can do serious damage to your boat. Thrashing fish have been known to damage the bottoms of small boats enough to cause them to leak badly. I once hooked a very large lingcod from our folding kayak but there was no way I was prepared to risk having it in the boat, especially as they are tough to kill. Luckily, there was a larger boat nearby who hauled it aboard and dealt with it for us.

Water Parasites

Swimmer's itch is an unpleasant disorder caused by minute parasites that inhabit warm, generally shallow water areas. They burrow into the skin, causing irritation, a rash, and possibly hives and blisters. They are found in both fresh and salt water but more commonly cause problems for fresh water bathers. Avoid shallow warm water. Towelling vigorously after leaving the water is usually sufficient to prevent the problem from occurring. If showers are provided at a public swimming area, use them. They may be there specifically to allow people to rinse off immediately after swimming to reduce the risk of swimmer's itch.

Problem Plants

There are some plants, which you should be aware of, that can make life very unpleasant and can turn your trip into a disaster.

Poison Ivy

This plant has ruined many a holiday. The resulting allergic reaction, pain and weeping sores after someone has unwittingly had contact with the plant are extremely unpleasant and difficult to treat. One of the worst features of poison ivy is that a hand used to scratch the initial irritation becomes contaminated with the irritant oil from the plant and spreads the oil to other parts of the body. The oil is also spread on clothes, equipment and pets' fur.

The key is to be aware of the existence of this plant, especially in temperate forest areas of southern Canada, and to know what it looks like. Treatment involves careful washing with soap and water of the affected area and any other surfaces that could have been contaminated. Preparations are available that are supposed to be helpful specifically for poison ivy, but the one I have seen is simply a topical anaesthetic containing benzocaine. Others such as Caladryl have the soothing effects of the antihistamine Benadryl in conjunction with calamine. Topical steroids are of limited value. Medical assistance is useful in serious cases.

Poisonous Fungi

Mushrooms and their relatives have negligible food value so eating them is an activity with lots of potential risk and without enough worthwhile benefit to justify the risk. "Experts" should be particularly careful about identifying supposedly edible varieties in parts of the country remote from their normal sphere of operations.

Devil's Club

This obnoxious thorny plant makes bushwhacking a thoroughly unpleasant experience in the wetter forest areas of the west, especially the Coast ranges. Time spent researching the existence of a trail or logging road can pay dividends. Do not hold out great hopes of bushwhacking more than one kilometre per hour in some types of coastal forest, and in some places that would be fast progress!

When choosing a river crossing location, take a look to see what is downstream in case you end up swimming. A log jam can be a death trap.

Water Hazards

The untamed waterways of wilderness areas can present serious barriers and hazards to the unwary or the uninformed. Accidents involving water can result in hypothermia and other injuries, as well as equipment loss or damage.

River Crossings

That thin, almost imperceptible blue line on your topo map can be a major barrier to your progress, even in quite populated areas. Although the creek or river may be across an obvious route into an interesting area, in Canada and Alaska it is quite possible that there is no bridge or easy way of crossing. This may be simply because the area does not receive the use to warrant the expense of a bridge, or it may be a deliberate omission in an attempt to discourage use. A trail or logging road shown on the map or on air photos as crossing a watercourse does not indicate that there is or even ever was a bridge there. The trail may be a winter-use-only trail. Foreign visitors should be aware that in Canadian and Alaskan winters, water levels drop and creeks and rivers can freeze strongly enough for vehicle travel. Or the trail

may be a summer exploration road used by vehicles capable of fording quite deep water. It may just be a horse trail—much of the west was traditionally travelled on horseback and horses forded deep water. Inquiries before your trip can save a great deal of aggravation. Officials of local forestry, parks or recreation areas can be very useful, as can local travellers. I know of two key trails that end in thigh-deep fords, but in both cases there is a bridge a short distance away, out of sight. I also know of two bridges that are seasonal—one is removed in the fall so winter avalanches do not take it out, another is only in place for the winter logging season and is removed before spring floods.

The many styles of improvised crossings are risky. If you intentionally or unintentionally end up floundering in the water, you must be aware that the force of the water on your whole body as opposed to just your legs is very large. If you are not used to swimming or floundering in rock-filled moving water, it can be a very unnerving experience, particularly when unexpected, when wearing boots, when carrying a pack and in cold water. It's dangerous to stand up in a fast current because if your foot becomes trapped between two rocks or in a crevice, the current will pin you down flat in the water. You are then in a helpless position in which you can easily drown. A kayak racer was drowned in front of hundreds of spectators in just such a situation.

Because a mishap can be so dangerous, the most important thing when planning a safe river crossing is to be aware of what could happen if your plan goes wrong, and to plan and act accordingly. If you slip on that key rock, what will happen? Which way will you fall? Will you injure yourself? Will that dry rock you jump onto be wet and slippery after the first person's passage? If while wading you are washed off your feet, will you end up soaked and hypothermic or swimming or washed over a waterfall? Will you have to abandon your pack to swim? If you don't reach that eddy with your raft or by swimming, where will you end up? In a log jam? Over the Killer Fang Falls? If you are driving a vehicle, what will you do if it stalls or gets stuck in the river? (See section on Fords and Flooded Areas, page 229.)

There is not necessarily a bridge where a map shows a trail crossing a river.

You also particularly need to consider whether the crossing will be reversible for your return trip. That easy downward jump may be upward on the return, or the water level may be higher with rainfall or afternoon snowmelt, so the easy wade of the morning may become a dangerous nightmare in the evening, with considerable risk of hypothermia, loss of equipment, wetting of equipment or personal injury. A long detour may be needed, or a long wait until the water level drops after the rain stops or the weather cools down if it is meltwater.

Safe river crossings therefore require careful risk assessment and a healthy respect for the power of moving water.

Getting yourself across is one thing, but dealing with a heavy pack is another. A pack will float if you can keep the water out of it. It takes a long time for enough water to get into it to sink it if the items inside are in closed stuff bags and the spindrift collar is well tied. Although a full-size loaded pack feels very heavy, its density is substantially lower than that of water, unless it is unusually full of climbing hardware. Carefully placing it inside a large garbage bag and tying the top of the bag securely may be all you need to float the pack across, particularly if you inflate your Therm-a-Rest to take up more room

This method is much safer than trying to balance on one of the logs.

in the bag. Double-bagging is safer, and try to establish which way up the pack will float and position the top of the bag accordingly.

Stepping stones. Stepping stones are great as long as you don't slip, so don't push your luck with long strides or hops. People subconsciously tend to aim for smooth flat surfaces to land on, but in reality, sharp edges are better. You achieve grip from an interlocking of the rock with a patterned boot sole rather than the unreliable friction between a smooth wet rock and rubber. Try to avoid splashing, so the rock is still dry for the next person.

People also try to keep their feet completely out of the water, which greatly reduces foot placement options and increases the risk factor. Many people do not make good use of the fact that a hiking boot will easily stand a few moments' immersion without leakage, and with a good gaiter will keep water out even if briefly immersed above the ankle. The elasticized Patagonia Instigaiters seal really well. Putting your foot down in gaps between rocks where it cannot slip, or walking quickly through shallows are available options, giving you more choices of safer routes across the creek. The more options you have the better your chances of avoiding those jumps where you have to hope your foot won't slip and deposit you full length and injured in the water.

Logs as bridges. Only occasionally will you find that perfect log to walk along across the river. They often slope one way or the other, are likely to be wet and slippery, and may have numerous branches and stubs for you to trip over. Falling off may have serious consequences—you could end up injured or unconscious in a fast-moving stream.

Two logs, one to stand on and one higher to hold on to, is a better option. Walking with one foot on each of two logs close side by side is yet another alternative.

If you have a long pole, you can use it as a third leg, alternately leaning on it and moving it as you move across the log. This is much easier said than done because the force of the current on the pole makes it hard to manoeuvre. Use it with its thin end down so it presents minimum area to the force of the current. Also, that way as much of its weight as possible is helping you hold it down against the force of the current and against its buoyancy.

Walking a log may get you across bone dry or it may get you into the water with a broken bone.

A pole can give you a lot more security when walking along a log or across stepping stones.

Yet another option is to hold on to a pole, one end planted in the middle of the river a few metres upstream of the log on which you are walking. Face upstream, leaning on the pole and shifting your grip down the pole as you shuffle sideways toward the centre of the stream and then up the pole again as you approach the other side. This only works if the stream is narrow, so the pole only swings through about 45 to 60 degrees as you go across the river. Attach a rope so the pole can be returned to the next person.

Straddling a log and inching your way across is not always practical because it is likely to be a coniferous log with numerous protruding branches and spikes. A small pocket saw could be used to remove the obstructions. Attach it to your belt or wrist with a lanyard so you can't drop it. Keeping your heavy boots on improves your balance by lowering your centre of gravity. Keep your legs hanging as vertically as possible but lean forward and keep your head low.

It will be difficult to keep your balance while wearing a pack. If using the straddling method, maybe make two trips with a half load each or try carrying your pack in front of you. Tie a rope to the pack so it can be retrieved by someone else on shore if dropped, but do not risk becoming tangled in it if you fall in with it.

The traditional tightrope walker's pole really helps, especially if it is bent and droops below the level of your feet.

Safer wading techniques. When wading you need to be particularly aware of the force exerted by moving water and of the difficulties imposed by invisible and loose, slippery footing. A small increase in the velocity of moving water produces a disproportionately large increase in the force it exerts on you. Therefore as you move into deeper and faster water, you can quickly be subjected to forces you would not have expected as you started to wade. Falling over in wading-depth water in a fast, rocky stream is an unpleasant experience because you get bumped around and it is difficult and dangerous to stand up. Also, it's barely deep enough to swim vigorously without banging into rocks. As with other types of crossings, look carefully before you start, to see what will happen if you run into problems. Choose a

Wading ice cold northern rivers can be excruciating unless you have neoprene booties and sandals to wear in the water.

A braided section of stream often provides fording opportunities.

place with a firm, gravelly bottom and where you will be washed into safer rather than more dangerous water if you fall in. Look for a place where the stream is slower, even if it means getting wetter higher up your body. This could be an outlet from a lake or an inlet (safer if you swim well), or the pool below a drop. You will stay drier by wading a lot of shallow, wide channels such as in a place where the stream is braided, rather than one deep one. However, in braided areas, although the water is shallow, the water may be fast and the bottom unstable.

If you have to return the same way, consider carefully before you cross what will happen if the water rises during the day as a result of snowmelt or rain. If you cross in the early morning you may not be able to get back in the late afternoon and may have to camp until the next morning's low water level.

Never wade barefoot, partly because you are more likely to stumble and also because you could end up losing your boots and be stuck in the middle of nowhere with no footwear. Some people carry shoes or sandals to use for wading, but these provide scant support and protection among the often moving boulders on the bottom of a stream. Removing your socks and putting your boots back on for the wade is a safer system. Dry them inside with a towel as soon as you get ashore. GoreTex socks over your regular socks will help keep your socks dry afterward in the damp boots, especially those with moisture-absorbing fabric linings.

Wading glacial streams is agonizing, particularly when your legs and feet start to warm up again. Added problems are that you cannot see the bottom through the silty water and you can't feel it either once your feet go numb.

If you have to wade glacial streams, it is well worth carrying some neoprene windsurfer/canoeing booties or socks to keep your feet warmer and to maintain some feeling so you can keep your footing better. You can wear neoprene socks in your boots or wading shoes.

Cheap quality and lighter grade fisherman's waders are used by some people, but they are still a bit heavy for backpackers. Cheapie vinyl "stocking waders" are basically waterproof pants with waterproof socks attached. You wear them over your socks and pants and inside your

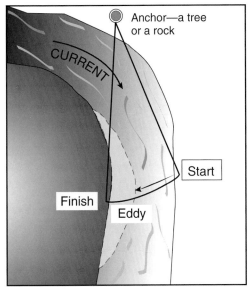

Pendulum River Crossing
With the anchor suitably located on a bend, the wader holding the rope reaches the riverbank downstream of his start. This makes wading easier than having to go upstream, which is what happens on a straight stretch with the anchor on the starting side.

boots, and they are much lighter than boot waders. Pants for water sports with latex ankle gaskets are lighter than waders, but like any waders they can be dangerous if you fall in and they fill with water. Keep a knife readily accessible to slit them if you have to in an emergency. Wading clothes and boots can be passed to and fro across the river so you only need one pair for the party. If you have a rope or long cord across the river, you tie the waders to the centre of it and keep it tight while one side takes in and the other side pays out rope. If you have a canoeist's dry bag to put the waders in, it doesn't matter if the rope sags into the water. Or you can throw the waders across—perhaps tied to a light safety line in case you have a bad throw! If you weight them with something, do not use a rock because if they land on a hard surface a puncture will result. Use a baggie of sand. We once camped near a fishing camp when one of the guides received an air-drop of his waders after he made the serious mistake of leaving them behind. He was relieved to see them land on target, but less than pleased to find them weighted with a pile of fish heads and guts by "friends." They weren't letting him off lightly from his mistake!

Practising a pendulum crossing. The person is holding on and leaning back against the rope attached to a rock upstream. DO NOT TIE YOURSELF TO THE ROPE.

Crossing a river in a group using the Conga sidestep method.

One way of wading with two people supporting each other in a four-legged structure.

Three people wading as a six-legged rotating stable structure.

Wearing rain pants and gaiters diminishes the rate at which cold water numbs your legs. However, avoid elastic cuffs because if you fall in, as with waders, the pants can fill with water through pocket slits and create a hazard.

Wading while facing upstream causes the force of the current to lock your knees rather than collapse them. Wading sideways with legs apart for more stability keeps one leg in the eddy of the other part of the time. Take a diagonally downstream route across the river. If you can find a stick strong enough yet not so thick as to be deflected by the water too much, use it as a third leg for support. Better still is to attach a rope to a tree or rock as far upstream as possible and lean back against the tension of the rope as you move in an arc across the river. Never tie yourself to the rope but hold on with both hands, perhaps to a stick tied to the rope as a toggle. If the rope is really long you can use it as a continuous loop between you and the anchor, and retrieve it once the party is across. Ideally, the fastest part of the current will be on the side where the anchor is. If you can choose an anchor on the outside of a bend so it is straight upstream along the line of the current at the middle where you are crossing, your task will be easier.

Another strategy is to wade with a partner, facing each other and gripping each other's arms. Put the stronger partner on the upstream side and move *only one leg at a time* so you always have a stable three-legged support. With more equal-sized partners some people find it easier for each to be sideways to the current, but then one person cannot see where they are going. A threesome can rotate their way across the river, two supporting the one who is moving. They can also walk across with linked arms, in a line parallel to the current. The largest person should be at the upstream end.

Yet another variant is the Water Conga where the entire party forms a line one behind the other, parallel with the current and holding around each other's waists or packs. Only the person at the upstream end is subjected to the full force of the current, and you have plenty of points of support because only one leg is moved at a time.

The problem with these multi-person methods is that although there is less risk of falling in, if you do so the consequences are more serious because there are multiple victims to take care of instead of one.

Wading problems are compounded by a pack, particularly if you fall in. Loosening or undoing the hip belt facilitates getting rid of the pack when swimming but increases the likelihood of falling over in the first place. Losing your pack is a significant possibility, so wear enough clothes to survive and make sure you have survival items such as matches in a waterproof container in your pocket.

Swimming. This may be your only option. Although it demands a higher level of commitment than wading, swimming in a suitably chosen place can be a lot less hazardous than a wade in fast shallows that suddenly becomes a swim in fast shallows! Ideally you choose a place with minimal current, but if you must swim in a current, choose a place where there are no hazards downstream for a long way, because you will probably end up much farther downstream than you think you will. Boulderfields, trees and log jams that water flows **through** to form deadly "strainers" are far more dangerous than rocks the water flows **around**. The force of the current can pin you helplessly in a strainer. It may bump you into a rock but it is unlikely to pin you.

Also, choose a place where there is a good landing on the other side such as a beach or eddy. Don't worry so much about the starting side—it's easy enough to get started in deep, uninviting fast water but much more difficult to stop!

If the water is cold, you must be aware of the fact that you will rapidly lose strength, so do not attempt long crossings in cold water. Swimming naked is faster than swimming clothed, but if there is subsequently a hold-up in getting your gear across or you lose it you are in big trouble! It's a good idea to tow at least some of your clothes and key survival items across with you in a sealed plastic bag. Clothes also protect you from abrasion and to some extent from cooling in cold water. Beware of water pooling in the arms and legs of rain gear with elastic cuffs. Only use garments with openable cuffs.

Swimming on your back with your feet downstream is the safest way to swim if there are rocks in the water. By swimming in an upstream direction at an angle to the current you can minimize your downstream progress.

If you present your body at an angle to the current and swim so as not to lose ground, the current pushes you across the river. This is the same principle as the "ferry glide" used by canoeists and of course by ferrymen. Do not risk putting your feet down until you can easily stand up, because of the risk of foot entrapment and drowning mentioned earlier. Swimming on a belay can be very dangerous because a combination of rope tension and current can force you under the water. The belayer with whom you cannot communicate may end up holding you helplessly in place when you want to be free to swim away downstream.

Of course, you still need to get your pack across the river. A log raft big enough to support it totally out of the water will be surprisingly big and not really the kind of thing you want to try to push as you swim. However, you might be able to wade with it if the current is slow, and it would be something you could pull across later with a rope.

Another solution is to waterproof your pack and float it across. Use a big garbage bag as already mentioned. Or place your tarp (or your tent, ground sheet side down), on the ground, place your pack on top and gather the fabric together above the pack and tie it with cord. Make sure your pack is heaviest side down, and you may want to increase the buoyancy by padding the bundle with moss, duff, bracken, soft branches, etc. This will also soak up initially any water that leaks.

River crossings, especially swimming and wading, do expose you to the risk of drowning. Although improvised "life jackets" can be more of a hazard than a help, you may feel the risk of rigging one is worth it. The biggest risks occur if the improvised garment does not stay in place and slips up and pins the arms like a straitjacket, or slips too low and lifts up the waist area, allowing the upper body to sink. Also, the improvised jacket may make it difficult to turn over or to swim. Most life jackets and buoyancy aids have the greatest amount of buoyancy on the chest, so you are turned on your back. A Therm-a-Rest, folded lengthwise and wrapped around the chest is a possibility. One way to keep it in place is to wear a shell garment over it with the waist string done up tightly. Bundles of clothes sealed in plastic bags can be similarly held in place. A U-shaped head hole can be cut with a sharp knife in a closed cell foam pad and the flap worn behind the head like a lifejacket collar. The foam pad is still perfectly usable and the hole is easy to repair with contact cement.

I repeat that improvised life jackets can be more hazard than they are worth if they hinder swimming.

Using inflatables. Cheap, light one- and two-person inflatable rafts have been used with success for river crossings. They are often available in department stores and sporting equipment stores. If the party is large, the five kilogram or so weight becomes less significant. For paddles you can just take with you 20 centimetre by 45 centimetre pieces of light plywood, pre-drilled with two rows of holes five centimetres apart so they can be easily laced onto convenient poles. If you have a rope you can attach the raft to the centre and pull it

A cheap inflatable raft is light enough to be carried among a large party for major crossings.

back and forth across the river. Don't trust the welded-on rings of cheapie inflatables to hold against the force of fast water. Rig a bridle around the raft to spread the load. If you leave it on the riverbank for your return, tie it down so it can't blow or wash away. Porcupines and other nibblers can play havoc with your inflatable, so it may be worth suspending it out of harm's way. Hide the paddles separately to discourage use of the raft by joy-riders.

Log rafts and other rafts. We've all seen those drawings of neat rafts made of straight logs, all the same diameter and length, etc. Great if you happen to be near a good supply of suitable dry dead logs and have an axe or saw and lots of rope. Easier said than done, but you might find some suitable stuff in a drift pile or an old burn or a lodgepole pine forest, but it's not easy. A folding saw is a great help. Leave some branches sticking up along the outside logs so that you have something to use for oarlocks, because you have far more power using the leverage of a sweep or oar than by using a paddle. If you are short of rope, clamp the logs together with a cross log top and bottom, tied together at each end. Notching will help produce a more stable structure but is not really necessary. See sketch.

Your raft will have very little freeboard and waves will wash over it, so make a platform to keep your gear dry. A bundle of brushwood will do. The raft will be very unwieldy, so if you are crossing a river, allow an enormous amount of room for downstream drift unless it is tethered to a rope across the river.

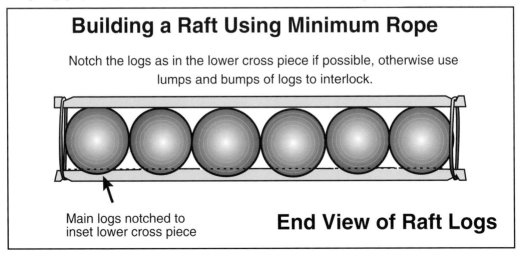

Building a Raft Using Minimum Rope

Notch the logs as in the lower cross piece if possible, otherwise use lumps and bumps of logs to interlock.

Main logs notched to inset lower cross piece

End View of Raft Logs

Rafts can be improvised using an upturned dome tent fly sheet filled with leaves or grass or bracken and then tied. Try to keep the middle a bit hollow so that the load is low. Hardly a sleek and easily managed craft, and not one to use unless you have a tent repair kit and feel the risk of damage is worth it!

Rope crossings. The "zip-line" is a way of using a rope to get swimmers very quickly and reasonably safely across a river. Because it is fast, chilling is minimized. It consists of a rope stretched across the river at less than a 45 degree angle to the current, leading downstream from the starting side and just clear of the water. The swimmer clips a carabiner or crevasse rescue pulley and a short sling onto the rope and enters the water on their back, holding the end of the sling to their chest. **Do not clip your body into the sling unless you have a system that allows instant release under tension**, such as a kayaker rescue harness. The downstream force of the current pushes the swimmer rapidly downstream along the rope, a direction that also happens to be across the river. The angle must be enough and the rope must be tight enough so that there is not much sag, otherwise there is not enough angle to the current once you reach halfway. A light rope can be used to return the pulleys and carabiners, which of course should not be thrown if there is any risk of them hitting a rock. Wet clothes could also be returned so that each person in the party can cross with the protection of clothing, but only one set of clothes in the party gets wet. Packs can be sent across on the zip-line. If the rope is doubled it can be retrieved once you are across.

Occasionally, small cable cars for river flow gauging purposes are found across rivers in remote places. These are usually padlocked to prevent unauthorized use. However, people have rigged their own pulleys or carabiners on the cables and pulled themselves across, usually ending up with their hands covered in grease off the cable and cut by worn strands of wire.

"Tyrolean traverse" types of crossings look very heroic in the photos, but unless you know exactly what you are doing and have a suitable rope, they can be a nightmare. If the system

Using a zip-line to cross deep, fast water. The person is holding on to a short length of rope attached to a pulley on the rope stretched at an angle across the river.

fails and someone is dropped from a height into a rocky river amid a tangle of rope, you have big trouble. Climbing ropes are very stretchy and prone to sagging unless tensioned to a very high degree. Also, the weight of a person in the middle of a taut rope exerts an enormous force on the rope and anchors, far greater than the weight of the person. A slacker rope produces less force, but when a person is in the middle of the river on a sagging rope, they often face a difficult uphill haul to the far side. Climbers' Prusik slings can be used to make that part easier. Because of the serious consequences associated with a system failure, constructing and using suspended systems requires a knowledge of rope work as well as suitable ropes, and specialized instruction beyond the scope of this book.

I hope after reading all this you will have more ideas to draw on and adapt to the particular situation you encounter. However, avoid the trap of using a more elaborate and risky system than you need to, just for the experience of using it. Keep a healthy respect for the power of moving water and a keen eye on the potential consequences of something going wrong. Be prepared to wait for the water to recede, to change the route or to change the plan.

Travel on Frozen Lakes and Rivers

Frozen lakes and rivers are the winter high-ways of the Canadian and Alaskan wilderness. However, they can present traps for the un-wary. Falling through the ice on a cold day is the worst-case accident for most winter travel-lers. You become soaked and so does your gear and you quickly become helpless—even if you do manage to get out. That's not easy with a full pack and skis or snowshoes on, and you can't afford to jettison the gear. You are in a life-threatening situation unless you have access to someone else's dry gear or have a reliable firestarter such as a Skyblazer Hot Shot fire-starter flare and lots of easily gathered fire-wood. Read Jack London's sobering short story *To Build A Fire*.

Opinions differ as to what is a safe ice thickness, but five centimetres is often quoted as a minimum for skiers who are well dis-persed and moving. Snowshoers may need a bit more, foot travellers still more. However, this is assuming it is solid blue-black water ice with no air in it, rather than a white, frozen, wet snow crust or springtime candle ice. You don't know how thick the ice is unless you cut holes every few metres. Just because it is five centi-metres in one place does not mean it won't be only two centimetres somewhere else. Also, you don't know what sort of ice is hidden under the snow, and actually, a layer of snow hinders the freezing process by its insulating effect. When constructing ice bridges for high-ways such as on the Mackenzie Highway across the Mackenzie River, they plow the snow off to promote deep freezing.

Ice will be thinner anywhere that the water is moving faster, which means at rapids, the outside of river bends, where creeks enter lakes and in narrows between lakes. Sometimes there are totally anomalous upwellings of warmer water or warm springs, though these are usually known to local people. If you have to cross some suspect ice, carry a long pole from the woods or rope up.

Ice rescue. If you do go through the ice and end up swimming, your pack will float for a while, especially if the contents are tightly packed in individual stuffbags. You don't want to lose its vital contents so you should try to get it onto the edge of the ice and roll it away. In cold weather on glare ice it may even freeze in place to give you something to hold and pull up on—but it might do it too thoroughly so it then becomes difficult to retrieve. If you can, kick and crawl or roll up onto the ice. Do not stand up until you are well away from the hole. The short ice daggers popular in Scandinavia for ice rescue provide grip to enable you to pull yourself out onto the ice. They can be impro-vised from pieces of dowel with a protruding nail and a piece of plastic tubing to guard the points when not in use. Cheap screwdrivers cut shorter with a grinder will also do. You can use your knife if it is accessible.

If your partners are in the vicinity, it is essential that they look after their own safety first—if everyone goes into the water, the party is likely doomed. If you have to rescue some-one with a rope, stretch it between two people and then walk so one person passes each side of the hole, then lower the middle of the rope to the victim. Keep on walking so the victim is then at the bottom of a loop, which is easier for them to hold on to with cold hands. A long tree (lodgepole pine is ideal) can be used as an alternative to rope.

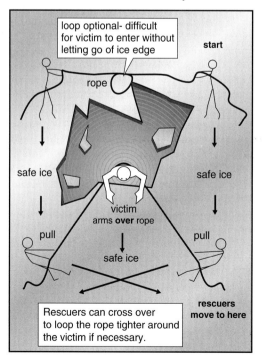

loop optional- difficult for victim to enter without letting go of ice edge

start

rope

safe ice

safe ice

victim
arms **over** rope

safe ice

pull

pull

rescuers
move to here

Rescuers can cross over to loop the rope tighter around the victim if necessary.

Slush. Frozen lakes and rivers do not always provide good travel conditions. Slush forms when the weight of snow on a lake causes the ice to sink and water to seep up through cracks and soak the snow above. Travelling in slush can be very frustrating. It can freeze to skis or snowshoes and quickly bring travel to a halt. If your skis or snowshoes sink through the dry surface snow into the slush, they will ice up. The same thing happens when the water level rises on a frozen river, perhaps because of a dam release, and water flows over the ice.

Skiers who encounter slush conditions can keep going longer by keeping the skis on the snow and shuffling. The moment you start "walking" on the skis you will rapidly build up an even bigger mass of snow on the bottom. Scraping with a scraper is of little use until you are back on dry snow. One trick that saves time is for the party to shuffle over the edge of the lead person's skis. The lead person stops and puts their skis at right angles to the direction of travel. They roll their ankles to raise one edge and allow the others to shuffle their skis across the raised edge. The person who was immediately behind the lead then ends up in the lead position. Not great for your skis but it keeps the party moving at a reasonable speed.

Snowshoers should carry a stick with which to strike the side of a snowshoe to dislodge slush. As soon as possible after reaching dry snow you should clear off all the slush before it freezes solid. If it freezes it might be worth dunking the snowshoe completely in water to melt off the slush and then shaking the snowshoe dry immediately, before it refreezes. Slush and ice adhere much less well to modern synthetic snowshoe materials and can usually be beaten off.

Sometimes the overflow forms a new layer of ice with water under it and above the main ice layer. I remember the story of someone who broke through the ice on skis, and in the split second as they sank into the water their life passed before them and they thought they were about to die. Then their skis landed on the next layer of ice and they were standing there, up to their knees in icy water but feeling rather relieved! Even getting out of that situation with skis on was enough of a challenge.

Navigation Hazards

Many rivers in Canada and Alaska are much closer to their natural state than are rivers in many other countries. Relatively few streams have flood and erosion control structures. Extreme high water can produce drastic changes in the character of the riverbed, making guidebook information inaccurate. As well as drastic changes in level, there can be a considerable amount of debris and active erosion, especially in mountainous areas. Logs and logjams can quickly change a normally safe section of river into a deathtrap. Rivers are not as heavily used as those south of the border, so it is unlikely anyone will know about a hazard, and the likelihood of someone taking it upon themselves to remove it is small. Paddlers must proceed with caution at all times. In more populated areas, barbed wire cattle fences are often strung across rivers. These are not a natural hazard, but they are a hazard to boaters, especially as they can be very difficult to see.

Floods

Because few wilderness rivers have flood control structures, they can rise quickly and inundate adjacent land in response to a heavy rain or warm days and snowmelt. This can come as a surprise to people who only see the regulated rivers of more populated areas. In areas that have been logged, erosion and quick runoff are common. However, some undisturbed rivers such as the Nahanni are notorious for rising rapidly. This is because of the geology and type of vegetation specific to the area. Runoff is also rapid in places where permafrost is close to the surface so rainwater and spring meltwater cannot percolate easily down into the ground.

The length of the rivers and the distance to their catchment areas is such that you could be unaware of stormy weather in distant headwaters. The river can rise and potentially flood your campsite in the middle of the night with no warning after a day of good weather. We once left our canoe on a sandbar on a mountain river in the N.W.T. while we went for a walk for a few hours, and returned to find it well and truly afloat. Luckily we had tied it to a tree so it and our three weeks' food and gear were still

When a creek or river starts to flow in springtime, the ice can jam and dam up the river to cause dramatic floods.

The river rose rapidly while we were away hiking.

there! Our mistake was partly that although we had hauled the boat a considerable horizontal distance from the water, we had not gained a significant amount of height **above** the water.

Hydroelectric power activities can cause wide water level fluctuations over short periods. This is particularly the case with "peak load" supply developments where vast amounts of water are drained in a few hours to supply a burst of power at peak times. Some of these systems are automatic and unmanned, and turn on the water without warning. Some of the Ontario rivers flowing into James Bay are of this type. Warning signs on dams should be taken seriously.

Beavers, with their dam-constructing activities, are often responsible for flooding that occurs surprisingly quickly. Similarly, areas that have in the past been flooded by beavers can dry up if the animals are trapped out or die off from disease. Depending on your mode of travel these changes can have very significant effects on your progress. Paddling your craft through beaver ponds is easier than wading through the muck of a dried-up pond, and frozen beaver ponds can provide easier skiing than a brushy swamp. A flooded area can be a barrier to backpackers, and beaver dams are not often easy to use as bridges.

Some of the rivers in Alaska and the western Yukon have glaciers calving into them, and the ice blocks can cause damming and temporary flooding. This is similar to what happens during spring break-up when river ice jams up and causes backups and flooding. Another cause of unexpected changes in water levels is strong winds blowing over a long stretch of a large lake, which can drive the water to the downwind end and cause a substantial rise in level, sometimes called a "wind set." Tidal ranges vary around the country, but the Bay of Fundy has some of the highest tides in the world and they are also high in Baffin Bay. Coastal hikers and boaters should obtain a tide table.

Friends lost their kayak in the Arctic Ocean when a combination of wind, tide and ice floe jams raised the level of water in an inlet enough to float the craft away. They were lucky to retrieve it by paddling an ice floe in pursuit.

Strong winds during the day may mean that you have to travel at night when it's calm. Ken Ellison photo.

Severe Weather Conditions

Because of the distances involved and the un-populated nature of much of the backcountry, there may well be no escape from severe weather. Consequently, you may have no option but to use your own skills and precautions to ensure your well being during adverse conditions. You must make sure that weather conditions do not damage equipment or injure people.

Hail

Hail is often associated with thunderstorms. Small hail is unpleasant and large hail can be very destructive and dangerous—hailstorms in Canada regularly injure livestock and damage cars. On one river trip we kept on paddling through some heavy rain that suddenly changed to 10-millimetre (1/2 inch) diameter hail that inflicted intense pain on heads and hands, leading to a disorderly yelping scramble for shore, where paddles could then be used as head protection. Had the hail been large (ping-pong ball size is not uncommon in Canada), it would have been very nasty. Cy-clists and hikers can stop more easily than paddlers and crouch down and protect head and neck with a pack or other convenient item.

Lightning

Summer thunderstorms are common in many areas. To avoid being struck by lightning you should shelter in appropriate places. Avoid being the highest object or near the highest object in the vicinity. Certainly keep off high ridges and away from solitary trees or the tallest trees in the forest. Avoid metal objects such as sailboat masts, metal tent frames, bicycles, ice axes and wire fences. Cyclists or hikers who drape a tarp over a roadside wire fence to make a shelter would be pushing their luck!

One day my wife and I were retreating fast off a ridge in a thunderstorm when we met some mountain bikers going **up** the ridge into the rain and lightning. There are suicidal practices and suicidal practices, but even that didn't beat the sight of a girl with shoulder length hair I once saw standing on top of a

A three-metre square of plastic sheeting can make a good cook shelter and socializing place in inclement weather.

survey pillar on a peak in thundery weather. Her hair was standing vertically on end and her friends were busy taking pictures! The day we saw the mountain bikers, a hiker was killed by lightning on an adjacent peak.

If you are caught in the open and you "hear the bees" and your hair starts to bristle or stand on end, it's a warning of an imminent strike. The charge hitting the ground during a strike has to dissipate into and across the ground. Humans are better conductors than the ground so you want to avoid being in a position that provides an easier pathway than the ground for the flow of current. Keep your feet together, otherwise the current may find it easier to go up one leg and down the other rather than across the ground between your feet. Do not lie down, but kneel down with knees and feet together, placing hands on knees and bending forward. If you are in a group, scatter so that there is more likelihood of there being survivors to help the injured.

In the mountains, don't lean against a rock face, otherwise the ground current could flow in through your hands and out through your feet.

Similarly, do not sit under overhanging rocks to provide an easier current pathway across the air gap into your head and out through your feet or seat. Although low points are good places to be, a rivulet down a mountainside may provide a channel for dissipating current.

A lightning strike is a potentially fatal event, so don't tempt providence. We once had a barbecue rudely curtailed by a thunderstorm. My wife had no sooner commented how evil we were being by illegally drinking wine in a picnic ground, than there was a deafening bang, a flash and an electrical smell, as a strike hit the picnic area! Providence must not be tempted!

Wind

The wind associated with a thunderstorm or other disturbances such as line squalls can quickly turn a calm lake or ocean bay into a frothing maelstrom. Canoeists and kayakers must go ashore and seek shelter in plenty of time if the wind is rising or a thunderstorm is approaching. Canoes, kayaks and rafts must be tied down securely or weighted down with heavy rocks, not just left in the open on the beach. Once the wind starts a boat rolling it keeps on going. We met people on the Nahanni whose canoe had been badly damaged in a windstorm, and they were only thankful it had not been blown into the river and lost completely. A friend once chased a pot blowing across a glacier in a blizzard and was lucky to catch up with it—and even luckier to find their way back to the tent again in the poor visibility. Tents, perhaps already rendered heavy by the precipitation, can be severely damaged by thunderstorm winds in exposed places. Sometimes it's best to collapse the tent before it breaks, or not put it up at all but to huddle instead under the fly until the worst wind is past. A tent with the usual aluminum poles is hardly a good place to be in an exposed place in a thunderstorm, anyway!

The chinook winds of southern Alberta blow strongly out of the west, rapidly removing snowcover and making cycling westward unpleasant. People planning extensive cross-Canada cycling usually go west to east. The Anchorage area is known for similar chinook winds that blow very fiercely down off the Chugach Range. Williwaws are another type of strong wind that comes up unexpectedly in mountainous areas in Alaska. The main thing is not to leave yourself vulnerable—don't wander off from camp with nothing tied down to see from a distance your drying sleeping bag blow into a pond and your dome tent roll off down the mountainside!

Although forested areas provide shelter from wind, they pose the problem of falling trees, and there is some risk of lightning strike if the wind is associated with a thunderstorm. Dense forest of relatively young trees of uniform height is likely to be safer than forest with a mixture of tall old trees and younger trees. The taller older trees are more likely to fall because they project above the main forest shelter and catch the full force of the wind. They are also more likely to be struck by lightning or to have dead parts that fall off. Some of the west coast campsites among the rainforest giants are magnificent, but they are places in which I would feel quite uneasy in a major windstorm.

You can attach string to a plastic sheet using (left to right) duct tape reinforcement with a grommet, duct tape over a paper clip, tying round a pebble in the plastic and just by tying around a handful of the plastic.

Heavy and Prolonged Rain

In heavy rain, parties can soon become miserable unless their outer clothing is waterproof and they are wearing the correct amount and type of garments underneath to avoid overheating, condensation and discomfort. See Chapter Five on clothing.

A large tarp to make a cooking/living shelter makes life more comfortable in camp, and can be a tremendous help for keeping people and gear dry. You have room to stand up, move around, cook, change and sort gear. You can even pitch or strike your freestanding tent under it, keeping the inner tent dry before moving it to one side once the fly sheet is installed. For summer backpacking I carry a three metre by three metre (10 feet x 10 feet) sheet of two mil polyethylene and some thin twine. It is quite light so it is no trouble to carry it "just in case." This weight of plastic is not very robust, but is fine as an "insurance" on the off chance of bad weather, as long as you are below treeline and can get out of the wind. For long trips, canoe trips, large group trips and trips where bad weather is more of a certainty or where you need to camp in exposed places, a strong nylon tarp or heavier polyethylene is required. Clear polyethylene has the advantage of making a less claustrophobic shelter. String is easily attached to polyethylene by bunching the plastic over a one-centimetre pebble and tying the string around the "neck" of the plastic below the pebble.

A recent conversation with a wilderness guide revealed that many of their kayaking clients were inept at basic camping skills such as staying dry in bad weather. People were careless about packing their gear so it would stay dry during the day, and worst of all, they would put on their one remaining set of dry clothing in the morning to travel in the rain.

Setting up a tarp provides lots of challenge for your ingenuity. Avoid draping a tarp over a pole because it will always chafe and the tiny holes that form will invariably cause a drip down your neck at the next site. The weight of the bipod and rock keep the rope taut enough.

Remember that when travelling you will almost inevitably get clothes wet with condensation, but at least you can keep warm by moving. If you have dry clothes sealed in a waterproof bag, they are something to look forward to at the end of the day. They are also your insurance if something goes wrong or someone gets hurt and you cannot keep moving to stay warm. Do not work too hard at camp chores so as to work up a sweat and soak your dry gear.

Blizzards

A true blizzard with its strong winds, heavy snowfall, blowing snow, low temperatures, poor visibility and high windchill creates serious problems. Travelling in a blizzard exposes personnel to the risk of frostbite, hypothermia and exhaustion. There is significant risk of becoming lost in the poor visibility, or of the party becoming separated. There is risk of straying into an unseen crevasse field, thin ice area or avalanche terrain. Travelling in the face of such conditions may therefore be unwise unless you are absolutely certain of the route

and **everyone** is fit, well clothed and well fed, and is monitored carefully and often. You must be absolutely certain of reaching shelter long before people start to succumb.

"Reaching" not only means getting to the general vicinity of the shelter, but also actually **finding** the hut, camp, vehicle or whatever. Plenty of parties have succumbed while very close to a shelter they could not find in a blizzard. If they'd stopped sooner they would have been without shelter but at least not too exhausted to build a good bivouac or to survive a bad one. Often a safer course of action in a blizzard is to dig in and build a snow cave or quinzee and wait until conditions improve.

If you are camping in a blizzard, a snow block wall to provide shelter makes for a more relaxed and quieter time in a tent as well as improving the tent's chances of surviving the winds intact. However, a wall that is too big will encourage drifting and burial of the tent. If drifting is a serious problem, a second wall 10 metres or so upwind of the first may be worthwhile. Beware of high winds eroding the bottoms of walls until they collapse. Even with a wall, tents are noisy in storms, leading to lack of sleep. There is then the danger of becoming fatigued and accident-prone. It is therefore often well worth the effort of building snow caves or igloos to wait out storms in peace and quiet. Beware of entrances becoming blocked with drifting snow. Winter travellers should practise building quinzees (see page 363) and other forms of snow shelters such as the snow cave, trench shelter and igloo so that they can do it quickly and easily when it really matters.

Tornadoes

Tornadoes are surprisingly common in Canada, 70-80 striking populated areas annually according to Environment Canada estimates. They usually require hot, humid weather, so they are more common in southern Canada, but they can occur as far north as Yellowknife, N.W.T. and Churchill, Manitoba. They are twisting funnel-shaped clouds that reach down to the ground at the base of thunderclouds and that contain winds as fast as 450 km/h. However, the cloud of flying debris can mask the shape of the funnel so it looks like a low cloud. The associated loud roaring noise like a jet aircraft or train is very characteristic. Generally they move from southwest to northeast, so if the tornado is moving that way across your field of vision and is not in your southwest quadrant, you may be out of its track. However, the movements can be erratic, so don't take chances by standing there watching! Seek shelter! The basement of a strong building may be a good choice. You don't want to be in a building with a floor that could be picked up in one piece (initially!) and thrown around with you in it. Mobile homes and vehicles are particularly bad places to shelter. You are much better off lying down in a ditch, as long as you are not hit by debris and you are far enough from your vehicle that it does not get rolled on top of you. Finding shelter under a low bridge or culvert is also a good choice if it does not flood, but beware of flash floods in thunderstorm weather. In the open, hanging on to a small tree, a stump or a fence post is a help, but avoid items that could be uprooted and thrown around by the wind.

You could read this section and end up feeling that the weather in Canada and Alaska

makes life outdoors unpleasant and hazardous. Although the weather does have the potential to make or break a trip, there is some truth in the saying that "there's no such thing as bad weather—the problem is just poor attitudes or inadequate gear." If you add "and lack of knowledge about how to use the gear effectively, coupled with poor planning" you are close to the truth.

A blizzard can be very unpleasant while it is happening and the aftermath can be very trying as well. Chic Scott photos.

Travelling on glaciers is always potentially hazardous. While pulks are a great way to transport gear on long trips, a crevasse fall with a pulk is a nasty situation.

Miscellaneous Hazards

There are a number of other natural hazards you should be aware of. While the likelihood that you will encounter them is small, the consequences of mishandling some of them can be catastrophic.

Forest Fires

A forest fire is a terrifying event, especially in a remote area where there is no help at hand. Because most people are not used to being close to such fires, they may respond inappropriately.

Fires are often regarded as being summer events. However, they are common in spring when winter-dried grasses are exposed and provide easily ignited kindling. A strong wind can rapidly spread a spring grass fire and ignite nearby forest. Also in springtime, fires from the previous season that have been smouldering underground in duff and stumps under the snow all winter may break out anew.

The intensity of a fire and its speed of progress will depend on wind strength, air temperature and humidity. It is also influenced by the type and amount of fuel available. In some areas, fire suppression activities have resulted in a buildup of unburned combustible materials. If a fire does start and is not immediately suppressed, it quickly attains a terrifying, catastrophic size and intensity. Windy, hot, dry days in coniferous forests where there is lots of dead underbrush present a high hazard.

Do not assume that just because it rained recently that the hazard has gone. It takes a large amount of rain to really wet down a coniferous forest and the ground and brush beneath the trees.

Don't start a forest fire. The fundamental principle to remember when fire hazard is high is to take extra care not to start a fire yourself. Even stoves are capable of starting forest fires, so be careful. Spilt fuel or heat from the burner can easily start duff or grass burning, and fire in dry grass will spread rapidly, particularly with a wind. Use a rocky or gravelly place to set up your stove, and if this is not available, thoroughly wet down the area where you will use it. If there is a lot of fuel such as dry grass, trample or remove it if practical to do so and the area is not too sensitive.

I remember one frightening experience where a stove ignited winter-dried grasses in a riverside meadow in the spring. The wind was gusty, and within seconds the fire spread. Frantic beating by eight people with wet spray decks, paddles and vehicle mats only just succeeded in stopping it from spreading completely beyond control.

Camp fires require special care to ensure that sparks do not fly to where they can start a fire, and that fires don't start smouldering underground. You must be extremely careful to totally extinguish the fire and wet the ashes and coals until they are cold to the touch. See Reducing Your Impact, page 244.

Smokers **must** stay in one place while smoking. They should preferably choose a rocky, sandy or gravelly spot. Make sure that butts are placed in a metal container and taken away. I once sat on a log talking with a smoker and watched out of the corner of my eye as a lump of his ash set the duff smouldering, and within a few minutes there was an area of burning duff at our feet 10 centimetres across.

Vehicle exhaust systems become very hot, especially when equipped with catalytic converters, so be particularly careful if you park in long, dry grass. If you are using a motorcycle or a quad for access, make sure it has a functioning spark arrester on the exhaust system.

Pay attention to fire hazard warning signs.

You can carry water for putting out camp fires in a plastic bag inside a stuffbag.

Other causes of forest fires. Having taken steps to avoid starting a fire yourself, you must also be aware of the possibilities of encountering fires started by lightning or other people, as we did on a canoe trip in the N.W.T. Pay attention to the current and previous weather conditions, and the forecasts, and consider how the weather will affect the fire hazard in your area. Pay even more attention if there is already a fire burning in the vicinity, especially if, given the right conditions, it might grow and spread your way. Local radio stations may provide vital information.

What to do near forest fires. Get out of the area if you possibly can and raise the alarm.

If there seems to be any risk of being trapped, or if the fire is moving toward you or is behaving in an erratic way, you must arrange for lookouts to watch it continuously. You don't want to wake up in the middle of the night with it getting "light" a few hours early!

Keep control of your group. At all costs avoid panic.

Plan escape routes and identify refuges such as large rocky areas, large gravel bars in rivers, large green (not dry-grass) meadows or swamps, and lakes. Make sure everyone understands where they are and how and when to go to them.

If you do find yourself close to a fire, planning your course of action to escape will be easier if you have some knowledge of the way it is likely to move and of the relative speeds of movement in different directions.

A fire will move more quickly **downwind** and **uphill**. A fire will spread more quickly if:

- there is a large amount of fuel—dense trees, brush, grass, etc. (This dense vegetation can make it very hard to travel and escape, too.)
- the fuel is dry and highly combustible—dead grass, pine needles and shrubs.
- the weather is hot with low humidity (so fuel has maximum combustibility).
- the winds are strong and gusty, as in thundery weather.
- slopes are steep (fire moves uphill).
- slopes are south or southwest facing (hotter and drier).
- the fire is in a steep gully or canyon (produces a chimney effect).

Having determined the fire's main overall direction of travel, move off to one side of it. Fleeing downwind in front of a fire is a common panic response that is seldom helpful, because the fire may move downwind faster than you can.

What to do if you are trapped. If there appears to be no chance to escape, you will be in a very scary situation and panic will be hard to suppress. Try to keep your head—this is the key to survival in any emergency.

Prepare wet cloths ready to hold over your face and don suitable clothing. You must cover as much of your body as possible when the fire reaches you. Wool is the most fire-resistant clothing you are likely to have, followed by cotton. Synthetics tend to be inflammable and to melt. Fuzzy surfaces ignite easier than tight weaves. Gloves or wool socks will protect your hands, and without functioning hands you are almost helpless even if you survive the fire. However, until the time the fire actually arrives, you need to guard against overheating, so keep cool and don't wear too much. You don't want to be too exhausted and overheated to be able to carry out decisive action at a critical moment. Don't wet all your clothing because it loses its insulation value when wet and you can get badly scalded by steam passing into the clothes.

You may need to be mobile and nimble at a crucial moment, so you need to shed much of your load. You should only be carrying equipment needed for surviving the fire, but if you have time, consider what will be essential for survival after the fire has passed. You might try to stash equipment in a creek or bog in a location you will be able to find again. Hedge your bets by spreading it to several locations, and bear in mind the place will look very different after the fire.

Do not run unless you can clearly see where to run to and are sure that running will be useful. Try to move to the sides of the fire and downhill of it. Try to do your travelling in plenty of time so there is less of a rush and no need for running and its attendant risks of falling and injury.

If you can get into an already burned area, do so. There is little or no fuel there anymore so it is a relatively safe area. You may have to pass through flames to get to it, but this can be done. Choose a spot on the side of the fire where there is less material burning, ideally where the flames are only a metre or so deep and the area inside is burned out. Cover all exposed skin and go for it.

If you are in an area where the fuel will burn away fairly fast (not dense forest), you can start your own fire in front of the main fire's advance. Once your fire has burned out or moved on, you enter this area from the upwind side. When the main fire arrives, it burns around your refuge. Depending on the size of your preburned area, you may be subject to intense heat radiation from the main fire as it passes.

Heat radiation is a serious hazard to people in the vicinity of a fire. Radiation protection is provided by sheltering in shallow trenches, crevices, behind rocks, in streams, ponds or lakes, and simply covering yourself with clothing, equipment, soil, damp moss, etc. Wells, caves, etc., are not necessarily good because the air in them can become deoxygenated by the fire. Lying prone in an area that will not burn is much better than standing up or running, though it takes some willpower to override the instinct to run. The sides of narrow valleys and canyons are not good places to be if there is much fuel on the opposite side because when it burns you will receive the full force of the radiation, rather as you do when sitting in front of a fire with a high log back.

Breathing in the intense smoke is of course very difficult, and eye irritation makes it hard to see. Avoid intense smoke if possible by staying low, and a wet cloth (towel, handkerchief, etc., wetted with urine in a pinch) over the mouth and nose will help. However, if the air becomes too hot, the moistened air from the cloth can carry more heat to the lungs and do more harm than hot, dry air.

If you are trapped near a building or vehicle, get inside them if possible because they will provide good protection from radiation even though they may *eventually* catch fire. Usually by that time the fire has passed and you can leave the building or vehicle reasonably safely. Time and again people have mistakenly fled from or failed to use such refuges and died, whereas those remaining inside *until the right moment* survived. The protection afforded by a building will depend on the materials from which it is constructed. A metal roof and siding is much more protective than cedar shingles and wooden siding. Protection is also affected by how much combustible grass, brush and forest there is close to the building. It will also depend on the extent to which you have time to seal it up properly and to wet the roof before the fire arrives.

Grass fire flame exposure is quite short at about 30 seconds, but a forest fire produces a much longer flame exposure of three to four minutes depending on the amount and type of fuel. Temperatures inside a vehicle rise considerably, partly because of the greenhouse effect of the glass, so occupants need to get low and cover exposed skin with mats and upholstery. The inside of the vehicle may start to smoulder too, but it's still better than being outside. As soon as the main fire has passed, vacate the vehicle. Fumes from burning vehicle trim are likely to be toxic. Hollywood has portrayed vehicle gasoline tanks as being far more explosive than they really are when undamaged, and in fact, experiments have shown that there is little immediate hazard of a vehicle gas tank explosion in a forest fire.

Forest fires are a very serious situation to encounter. However, if you follow the basic precautions outlined and particularly as long as you do not start the fire yourself, the likelihood of becoming involved is quite low. Every fire situation is different, and it is impossible to anticipate specific circumstances or advise specific courses of action. With this information, you should be able to formulate an appropriate and successful plan if the need arises.

Avalanche Hazard

Avalanches are a serious threat to backcountry skiers and a knowledge of routefinding in avalanche terrain and the ability to do your own snow stability evaluation is essential.

The snowpack is dramatically different in the Rockies compared to the B.C. Interior or Coast ranges. Climatic conditions in the Rockies and the cold eastern sides of the western mountains are particularly notorious for producing a shallow, unconsolidated snowpack with many potential sliding layers. Climatic differences in different parts of Alaska similarly produce dramatically different snowpacks in different regions.

Valuable sources of avalanche information are the stability forecasts provided by the personnel of national and provincial parks and other land management agencies. They can often provide snowpack records and other more detailed information. Telephone Avalanche Hotlines exist and can be found in local phone books or ski stores.

Do not expect definitive information about whether to ski a particular slope, other than perhaps whether it has slid recently and maybe how deep. The information they provide is all useful additional information to help **you** make appropriate decisions by complementing the information you gather in the field yourself. Hazard and stability forecasts are available for much of western Canada and Alaska. However, because conditions will change during a long trip you must be knowledgeable enough and tuned-in enough to read "nature's billboards." These natural signs and indicators stare you in the face if you know where to look. You must also take the trouble to dig snowpits and do snow stability tests to gather enough information to make an informed decision.

Tracks into the backcountry are often made by people unskilled in routefinding. Never assume that the broken trail is following a safe route, and always be prepared to do the extra work of breaking a new but safer trail. Remember that the route may have been made in a whiteout by someone who was later horrified when the weather cleared and they saw where they had been!

Your party **must** be equipped, trained and **well practised** in avalanche rescue, because in the wilderness you are the only people who stand any chance of recovering a victim alive.

Ice climbers must be very aware that their favourite routes are often in gullies below substantial snow-filled bowls. Conditions above the climb can be totally different from those lower down, leading to the possibility of disastrous avalanches. Remember that while you are freezing in a cold, dark gully, the sun could be dangerously heating the snow field above, and even without sun, temperature inversions are common.

Rockfall

Natural rockfall in wild mountain areas is common because the harsh weather conditions of northern winters produce much new loose material each year. It doesn't get cleaned off as quickly by numerous people as happens in, say, the busy parts of the Alps. On the other hand there is less likelihood that people will be above you and kicking material down on to you. Loose rock creates problems not only for climbers but also for scramblers. Large groups must be very careful when ascending or descending long, steep routes to avoid kicking rocks down on to people below. Either spread out across the slope and descend grouped together or keep the party close to each other so dislodged rocks have no space to gain dangerous momentum. Wear helmets!

Surface hoar is one of nature's many billboards that warn of avalanche danger. The next snowfall on this layer will bond very poorly and slide easily.

Chapter 12

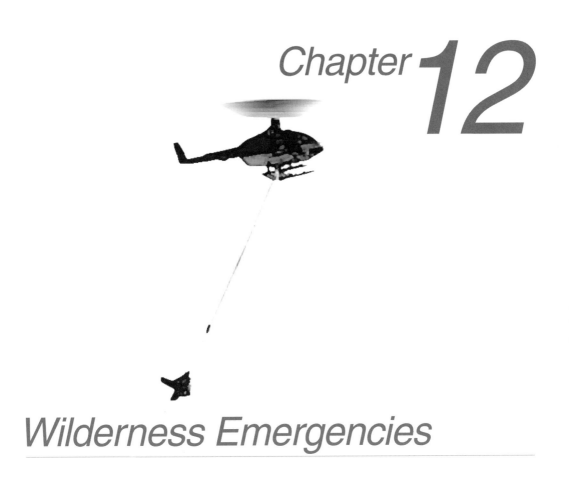

Wilderness Emergencies

"There is always a certain risk in being alive, and if you are more alive there is more risk." Ibsen

It's easier to avoid emergencies if you are aware of the hazards described in the previous chapter. You can further reduce the likelihood of emergencies by conducting your trip using safe practices and risk control strategies. You should recognize that your precautions are not infallible and that you must still be prepared to handle an emergency. You must be practised in rescue skills and equipped with appropriate gear. Wilderness emergencies are quite complex events, often involving a number of people, so it is also important to know how to organize and handle them. Because they may happen in remote locations, it is also important to know how to survive the aftermath.

Planning Ahead to Reduce Risk

To minimize the likelihood of an emergency you should plan, organize and conduct your trip using safe practices right from the start. The possibility of a serious mishap is much reduced if you have the **Right People** in the **Right Place** at the **Right Time** with the **Right Gear**.

On a private trip with friends whom you know well, it's easy to make sure the above "**rights**" are present. With other groups, group trips, expeditions or commercial operations you must take the extra time to ensure you have all of the **four rights**. You should also discuss specific safety practices to be followed.

The Right People

There are three questions to consider when deciding on the right people for a safe trip:

- Is everyone able to meet the fitness, mental and skill demands of the trip?
- Do you have the right number of people for safety and speed?
- Will everyone communicate well and bond closely together as a group, possibly under stress or difficult conditions?

These issues were explored in the discussion about the general success of your trip in "Assembling a Compatible Group," page 62, but they also drastically affect safety.

There are numerous situations in which the fitness and skill of individuals can affect safety. Obviously people who are constantly falling or capsizing or are exhausted certainly increase the risk level on a trip. However, safety can be compromised in a less direct way. I can think of an incident where a physically unfit individual slowed the party down so much that they were unable to reach a creek crossing before the afternoon snowmelt made the crossing dangerous. Someone who slows a party because of a skill problem (paddling, climbing or skiing) can also put a party in jeopardy. I know of an incident where an unskilled member of a ski party slowed the group to the point where they had to cross a slope late in the day when it had become sun-softened and avalanche-prone.

At the planning stage you must not just consider the "rightness" of people for the trip under "ideal" circumstances. People who will be at their limit under "ideal" circumstances will have no margin for error and no reserve of skills and energy for dealing with less than ideal circumstances. They may not have the skill to reach a fallen climber or trapped canoeist, or the navigational skills to find their way in poor weather, or the ability to carry a pack along the trail in wet or slippery conditions. You must therefore build in a skill margin to allow for such circumstances. If necessary, you can widen the margin by conducting a training program, provided that you allow time for enough training before the trip.

The right number of people in your group is a crucial consideration. For one thing, speed is approximately inversely proportional to the size of party, and there are trips where speed undoubtedly means safety. On the other hand, on some trips a small, fast party is inherently at risk because of its limited ability to respond to emergencies. For example, a canoe party of two tandem canoes cannot continue the trip after the loss of one canoe whereas a party of three canoes can. A party of two has considerable difficulty handling a crevasse rescue. If someone is immobilized by injury and there are only two people, there is only one person to go out

A lot of mishaps can be avoided or mitigated through good assessment and discussion of the hazards among the group.

Try to cultivate an atmosphere in your group where it is okay to do the "chicken wing flap" and retreat from or circumvent a hazardous situation.

for help and no one to stay with the injured victim. At least with four people, one person can stay with the victim and two can travel relatively safely for help.

For ideas about how to select your party effectively, see Chapter Two, page 61.

The Right Place

If you are the leader, safety will be enhanced if you ask yourself whether it is the right place for a person of your skills to be taking a party. Then consider if it is the right place for the party you expect to assemble. Once a team is assembled, you must have the knowledge to decide whether the skills, attitudes, expectations and equipment of the people who ended up joining it really are appropriate. If you end up having assembled a team that is not right, change the venue to one that better suits their capabilities. After all, going somewhere with a strong party is a different matter compared to going to the same place leading a weak party.

Participants also have a responsibility to consider where they are going and how their own abilities and those of the leader and the rest of the party affect the safety of the group and its ability as a whole.

For example, if the highly technical Little Nahanni isn't the place to be taking the team you finally ended up with, start on easy water lower down the Nahanni at Island Lakes or Rabbitkettle. If the East Ridge of Logan isn't really the place for your team, consider the King Trench route instead.

Also, bear in mind how the "rightness" of a place for your particular party can be significantly affected by changed conditions. Be careful that your assessment of the seriousness and demands of an area was not distorted by your previous experience with a strong team when the weather was great, the snow powdery, the water level perfect or navigation was easy.

Most of all, be careful that another person's assessment of the seriousness of an area hasn't dangerously misled you. A local team exhibited a slide show of their very successful Logan East Ridge climb that was blessed by many things, including great weather. As a result of the impressions given by their show, they had numerous inquiries from much less able people about doing the route.

Build in some flexibility about your destinations. An ex-SAS mountain troop instructor who was one of my first outdoor leader instructors always said, "Don't tell people too much so you won't have to disappoint them if you make a change in the plan." In the Logan example above, you might follow this advice by first assembling a group for "Mount Logan, route unspecified" and then decide whether their skills were good enough for the East Ridge.

The Right Time

The right time refers not only to the overall time of the seasons but also to the particular weather conditions on the day in question. Remember that you can have spring weather in January, and January weather in May! Good prior research will lessen the likelihood of arriving in an area at the wrong time, but conditions are not entirely predictable, especially as some trips tend to be organized long in advance. Weather, snow conditions, ice conditions, avalanche hazards, water levels, forest fires or bear activity may make the appointed time the wrong time when the time actually comes. You may have a group of people who have been looking forward to the trip for months and who may have their hearts set on the established objective on a particular date. This type of trip, which has a lot of momentum, and club group trips especially, is more difficult to cancel or divert than a small, spontaneous private trip. **Don't** let yourself be swayed by momentum and by people pressures, especially from uninformed people, into going anyway at the wrong time, and then end up getting into trouble. Many "organized" groups get into difficulty because they continue in the face of unfavourable conditions and sometimes in opposition to people's better judgement.

The Right Gear

Successfully completing the trip as planned depends on the party being properly equipped, and particularly on the gear of the *least* well-equipped person. You will have a problem if even only one person is, for example, without adequate raingear or has no ice axe or has worn boot soles or no helmet. So make sure someone advises all participants well in advance what gear is needed, **and** checks (tactfully) that everyone has what they need. You don't want to be in the position where one of your group attempts a section of your route with inadequate equipment just because the others have completed it and the person feels they have to keep

up. They would probably not try it with their equipment if the peer pressure was absent. This changing of people's acceptance of a risk under the influence of peer pressure is known as the Risky Shift phenomenon, and is a frequent cause of problems.

"Right gear" also means food and particularly drink. On one glacier traverse two members of our group who should have known better had a totally inadequate stove that could not melt enough snow to keep them hydrated. They became dehydrated to the point of impairing their performance.

Of course it is one thing to set off with the right gear, but it is another thing to make sure you do not lose equipment along the way. Be particularly careful if you are using drab-coloured gear—it's very easy to put it down and lose it. A spray can of fluorescent paint, some flagging tape and some self-adhesive fluorescent tape to mark items will save a lot of grief. My brown spectacle case has a strip of fluorescent tape attached, and the green handle of my Swede saw has been sprayed orange. I have pieces of orange flagging tape attached to a dark blue waterproof bag containing the first aid gear. My pack is made of Spectra, which is white and cannot be dyed, and was a liability in winter until I sprayed it with red paint. It now looks horrid, but you can see it in

The avalanche hazard meant this particular week was not the right time to be skiing much around this particular hut, so we spent more time like this and all lived to tell the tale.

the snow and no-one would think of stealing it! The last person to leave a lunch spot, campsite or other stopping place should always check around, behind logs or rocks, used as seats, on the ground and up in trees where people hang things.

Be aware that some of the **rights** may be a bit "less right" on a trip with a club or other organized group. You need an extra margin of safety than with your own hand-picked group of friends. A club group might not have the same reserves of skill or gear to keep themselves out of trouble, so more preventive planning is needed. It is important, however, to avoid over-planning to the point where you lose the flexibility to roll with nature's punches.

Consider these Safety Practices

Staying out of trouble may well impose constraints on your fun. You may have to ski roped, or ski a less steep slope or climb an easier route. You should discuss as a group the safety precautions and practices to be followed on a trip. If you suddenly spring constraints on the group part way through a trip, you may have a revolution on your hands.

When discussing these precautions you need to make everyone aware of the seriousness of a mishap. Factors may include remoteness, difficulty of evacuation, steepness of terrain, weather conditions, water temperatures, amount of daylight, and availability of professional rescue or medical care.

Here are a few examples of safety practices you could discuss with your group:

- always wearing a helmet when climbing, paddling or cycling; in single file
- never hiking alone
- always roping up on glaciers and always belaying when climbing
- boiling or treating all drinking water
- always wearing a wet suit or dry suit
- always carrying a bright-coloured garment
- always wearing shoes when swimming
- always wearing gloves when gathering wood or cooking
- always scouting rapids
- always hoisting food into a cache

- not cooking in the tent no matter what the weather
- wearing gloves, boots and eye protection when chopping wood
- not eating shellfish and risking PSP
- climbing two points below your best lead level when in a remote area
- running rapids one class below your best in a remote area
- not skiing avalanche terrain in whiteouts
- always wearing nonslip/protective gloves when filleting fish
- making lots of bear-scaring noise but not seeing any wildlife as a result
- always dividing essential gear among different members of the party.

You should be able to add to this list!

It is most important to realize that many mishaps occur when people are tired. For this reason, you may want to make a rule that you will not carry out higher risk activities late in the day, or will at least take extra special precautions at those times. If you have had a poor night's sleep, you should take special care. After a morning of difficult rapids, hard climbing or demanding skiing, you may decide to shorten the day and should certainly be conservative in the afternoon.

Some friends on a very remote trip in the north made a rule that they would not run any difficult or long rapids after 2 pm. A good rule, and sure enough, when it was broken, a capsize in a long, hard rapid resulted. By the time everyone was together again and in camp it was 8 pm. I can remember camping early in the afternoon on a demanding northern river, having recognized that after spending all morning running technical grade 3+ rapids with a full load of gear, we were becoming tired and accident-prone. It was only when we actually did stop that we realized just how tired we really were and what a good decision it was.

Controlling Risk on the Trip

Now that you have done all the planning for a safe trip, you must follow through by carrying out safe practices on the trip itself.

Likelihood and Consequences of a Mishap

As you proceed through your day in the outdoors, it is essential to continually consider **not just the likelihood** that your actions or omissions could cause a problem, **but also the consequences** as well. Maintaining an acceptable level of risk requires you to strike a balance between likelihoods and consequences. It must be a balance with which you and all the group feel comfortable.

Preliminary discussions of risk tolerance should have occurred in the early stages of planning, because risk management may impose constraints with which some people are uncomfortable. For example, suddenly announcing half a day into the trip that the group will be roped at all times on the glacier may cause serious dissension from the people who came expressly to make turns in the powder.

There are four steps when balancing likelihoods and consequences:

The first step is to learn what the hazards are and to recognize them in the field. If you don't recognize a hot, steaming grizzly scat for what it is and deduce that there is probably a hot, steaming grizzly nearby, you are heading for trouble. If you can't distinguish an avalanche slope from an asparagus patch, your days are numbered.

Having recognized a hazard, the second step is to consider what constraints on your activity you can tolerate to control the likelihood of a mishap occurring. Will you about-turn and abort your trip at the grizzly turd, or will you proceed, while taking certain precautions? Having recognized the avalanche slope, will you ski it, avoid it, or take the time to dig a snowpit and do assessments to decide if it will slide **today**?

The third step is to consider your ability to control and deal with the **consequences** if something goes wrong. If you encounter a griz, are there any suitable trees to climb? If the slope slides, will it be a big slide, or is there a reasonable runout, or will it carry you over a cliff? And is the party good at avalanche rescue?

An injury that does not have serious consequences in the city will have particularly serious consequences in the backcountry if:

- it is very painful
- it prevents the victim from continuing
- it will get much worse if not professionally attended to soon
- the immobilized victim will become hypothermic or frostbitten.

For example, the consequences of a relatively minor cut on the hand from careless fish-cleaning could be that paddling becomes difficult or impossible. This would create a major problem for a wilderness canoeist or kayaker who is a week's paddling from civilization. A badly cut foot from swimming barefoot could be disastrous for a backpacker with no choice but to walk the 50 kilometres back to the trailhead. Both these examples become even more acute if the wound becomes seriously infected and you have no antibiotics with you.

Besides "people breakdowns," equipment breakdowns or loss can have very serious consequences. A broken ski in two metres of backcountry snow is much more of a problem than when on a packed trail, and a lost canoe has more serious consequences when you are 50 kilometres from the nearest road than when there is a riverside road nearby. Even a broken hipbelt buckle could make life very difficult for a backcountry skier or backpacker.

I know of one outdoor educator who, when out in the field, would often ask his students "what if?" questions to train them to consider consequences. For example, "What would happen to Fred over there if that slope avalanched?" or "If we capsize here, where will we end up?"

The fourth step is to consider what potential consequences you can live with. Could you justify the small risk of getting mauled—is the trip worth it? Is the slope going to provide good enough skiing for you to justify the risk? As someone once said, it's a pity to get hurt if you aren't even having any fun!

Communication and Safety

You must talk to each other on the trip. Ineffective communication within the group can adversely affect safety. On a number of memorable occasions (actually ones I would much prefer to forget), we have found ourselves saying later, "How did we all end up in that crazy situation?—we all knew better than to do that." On most of those occasions the problem was that we were not communicating effectively. If we had stopped and discussed the situation, it would have become clear that everyone was worried and an alternative safer plan would have been made.

Interpersonal Relationships and Decision Making

If the interpersonal relationships are not working well, decision making can be seriously affected. The problem can be particularly pronounced when good advice comes from an individual who is not liked or respected. Unfortunately, the advice is not acted on because of this person's low esteem within the group, or perhaps because of the manner in which the advice was given. Worse still, the group may deliberately go against the advice, even though they know it to be sound.

Peer Pressure

In some groups, peer pressure, either spoken or unspoken, is a powerful influence that all too often overrules the good judgement of each individual and leads even a well-chosen party into trouble. A classic example of peer pressure effects is described by surveyor G. V. Copley and recounted by R. M. Patterson in *Finlay's River*. It concerns a surveying party in the fall of 1914 descending the upper reaches of the Finlay River in a heavy dugout canoe. Copley writes: "(If) we ran this canyon (it would be) at the peril of our lives—we were very short of grub and we didn't want to take the time to portage, which would have delayed us two days. We looked the water over carefully, then walked back to the upper end and

went *into conference*—and finally decided to take a chance. If we had upset we would all have been drowned as no one could possibly have lived in that turbulent water."

Of course, in a conference all sorts of decisions can end up being made under the influence of peer pressure, egos, etc. No one wants to be the chicken! However, the striking part of this incident was that the boat leader then took each man aside and asked him *individually* if he was prepared to take the chance to run the rapid with him. Even that technique is not infallible because one man's reasoning for his decision assumed that everyone else would run the rapid. He commented that "he might as well go and be drowned with the rest of them because if they drowned he'd die by himself anyway out there in the middle of nowhere."

A friend recently recounted a ski touring situation in which there were some interesting dynamics. They had ascended a peak along a ridge and were discussing the ski descent off the side of the peak, which was certainly steep enough and loaded enough to avalanche. Everyone was agreeing to ski the slope until the last person announced that he was not going to ski it and was planning to ski back down the ridge. As he set off thinking he was alone, he realized that three others had suddenly changed their minds and were hot on his heels.

Is the Risk Level Increasing?

When assessing a hazard and its potential consequences, you must be careful not to look at it in isolation. A serious mishap rarely happens as the result of a lone event. It is more likely that the trip had been heading for trouble for some time. When one more, even relatively minor incident occurred, all the problems suddenly became much more significant, compounded, and finally created a big problem.

The often-cited classic example is the group of young people whose canoes capsized on a northern lake, resulting in the deaths of 11 people. The coroner observed around 15 factors that came into play and compounded the problem once the capsize occurred. These included lack of sleep, not enough food, no prior knowledge of the area, lack of physical fitness, lack of paddling skill, poor swimming skills and lack of planning for a capsize. When the first capsize occurred and people were in the water, the numerous factors working against them became very significant.

The trick for staying safe is to recognize the strikes you already have against you and to realize their significance if a mishap occurred. You may well change your mind about, say, risking a river crossing, running a rapid, climbing a route or skiing a slope, because you realize that the consequences of a mistake may be very serious.

J. Raffan used the One-Armed Bandit ("fruit machine") in a marvellous analogy. On these machines there were randomly spinning wheels with various fruits depicted around their perimeters. If they come to rest with all the same fruit in a line, you win the jackpot. If only the first four fruits in the line are the same, nothing happens. In his model, winning the jackpot represents getting into a full-scale emergency in the outdoors. Imagine that each strike against you on your trip is a lemon in a line on the slot machine. You can have four in a row and nothing happens—no winnings at all and the lemons are not affecting anything and the trip continues. However, if and when the fifth lemon comes up, in conjunction with the other four, you hit the jackpot. A relatively minor event occurred (the last lemon), but in conjunction with the other lemons (other strikes against you), you have a major problem.

For example, it is late afternoon on a backpacking trip. One of your party has blisters and has been slow all day so you have not gone as far as you would have liked and have not reached the intended campsite. Everyone is tired and hungry. You have arrived at a river crossing that, because it's late in the day, is now swollen with icy water in the late afternoon glacier melt. It looks risky, particularly as there is a nasty logjam just downstream. The side where you are is flat and pleasantly wooded but the other side is steep straight out of the water and there will be several kilometres of hard going to the intended campsite.

Identify the "lemons." They are the slow person with blisters, the resulting lateness, fatigue, hunger, cold water, the logjam, the lack of a suitable camping spot on the other side and rough terrain. They will all make the incident more serious if someone falls in while crossing. You should probably decide to camp in the

good place and cross the river next morning when the water is low, everyone is fresh and better able to handle an emergency, and there would still be time to dry out if someone fell in.

Another example: It's late in a long, hard day of paddling. It is raining, the party members are chilled and it's been a long time since lunch. You arrive at some rapids and go ashore to scout, noticing that the camping spot you hoped to find at the end of the rapids doesn't exist. When deciding whether to portage or risk a capsize, you should recognize how the significance of all the factors (winning numbers or lemons) will suddenly increase if someone capsizes. The lemons are that the group is tired, already cold and their energy reserves are depleted, so a swimmer will become helpless in the cold water more quickly. The tired group will respond less effectively, and the wet weather will make lighting a bonfire to warm and dry the victims more difficult. There is also no obvious place to camp and dry out at the foot of the rapids.

Staying out of trouble in the outdoors therefore requires you to have the skill to recognize "lemons" and to weigh their significance. Often the most significant lemon is the weather and changes in the weather. Sometimes it accounts for several lemons! See Chapter Four on weather.

Many lemons can be recognized and neutralized before the trip and during the planning stages, but keep watching for lemons during the trip. Always be thinking "what if...?".

Assessing Your Ability to Cope with an Emergency

You must consider your ability to handle an emergency and then modify your activity accordingly. If you recognize that for some reason your ability to cope is impaired, you know that the consequences of a mishap will be far more serious. For example, if you already know that someone's avalanche transceiver is not working, you must take extra care to avoid any risk of being avalanched. If you are already using all the spare paddles, you don't want to risk another capsize and the loss of more paddles so you may portage or appoint a paddle retrieval crew. If you are barely able to summon the energy to keep travelling, you are likely to have the utmost difficulty carrying out a crevasse rescue so you may decide to stop and camp.

Can You Live With the Consequences?

Deciding whether the game is worth the potentially serious consequences of a mishap is a personal decision that should not be taken lightly. It should not be a decision you take under the influence of peer pressure. Really stop and ask yourself how you will feel if the worst case scenario occurs.

Developing Judgement

It takes training, practice, experience and the development of good judgement to reduce the likelihood of mishaps occurring. The training comes from formal courses, associating with well-trained, competent individuals and reading. There are plenty of publications specific to various sports. However, just reading or hearing about skills and techniques and about hazards isn't enough—you must go out and practise and gain experience.

Training must come first, however, because there is no point practising or becoming experienced in using incorrect, unsafe or inefficient techniques. I was once on a trip with a group I had been assured were "very experienced." In fact, they were experienced in carrying out some questionable techniques and "experienced in being very lucky." Many of their techniques did not follow current mainstream thinking, so choose your mentors wisely.

By following the steps in this section you will go a long way toward keeping out of trouble, but there is still some likelihood of mishaps occurring.

Preparing for an Emergency

Even if you have taken steps to reduce the likelihood of a mishap, you must accept that your efforts are not infallible and that wilderness emergencies can still happen. If something happens to you in the backcountry, you will probably have to deal with the incident on your own. Your ability to cope with a mishap and reduce its consequences is very much influenced by the thoroughness with which you have prepared and planned for emergencies.

Why You Must Be Prepared

Life in populated areas conditions people to think that even if "It" happens to them, they can rely on emergency rescue services. This is not the case in the backcountry, and a widely publicized case recently underlined the way many people today have unreasonable expectations about rescue and ambulance services. There was public indignation that it took an hour for a technical rescue team to arrive at a remote tourist spot, regardless of the fact that it was 100 kilometres from the nearest town!

Emergencies that would be minor in places with quick rescue and evacuation to medical care can be very serious in the wilderness, unless you can deal with them yourself. Planning for a safe trip must include rescue and first aid training, and inclusion of appropriate safety equipment.

The single most important part of the planning process is telling someone where you will be going and then navigating well enough that you do actually end up going there. Also, tell them your emergency or alternative route and what to do if you don't return on time.

Why Practice is Important

The big advantage of detailed planning and sufficient practice is the reduction of stress in an emergency. If you are highly stressed, tasks that are easy under low stress conditions become more difficult, so your ability to do what is needed to deal with the emergency is reduced. A high stress level often results in poor decision making, too much haste, ineffective actions, poor group management, wasted time, rage, panic, fear, denial, tears, vomiting or fainting.

The graph overleaf shows how stress levels change over time during an emergency. The top line shows stress in a person who has not been well trained to manage an emergency. Their stress level immediately skyrockets—they have good reason to be stressed because they

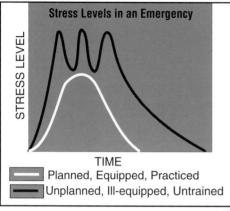

Stress Levels in an Emergency

STRESS LEVEL

TIME

▬ Planned, Equipped, Practiced
▬ Unplanned, Ill-equipped, Untrained

Source: J. Raffan

don't know what to do or how to do it. They may be further stressed by feeling guilty about their unpreparedness, too! Stress diminishes as they try their first solution to the problem, but climbs again if they realize their solution is not working. There are several peaks and valleys in the overall high stress level during a possibly quite long period of trial and error. Eventually they hit on a workable solution, and their stress level finally diminishes back to normal.

The bottom line shows stress levels for a well-trained and equipped person who had planned for dealing with emergencies. For several reasons, their stress level does not rise as high, and then drops back to normal levels sooner. Their maximum stress level is lower because they know what to do and know *they can do it* because they practised. Also, their planning made them realize that there was potential for emergencies to occur and therefore made them less likely to react to the emergency with denial. They are also less stressed by surprise or shock. During planning they identified and practised solutions to various problems and therefore had more chance of coming up with a suitable solution. They seized on the correct course of action right at the beginning and were able to execute it successfully. Their confidence level was raised and their stress level returned back to normal more quickly.

As well as influencing the outcome of a mishap, practice will make you realize the difficulties of dealing with a wilderness emergency, and can make you doubly careful about keeping out of trouble in the first place!

Practising for Emergencies

How do you plan for emergencies? Start with the first stage of risk management, which is finding out about the hazards of the area to define what type of emergencies you might have to face. You should assume that your party must be self-sufficient and must deal with an emergency without outside help.

Practice and simulation are the best training. If you can't organize a practice, doing verbal walk-throughs of scenarios and doing "what if?" sessions is a help. Reading books helps increase your repertoire of ideas so you will not be totally clueless as to how to handle an emergency. However, I always remember the words of a national park rescue warden, "It doesn't always work like it shows in the books!"

Hands-on training sessions with simulations are of the most benefit, because they not only hone people's skills but also teach them to properly organize the people who carry out a rescue. Often the success of a rescue hinges more on how well the group is organized than on the technical skills of its members. Speed can be important in some rescues, and practice will ensure that you can operate quickly *but still safely* when needed. I know from experience that there are some very useful river rescue techniques that many people dismiss as "too slow to set up" or "too complicated" to be of use in a real emergency. In reality, the techniques are only too slow if people do not practise enough to become quick, slick and proficient.

Remember that practising rescue techniques can be hazardous to participants if they are using a procedure for the first time, so don't practise river rescue procedures in the middle of a Class 3 rapid, or a crevasse rescue in a crevasse that narrows to unfathomable depths. Choose a safer place.

If you are using people as "victims" they must be instructed to say "this is real" if they are in fact being hurt by the rescuers. It's also a good idea to warn the authorities that you are having a rescue practice in case a passerby thinks it is a real emergency and summons police and rescue professionals!

Simulations are always good learning experiences and can be fun if you choose the right time when the group is amenable. Bury some chocolates with the transceivers when doing avalanche transceiver exercises. Throw your throw bags at a well-padded bottle of wine, which is the prize for the best shot. You must also make sure your practices require people to learn to deal with the group dynamics of the situation and to maintain adequate control, safety and organization, and use all personnel efficiently. Make sure someone is taking notes and observing, so that a thorough debriefing can be done afterward.

Emergency Services

Although you should plan to be self-sufficient, there are emergency services available that can be very helpful **if** you can summon them. Find out during your pre-trip planning the **services available**, **how to contact them** and their **likely response time**. Response time is important because it will have considerable bearing on your course of action if a mishap occurs. Don't make the mistake of carrying pride in self-sufficiency to extremes. If you can quickly summon a well-trained and equipped professional team to provide safe, speedy rescue and evacuation, there is no sense risking further injuries to the victim or to the party by performing a lengthy or dangerous improvised rescue and evacuation.

For example, if flying conditions are good and you know that a helicopter sling rescue system is available, you probably won't risk lowering an injured climber in an improvised stretcher from a wide ledge where he would be in no further danger if left until rescued by helicopter.

Radio communications can have a dramatic effect on the outcome of a wilderness emergency. However, relying on radios exclusively is not a good idea because you may not be able to make contact when you need to. See Chapter Five on Radio Communications.

Finding out ahead of time what help is available is particularly important if you are engaging in an activity, such as caving or climbing, that requires technical rescues. The local police can usually tell you what is available. In parks, inquire of the park wardens or rangers. In coastal areas, the Coast Guard is responsible for rescues. There may also be a local search and rescue group, sometimes affiliated with the military, mountaineering and caving clubs, horseback riding groups, flying clubs, even snowmobile and ORV clubs. I have met emergency services (fire, police, ambulance) personnel on a river rescue course who had convinced their area chief of the need for technical river rescue training. One of

If you have practised rescue techniques, it will be much easier to do them properly when you have to.

them was also a climber, and he had made it his business to train in high-angle rescue techniques that would be useful in a local oil refinery.

Not only does the availability and sophistication of rescue services vary considerably from place to place, but also the quality of ambulance services once you are rescued. In some areas the ambulance personnel have a low level of training and rudimentary equipment, in others the ambulances are state-of-the-art and the personnel are EMTs or paramedics. In B.C. especially, where the Industrial First Aid program is very comprehensive, there are likely to be well-trained first-aiders at backcountry work sites such as logging operations.

An example of an excellent rescue organization is found in Banff, Jasper, Yoho and Kootenay national parks in Alberta and B.C., Canada. When a backcountry incident occurs, a call to the warden's office will trigger a rapid response by highly trained personnel who are equipped to deal with most types of wilderness accidents, including searches, avalanche rescue, high-angle mountain rescue, water and swift water rescue. The response is often by helicopter, with foot, vehicle, snowmobile, horse or jet boat backup.

Helicopters generally provide the quickest and most overall cost-effective rescue, but are limited by the weather and daylight. Within a short time of the alarm being raised, the parks' rescue helicopter may be able to bring to the scene a trained team equipped to stabilize, extricate and evacuate the victim. In the above parks, the machine is equipped to carry out sling rescues without landing. Even if the helicopter is not waiting on call but is at a work site, it can be summoned very rapidly as rescues have priority.

Denali Park has been the scene of some daring high altitude helicopter and fixed wing rescues. More so than most rescues, these often put the crews at considerable risk because the machine's capability is pushed close to the limits by the altitude and wind. The line between a heroic successful rescue and a tragedy is often very thin. One helicopter pilot described landing a Chinook helicopter on Denali as being like "driving a car into a garage at 65 km/hr (40 mph) and trying to stop before you hit the back wall." Rescues are always subject to risk.

However, large parts of Canada and Alaska are not served by highly trained technical rescue specialists on call at short notice. You may be lucky and there may be a suitable helicopter around, but don't bank on it. In many areas it could take hours or days to locate one.

A call to the nearest police detachment will activate whatever rescue resources are available. However, police can be very cautious (understandably) about immediately setting in motion a large and expensive technical rescue operation. This is particularly the case if there is no local standing rescue unit and other agencies from afar must become involved. The key to getting a technical response is to convince the authorities that there really is a need for a "technical" rescue. You need to be prepared to explain in a reasoned, logical way why the rescue requires technical expertise, if in fact it does. This means that the messenger must take a **clear, concise, complete and rational** message to the responding authorities. You must always, therefore, have a paper and pencil in your gear, perhaps in your first aid kit. Better still is an Incident Report form.

A helicopter sling rescue is very effective, but it is not available everywhere and is limited by weather.

Repairing Equipment

It is important to be prepared to repair gear in the field. People are becoming more and more dependent on exotic gear to travel enjoyably fast and light in demanding environments. Failure or loss of this crucial equipment during a trip can therefore create major problems or even an emergency.

Repair Principles

Modern gear is not as easy to repair as some of the old traditional items. For example, replacement parts for an old style wood and canvas canoe could be made in the bush quite easily with a knife and perhaps an axe, and the canvas could be repaired with a piece of handkerchief and some spruce gum. A Kevlar or ABS canoe requires more tools and supplies to do a satisfactory repair. If a wooden tent pole broke, you just whittled another, but you can't whittle a replacement for a seven millimetre diameter high tensile aluminum tube to fit into a long narrow sleeve.

The idea that "the more skilled you are, the less gear you need" applies to equipment repairs, just as it does to survival. Repairs are easier if you are ingenious and have a good engineering mind. However, certain ways of looking at the problem and thinking about it can help anyone come up with an appropriate improvised solution to loss or breakage of equipment.

Some ways of thinking when needing improvised repairs are:

- What really does it do?
- How does it work?
- Can I make do without the item anyway?
- What did our forefathers or so-called "primitive" cultures use for the same purpose as the broken or missing item?
- What are the essential aspects of its design relative to its function?
- How did our forefathers make the item or whatever they might have used instead?
- How can I improvise?

For example, a ski comes off and disappears down the hill to be lost forever in the woods. The thought process you might use is as follows:

- The most important thing a ski really does for us is to stop us sinking in to the snow. Sliding forward is not so important.
- The ski stops us sinking by presenting a large surface area to the snow surface to reduce the pressure of its wearer on the snow.
- Perhaps you can do without it because the other ski provides enough support and you can scoot on one leg, as did a friend for 15 kilometres across an icefield after losing a ski in an avalanche. (Transfer the ski to the other leg occasionally.)
- In North America, the traditional method of snow travel was with snowshoes rather than with skis.
- The essential aspect of the design of a snowshoe is a frame with something snowproof across it. The holes between the lacing are only for lightness and to prevent snow accumulating on top.
- Traditional snowshoes were wooden with animal skin lacing to make them light but snowproof. Some frames were made of one piece of wood bent at the front into a hoop. The Ojibwa pattern was pointed at both ends and made of two pieces of wood tied together at front and back and spread apart in the middle. It therefore did not need much bending or steaming.

The improvised snowshoe below is two sticks lashed fore and aft, two spreader bars for footrests and a stuffbag over each end for support.

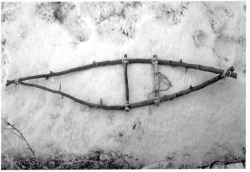

A simple snowshoe frame can be constructed without bending sticks in 10 minutes with some string. Cover the frame with stuffbags or spruce boughs.

Cord will do for a harness because in this case it is for someone using a stiff ski boot who doesn't need straps to spread the pressure. An evergreen branch makes a good snowshoe without any construction work.

If you are above treeline you might make a frame with your tent poles or your glacier wands. A friend who was assisting in a rescue on Mount McKinley was separated from his skis and travelled a considerable distance with an ice axe tied to each foot. A piece of closed cell foam sleeping mat can be attached to the boot, and in spite of its flexibility it will produce a useful surface area increase. "Weaving" a few sticks or wands through the mat will stiffen it to enable you to use a larger piece. They also provide grip. You can still use the foam pieces to sleep on.

So, what you end up with is a far cry from being a ski, but it does most of the job of the ski and gets you out of trouble.

Another example of open-minded thinking is the case of a group in the African desert in a vehicle that was leaking oil rapidly through a failed engine seal. The engine was going to lose all its oil and seize up long before they reached the next oasis. Rather than focus on mending the seal, which would have been next to impossible anyway, they analyzed the problem more broad-mindedly. They realized the problem was more fundamentally one of losing oil onto the ground rather than of having a leaking seal. The cure to the oil loss problem was to suspend a hubcap under the engine to catch the leaking oil. They then stopped periodically and strained the oil through a cloth back into the engine.

Ingenuity and improvisation are all very well as a satisfying intellectual and handy person challenge, but carrying replacements for some key items is still highly advisable. Key items are those that are important to the trip and especially prone to failure. Carrying them can save a lot of time, and can ensure that a trip continues as planned with minimum delay.

Ingenious people can use almost anything to do the job of a snowshoe, which is simply to spread your weight out over a wider area. It doesn't have to look like a snowshoe.

Repair Tools and Supplies

A good repair kit will prevent a lot of delays and difficulties. You need a general kit for all activities and must supplement it with items specific to the activity and the equipment you are using.

General. This is the equipment needed for all backcountry activities, and items from the lists following should be **added as needed for the specific activity.**

- Stove repair kit and tools. Find out what tools you need by dismantling it once at home.
- Stove jet cleaner if applicable.
- Stove washer oil. Use gear oil in a small, old pharmaceutical product dropper, suitably relabelled.
- Duct tape for tent repairs. Rub the repair with the back of a spoon against a hard object to drive the adhesive into the weave for good adhesion.
- Therm-a-Rest repair kit
- Tent zipper sliders (Mountain Hardwear brand)
- Zipper repair kit
- Sewing awl with a variety of needles for boot repairs, tent and pack sewing, etc.
- Variety of strong threads—braided fishing line, button thread, polyester topstitching thread, etc.
- Needles—assorted
- Small pliers
- Swiss Army knife (Camper model has most of what you need without weighing a ton.)
- Braided nylon cord
- Mason's line
- Brass wire ("Snare wire")
- Spare flashlight bulb and batteries
- Tent pole repair sleeve
- Tent pole spare section
- Hip belt buckle (tend to be lost in transit or broken when trodden on).
- Contact cement

Backpacking. Items from General list, plus:
- Spare clevis pins if used in pack.
- Hip belt buckle

Canoeing. Items from General list, plus:
- More duct tape. Keep it dry.
- Awl capable of making holes in hull material so splits can be stitched with wire before taping. Nail heated in stove will suffice for plastic boats. Drill bit.
- Mechanic's wire for stitching splits.
- Screwdriver and pliers for trim and seat screws.
- Fine sandpaper for rough paddle handles, gunwales.
- Coarse sandpaper for roughening repair surfaces before fibreglassing. Keep dry or use waterproof variety.
- Five-minute epoxy for quick, clean repairs of fibreglass tears. V-notch the tear with a knife point and fill with epoxy and you'll have reasonable structural strength, especially if stitched with wire or nylon cord.
- Fibreglass repair kit—cloth, resin (epoxy if you wish), hardener, mixing and measuring containers, spreader, disposable gloves, stretch-wrap to spread over repair to hasten curing and provide a smooth surface without sanding. Resins and hardeners may be prohibited products for air transport. Container lids may pop off in heat or with reduced pressure at altitude. Pack resin and hardener containers separately. Place each container in its own additional sealed container such as a Nalgene bottle or two separately sealed heavyweight plastic bags.
- Assortment of screws and bolts
- Hacksaw blade
- Spare latex dry suit gaskets and glue. Kokatat kits and instructions are great. Sandpaper and Comet for removing silicone seal saver compounds so glue will stick.
- Spare paddles

Rafting. Items from General list, plus:
- Hull material adhesive and lots of patching material.
- Sandpaper, kept dry or waterproof sandpaper.
- Spare valve, valve cap
- Spare pump or pump parts
- Duct tape
- Spare oarlock parts
- Sewing awl, strong thread
- Spare oars or paddles

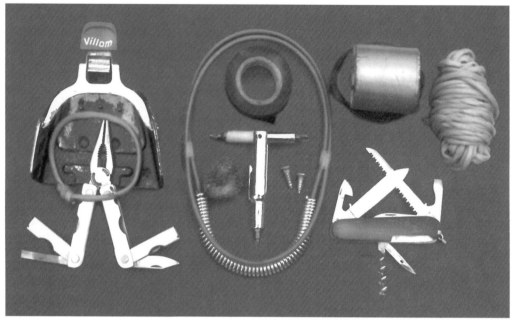

A ski repair kit for backcountry skis.

Ski touring. Items from General list, plus:

- Ski binding
- Ski binding bail and screws
- Ski pole basket
- Spare cable
- Screwdriver that fits binding screws— Posidriv tip, Phillips #3 is okay, #2 Phillips for Voile releasable, also Allen wrench.
- Screwdrivers need to have lots of leverage for removing glued screws. T-type or parachute cord wrap and lever, see photo.
- Binding screws and assorted wood screws
- Coarse steel wool to jam in stripped holes before replacing screws.
- Mechanic's wire
- Awl or Swiss Army knife to drill holes.
- Five-minute epoxy, contact cement
- Boot-toe reinforcing plate for three-pin.
- Duct tape, fibreglass tape, low-temperature electrical tape
- Small vice grips or pliers such as a Leatherman tool or Gerber.
- Long crampon strap to hold boot into binding if slotted.
- Small file or hacksaw blade to cut metal ski edges if needed.

Mountain biking. Items from General list, plus:

- Spare tire and tube and repair kit.
- Chain repair parts and tools
- Pump
- Brake cable
- Spare spokes
- Comprehensive set of tools

Mountaineering. Items from General list, plus:

- Crampon adjustment tools, spare screws and nuts
- Ice tool spare parts and attachment tool
- Crampon strap

Repair Techniques That Work

You need to return your gear to a usable state quickly and efficiently, and possibly under unfavourable conditions. The following are some tried and true, quick and practical methods that involve a minimum of extra equipment.

Drying wet gear. Drying your gear, although not really a repair, does return otherwise useless gear to a useful condition and you should dry wet gear whenever you have a chance. The process is easier if you can build a good fire. A good reflector fire makes the drying process more efficient and less hazardous. However, stories abound of clothing falling into fires and of holes being burned in boots. Don't take chances when you are as dependent on your gear as you are in the wilderness. I heard one horror story of a winter traveller standing his wooden freight toboggan up in the snow near the fire to warm and dry the base ready for waxing. When he came back from the forest with more firewood, he found his toboggan had fallen across the fire and burnt in two!

If you are drying your gear in the sun and wind, you may not have much time to complete the task before nightfall or before you have to move on. It is therefore worth putting care and effort into the job so that the gear dries as fast as possible.

Start by squeezing and wringing as much liquid water out of the items as possible. You can remove a tremendous amount of water from socks, sweaters, etc., by shaking them with a whip-cracking motion. This is especially the case with synthetic piles, fleeces and wool, but does not work with cotton. Swinging and beating socks against a smooth rock or the bottom of an upturned canoe removes water very well. Repeat the procedure until no more wet patches form, then pull the sock back into shape and hang it to dry. Rolling and twisting wet garments in a cotton towel works especially well with wool and synthetic materials. When wetter spots form at the bottom of hanging items, squeeze the water out of them.

For maximum heating by the sun and therefore faster drying, wet items should be placed so that their surface is at 90 degrees to the direction of the sun. Dark-coloured items dry substantially quicker than pale ones because they absorb more heat from the sun, so take a dark-coloured towel, keeping in mind that a large thin one dries quicker than a small thick one.

Arrange items so the wind blows **through** them rather than just draping them over a log, boat or tent. Socks dry much more quickly if they are placed over two sticks stuck in the ground. Setting up a good "washing line" and attaching the items with the knot shown in the photo is well worthwhile. On a canoe trip, the weight of some wooden or plastic clothes pins is small and they can be very useful.

It is even better if you attach items so they act like sails, forcing the wind to blow through them. Use small rocks in pockets and socks to prevent items from streaming like flags in the wind. Always make sure your sleeping bag is tied to something solid so it cannot blow away. I have seen sleeping bags blown into lakes or half a kilometre down a glacier. Our guide on a glacier tour could not find his sleeping bag at the end of a rest day. He spent half an hour looking in all the tents and quizzing us all before he was convinced we hadn't hidden it as a prank—it was that sort of a group! We eventually found the bag half a kilometre down the glacier in a hollow. Luckily, it hadn't gone into a crevasse.

Gear will dry much more quickly if it hangs single thickness. You can attach it securely to a line using either of these two methods.

Repairing Ski Gear.

- Ski broken in half under foot. Break completely, move binding to front half and use as a short ski. Breaking or cutting ski edges is difficult and nicking with a small file or piece of hacksaw will help. One party screwed a cribbage board to the ski over the break and continued. Taped-on splint.
- Bail broken, lost. Strap over toe through slots in binding sides, cord around heel to hold boot forward. Crampon strap works very well.
- Binding torn off ski. Plug hole with coarse steel wool jammed in *tightly* with screwdriver, reinsert screws. Match sticks are useless. If screws are lost, use spares or one from each of several other bindings. If screws are glued in too tight, heat screw head in a candle flame to loosen.
- Binding plate broken. Remove and replace with spare. If no spare, tape boot to ski with lots of duct tape. Screw boot to ski with wood screws. (Remove foot, cut slit in toe cap, insert screw and screwdriver. Close slit with duct tape when finished.)
- Delaminated ski. Wedge the opening apart and place in warm area to dry. Test small area to check that epoxy does not dissolve the ski's core. Insert glue into all the cracks. Use a piece of thread, dental-floss style to work adhesive into smallest parts of crack. Close and apply pressure if possible. Tape will work in a pinch, but blunt the steel edge of the ski thoroughly with a rock so tape does not wear through on the edge too fast. Wind the tape around ski, working from rear to front so that overlaps allow ski to still slide forward over the snow.
- Tip broken. Reinforce with spare tip. Glue and tape. If it breaks off totally, and no spare tip is available, cover jagged ends with stuffbag, plastic bag, tape, sock, glove, etc., so it glides better.
- Broken pole. Use a long splint of wood, 70 centimetres at least, or a tent pole or several glacier wands. Attach with tape. Do not entertain ideas of using a stick inside a hollow pole. Exotic devices made of split tube and hose clamps are extra weight and have no other functions, whereas tape and wands are things you have anyway. For a lost basket use

a margarine container lid, tied on with shoelace. Three 15-centimetre sticks or pieces of glacier wand lashed to the pole in a * shape with string or tape also works well.
- Handles on probe poles that will not come off. Use WD-40 to remove initially, then clean and lubricate with graphite powder so they will come off easily in an emergency.
- Voile releasable binding piston assembly failure. Carry a spare. Or remove binding from release assembly and screw it directly to the ski. You need your Allen wrench to do that. If the binding and release are integral, you may want to predrill screw holes, at some risk of weakening the structure.

An equipment failure like this in the backcountry can be very serious unless you know how to do emergency repairs.

If a repair is difficult, always get right down to the basics of what you need to achieve. Do you want to mend a binding or do you really need to fix a boot to a ski?! Courtesy Norseman Ski Shop, Calgary.

Be imaginative and resourceful when mending gear. Courtesy Oavel Miskiw.

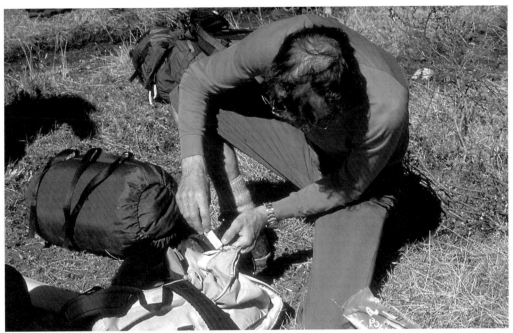

Equipment failures can delay a party seriously, so you need to have repair gear handy to be quick with your repairs.

Backpacking repairs.

- Boot repairs can be done with a sewing awl, though doing the lock stitch inside close to the toe is difficult unless you have a mirror, tweezers and someone with small hands. If the stitch is exposed to wear, cut a groove with your knife so the stitches can lie in it below the surface.

- Pulled-off D-rings or hooks on boots can be substituted with small loops of cord. Make an extra hole, thread cord ends through both holes from the inside and tie on outside. Thread lace through resulting loop. If the metal "washer" is still on the inside of the boot, tie a small loop in nylon cord, thread the tail of the loop inward through the washer and melt the end of the nylon on the inside of the boot into a blob so it won't pull back out.

- Collapsed shoulder strap padding can be improved with strips cut from a closed cell foam sleeping pad. You can always glue them back to the pad, edge to edge with contact cement, when you return home.

- Broken or lost hip belt buckle. Use spare. Or scrounge some Velcro from noncritical fastenings on other gear. Sew on the Velcro so that the belt passes through a ring and is velcroed back on itself. Ring could be a redundant slider or made up from wire or a tent peg. Or you can attach thin rope pieces to each end of the belt and tie them together with a quick release bow knot. You may have to make holes in the webbing of the belt to attach the rope.

- Fractured frame joint on external frame pack. Splint with T-shaped stick, use duct tape or fibreglass tape. If it is the shoulder strap bar, brace with cord to next lower bar. Lash on sticks as additional verticals.

Canoe repair tricks.

- Stitch long hull fractures with snare wire or mechanic's wire before taping or fibreglassing. Sailmaker's "Figure 8" stitch is often best for holding thin edges in alignment, see page 347.

- You need a drill of some kind—a Swiss Army knife awl will do. Twist it fast — do not push it in until it jams and then twist, because it will break. A hot nail also works on plastic canoes. Hold it between two scraps of wood in your pliers so the pliers don't take away all the heat. Aluminum requires a better drill, particularly if it is good quality aircraft alloy

Canoeists should carry a big roll of duct tape—some repairs need a lot of tape!

such as is found in Grumman canoes. If you carry a drill bit, you can always epoxy it into the end of a split stick, which you then use in a bow-drill. Make sure the stick and drill are in a straight line while the glue sets and that only a short length of the bit protrudes, otherwise it will break. Only use it for thin material.

- Broken seat hanger bolts can be replaced with strong cord, but remember that seats are structural features of many canoes and a replacement bolt you brought with you would be better.
- A fractured gunwale can be lashed or splinted if you can drill holes in the hull just below the gunwale.
- Make sure you have the tools to undo seat and thwart bolts so you can replace broken seats or thwarts.
- Dry suit gaskets damaged in the field are difficult to repair because nothing sticks to the silicone protectant you should have been using on them. You may be able to clean them enough if you carry some powdered cleanser such as Ajax or Comet in a film canister. Then you can use a bike tire repair kit or duct tape. If you have to replace the gasket, it is sometimes easier to do the job by leaving about 15 millimetres (1/2 inch) of the old one still glued to the suit. Clean any silicone or other protectant off with sandpaper and detergent. Stuff the part under repair tightly with clothes in a plastic bag to hold it in shape while gluing the new gasket on. Kokatat repair kits have great hints to make the job easier.

Raft Repairs.
- Long slits are probably best stitched before patching. Use Figure 8 stitch, in the photo on page 347, so that the edges are properly aligned. Sandpaper before stitching!
- Make sure you have the tools required to repair or replace the valves.
- Be scrupulous about cleaning and drying surfaces before attempting to glue.

General repairs.
- Failed zippers on tents and sleeping bags. If the zipper is opening up on the wrong side of the slider, you may be able to work the slider backward to the starting point. Then take your pliers and **gently** squeeze the slider as in the photo, across the thickness of the zipper. This reduces the height of the channel the teeth slide through so that they can no longer move through without meshing properly. If you could not work the slider backward, you will have to take it to the end of its travel, remove the stops, take the slider off and back to the other end. Remove the stops so you can reinstall them, and once the teeth are starting to mesh, squeeze as above. Use stitching to form new stops if you can't reuse them. Mountain Hardware make a great devise that makes removing stops unnecessary.

  If your tent door/bug net uses two completely separate zippers, you have a built-in replacement for a failure. If the bug net zipper fails, just use the door to keep out bugs, and make do with less ventilation. If the door zipper fails, simply stitch the door to the bug net and use the bug net zipper as a door zipper. Again, you don't have as much ventilation, but you have a serviceable bugproof/weatherproof door. You cannot do this if the zippers are not independent and the bug net is, in effect, a window in the door. A spare tent zipper could be worth the weight for a party to carry, especially if the tent zippers are old or worn or the tent is not of the highest quality.

- Duct tape adheres better if it is firmly pressed down with the back of a spoon or similar object. This is particularly important with fabric repairs—press against a hard, smooth surface such as a plate or pot.
- Stove and pressure lamp pump failure. Usually the problem is caused by poor lubrication and maintenance of the pump washer so it becomes dry and brittle. You may be able to revive it with cooking oil, butter, suntan oil, lip balm, etc. If not, you can remove the pump piston from another stove while it is running and pump up the faulty stove, assuming they are the same type. There is a lot to be said for having all stoves in a group the same so they can be cannibalized for parts if necessary! New washers can be made from a scrap of leather. I once took a reinforcing patch off a pack to do this. To insert it more easily into the pump cylinder and to get it to form a good cup shape, push it in backward (open side out) a few times to get it to mould to shape. Then turn it round the other way on the piston and insert it open end inward. It's much easier to keep pumps oiled and to carry a spare piston than to make one.
- Clogged Stoves. Clogged stoves are difficult to clean, especially if clogged by deposits from motor gasoline or the gum from poor quality kerosene. Carry a spare generator for stoves such as Coleman, and cleaning needles and a full repair kit for MSR stoves such as Whisperlite and XGK. Maybe a spare generator for Whisperlite, too. Carry enough tools to totally dismantle your stove.

Most stove problems are from dirt entering via the fuel or via joints when two-piece stoves are separated. Make sure open joints are kept clean and capped, and do not separate the stove unnecessarily.

Carry a spare tank cap/safety valve assembly for Optimus stoves because they do not always reseat properly if the valve blows, especially if the valve catches fire.

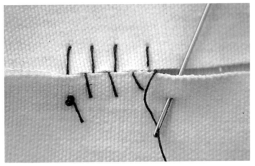

The sailmaker's Figure 8 stitch is a good way to keep edges aligned so stresses are equalized. It enables you to stitch from one side of a large panel such as a tent.

Squeezing a zipper slider at the narrow end as shown may restore its effectiveness. See text. Don't crush the teeth.

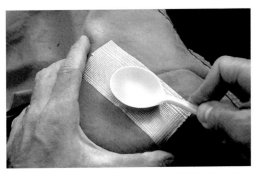

Making adhesive tape adhere better by rubbing it into the fabric with a hard, smooth object.

First Aid Kits

The wilderness environment places a heavy responsibility on recreational travellers to be well trained in first aid. Most "standard" first aid courses are designed with the assumption that professional help will arrive very soon. They are, of course, much better than nothing, but they hardly prepare you adequately for the wilderness emergency where you are often faced with providing long-term care for the victim.

Once travellers have a grounding in standard first aid, they should take a wilderness first aid course. Consult outdoor education programs, guides associations, and park rangers or wardens to locate a wilderness first aid course in your area. A very important part of these courses is the simulation training in the overall management of a wilderness emergency. AR/CPR certification should be mandatory for water-based activities.

There are many good first aid books. Make sure you obtain one that addresses first aid in the outdoors and in remote locations. There are also specialized books on frostbite, hypothermia and altitude sickness available.

First Aid Supplies

Wilderness first aid supplies must be well chosen and comprehensive. Unfortunately, you often end up in a group where everyone has a basic kit, and you have a zillion Band-Aids and an acre of moleskin. You have a couple of kilograms of stuff between you, but no one has the items you expect in a single, more comprehensive one- or two-kilogram kit. Take the time to find out what everyone has and organize a more complete kit for the party if necessary. You should not have everything in one place so ideally have two kits. Do not carry items you do not know how to use.

It is very important that the kit be in a suitable container to protect the contents from flexing, dirt, puncturing and particularly from water. A rigid container with a screw top gasketted lid or a Pelican box should be used for boating trips. When a warm container is immersed in cold water, a partial vacuum forms, drawing water inward through the smallest leak. Soggy dressings are no longer sterile!

First aid kit contents must be properly protected from water and damage using suitable containers.

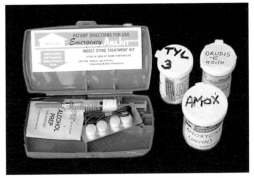

Make sure that all members of the party have an adequate supply of necessary personal medication. If medication is essential, such as insulin or asthma medication, a reserve supply should be carried in a different pack or canoe.

When there is a large group with only one first aid kit and rescue kit, label the pack or canoe containing the kit using a hang-tag such as these ones made from a margarine container lid.

Make sure everyone knows where the first aid supplies are—make a "+" with tape on the outside of the pack containing the first aid, or make a distinctive hang-tag that everyone in the group recognizes, and attach it to the appropriate pack. Major problems were caused at a recent air crash site because the survival and first aid equipment could not be identified in the jumble of baggage that all looked the same.

First-aiders are not supposed to administer drugs, yet certain drugs can be extremely useful in the wilderness. For example, painkillers can be of considerable benefit if a victim has to wait for a long time before evacuation. Antibiotics can control serious infections from cuts, animal bites or abscesses. For a long trip in wilderness environments it is advisable for each member of the party to obtain key emergency prescription medications from their **own** physician before the trip. That way they can use their **own** medication rather than medication prescribed for someone else. My experience has been that if people approach their family physician and explain the risks to which they will be exposed and the distance and time from help, there is little problem in obtaining a supply of prescription antibiotics and painkillers. If you've also done your reading and research and have a reasonable knowledge of the capabilities of drugs, your doctor may feel better able to trust your judgement about when to take them.

People who depend on regular medication should carry double the amount needed for the trip and split the supply between two separate places—two packs, two canoes, etc. People with allergies, especially to foods, should take special precautions and bring appropriate antihistamines or an anakit. Remember, there is more likelihood of making a mistake on a trip where you will probably be eating other people's cooking.

First Aid Kit

This is a suggested list that *should be modified to suit your particular type of trip and the number of participants.* All items must be in a waterproof container, which should preferably be rigid.

- Wilderness first aid manual
- Pencil, paper and accident report form
- Soap or Hibitane hand cleanser
- Disposable latex gloves to wear when administering first aid or to wear temporarily over dressings on an injured hand in wet or dirty conditions.
- Tensor bandage five centimetres (two inches) wide
- Triangular bandages (two-three)
- Assorted Band-Aids
- Moleskin, at least 200 sq. centimetres (30 sq. inches)
- Seven centimetres (three inches) wide adhesive dressing strip 20-30 centimetres (8-12 inches) long
- Butterfly adhesive strips (six) in two sizes
- 10 assorted size Telfa pads
- Adhesive tape 1 metre x 25 millimetres (three feet by one inch)

- Large wound compress dressings 10 centimetres by 10 centimetres (four inches by four inches) and seven centimetres by seven centimetres (three inches by three inches)
- Eye pads
- Antiseptic cream, e.g., Savlon
- Tweezers, scissors, sewing needles for splinter removal
- Eye drops (Murine), Aspirin, acetaminophen, Tums, laxative, seasickness tablets, antihistamine pills, Calamine cream, safety pins
- Pocket artificial respiration mask e.g. Laerdal mask
- Antiseptic concentrate such as Savlon liquid concentrate to add to water for cleaning large areas of skin such as the first aider's hands, large grazes, etc. Research indicates that these substances are less effective than first supposed, so gloves are handy.
- Large syringe (30 millilitres) and #19 needle if possible for irrigating deep wounds. Do not irrigate with antiseptic scrubs that contain detergents. Use plain water or saline if in doubt.
- Cavit or similar temporary tooth cavity stopper (dentist)
- Tooth anaesthetic such as oil of cloves or a topical tooth anaesthetic ointment such as Ora-Jel.
- Antiflatulence preparations; either Beano to put on food or simethicone (Ovol-80) tablets.
- Contac-C or other cold symptom relief tablets
- Cough suppressant tablets
- SAM splint or wire splint
- Finger cots (like miniature condoms to protect bandages and dressings on fingers from becoming wet). Do not leave these on for a long time because the warm, damp conditions inside promote bacterial growth.
- Antifungal powders for athlete's foot and jock itch.
- Broad spectrum antibiotic for long trips in remote places. Approach your doctor explaining why you might need it and what sort of injuries you might use it for (animal bites, deep cuts, abscesses—tooth abscesses especially, etc.). Make it clear it is for your use only.
- Strong painkiller such as 292, Tylenol with codeine. Explain to your doctor where you are going and why you might need it. Make it clear it is for your use only.
- Earplugs. They may help a sick or injured person sleep while others are up and active. Also useful for you if you find yourself in a hut or tent with snorers or coughers. Be aware of the dangers of sleeping with these in—you are less alert to the sounds for which you maybe ought to wake up!

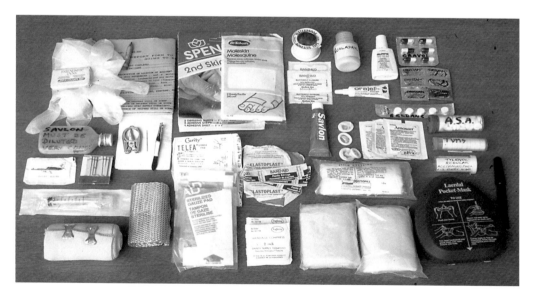

Survival Kits

You can do a lot with virtually nothing if you are a highly skilled survival specialist who has devoted a large amount of time and effort to becoming well trained. By all means read some books, take some courses and practice. However, until you have acquired enough skills to make do with almost nothing, you should make sure you always have certain key survival items with you **on your person** at all times. Also, do not avoid the trap of spending so much energy on learning survival skills that you neglect to learn the skills that will keep you out of trouble in the first place! Some outdoor groups and youth groups in particular seem to put a lot more emphasis on survival than on basic skills and prevention.

The key items must be actually on your person. It's no good having nothing in your pockets but lots of survival gear in the pack you just lost in an avalanche or down a crevasse, or that you last saw disappearing down the trail in the jaws of a bear. Obviously you cannot carry a lot of gear on your person at all times, but a few key items kept in your pockets will make a big difference.

The key items are firestarting equipment, and some insect repellent and a frameless head net in summer. A "disposable" foil space blanket is very useful, too, relative to its weight and bulk. These items together weigh less than one Rambo-style "survival knife." They are going to do you far more good, too, unless you go in for combat with grizzlies or with the forces of evil and darkness.

If you are travelling lightly clad, for example, canoeing or hiking in shorts, make sure you always have at least a light nylon shell with you all the time. Its ability to keep out wind, insects and to some extent water, coupled with the possibility of stuffing it with natural insulation, make it the most versatile and useful item for the space and weight. We tie the shell and pants neatly around our waists when canoeing scantily clad.

There are lots of other useful items, but they all add up in weight so that you may not always have them with you. I have met people whose "survival kit" weighed enough to sink a battleship and certainly enough to exhaust them so that they would probably end up needing it!

Survival Kit

The following are my suggestions for the contents of a survival kit. The first three items and a good utility knife are the key ones to keep on your person at all times. You can add or delete the others as you think fit, but will probably not want to keep all of them in your pockets. You will also need to modify the kit to suit the season and the environment.

Firelighting equipment. There is virtually no excuse for being caught without functioning matches or a lighter, and they are quick, reliable technology everyone knows how to use. Stash them in several places in your gear. You have probably got better things to do with your time than worry about learning to use flint and steel and fire drills, particularly under damp conditions. Certainly you can light an infinite number of fires with flint and steel or a drill, but usually you stand a better chance of surviving if you stay put, so you only need to light one fire anyway and keep it going.

Coghlan's Fire Sticks are an excellent firestarter. They are unaffected by water and have no smell. A piece two centimetres long is usually enough if the kindling twigs are small.

Keep at least one set of firestarting equipment sealed and complete just for emergencies and use another set for day-to-day use.

Don't rely on waterproof matches to be waterproof, no matter what the label says. They might be waterproof, but the box or striker often isn't! Use a good quality waterproof container that can be easily opened with cold hands—some traditional captive-lid metal containers are awkward to open.

Kodak film canisters are okay, especially if you tape the lid on, but a small size (30 millilitre) Nalgene bottle is much better. Some commercial plastic match cases are camouflage coloured so that you can lose them easily. Choose the bright orange ones instead. If you are putting the striker from a match box in your match case, include a fold of card to stop the match heads rubbing on the striker in your pocket, or you could have a nasty surprise!

Disposable cigarette lighters work well as long as they are kept warm in your pocket so the butane liquid will still change to a gas. To prevent the gas valve being turned on in your pocket or gear and leading to loss of the gas, jam it with a wide elastic band wrapped around the top of the lighter or with a small wooden chip held in place with duct tape. The new childproof lighters make this unnecessary.

As with match cases, choose a conspicuous colour so you don't lose the lighter.

A small amount of firestarter will greatly assist your fire lighting efforts under windy or wet conditions, which is when you most need the fire anyway. Coghlan's Fire Sticks are an excellent product. They do not smell or disintegrate, and are unaffected by water. You only need a piece two centimetres long, not a whole stick. A couple of birthday-cake candles in your match case or held onto the lighter with the elastic band is another handy help. Skyblazer firestarters are very hot mini road flares that burn for about two minutes.

Insect protection. Insects can cause enough stress to seriously impair your ability to think and function in an emergency. A small plastic bottle of concentrated repellent should always be with you if you are in serious bug country. If you are on the water and away from the bugs, still keep it on your person in case you end up ashore unexpectedly minus your boat and gear! A frameless head net is simply a large bag, easily made of mosquito netting. The Bug Hat made by Lynn Valley in Ontario has good features including a Lycra neck seal. You can always improvise a frame from thin twigs.

Space blanket. For your survival kit choose the very thin disposable variety. They will last you through the emergency if you are reasonably careful. Space blankets are totally windproof and waterproof for use as a cloak or lean-to. The shiny foil reflects radiant body heat back inward, though the effect of this is small compared to the benefits of the windproofness and waterproofness. They can produce a considerable reduction of evaporative and convective heat loss.

The most dramatic reflective effect is felt if the space blanket is used to reflect heat from a fire onto your back when sitting facing a fire. A lean-to lined with a space blanket is like a reflector oven.

Space blankets must be kept dry during storage otherwise the metal coating comes off. Double-bag them if they are in, say, a lifejacket pocket or any other place where they will be exposed to moisture. Some brands are packaged with an envelope of silica gel desiccant to keep them drier, but this only works for atmospheric moisture, not liquid seepage.

Metal water container. Many people use a tin can as the container for their emergency gear so they also have something in which to sterilize water or to melt snow. The plastic snap-on lid that comes with some cans can be taped on to keep the kit intact and dry. However, a "tin" (steel) can is 60 or more grams heavier than an aluminum can such as a pop can or Maple Leaf ham can.

Cord. Useful for setting up shelters and for repairs. Strong nylon utility cord, preferably orange, is a good choice. You are better off with lots of thin cord than with a small amount of thick cord—it's easier to double up thin cord than it is to separate the strands of thick cord!

Water purifying chemicals. A small container of purifying tablets is the most practical item for a survival kit because it is small and light.

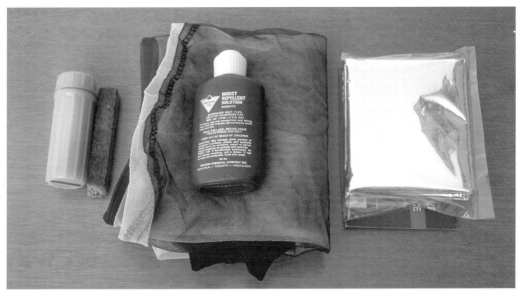

Basic survival items to have on your person at all times—firestarter, insect repellent, head net (spring and summer only) and a foil blanket.

Signalling devices. A good whistle. The Fox 40 is probably the best. A signalling mirror. Signal flares and smoke projectors. See section on "signalling equipment," pages 365-368. Remember that you cannot fly on commercial airlines with pyrotechnics in your luggage.

Repair items. See section page 341.

Emergency food. A shortage of water will produce serious adverse symptoms long before a shortage of food will. Provision of adequate water is far more important than provision of food. That said, it is still good to have some emergency food, particularly to get you through the hectic time of dealing with the emergency and setting up your bivouac.

The rations you choose must be non-perishable, and marked with the date so they can be periodically replaced. If you have a weak will like mine, choose a nutritious item in a flavour you dislike so that you will not be tempted to raid the survival kit in a non-emergency and devour the emergency food. Specially packed emergency rations can be bought from survival equipment suppliers, or you can use athletic sports bars.

Fishing hooks and line. In some places fish are easy to catch, particularly once you have the first one and can use its eggs or other parts as bait. Anything goes in an emergency! A variety of different sized hooks with leaders attached should be included along with some line. If you use a pop can with a rounded bottom as your kit container, you can wrap the line around it and use it to cast. With practice you can cast with the line running off the bottom of the can like an open-faced reel. (At least the Inuit kids I once watched could!)

Brass snare wire. Probably more useful for most people as part of the repair kit, but can be used for snaring animals **if** you know how. You also need to know how to do it in the environment in which you find yourself, which may not be a familiar one.

Swiss Army knife. The Camper model is small enough to keep in your pocket at all times and has a couple of good blades, a very sharp saw, an awl/needle, screwdrivers, etc. Beware of the nasty imitations made from low-grade steel, and don't buy a knife that has so many gadgets that it's too heavy to keep with you **in your pocket** all the time. Some people feel they must have a 25-centimetre, 500-gram knife dangling from their belts before they head off into the woods. This may boost (falsely) their fragile self-confidence and reduce their level of insecurity. However, it is often a source of much derisive amusement to other travellers who go lightly and with skill in the backcountry. An entire survival kit, including a Camper model genuine Swiss Army knife, weighs about as much as one of these macho daggers.

Axes and saws. These are, of course, heavy, particularly the axe. The axe is a great tool to hurt yourself with and to thereby compound the seriousness of the emergency. A saw will do everything an axe will do except split wood, and it is a lot less dangerous. Together they enable you to use large driftwood on beaches where all the small wood has been picked over by other campers. A saw and axe are desirable in a canoeing or rafting party for cutting people free of tree or boat entrapments. Carry a hacksaw or hacksaw blade for your saw if you have metal frames on your rafts or canoes. Then you can free people, especially when legs are trapped under metal seats in a boat wrapped round a rock. You can buy a length of metal-cutting bandsaw blade to fit any saw.

A selection of firestarters and match containers. The metal captive lid container is difficult to open with cold hands.

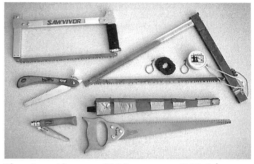

There is a wide range of folding saws available for recreationists. Even the small Opinel (bottom left) is very effective. The pruning saw, bottom right, makes a good snow saw and cuts wood, too.

A selection of survival kit items.

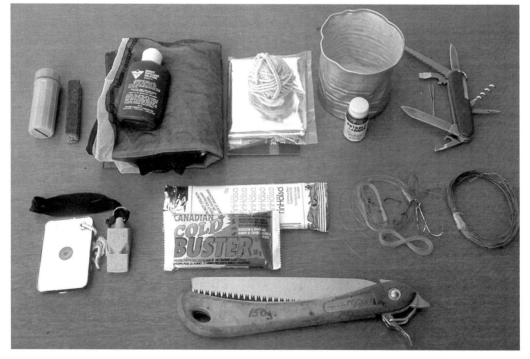

Handling Emergencies Effectively

In spite of your preventive efforts, sooner or later a wilderness emergency will occur. Because you don't encounter emergencies every time you go out, you'll probably be quite scared and close to panic, even with good advance planning and practice.

The key to handling an emergency well is **good organization** so as to use your skills and resources as efficiently as possible. Although every situation is different, the following framework for handling wilderness emergencies will help you deal with a mishap in a logical, methodical manner, with minimal danger to yourself and the rest of the party.

Handling Emergencies

Don't Panic! Calm yourself—count to 10, take a few deep breaths and then get on with the job as methodically as you can.

Somebody must take charge of the situation! Volunteer yourself, designate, order or somehow obtain a person to fill this role and do it **immediately!** The first person on the scene of the mishap will lead, at least initially.

Inventory the gear and equipment so that you know what you have to work with.

The continued safety of the leader and the **safety of the rest of the party** is the top priority. This is not selfishness—rescuers are no use to the first victim if they get into trouble, too!

The first job of the first person on the scene is to **stop the rest of the party** and **warn them of the hazard**. They should check for **further hazards** and take appropriate action to prevent further mishaps to themself or the party.

Take **time** to **properly assess** the problem—few crises require an absolute split-second response. The first assessment may have to be done at a distance from the victim to plan your safe approach. If you feel yourself panicking, rushing or becoming overwhelmed, pull back, think, "count to 10," then get on with the job carefully and methodically.

Remember the **C-ABC first aid priorities**: C-spine, Airway, Breathing, Circulation. Non-breathers need quick response, serious bleeders likewise. Screamers at least have an airway, so their actual priority may be relatively low. However, they are disconcerting, and people tend to find them alarming and want to deal with them first.

When you are planning a course of action to solve a problem, try to keep an open mind and not have too many preconceived ideas. Most of us have deep-rooted ways of thinking. For example, when you look at the box in the photo you probably blink and wonder how it was made with two dovetails at right angles. Look at the photo on the opposite page.

Inventory the group skills and equipment. (If it was done at the start of the trip, you don't have to do it again in a hurry in a crisis.) Inventory the immediate surroundings for useful resources, too. In your trip planning you should have made yourself aware of what external rescue resources are available, how and where to activate them, their capabilities and their approximate response times.

Plan and communicate a plan of action for first aid or rescue on the basis of priorities and available skills and resources. Make sure that **everyone understands** the plan. The leader should delegate jobs—use people effectively. All actions must improve the situation; do not risk making it worse for the victim or rescuers by hasty, ill-conceived or carelessly executed actions. Your initial assessment should have established whether there is any need at all for rescuers to be in a high-speed (and possibly risky to themselves or the victim) "rescue" mode versus the slower, safer "recovery" mode. Switch to the "recovery" mode as soon as possible. Remember that **hypothermia** is very likely to develop as a result of even a fairly minor injury, and it is a significant threat to life in a wilderness emergency.

Carry out the plan. Make as much use of the group and its skills and equipment as possible.

Depending on the level of skill within the group, it is usually best for the **leader to stand back**, keep hands off, delegate/coordinate/supervise the group, and maintain an overview and control of the **whole situation.** This will nearly always be better than the leader becoming involved in the actual tasks. It also gives the leader a chance to formulate alternative plans in case the first one does not work.

When the situation is stabilized, **regroup, take stock of the situation**, make sure that all problems are taken care of and that all available equipment and resources have been used to advantage. A checklist (page 357) and an Accident Report Form (page 377) are useful reminders that you have done everything. **Assess the condition of the party**, and act accordingly. People tend to neglect themselves in the heat of the action. After a recent Arctic air crash it was recounted how someone had systematically gone the rounds of all the survivors so everyone was spoken to regularly and no one was forgotten or left to "stew" for too long.

Decide whether to **evacuate the victim, bivouac or send for help**. Consider the time of day, travelling conditions, state of the rescuers, state of the victim, how soon you'll be missed, whether you are where you said you would be, capabilities of rescue services, your equipment and the skills in the group.

If you decide to send for help, you should send at least **two people**; the fittest and most competent who can be spared without jeopardizing the rescue. They must be fed and watered, equipped for an emergency overnight, and they must have a map and well-planned route they can be sure of successfully completing under the conditions. They must have **very clear written instructions** and information about the incident:

- where they should report to
- where, when and what type of accident
- number of victims, condition of the victims and who the victims are
- condition and capability of party
- landmarks, how to find the site.

A report form to accompany the party going for help is a useful checklist—you'll probably be rattled by the situation and a checklist reduces risk of oversights. Beware of people prematurely running off for help. Sometimes this is the response of people who cannot face the accident scene, and is more an excuse to get away than a well thought-out, helpful action.

If you are reasonably skilled and equipped, the bivouac/message party option may be the safest for all concerned. If the amount of bivouac equipment is limited, you might consider having most of the party continue the trip, leaving some of their equipment for the victim and a few helpers. This would generate some risk—it would only be okay if the rest of the party can be sure of getting out before nightfall and without having another accident!

If you make a **decision to evacuate**, you must take into account such factors as how urgently medical attention is required, type and extent of injuries and therefore hazards to victim, hazards to the party, distance, terrain, time of day or year, equipment available, and size and strength of party. You will also need some information concerning the availability and type of external rescue service available, its capabilities and response time. There is no point in carrying out a hazardous improvised rescue if a fully equipped rescue team with a short response time is readily available. Consider the effect of weather or darkness on helicopter rescues.

Even with a large fresh team with good equipment, a ground evacuation is **exhausting** and therefore potentially hazardous. It is hard on the victim, too, and may aggravate injuries. An improvised ground evacuation with your own tired party is worse. You should consider the possibility of the slightly injured victim assisting in their own slow but sure, assisted self-evacuation. For example, one injured arm does not immobilize the victim completely and make them into a stretcher case. I often see a one-armed cross country skier on my local backcountry trails, and I have twice met a one-armed paddler on wilderness trips.

Key points to remember
(maybe write them on a card)

- **Don't Panic**. Slow down
- **Leader**—Appoint, designate
- **Safety**—yourself, party
- **Assess** the situation
- **Inventory** skills, equipment, surroundings
- **Think, plan, communicate** a course of action
- **Delegate, supervise, leader's hands off**
- **Alternative plan**
- **Take stock of situation, checklist**
- **Logbook/Report Form** as soon as possible
- **Assess party's condition**
- **Plan bivouac/evacuation/message**

Our preconceived ideas and narrow thinking probably had us assuming the dovetails were at right angles to the surface and wondering how the lid could be removed. They do not have to be at right angles!

Sending for help. Whatever type of rescue organization you are trying to bring to your assistance, the better the information you can provide for them the better they can respond. If complete, detailed information is available, they can assess the situation without having to do their own time-consuming research, and will be able to respond more immediately and more appropriately. The sample form on page 377 shows the amount of detail rescue people like to receive. I carry one of these, printed on coloured, waterproofed paper (see section on waterproofing maps) in my field book and in the first aid kit. Even if you are not physically going out for help but are using a radio, this information should be completed, ready to transmit to the emergency services operator.

The leader should keep their hands off and maintain an overview of the whole situation.

Collaborating With Emergency Services and Other Groups

Problems can arise if emergency services personnel without technical expertise arrive at a technical rescue site and want to take over completely. They may be reluctant to use members of the party or of the public who are experts in the activity such as paddlers or climbers. They may, with good reason, be reluctant to mix their comrades up in a high risk environment with unknown people. In these cases careful and sensitive communication should result in a cooperative effort to combine the skills and resources of both groups to successfully effect a rescue. A technical rescue team will usually want to take over completely—be prepared to stay clear or assist only as asked. You may feel "left out"!

Other wilderness travellers, operators and guides may be very well trained and able to assist at an emergency on a voluntary basis if needed. They may even have the trump card of radio communication with the outside world. I was out ski touring with a guided group when our guide saved the life of a heli-ski guide in a dramatic avalanche rescue in response to a radio call.

Paying for Rescues

You may be asked to pay for some types of rescue. One wild incident in the north involved a group of four would-be paddlers who had left a trail of errors and destruction behind them on a remote river. They decided they had had enough and wanted to be flown out, and found a ranger with a radio. It was not a real emergency since they were not at risk of anything worse than being a bit hungry and uncomfortable for a week, so it was certain they would have to pay for evacuation. The air charter company they radioed was wary of incurring some potentially unrecoverable costs, particularly as the people were foreign visitors. Eventually after protracted radio negotiations they were required to put up their rifles as collateral for a loan before the plane would come!

Carrying your Visa, Mastercard or traveller's cheques with you on the trip could greatly facilitate evacuation, especially a marginal or nonmedical evacuation. Being able to pay first and recoup your money later can often be much quicker and less hassle than persuading a doctor to authorize a medical rescue on a patient he hasn't seen and can't communicate effectively with.

At time of writing there is talk that adventurers in the far north may be required to have insurance to cover rescue costs. This has been proposed as a result of an expensive, hazardous and probably unnecessary search for an Arctic adventurer who claimed he was not actually lost, missing or in trouble.

(Costs of) evacuations from real medical emergencies are usually covered by your insurance, see page132. However, medical insurance is unlikely to cover the evacuation of the rest of the party. Also, the evacuation flight might not be able to take out equipment, so the expense of a flight to retrieve gear may be incurred later. It might increase your options if, while awaiting the rescue flight you pack your gear up small and tight and decide what it will be least costly to abandon if you can't take everything.

Remember that if you do call for a medical evacuation, you must go to a medical facility if you expect the evacuation to be paid for. One incident I know of involved an individual with an injury that had the potential to be serious if they continued the two-week trip. The outfitter was able to arrange for the person to be flown out. However, once back in civilization, the victim suddenly saw the injury in a much less serious light and went home to the other side of the country without visiting the hospital. The outfitter was then stuck with the bill for the flight!

Dealing with the Press

The press may possibly wish to interview you after a rescue when you are exhausted, emotionally drained and perhaps trying to deal with the injury or even the death of a good friend. You will probably not be at your best or your most patient, and may be inclined to ignore them or be rude. However, it is usually best to give them a brief statement to make sure they obtain a true picture from a person who was actually there. This is better than having them piece together a less accurate story from snippets of information gleaned from less informed sources. However, you should be very careful about what statements you make because they could be used in a later lawsuit. It is not easy to think clearly about what you say at a time when you are stressed and tired. Ideally, the rescue authorities will provide the bulk of the information needed.

Survival After an Emergency

A wilderness emergency can easily lead to loss of equipment and food such that your continued survival is a problem, even though you survived the initial incident. Once the initial crisis is over, you may be have to remain in the backcountry for some time until rescued. You may, in fact, be just beginning your difficulties if you have to survive with few remaining resources. The situation is less serious if someone knows where you were going, when you were to return and what to do if you are not back on time. As long as you are actually still on your planned route and there are people with the capability to find you and the conditions allow them to find you, you just have to wait it out. However, if the mishap occurs on, say, the third day of a two-week trip, you will have a long wait before someone realizes there is a problem. Below are a few survival pointers. However, for more detailed information you should consult books specifically on survival.

General Procedures

Make a thorough inventory of all the gear and food and the surroundings and then make sure that everything is used to advantage. You may have to deal with the problem of some people saying, "I carried emergency gear and put up with a heavier pack while you were having an easy time so I am going to use it." I was once on an unintended bivouac because one of the party was too slow and we didn't get off the climb before dark. Other party members had often ribbed me unconstructively about the size of my pack and my emergency gear. They were all of a sudden very interested in what I had with me. You can be sure I was not keen to share it unless someone really needed it.

Keeping warm and dry to prevent hypothermia is a priority. Get out of the wind into a sheltered place, or use your tarps, bivouac sacs, etc., to build a shelter. If you can get to a place where there is fuel, build a fire to dry out, warm up and particularly for the morale-boosting effect. The smoke may also alleviate insect problems.

Good shelter can often be found with no need for a major construction project by keeping your mind and eyes open.

You may have to contend with people in your group who have never spent a night out in the open and who may need considerable reassurance and calming down. They may have all sorts of fears and phobias that you as an experienced backcountry person would not even have imagined.

Liquid is far more important than food, so melt snow or boil water in whatever containers you have available and make sure people drink plenty. People of my ancestry say, "Where there's tea there's hope." Actually, the stimulant effect of the caffeine is only a

Building waterproof shelters from natural materials is a lot of work even if suitable materials are on hand. You can save work if you spot a partly built natural shelter or if you have a tarp with you.

transitory benefit and the diuretic effect leads to poor retention of the liquid and possibly to dehydration as well.

Living Off the Land

Living off the land should only be done in emergencies. It is easier said than done. Patrick McManus, in *A Fine and Pleasant Misery* published by Owl Books, wrote: "Don't worry," I said, "we can always live off the country. Then I looked around. The country didn't seem to be very edible. Perhaps this trip would be harder than I expected."

Unless you are very skilled at hunting, fishing and foraging in *similar terrain* with improvised equipment, living off the land is likely to be unproductive, frustrating and energy consuming. You might well be better off to conserve your energy by staying inactive. Familiarity with the type of terrain and its flora and fauna is very important. Samuel Black's account of his 1824 exploration of the headwaters of the Peace River recounts how even his expert Chipewyan hunter from the Peace Delta was almost useless as a food provider in the unfamiliar mountain terrain traversed by the expedition.

However, if you have a gun you are generally entitled to use it for survival purposes. For example, the N.W.T. Wildlife Ordinance section 41 (1) states that a person, "May hunt wildlife and take the eggs of birds for food where it is necessary to prevent his or another person's starvation." However, the following section adds that, "A person commits an offence who, **through mismanagement or poor planning**, requires to invoke subsection (1)."

The "mismanagement or poor planning" phrase is open to interpretation, of course, and the level of incompetence permitted is open to conjecture. I would suggest that if food was left unattended and in an insecure place and was lost to a bear, that would rate as mismanagement. A competently organized group doesn't often lose all its food because it would be distributed among different canoes, packs, sleds or locations. Unforeseeable delays that resulted in food being used up before the end of a trip might be an excusable reason to live off the land, but simply not allowing enough time and running out of food would probably be inexcusable. But, in the Alaskan and Canadian wilderness what is an "unforeseeable" delay?! It's a place where you should expect the unexpected!

Similar regulations exist in Alaska. You may kill game for food if you are in a dire emergency, which means if you are in a remote area, you are unintentionally out of food, you will seriously risk death or permanent health problems if you do not take an animal, and you cannot expect to get more food from any other source in time to save you. You must surrender leftovers to the state after rescue and make a statement about the circumstances.

If you are in a location and time of year where plant foods are available, you may be able to feed well without killing animals. This requires a good knowledge of edible plants.

Fires for Emergency Use

A fire has several benefits in a survival situation.

- It is a major psychological boost to have a roaring fire in an emergency. It evokes deep-rooted feelings of warmth and security. It provides interest with its movement and flickering light, and its need for tending.
- Light and/or smoke from the fire can alert rescuers to your position.
- Gathering wood is a relatively unskilled job to keep the party occupied doing something

useful so they are less likely to feel helpless and become panicky.

- Fires can be used to keep warm, heat lean-tos, dry clothing, cook food, melt snow for water and sterilize water for drinking.

In practice there may not be enough fuel available and it may be difficult to light a fire under the prevailing conditions. Conditions are often foul and you probably aren't at your best. Gathering wood for a big enough fire to keep you warm all night in winter is difficult in the dark, on uneven ground, in thick woods, in a crisis, when tired or injured, and especially if you do not have a good saw or you are in deep snow. Smaller, more efficient fires for drying gear and heating food and drink before retiring to a snow shelter can be a more practical proposition in winter. Even in summer with the shorter nights and no snow, it is still a major task to obtain enough fuel to keep a fire going all night.

There are, however, a few places where you can reasonably easily gather enough wood for an all-night bonfire. One of these is in an old burn, where there are plenty of dry dead standing trees in a small area. They can usually be knocked down fairly easily, especially with a saw. In winter, beaver-flooded areas also yield plenty of dead trees, conveniently rotted at ice level, and it may be easy to move around in the open level terrain of the frozen pond. A drift pile on a riverbank or a pile of avalanche forest debris may yield a good supply of wood or a ready-made bonfire pile. In R. M. Patterson's *The Dangerous River*, there is a wonderful scene where his partner fired a drift pile and he and the dog team cavorted around it after a midwinter capsize in the Nahanni canyon. If you gathering a lot of long wood you can't cut up, just burn it through in the middle to make shorter and shorter lengths.

You should **always** have matches or other firestarters, sealed in waterproof containers, for emergencies only. Place them throughout your gear—in pockets, packs, lifejacket pockets or attached to your canoe.

In winter you will have to dig down to ground level or build a base for your fire on the snow if digging is impractical. A base should be built from wet, green or rotting wood that will be no use as fuel. The pieces should be as thick as possible and in several crisscross layers so that they do not burn through too fast.

You can often break quite large diameter wood by levering it between two standing trees. If you put a layer of snow and debris between the layers, it will retard burn-through.

Before trying to light a fire, take the time to get organized. Gather all the material you need to light it and keep it going once lit. A supply of dry kindling is almost always found in the bottom branches of spruce trees, and birch bark is always reliable. Fuzz-sticks made by shaving a twig so the shavings protrude from it are useful if you have a knife good enough to cut them safely, but the inner parts of sticks are not necessarily drier than the outside. Candles, fire starters, oil, rubber and fuel can all be used to reduce the need for really dry kindling. If you are using fuel, conserve it by placing it in a container rather than sprinkling it over a pile of wood. A tuna can, piece of foil, tin lid, etc., will do, and then build a neat, organized pile of kindling over it. If you can put sand in the can along with gasoline it will burn longer and in a more controlled manner. Break the wood up so that it will lie close together, otherwise flames from already burning material will only heat up air spaces instead of catching on to more wood. Don't pack it so tight as to impede airflow, however.

Build up a high back to your fire with rock or logs, so that you have a tall, glowing, heat-radiating surface. Flat rocks tend to shatter with the heat so be careful. Unless the fire is tall, most of the heat radiates upward, instead of forward onto you. In a winter emergency, you could in a pinch locate your fire against a

In emergencies build your fire up against a large log or rock so the heat is thrown forward toward you. This leaves a mess so it should only be used in an emergency. Note how a bail handle enables the pot to be easily suspended in the fire.

If there is a good supply of easily gathered, ready-made firewood nearby, such as a riverbank log jam or this avalanche debris, keeping warm with a fire is a much more practical option.

stump or a big fallen tree so you do not need to build a fire-back. The stump or fallen tree will probably glow and radiate heat horizontally for a while even after the flames from the fire stop licking up onto it. If you just have a big pile of burning wood, you will be working all night to supply the monster with fuel. Remember the saying—skilled woodsman stays warm by small fire, greenhorn stays warm working to cut fuel for a big fire!

When sitting or lying in front of a fire, you should arrange some kind of reflector behind you. A rock wall, the roots of an upturned tree or a space blanket hung between trees or skis will help considerably to warm both your front and back. It will reflect fire heat onto your back. Beware of burning your boots or clothes when sleeping near a fire—it really does happen.

If you are lying crosswise to the fire and the fire is long, more of your body will be warmed than if you are at right angles to a compact fire.

Think carefully about the forest fire hazard before lighting up your fire. Large survival fires are difficult to extinguish. A forest fire will attract lots of planes and potential rescuers but you might just get doused with fire retardant or you may be "done to a turn" before they even arrive!

Emergency Snow Shelters

The quinzee or Algonkian snowhouse is the most useful type of snow shelter to learn to build. It is built using loose snow, so you can build one virtually anywhere. You can build it right beside an injured person and drag them in on a ground sheet or bivy bag. A big advantage of this type of shelter is that the whole group can work at it without any great skill and can feel useful and involved. While you are working, the leader can brief and reassure the whole group.

To build a quinzee, pile up a mound of snow in such a way that it will quickly harden at the surface, and then hollow it out. Many people believe incorrectly that you cannot make these shelters with loose sugar snow. I even had a highly qualified guide pooh-pooh my suggestion to build this type of shelter in some sugary snow. The key to success is to mix the snow thoroughly. This mixes the different layers of snowpack that have different temperatures, moisture contents and crystallization states.

When the snow is well mixed, hardening of the pile can be very rapid and you can often start hollowing immediately the pile is finished.

Inspect your intended site carefully for rocks, stumps, small trees, etc. It's annoying to end up with a Christmas tree in the middle of your abode! Plant an inverted ski pole as a centre marker. The size of the mound you need to build depends on the degree of emergency and the amount of comfort you need, but approximately three to four metres diameter will suffice for three people to stretch out, four or five people to huddle. For a group, several smaller shelters, possibly interconnected, is better than one large one. There is less snow to move, less chance of collapse, collapse does not deprive you of all your shelter and the shelters are warmer.

Trample, mix and consolidate the snow where the walls will stand. Work around the marker, throwing snow at the centre of your chosen site. Dig with shovels, folded foamies or dog-style with big mitts on, or with arms in a stuffbag. If the snowpack is shallow, it is easier to gather the required quantity of snow on the even surface of a lake or pond. Use your skis or logs or even folded foam pads as a bulldozer blade. Dig right down close to the ground before you move to another spot so that you get a good mix of snow temperatures. If you are dealing with predominantly sugary snow with a little bit of powder, you may do better by making the mound mostly with sugary stuff and saving the powder to mix with sugar in the final layers.

When the pile is approaching completion, compact the final layers to consolidate them better. There's no point in compacting any sooner because you don't want to harden the stuff you will be digging out! Beating with a shovel is no good. Use outstretched flattened hands or fists. Make sure you break up and mix any lumps at this stage. Leave the pile until the outer layer feels stiff when you try to push the straight fingers of a gloved hand into it. Usually you can start digging almost immediately you have completed the pile if you have done the mixing and surface compacting properly. Unless the temperature is very warm and rising it should never take more than an hour for the snow to set up.

While the pile is hardening, gather fuel, cook, drink, inventory and dry out your gear, and in emergencies gather evergreen boughs for floor insulation. Insert sticks approximately 25-30 centimetres into the pile so that the excavator inside can gauge wall thickness by spotting the ends of the sticks. The excavator should remove most of their clothes except outer, shell garments. Excavate the interior through a relatively large hole—you will stay drier. Fill this hole in later. Excavation must progress in stages as shown by the dotted lines below. Avoid the tendency to tunnel in too far too low too soon—this results in thin walls, a thick heavy roof and collapse.

When the interior is excavated, make a new, small, low entrance on the side at 90 degrees to the wind so the entrance does not become drifted in. The second diagram shows the excavator taking a well-earned rest, their back holding packs up against the original excavating entrance while the outside person piles snow against them. The outside person then excavates a new, low entrance whose top is **below** the level of the floor. This difference of level is **crucial** if the shelter is to be warm. The floor can be built up and levelled with snow from final interior trimming. If you build the quinzee on a slope and the entrance is on the downhill side, it is easier to make the floor higher than the top of the entrance. What you are trying to do in this or any snow shelter is to make a trap for the warm air. Warm air rises, and if the top of the entrance is below floor level, warm air cannot escape and you will have warm air down to floor level. All too often one hears people referring to digging a "cold air sink," but this is a backward way of viewing the situation—think instead of making a warm air **trap**. A roof vent is crucial if you are using a stove in the shelter. When you are not using the stove, block the vent with a crumpled plastic bag to keep body heat in.

Once you have mastered this shelter, try some of the other types that require more specific sites and conditions.

If you mix the snow and compact it properly, it will set up very quickly. These people stood on a quinzee roof within a few hours of building it.

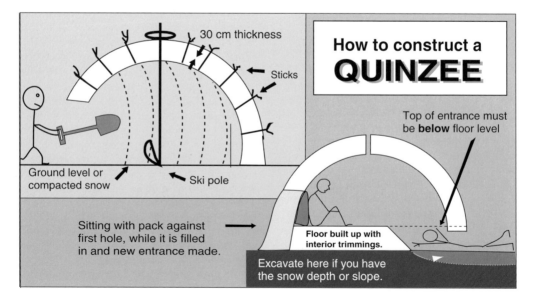

30 cm thickness

Sticks

How to construct a
QUINZEE

Top of entrance must be **below** floor level

Ground level or compacted snow

Ski pole

Sitting with pack against first hole, while it is filled in and new entrance made.

Floor built up with interior trimmings.

Excavate here if you have the snow depth or slope.

Signalling to Attract Attention

There will be occasions when you must be able to make yourself conspicuous and easy to find. This may be necessary in an emergency but also if you simply need to be picked up at a rendezvous by an aircraft or boat or want to meet up with other members of your party.

One of the most useful contributions toward making yourself easy to find is to make sure that someone knows where you are going and that you navigate well enough to actually go exactly where you said you were going. The smaller the area they have to search, the better.

The colour of your clothing is a very significant factor in making yourself easy to find. During my youth in the U.K. everyone wore dull khaki outdoor clothing, and this led to some horrendously long searches for lost and injured wilderness travellers. The eventual response was to encourage people to wear safety orange and fluorescent garb, especially in bad weather. In many areas, especially popular ones, bright clothing can be an annoying visual intrusion, and for this reason many people now choose less conspicuous colours. If you only have inconspicuous coloured clothing, keep a tightly rolled orange garbage bag or something else that is bright and easy to see in your pocket at all times, ready to be deployed in an emergency. You must wear bright colours in hunting season all the time.

Many bug jackets are a dull green camouflage colour, and I used to ask my clients who were leaving camp in these garments for tundra hikes to be sure to carry something bright coloured with them. I also stitched orange panels to mine so I was more visible and also to make the garment more difficult to lose if I put it down. PFDs worn by canoeists and kayakers are often seen in purple, dark red and blue, which are not very conspicuous. They are therefore not government approved. If on spring ski tours you wear white shirts, nighties and hats for sun protection, you might consider applying a bright-coloured panel for visibility and safety.

Other items of equipment can also improve your visibility if they contrast well with the surroundings. My grey tent is inconspicuous against beach gravel, moraines and snow, but shows up reasonably well against bush. Or-ange and yellow would be more conspicuous under a wider range of conditions. A red or bright blue pack also helps. For our sleeping bags and liners we chose orange and red so we would have good signalling materials if needed. My folding kayak is dark blue on top so I made a point of using bright red material for the spray deck. When I applied rubbing strips to the grey underside I used orange material. Kayak hulls of any colour are difficult to see among the waves from water level, but bright colours do help an air search.

In summer conditions white is very conspicuous and a sheet sleeping bag liner is a useful signalling device. I have seen aerial survey parties using strips of white cloth to make a conspicuous "X." A canoe party who had come to grief on an Arctic river made their presence known to us from a considerable distance with a white sheet laid out on the rocks and SOS in strips of white cloth taped to an upturned canoe. Strips of white toilet paper are amazingly visible from the air and can even be used to write SOS.

A forestry ranger told me they use toilet rolls dropped from helicopters to mark all the smoking lightning strike sites immediately after thunderstorms. They could then return later to do a thorough check and still find the sites even though they might be less conspicuously smoking by that time.

The white SOS made with toilet paper is quite readable, bottom left, and the white smoke from burning greenery is conspicuous. White contrasts well against the dark background. The black smoke from a burning tire (flame shows centre) is invisible against the dark background. The large +, top right, made of various bright coloured garments does not show up well because the garments are different colours.

A properly built signal fire will quickly produce a towering tight column of smoke that will penetrate up through thick forest without becoming too dispersed.

Against snow, green boughs laid out in a large "+" are very conspicuous. Ground-up charcoal can also be used to darken the snow, as can some marine dye markers. A "+" is much easier to make than SOS and is very conspicuous from the air because it is so unnatural with straight lines and right angles.

The See/Rescue device is a tightly rolled 13 metre orange plastic strip available in 15, 28 and 44 centimetre widths and is designed to float flat on the surface of the water. It is very conspicuous from above and can also be used on land.

These are all passive ways to mark your position. Movement greatly improves your visibility, especially to people who are looking for you already. Waving is a help, but running to and fro is much better. A bright object such as an orange garbage bag or a jacket is much more visible if it is waved rather than being stationary. Waving it on a long pole or paddle or ski makes the length of the wave bigger and more conspicuous. Wave in such a way as to be at right angles to the direction of the rescuer's vision—a semicircle over the head to people level with you on land, and horizontally like a helicopter rotor if rescuers are more overhead. Take the trouble to attach the "flag" so that it opens out as much as possible into a big flat area that is as exposed as possible to viewers. Splashing in the water makes you more visible from aircraft, especially if the water is calm.

Smoke can be a good signal, either from signal fires or from smoke flares. Building a signal fire and keeping a good plume of smoke going is a lot of work, which you may not be able to do as a result of injuries, exhaustion or lack of suitable fuel. If no one is looking for you because you aren't overdue yet or because you didn't tell anyone you were going, you have to make the distinctive distress pattern of three fires in a triangle, and this is even more work. Under these circumstances, a single plume of smoke, which could just be a camp fire, wouldn't attract much attention.

However, in forested areas smoke may attract the attention of a fire watch tower or a fire watch aircraft. Hopefully, the bush is not so dense and your gear so dull in colour that they fail to see you and they just bomb your fire from the air with fire retardant and go on their way!

To keep a good column of smoke going for a lengthy period, you need plenty of fuel for a hot fire and plenty of duff, grass and leaves to pile on it. Even then, in dense forest with tall trees, the smoke can end up being dissipated on its way up through the canopy.

Special signal fires can be built to produce an intense narrow column of smoke that will penetrate up through the trees as a distinct column. Keep a general fire going as best you can but build a special signal fire or trio of fires ready to light when you hear an aircraft or boat approaching. Build a "teepee" of poles two to three metres high, and one third fill it with dry kindling. Then fill it up with green boughs, pine needles and duff, and thatch it with more green boughs. These help keep the rain off and produce a chimney effect. If you do a careful job it will produce a narrow towering column of smoke within a few moments. You need to be very quick when you hear an aircraft approaching because the pilot's field of vision of the ground is a considerable distance ahead. If you have some fuel, use it to get your fires going quickly.

The large cross made of boughs is the most conspicuous feature because of the colour contrast, the unnatural shape and the uniformity. The white smoke shows against the trees but not where it drifts across the snow. The trampled SOS is almost invisible even though kicked down to the ground. The vehicles and tracks show well.

Always consider the background against which rescuers may see the smoke. White smoke shows up well against a clear sky and against a dark background of rock or conifers. It may not show up well against pale dry grasses, snow, sand or river gravel. Black smoke from burning tires, mud flaps, plastic canoe fragments, asphalt shingles, oil, birch bark, etc., shows up better against an overcast sky or a pale background such as snow.

Orange smoke flares are commonly carried for marine use. They are effective particularly when seen from the air. They are generally designed to be held by someone on a foundering vessel or in a lifeboat. Operating the lighting striker and holding the flare up is not easy for a swimmer or someone trying to hold onto an upturned kayak or canoe in rough water. Under these conditions it can be easier to use aerial flares or smoke projectiles fired from a "pen" projector or a flare pistol. Coloured smoke can also be used on land, but again consider the background—orange smoke would not be very good in an Ontario maple forest in September! Marine dye markers are also effective when viewed from the air.

Flares are another option, though they are more visible at night when it is less likely anyone will be outside to see them. The pen type flare guns commonly available and used by prospecting geologists to attract the attention of their helicopter flight back to camp work well and are light and compact. As well as firing flares they fire "crack shells" or "bear bangers" to scare away bears, so they have two purposes. A crack shell to gain people's attention followed by a flare shell could be a very effective combination. Smoke projectiles used to be available for these flare guns but the distributor tells me they no longer carry them. Be aware that the working mechanism of the pen projector can corrode so that the firing pin does not strike hard enough to fire the projectile. Keep it dry, lubricate it with WD-40 and check it often for free movement. Do not store it in the cocked position.

Remember that all types of pyrotechnics are subject to restrictions on their transportation by public conveyances (see page 212). Also be aware of their ability to cause forest and grass fires, and to damage equipment or even the operator if incorrectly used. Because of the fire hazard some flares may not be approved for land use. Flares also have an expiry date on them, and even within the expiry date they can be unreliable, so carry plenty.

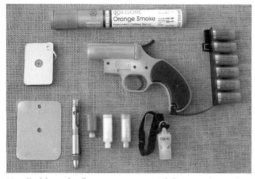

Handheld smoke flare, 12-gauge aerial flares and pistol-style flare projector. These are much larger but correspondingly more effective than the pen flare, below left. Remember that the whistle and signal mirror last forever and there is nothing that can go wrong with them.

Small signalling devices. Clockwise from top left: pencil flare gun, red flare, orange smoke, bear banger, orange smoke canister, signal mirror with sight, conventional mirror with sighting hole, Skyblazer firestarter/hand flare. Centre Skyblazer aerial flare.

Signal mirrors are very effective if the sun is shining and if they are correctly aimed. Signal mirrors have very effective aiming devices built-in and they are well worth carrying. Geologist friends tell me helicopter pilots claim the mirrors are the most effective signal devices, and can actually be dazzling if the people on the ground are overzealous with the mirrors.

Compass mirrors can also be used for signalling but lack the sophisticated aiming device of a signal mirror. Hold the mirror in one hand close to your face and project the bright light onto the other hand at arm's length. Sight across the corner of the mirror and line up the corner, the corner of the patch of bright light and the target, and then remove your arm's length hand. Vibrate the mirror and recheck your aim frequently. Practise by aiming at objects on the wall of your house. Cookware can be polished to a high shine with toothpaste.

For marine and open country use, strobe lights powered by batteries have a number of advantages. First of all, they are subject to less transportation restrictions, though lithium batteries are frowned upon, especially if large, by airlines. Second, they are easy and safe to operate. Third, they will operate for a lengthy period, unlike flares and smoke, which are short-lived. If someone wasn't looking during the few seconds or a minute of your flare, you are out of luck. Several models of strobes are available, some quite small and compact for attaching to lifejackets, others larger and more powerful. The ACR 4F from marine safety suppliers has a range in daylight of 3.5 kilometres,

10 kilometres at night. A lanyard or Velcro system to allow easy attachment to a paddle would be useful to help you keep the unit up out of wave troughs. The batteries have a finite shelf life, but so do pyrotechnics. A much smaller, lower cost strobe that uses a D-cell is available from MPI Survival equipment.

Don't forget that most simple, reliable and basic item of signalling equipment, a whistle. The Canadian invention, the Fox 40 whistle, has revolutionized the meaning of loud as it pertains to whistles. This whistle was developed by a Canadian soccer referee whose whistle to call a foul at a soccer match was not heard above the roar of the crowd. The game continued and a crucial goal was scored. This turn of events put his life at considerable risk since the game was in South America, and led to his decision to design a better whistle, which he certainly did! Spend the money and buy one—don't mess about with the inferior 99 cent plastic whistles.

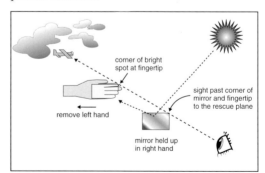

Sighting a one-sided mirror for signalling.

Useful Information

This section contains addresses and phone numbers of state and provincial tourism departments. From these departments, you should be able to obtain further information on the area you propose to visit and how to get there. These sources will also be able to provide you with the addresses of guides and outfitters. There is also a list of sources for maps, charts and air photos. Allow plenty of time for delivery. Other information covers animalproof containers, butane-propane adapters, addresses for booking hostels and backcountry huts and sources of information for rail travel.

If you use an outfitter, or are organizing a commercial trip, you may be interested in the sample waiver used by commercial outfitters.

The accident report form is intended to be photocopied and taken with you on your trip.

Provincial and State Tourism Depts.

These addresses are *starting* points for digging up the information you need. They vary considerably in the services they provide. Allow lots of time for them to respond and for you to follow up on the "leads" they provide.

Alaska Dept. of Commerce and Economic Development
Division of Tourism
PO Box 110801
Juneau, AK 99811-0801
907-465-2010
http://www.travelalaska.com
e-mail gonorth@commerce.state.AK.US

Alberta Tourism
Commerce Place
10155 - 102nd Street
Edmonton, AB T5J 4G8
Tourism Visitor Assistance
800-661-8888, 403-427-2280
http://www.discoveralberta.com/ATP
e-mail ATP.BOOKNOW@worldweb.com

British Columbia Ministry of Small Business Tourism and Culture, Visitor Services Unit
Box 9830, Stn. Provincial Government
1117 Wharf St.
Victoria, BC V8W 9W5
800-663-6000
Overseas calls 250-387-1642
http://travel.bc.ca, no e-mail

Manitoba
Travel Manitoba,
155 Carlton St., 7th Floor
Winnipeg, MB R3C 3H8
800-665-0040, 204-789-0050
http://www.gov.mb.ca/travel-manitoba
no e-mail

New Brunswick
Ministry of Economic Development and Tourism
Centennial Building, Box 6000
Fredericton NB E3B 5H1
800-561-0123, 506-453-3984
e-mail nbtradeinv@gov.nb.ca
http://www.gov.nb.ca/tourism/

Newfoundland and Labrador
Visitor Services
Box 8730
St John's, NF A1B 4K2
800-563-6353, 709-729-2830
http://www.gov.nf.ca/
e-mail info@tourism.gov.nf.ca

Northwest Territories Dept. of Economic Development and Tourism
Tourism Information
Box 1320
Yellowknife, NWT X1A 2L9
800-661-0788, 403-873-7200
http://www.edt.gov.nt.ca/guide//index
e-mail tourist@edt.gov.nt.ca

Tourism Nova Scotia Information,
PO Box 130
Halifax, NS B3J 2M7
800-565-0000, 902-425-5781
http://explore.gov.ns.ca/virtvalns
e-mail nsvisit@fox.nstn.ca

Ontario Tourism
1 Concord Gate 9th Floor
Don Mills, ON M3C 3N6
800-668-2746, 416-314-0944
No web or e-mail

Prince Edward Island Tourism
PO Box 940
Charlottetown, PEI C1A 7M5
800-463-4734, 902-368-5540
http://www.gov.pe.ca/vg/index.html
e-mail mcentre@cycor.ca

Quebec
Tourisme Quebec
CP 979, Montreal, PQ H3C 2W3
800-363-7777, 514-873-2015
France 05.90.7777
http://www.tourisme.gouv.qc.ca
e-mail info@tourisme.gouv.qc.ca

Saskatchewan
Tourism Saskatchewan
500-1900 Albert St.
Regina, SK S4P 4L9
800-667-7191, 306-787-2300
Fax 306-787-5744
e-mail travel.info.@sasktourism.sk.ca
http://www.sasktourism.sk.ca

Yukon Tourism
Box 2703
Whitehorse, YT Y1A 2C6
800-661-0494, 403-667-5340
Fax 403-667-3546
http://www.touryukon.com
e-mail yktour@yknet.yk.ca

Note: Phone numbers with an 800 prefix are toll free within North America.

Maps, Charts and Air Photos

Canada

Ordering from the federal government

Canada Map Office
130 Bentley Avenue
Nepean, ON K1A 0E9
U.S. and Canada 800-465-6277
International 613-952-7000

Ordering from Ottawa takes two-three weeks. The index sheet indicates that you should order from provincial map offices or from map specialty stores. In my experience, ordering from map specialists is much quicker, as long as the item is in stock. They are private businesses and have an incentive to satisfy customers. If you know the number of the sheet you want, mail ordering can be as simple as a phone call, giving your credit card number and address. Dealers can also be tracked down using the Yellow Pages of phone directories, which are available in major libraries for the entire country.

Provincial Map Offices

British Columbia

B.C. Ministry of the Environment
Surveys and Mapping Branch
Parliament Building
Victoria, BC V8V 1X4
604-387-1441

Alberta

Maps Alberta
Forestry Lands and Wildlife
Land Information Services Division
2nd floor, North Petroleum Plaza
9945-108 Street
Edmonton, AB T5K 2G6
403-427-3520 Fax 403-422-9683

Saskatchewan

Saskatchewan Supply and Services
Central Survey and Mapping Branch
2045 Broad Street
Regina, SK S4P 4V4
306-787-2799

Manitoba

Dept. of Natural Resources and
Transportation Services
Surveys and Mapping Branch
1007 Century Street
Winnipeg, MB R3H 0W4
204-945-6784

Ontario

Ontario Ministry of the Environment
Cartography and Drafting
40 St. Clair Ave. W., 6th Floor
Toronto, ON M4V 1P5
416-965-1123

Quebec

Cartography Service
Dept. of Energy and Resources
1995 Boul. Charest Ouest
Sainte Foy, PQ G1N 4H9
418-643-7704 Fax 418-644-4935

New Brunswick

Dept. of Natural Resources and Energy
Hugh J. Fleming Forestry Centre
Regent St. Extension
PO Box 6000
Fredericton, NB E3B 5H1
506-453-2764

Nova Scotia

Nova Scotia Information Service
Box 637
Halifax, NS B3J 2T3
902-424-2735

Prince Edward Island

Land Registration and Information Service
120 Water Street
Summerside, PE C1N 1A9
902-436-2107

Newfoundland

Dept. of Forestry Resources and Lands
Howley Building
Higgins Line
St. John's, NF A1C 5T7
709-729-3304

Yukon

Geoscience Information and Sales
345, 300 Main Street
Whitehorse, YT Y1A 2B5
403-667-3204

Northwest Territories

Municipal and Community Affairs
Surveys and Mapping Division
(municipal and land ownership maps only)
Box 21 NW Tower
Yellowknife, NT X1A 3S9

Natural Resources Canada
Map Sales Office
PO Box 668
Yellowknife, NT X1A 2N5
403-920-8299

Air Photos

Maritime Resource Management
Service Inc.
PO Box 310
Amherst, NS B4H 3Z5
902-667-7231 Fax 902-667-6008

Marine Charts

Hydrographic Chart Distribution Office
1675 Russell Road
Box 8080
Ottawa, ON K1G 3H6
613-998-4931 Fax 613-998-1217

Pacific Coast Charts should be ordered from:
Dept. of Fisheries and Oceans
Hydrographic Charts
Institute of Ocean Sciences
Patricia Bay
9860 West Saanich Rd.
PO Box 6000
Sidney, BC V8L 4B2
604-363-6348 Fax 604-356-6390
Tide tables are available from chart dealers.

Rights-of-way and Private Land

Information from:
DIAND Inuvik District Office
Box 2100
Inuvik, NT X0E 0T0

Alaska

Within Alaska, maps can be obtained over the counter or by mail order from:

Alaska Distribution Section
USGS
Box 12
Federal Building
101 Twelfth Avenue, Room 126
Fairbanks, AK 99701

Outside Alaska, mail orders must be directed to:
USGS Office
Western Distribution Centre
Box 25286
Federal Centre Building 41
Denver, CO 80225

USGS' annual list of the year's publications:
USGS
Box 25286
Federal Centre
Denver, CO 80225

Orthophotoquads should be ordered from:
Lakewood-ESIC
USGS
Box 25046
Federal Centre
Denver, CO 80225

Native Lands and Private Lands

A small-scale map that shows approximate locations of native lands is available for $1 from:

Public Information Centre
Department of Natural Resources
PO Box 107005
Anchorage, AK 99510

More detailed information is available from Status Plats, which are large-scale and available at the same address, or from the Bureau of Land Management. Also make local inquiries.

Specialty Recreation Maps

Trails Illustrated
PO Box 3610
Evergreen, CO 80439-3425
800-962-1643 or 303-670-3457

Road and Recreation Maps

Available for $3.95 each (1993) from:

**Alaska Natural History
Association (ANHA)
605 West Fourth Avenue, Suite 85
Anchorage, AK 99501
907-274 8440**

Forest Service Maps

Available for $3 each from:

**Tongass National Forest
Forest Information Centre
101 Egan Drive
Juneau, AK 99801
907-586-8751**

Marine Charts

Order ahead of time by mail order, as they can be out of stock at busy times of the year. Ask for Index #3 for Alaska. Mail order within U.S.

**National Ocean Survey
Chart Sales and Control Data
632 6th Avenue, Room 405
Anchorage, AK 99501**

Foreign mail order is only available through:

**Distribution Branch N/CG33
National Ocean Service
NOAA 6501 Lafayette Avenue
Riverdale, MD 20737
303-436-6990 for mail order using
Visa or Mastercard.**
Charts cost $14 and tide tables $10 (1993).

In Canada, charts for Alaska can be obtained at a number of outlets, including:

**Alexander Marine
570 Davie Street
Vancouver, BC V6B 2G4
604-689-5972**

**Maritime Services
3440 Bridgeway Street
Vancouver, BC V5K 1B6
604-294-4444**

Alaska Air Photos

U.S. air photos can be selected by ordering the USGS Index to National Aerial Photography Program (NAPP) from USGS. There is also an index to National High Altitude Photography (NHAP I) and another to National High Altitude Photography (NHAP II) Leaf, for air photos available from USGS.

**USGS Office
Western Distribution Centre
Box 25286
Federal Centre Building 41
Denver, CO 80225**

Aerial Obliques of the Alaska Range

Copies are available from:

**Bradford Washburn
Museum of Science
Boston, MA 02114**
Send for information and a price list.

They are also available from:

**Alaska and Polar Region Dept.
University of Alaska at Fairbanks
Fairbanks, AK 99775-1005
907-474-6773**

Radio Weather Transmissions in Alaska

The *Marine Weather Services Chart MSC-15* is available from:

**The National Weather Service
222 West 7 Ave. #23
Anchorage, AK 99513-7575**

Animalproof Containers

They are available from the manufacturer:
**Garcia Machine
14097 Avenue 272
Visalia, CA 93277
209-732-3785**

Cabins and Huts

Alpine Club of Canada

Bookings must be made to obtain a key. At least one person in the party must be an ACC member if there is no custodian present.

ACC
PO Box 2040
Canmore, AB T0L 0M0
403-678-3200

Quebec Mountain Federation

A chain of huts in the Charlevoix region is operated by the Quebec Mountain Federation.

Federation Quebecoise de la Montagne
4545 Av. Pierre-de-Coubertin
CP 1000, Succursale M
Montreal, PQ H1V 3R2
514-252-3004

Hostelling International Canada

Hostelling International Canada
Suite 400, 205 Catherine St.
Ottawa, ON K2P 1C3
613-237-7884

Hostelling International U.S.A.

Hostelling International U.S.A.
733 15 St. N.W., Suite 840
Washington, DC 20005
202-783-6161

There are about 200 cabins available for public use in Alaska, operated by various agencies.

Bureau of Land Management

Fairbanks Support Centre
1541 Gaffney Road
Fairbanks, AK 99703-1399
907-356-5345

Fish and Wildlife Service

Kodiak National Wildlife Refuge
1390 Buskin River Road
Kodiak, AK 99615
907-487-2600

Alaska Division of Parks and Outdoor Rec.

PO Box 107001
Anchorage, AK 99510
907-762-2261

Chugach National Forest

201 E. 9th Ave., Suite 206
Anchorage, AK 99501
907-271-2599

Tongass National Forest

PO Box 309
Petersburg, AK 99833
907-772-3871

Butane-Propane Adapters

An adapter that allows you to run a variety of stoves on the ubiquitous blue Camping Gaz cylinders can be obtained from:

Liberty Mountain Sport
PO Box 306
Montrose, CA 91020

Rail Travel

Algoma Central Rail Road

129 Bay St.
Sault Ste. Marie, ON P6A 5P6
705-946-7300

B.C. Rail

Box 8770
Vancouver, BC V6B 4X6
604-984-5246

Ontario Northland

555 Oak St.
North Bay, ON P1B 8L2
800-268-9281

Quebec North Shore

PO Box 1000
Sept Iles, PQ G4R 4L5
418-968-7495

White Pass and Yukon Railway

PO Box 4070
Whitehorse, YT Y1A 3T1
403-668-7245

Alaska Railroad Corporation

Passenger Services
PO Box 107500
Anchorage, AK 99510-7500
800-544-0552 or 907-265-2448

Sample Waiver Form

This is a sample of the type of waiver form often used by outfitters in western Canada. **Do not use verbatim for your organization without consulting your lawyer.**

RELEASE OF ALL CLAIMS AND WAIVER OF LIABILITY

BY SIGNING THIS YOU GIVE UP CERTAIN RIGHTS, INCLUDING THE RIGHT TO SUE.
  (*This is plain language, makes signer take notice!*)

TO: DEATH MOUNTAIN OUTDOOR EPICS LTD. and HER MAJESTY THE QUEEN IN RIGHT OF THE PROVINCE OF ....
  (*The province is mentioned so that they cannot be sued on the basis of such ridiculous, but legally possible arguments as, "they are the landowners where it happened" or "they were allowing the operator to operate."*)

In consideration of my decision (*"since I have decided"*) to attend a course or outdoor excursion led or instructed by DEATH MOUNTAIN OUTDOOR EPICS LTD., I AGREE to this Release of Claims, Waiver of Liability and Assumption of Risks (collectively "this AGREEMENT").

I WAIVE ANY AND ALL CLAIMS I may have against, and RELEASE FROM ALL LIABILITY, and AGREE NOT TO SUE DEATH MOUNTAIN OUTDOOR EPICS LTD. AND THE PROVINCE AND THEIR DIRECTORS, OFFICERS, EMPLOYEES, GUIDES, AGENTS AND REPRESENTATIVES, (henceforth "The Releasees") for ANY PERSONAL INJURY, DEATH, PROPERTY DAMAGE OR LOSS sustained by me as a result of my participation in any kind of activity, course or trip with "The Releasees," DUE TO ANY CAUSE WHATSOEVER, INCLUDING WITHOUT LIMITATION, NEGLIGENCE ON THE PART OF THE RELEASEES.

INITIALS............
  (*Initial to indicate the signer has read it and understands there is no one he can sue, even if people are negligent.*)

I AM AWARE that outdoor recreational activities have certain inherent RISKS associated with being in the natural environment. These include, but ARE NOT LIMITED TO, rapid and extreme weather changes, terrain hazards and obstacles, wild animals, other people, fast water, changes in river beds and rapids, falling trees, avalanches, floods, use of stoves and possible adverse effects of food. I also understand that the outdoor environment is continually changing and that Death Mountain Outdoor Epics' staff and the Releasees may fail to predict natural hazards, including, but not limited to, unstable snow, avalanches, rockfalls and water hazards. I am also aware that ACTIVITIES MAY TAKE PLACE IN LOCATIONS WHERE MEDICAL TREATMENT OR RESCUE MAY NOT BE AVAILABLE due to such factors as remoteness, communication difficulties, poor travelling conditions, bad weather, etc.
  (*Puts some onus on the participant, and also prevents them bringing forward stupid, but potentially legally acceptable arguments, such as "I didn't know there were wild animals in the park." A waiver for a specific activity might go into a lot more detail of the hazards of that activity.*)

I FREELY ACCEPT ALL THE RISKS associated with the course or trip in which I have agreed to participate.

INITIALS............
  (*Initial to indicate they have read this paragraph. "Freely accept" is a key phrase.*)

I ACKNOWLEDGE that the inherent risks of many outdoor activities contribute to the enjoyment of such activities.

I am freely entering into this Agreement, and in doing so I am NOT RELYING ON ANY ORAL OR WRITTEN STATEMENTS made by the Releasees, including those in brochures or letters of correspondence, to induce me to participate in a course or excursion organized, led or instructed by "the Releasees."

("Freely entering" is a key phrase—if people are forced into signing a waiver, it may be less valid. Many outfitters now send out waivers with booking information, and may require them to be signed at that time. If you sign at the outfitter's location after booking and at the start of your trip, there could be deemed to be some coercion.)

I confirm that I am nineteen or more years of age and that I have READ AND UNDERSTAND THIS AGREEMENT PRIOR TO SIGNING IT and that this Agreement shall be BINDING UPON MY HEIRS, NEXT OF KIN, EXECUTORS AND SUCCESSORS.

Signed this .... day of ...., 19.......

In presence of Witness (Parents if younger than 19 years of age):

Signature: .... Witness: ....

Please PRINT full names and mailing addresses:

....

....

....

(The witness is important, and a prudent operator will be very careful to check that all the signing is done completely and correctly. Some people seem to try to hand in incomplete waivers and operators must watch for this!)

ACCIDENT REPORT FORM TO ACCOMPANY PARTY GOING FOR HELP - PAGE 1

Rescuers can respond more quickly and more appropriately if they have complete and accurate information. Take time to complete this form carefully!

Answer y or n or write, as appropriate.

Day report completed .... Time report completed ....
Day of incident .... Time of incident ....
Number of victims ....

Description of location of accident. See back of this sheet.
Description of accident ....
....
....
....
....
Description of injuries, symptoms and severity ....
....
....
.... (over if necessary)

Vital signs in victim prior to message party departure:

time of recordings									
pulse									
respiration rate									
respiration quality									
pupils									
skin colour									
skin moistness, temp.									
level of consciousness									

Victim's medical history, medical alert tag ....
....
....
....
Any medication taken by the victim? .... What? ....

Victim's name .... age ....
Address .... phone ....
Weight .... height ....
Treatment provided for victim ....
....
....
....
....
Number of helpers still on scene ....
Condition of helpers still on scene (physical and mental) ....
....
Can helpers stay safely overnight? ....
Competence of helpers still on scene - first aid .... bivouac .... survival ....
self rescue....... return to trailhead unaided....... comments ....
....
....

REPORT FORM TO ACCOMPANY PARTY GOING FOR HELP - PAGE 2

Special equipment thought to be needed for extrication or treatment of injuries....................
....
....

Which of the following in your opinion could reach the site - horse .... 4x4.......
snowmobile......... mountain bike........ motor quad & trailer......... foot party with
stretcher.......... raft.......... motor boat......... jetboat............ floatplane............ helicopter.........
(Needs approx. 30 metres to land, depending on type of machine, temperature, altitude,
approach angles and wind. Not all can use a sling.) Could the victim be carried to a location
accessible to any of the above......... easily?............ how far?......... which of the above?
....

Weather conditions at site—wind, precipitation, snow conditions, visibility, temperature, trends
....
....
Name of person providing information for this form ....
Description of accident location...
....
....

Grid reference ("UTM") .... Mark location on topographic map and bring it out with you.
Draw a sketch map below. Be precise. Include distinctive land marks and any marks or signals
you can make to render the site easier for rescuers to find (flagging tape flares, smoke, coloured
tarps, etc.).

Terrain: glacier..... snow..... rock..... talus..... brush..... timber..... trail..... flat......

moderate..... steep...... gully..... cliff base..... river..... gravelbar/ island..... beach...............

Remaining hazards at site:

Avalanche .... Rockfall................... Animal .... Other ....

Draw sketch map below

Index

Available from Rocky Mountain Books

GPS Made Easy, Lawrence Letham, 112p., $14.95
Includes practical examples of how to use handheld GPS receivers in the outdoors.

Canoeing Safety and Rescue, Doug McKown, 128p., $12.95
Essential reading for recreational open canoe paddlers who need to be self sufficient.

Avalanche Safety for Skiers and Climbers, Tony Daffern, 192p., $14.95
Addresses recognition of avalanche terrain, stability evaluation and good routefinding.

Nahanni: the River Guide, Peter Jowett, 224p., $15.95
A comprehensive guide to the South Nahanni and Flat rivers.

Summits and Icefields, Chic Scott, 304p., $15.95
Alpine ski tours in the Rockies and Columbia mountains of western Canada.

Ski Trails in the Canadian Rockies, Chic Scott, 224p., $14.95
Cross-country ski trails: groomed, backcountry and well-established tours above treeline.

Waterfall Ice Climbs in the Canadian Rockies, Joe Josephson, 272p., $19.95
A wide selection of ice climbs on both sides of the Canadian Rockies.

Selected Alpine Climbs in the Canadian Rockies, Sean Dougherty, 320p., $19.95
An up-to-date guide to the best mountaineering routes in the Canadian Rockies.

Scrambles in the Canadian Rockies, Alan Kane, 208p., $14.95
A guide to 102 non-technical peaks for mountain scramblers.

Kananaskis Country Trail Guide, Gillean Daffern, 2 vols., 272p., $15.95 each
The third edition of this popular guide to Alberta's Kananaskis Country.

Kananaskis Country Ski Trails, Gillean Daffern, 296p., $14.95
Ski opportunities from groomed trails to ski mountaineering routes and telemark hills.

Backcountry Biking in the Canadian Rockies, Eastcott & Lepp, 352p., $16.95
Over 200 trails and old roads in the Rocky Mountains of Alberta and British Columbia.

To order write or fax to:
Rocky Mountain Books, #4 Spruce Centre SW
Calgary, Alberta T3C 3B3, Canada
Fax: 403-249-2968, Tel: 403-249-9490
If you live in western USA or Canada phone **1-800-566-3336**
We accept cheques or Visa (sorry we do not accept other credit cards)
Visit our web site at: http://www.culturenet.ca/rmb/